BOB HOPE
A Tribute

BOB HOPE
A Tribute

Raymond Strait

Pinnacle Books
Kensington Publishing Corp.

http://www.pinnaclebooks.com

Dedicated to . . .

Mrs. Bob Hope . . . a devoted wife and mother

and to

The World of Celebrity . . . without which I would still be wondering what to do when I grow up . . .

ACKNOWLEDGMENTS

I owe a very special thank you to Robert F. Slatzer and Arthur Marx for their more than generous cooperation and kindness in allowing me access to their research and books, and for directing me to important sources which helped bring this project to life. Thanks also to William Faith, a walking encyclopedia of the life and times of Leslie Townes "Bob" Hope, and to John Austin, a walking encyclopedia of Hollywood, California.

I am also deeply grateful to three women: The late Barbara Payton and Marilyn Maxwell (for their willing and forthright responses during our interviews in the 1950s and 1960s) as well as Jean Carmen, the greatest woman trick golf artist in the world, who provided strategic pieces of the jigsaw puzzle that was the psyche of Bob Hope.

And my thanks to the following, some of whom have passed on yet contributed important bits and pieces during interviews over the years: Leo Guild, Paul Blane, Nancy Bacon, Robert Ellison, Eric Root, Joey Barnum, Sue Terry, Mark Anthony, James Bacon, Earl Wilson, Lucille Ball, Milton Berle, Joey Heatherton, Tony Romano, Doris Day, Rosemary Clooney, Dorothy Lamour, Phyllis Diller, Zsa Zsa Gabor, Edith Head, Fred Otash, Fred MacMurray, Jack Oakie, Martha Raye, Jane Russell, Dinah Shore, Danny Thomas, Rudy Vallee, Steve Allen, Constance Bennett, Jayne Mansfield, Mamie Van Doren, Joan Collins, Cass Daley, Anthony Quinn, Roman Gabriel, Hedy Lamarr, Harry James, Rosey Grier, Mickey Hargitay, Sonja Henie, William Holden, Walter Winchell, Hedda Hopper, Ed Sullivan, Irv Kupcinet, Adela Rogers St. Johns, Sidney Skolsky, Rona Barrett, Toni Holt, Dorothy Manners, and Louella Parsons. I also want to include George

Jessel, Margaret Whiting, Keenan Wynn, Jim Backus, Maxine Andrews, Jerry Colonna, Jimmy Durante, Judy Garland, Tommy Howard, George Montgomery, Lana Turner, and Jan King.

REFERENCES: *Don't Shoot, It's Only Me,* (Bob Hope and Melville Shavelson); *Have Tux, Will Travel,* (Bob Hope and Pete Martin); *Bob Hope, A Life in Comedy* (William Robert Faith); *Bob Hope, Portrait of a Superstar,* (Charles Thompson); *Bing Crosby, The Hollow Man,* (Donald Shepherd and Robert F. Slatzer); *My Side of the Road,* (Dorothy Lamour with Dick McInnes); *The Last Christmas Show,* (Bob Hope and Pete Martin); *Long Live the King,* (biography of Clark Gable by Lyn Tornabene); *The Lucille Ball Story,* (James Gregory); *Going My Way,* (Gary Crosby & Ross Firestone); *A Child of the Century* (Ben Hecht); *Desi Arnaz, a Book,* (Desi Arnaz); *March of Democracy,* (James Truslow Adams); *No People Like Show People,* (Maurice Zolotow); *Show Biz, from Vaude to Video,* (Abel Green and Joe Laurie, Jr.); *The Amazing Careers of Bob Hope,* (Morella, Epstein and Clark); *Milton Berle, an Autobiography,* (Milton Berle & Haskel Frankel); *A Hell of a Life,* (Harry Richman); *The Brothers Shubert,* (Jerry Stagg); *Who Could Ask For Anything More,* (Ethel Merman and Pete Martin); *Merman, An Autobiography,* (Ethel Merman and George Eels); *They Got Me Covered,* (Bob Hope); *The Road to Hollywood,* (Bob Hope and Bob Thomas); *The Incredible Crosby,* (Barry Ulanov); *Didn't You Used to be George Murphy?* (George Murphy and Victor Lasky); *Out Without My Rubbers,* (John Murray Anderson); *Schnozzola,* (Gene Fowler); *Cole Porter, The Life That Late He Lived,* (George Eels); *The Great Movie Comedians,* (Leonard Maltin); *I Never Left Home,* (Bob Hope); *None of Your Business,* (Carroll Carroll); *The Complete Crosby,* (Charles Thompson); *So This is Peace,* (Bob Hope); *Doris Day, Her Own Story,* (A. E. Hotchner); *Here's to the Friars; The Heart of Show Business,* (Joey Adams); *I Owe Russia $1,200,* (Bob Hope); *Five Women I Love,* (Bob Hope); *Kissinger,* (Marvin Kalb); *Dear Prez, I Wanna Tell Ya,* (Bob Hope), *Jack Benny, an Intimate Biography,* (Irving Fein); *Call*

Them Irreplaceable, (John Fisher); *The Secret Life of Bob Hope,* (Arthur Marx).

OTHER REFERENCES: *The New York Times, Los Angeles Times, Library of Congress, Congressional Record,* Academy of Motion Picture Arts & Sciences, American Film Institute, *TV Guide, Saturday Evening Post, Modern Maturity, Variety, Hollywood Reporter, Film Comment,* Associated Press, *Stars & Stripes, Cleveland Press, Chicago Tribune, Playboy, Dallas Times Herald, Washington Post, Washington Star,* United Press International, *Family Weekly, New York Times Magazine, Los Angeles Times Magazine, Los Angeles Herald-Examiner, Hollywood Citizen News, Boston Herald, St. Louis Globe-Democrat, Houston Chronicle, Life, Time, Newsweek, U.S. News & World Report, Facts on File, Liberty, Look, Seventeen, Ladies Home Journal, Seattle Times, Riverside Press-Enterprise,* NBC Archives, CBS Archives, ABC Archives, *Confidential, This Week* Magazine, *Family Circle, London Times, The New Yorker, Woman's Home Companion, Cosmopolitan.*

Prologue

Bob Hope's face is one of the most recognized faces in the world and has been since World War II. His national acclaim began with radio and segued into movies, USO tours, and television. Although a British import, he belongs to the United States. He is a beloved and respected American icon. That is not to say he doesn't have detractors; he does. It's a by-product of "celebrity."

Bob Hope, Bing Crosby, and Dorothy Lamour became the most famous trio in the history of American show business. All three had separate careers; Dorothy Lamour was known more for the sarong she introduced in her first film, *Jungle Princess,* than for any acting ability; Crosby was best known for his crooning; Hope shone as a comedian, leaping out of vaudeville, Broadway, radio, television and movies right into the hearts of fans throughout the world.

Dorothy Lamour's famous sarong is now enshrined in The Smithsonian Institution, Crosby's recording of "White Christmas" has become as popular as "Silent Night," and Bob Hope's USO tours are as legendary as the invasion of Normandy.

At this writing, Bob Hope is approaching 95 and counting.

While watching him on television recently during a PBS celebration honoring big-band leader Les Brown, it came as a sudden shock that Bob Hope is now an old man—a young man turned old overnight. Coming, as I did, from a generation that revered Franklin D. Roosevelt as a member of the family, Bob Hope has always been like a big brother, the family clown.

I watched that PBS special as Dolores, his wife since 1934, tenderly escorted him off the stage after they sang a duet together. Dolores had warbled like a young band singer; Hope seemed to be remembering some previous generation. I felt sad. I remember Bob Hope from radio, films, television, and many USO encounters during my military service in both World War II and the Korean conflict.

As press secretary for ten years to the late Jayne Mansfield, I encountered Mr. Hope personally in other ways. Jayne and Bob were great friends and I met and spoke with him on many occasions as well as with others who have known him well. In addition to being a unique personality who represents everything we thought we stood for throughout the 20th century, Bob Hope happens also to be human. He aspired to and accomplished great human deeds within the scope of his life.

However, being human, he committed human errors. I wish the reader to understand that at no time have I made any endeavor either to glorify Mr. Hope or to demean him in any way. I merely wish to present the man in his entirety.

This, then, is how I remember Bob Hope.

Raymond Strait
Hemet, CA

Chapter 1

"I never wanted to be anybody," Bob Hope responded to an interviewer who asked the great comedian about his childhood ambitions. He might well have reached that not-so-lofty goal had he remained in Eltham, London, England, where he entered life on May 29, 1903, as Leslie Townes Hope, the fifth of seven sons born to William Henry Hope, an English stonemason, and Avis Townes Hope, daughter of a Welsh sea captain. The first boy, Ivor, was born in 1892, James Francis II came a year later, daughter Emily in July 1895. In 1897 came Frederick Charles. While pregnant with her fourth child, William John, Avis lost Emily to diphtheria, one of the most dreaded childhood diseases of the time.

The elder Hope took to drinking and carousing with other women, neglectful of the family as his wife continued bringing forth heirs into what looked like a future of poverty. Due to Harry's inability to stay put, the family became a band of nomads, moving from one town to another. During this time, the man we have come to know as Bob Hope was born to a family already grown too large for its income. Mrs. Hope was forced into the labor market to help put food on the table. Even the older boys had to pitch in, taking whatever jobs could be found.

Having no one to look after him, Avis took young Leslie along with her to work. Barely two years old in 1905, Leslie welcomed a new brother, Sidney, into the clan.

Harry Hope's brothers, Fred and Frank, had already sought a better life in the United States. America seemed to be the best place to provide for such a large family, so Harry decided that he, Avis, and the children would join his brothers in Cleveland, Ohio. He assured her that there would be work and an idyllic life for one and all across the Atlantic.

A skeptical Mrs. Hope did not wish to leave England. She had no blood relatives in America. However, Harry left her no choice; he departed for America without his family.

Avis sold whatever she couldn't take aboard the filthy steerage accommodations that brought her and the boys across the Atlantic to Ellis Island in New York Harbor. They had hardly any money and very little food. It was rumored that they literally sang for pennies in order to sustain themselves during the voyage.

Harry, having found only part-time employment, could not afford to meet his wife and children in New York. Instead, he and his two brothers were waiting when they arrived by train in Cleveland along with other immigrants from Europe. As always, Harry put up a big front, showering his frightened wife with promises of grandeur when, in fact, he had been disillusioned by his own brothers as to the "milk and honey" conditions in Cleveland.

When work could be found, immigrants received the worst of it. They toiled 12-hour days, six and seven days a week, for very little pay. As a stonemason, Harry earned above the average for an immigrant—when he could find employment.

Unable to live like sardines packed in with Harry's relatives, Avis soon located a house with three bedrooms and inside plumbing for her brood. The rent, $18.50 per month, seemed beyond any budget plans she may have devised, since Harry didn't have steady work, but she was determined to manage.

Harry continued his old pattern of drinking and carousing

which Avis, as a good wife of the times, accepted without open complaint.

Instead of making an honest effort himself, Harry sent his three oldest boys out to look for work. Two of them soon found permanent jobs at a local ironworks factory. After a while, Avis rented an even larger house at 1925 East 105th Street, where she took in boarders.

A frugal woman, she mended and patched items of clothing, passing a garment down to the next son as the older one outgrew it. In 1909 a seventh and final son, George, who was born an American citizen, completed the family circle. That same year, Harry became a naturalized American citizen and as a result the rest of the family was granted citizenship.

With the two older boys working at full-time jobs, the other four sold newspapers at the four corners of Euclid Avenue and 105th Street. It was Leslie's first job and he immediately showed an interest in making money. Although most of his earnings went directly to his mother, being a wage earner made him feel "more like a man."

Avis, a possessive and indulgent mother, never had any real problems with her sons. She would instigate competition between them from which she received the benefits. She tolerated Harry and his bumbling, but she drew her emotional and, more often than not, financial support from her sons.

Avis managed to scrimp and buy a piano so the house was always filled with music and singing. Leslie's voice, definitely soprano, and his English-style clothes brought snickering and ridicule from classmates at school. Out of necessity, he became proficient with his fists. A good runner with natural athletic ability, he often competed in and won at track meets.

During his stint at Doan's Corners selling newspapers, Leslie received his first bit of sound financial advice. It came from a man who stopped every day, rolled down the back window of his chauffeur-driven private car, reached his hand out with the correct change, and bought a paper. Without a word, he would roll the window back up and drive off. One day he called the boy over to the car, took his paper, and handed him a dime. ope had to go inside the corner store to get change. When he returned with the man's money, the gentleman said to him, "Listen to me, young man. I'm going to give you some advice. If you want to be a success in business, trust nobody, never give credit, and always have change in hand." Someone later identified the man as John D. Rockefeller.

Leslie drifted from one job to another, and then another. His mother voiced her concerns to his older siblings and may have worried that he might have inherited a bit more of his father's dark side than necessary.

Mrs. Hope didn't have time to dwell much on young Leslie's flightiness. She had a husband and other children to attend to, and boarders who required meals three times a day and laundry on weekends. Had she been more dependent upon Leslie's income for the survival of the family, she would probably not have allowed him so much freedom.

By the time Europe erupted into flames at the onset of World War I, Leslie had made a decision to enter the world of entertainment. It soon became an obsession. Charlie Chaplin was his idol and he emulated "the little tramp's" every gesture. He became so proficient at "doing" Chaplin, that his brothers entered him in local Chaplin contests, which were the rage.

Winning a Chaplin contest at Cleveland's old Luna Park, Leslie took home enough prize money to buy his mother a new stove. Endowed with his father's gift of gab and being quick of wit, young Hope saw the benefit of being popular and developed an early skill for making others laugh.

Although he still maintained a vagabond's attitude about work, each new job gave him ideas for comedy routines which would serve as a foundation for his unparalleled success as a comedian throughout the 20th century. Nevertheless, Leslie seemed always just half a note on the dark side of the law. He never committed crimes, but he became adept at con games. For instance, he learned how to get just a little more change from customers when he had a delivery job. Women in particular felt compassion for a young man who either lost his bus fare or had it taken away from him by a gang of bullies. Plaintive dissertations in which he requested directions, for which he already knew the answers, to his uncle's butcher shop—a good three miles away—played on the heartstrings of mothers and housewives. Many purses were opened wider out of compassion for a most undeserving conspirator.

Such shenanigans came to an end when he went into his routine a second time with a woman who'd fallen for it before. She reported him to the butcher shop and his uncle fired him. Unconcerned, he went on to another part-time job. He intended to become an entertainer and if he could not combine his routines with mundane work, he would find other ways to utilize his talents. He never once doubted that one day he would be a major success as a comedian.

He dropped the name Leslie and adopted the more masculine Lester, soon shortened to Les. He would drop out of school for weeks at a time and began hanging out with unsavory characters. He became part of a scheme cooked up by a couple of pool players who lured unsuspecting suckers into a game of eight ball with "this kid who thinks he can beat anybody." Hope loved the game and had no sense of guilt about tricking grown men out of their money on the pool table. He became an expert with a cue stick, losing just often enough to keep from being labeled a "hustler" like his two friends Charlie Cooley and Johnny Gibbons.

Les had something more than pool in common with Charlie and Johnny. They, too, were performers. Along with Hope's best friend, Whitey Jennings, the three of them haunted Zimmerman's Dance Hall, where Hope met girls and improved his footwork.

From Zimmerman's, Hope and his buddies segued over to 79th street and Charlie Marotta's Athletic Club. Whitey confided to Les that he had already decided to enter the featherweight division of the Ohio State Amateur Boxing Matches under the name of Packy West.

Dumbfounded, Hope felt assured that his fists better fit the ring than Whitey's. With more jealousy than envy, Hope adopted the name of Packy East.

"We'll be a one-two punch," he grinned as he and Whitey shook hands without the slightest idea of what to expect in the ring. Hope just missed the 128-pound featherweight limit and was shifted up into the lower register of lightweights, which made him smaller than his second, and last, opponent. Having won the first fight by a lucky punch when the other guy turned to look toward his corner for advice, an overconfident Hope faced a more seasoned fighter in his next fight. The guy quickly made history of Packy East—and Les's fighting career came to an abrupt end.

Failure in the ring did not deter him, nor did losing one job after another. He once explained in an interview that "I never had a civilian gig that didn't teach me something about comedy. Life is one comedic episode after another, so nothing ever got lost in the process. I started filing away jokes at a very early age. Jokes about life."

More than 75 years since he first thought he was funny, Hope stood convinced that his lack of real formal education only sharpened his perception of what made people laugh. He barely graduated from high school, followed by a few sporadic weeks at Western Reserve University.

He saw every mundane job, and there were many of them, as another stepping stone to comedic success. He obtained a nighttime job in the spare-parts department of Chandler Motor Company in Cleveland where he and three other guys formed a barbershop quartet. They spent as much time harmonizing as they did filling orders. One night Les thought it would be interesting to record into the boss's dictating machine, "just to hear how we sounded," Hope said. The following day, when a secretary turned on the machine to transcribe a letter dictated the previous day by her boss, she heard, instead, a scratchy recording of "Ole Black Joe."

The foursome hit a sour note with their employer and were quickly dismissed. Hope, never one to let a pink slip distract him, found another temporary job as a shoe salesman. The shoe store had a policy that rewarded salesmen who could pawn off out-of-date models that weren't selling. Selling last year's model earned the salesman a twenty-five cent bonus; getting rid of earlier styles earned the industrious huckster fifty cents.

Hope became the star of the store until a number of dissatisfied customers showed up at the same time to complain that they'd been hoodwinked. Fired again, he explained to his mother that they just didn't understand. Yes, she would agree, they just didn't understand her Leslie.

Chapter 2

The Hopes moved even more often than they had in England. By the time he entered high school, Bob remembers having lived in a number of different houses and apartments.

"Each new home was like opening in a new theater," he said. "The bathrooms were always cold."

He met many girls in the dance halls he haunted as a teenager, but never took any of them seriously. His first priority was his career. Everything else took second place—even his mother, who inserted herself into every aspect of his young life and warned him constantly to be on the lookout for "conniving females."

By the time he was seventeen he'd been thoroughly bitten by the stage bug and knew that meat markets, shoe stores, and automobile parts factories did not lead to Broadway. He entered talent contests which were held every Saturday night in various locations. The first place prize of ten or fifteen dollars for a few minutes on stage looked like easy money. That was more than he'd make in two or three days working at a regular job. Besides, he had fun doing it.

Always ready to improve his public presentations, he quickly realized that the guys with dance partners usually took first place. He'd worked up some routines with a girl he met at a local dance hall and invited her to join him in one of the competitions. Her name was Mildred Rosequist, a slender and willowy blonde. Mildred loved to dance and liked being with Les. Something more serious might have developed between them had she been interested in a stage career.

The two of them began to work theaters around Cleveland, often picking up ten dollars a night. Hope thought they were good enough to take their act on the road, but Mildred's mother put her foot down. Years later, when Bob Hope had become one of the highest paid stars in show business, he ran into Mildred. She confided, ''I just wish my mother had kept her big mouth shut!''

He chose Lloyd Durbin as his next partner, a buddy from the old Euclid Avenue gang. They put together a pretty good song and dance routine, but it didn't seem to be going anywhere until another famous comedian saw them perform.

Roscoe ''Fatty'' Arbuckle, once the highest paid comic in the business and ranked with Chaplin, Harold Lloyd, and Buster Keaton, had become involved in a sensational sex scandal in San Francisco. Fatty, a household name to American filmgoers, threw a big party in his hotel suite. Though prohibition was the law of the land, whiskey flowed freely for anyone who could afford it and Arbuckle could certainly do that.

Virginia Rappe, a party girl from Hollywood, had been found bleeding to death in Fatty's hotel bedroom. Accused of assaulting the starlet with a Coke bottle in a fit of rage, Fatty had originally been charged with her rape and murder. By the time the case went to trial the charges had been reduced to one count of manslaughter.

After 42 hours of deliberation, the jury deadlocked at ten to two in Arbuckle's favor. Although later completely exonerated, his film career was destroyed. He attempted a comeback on the vaudeville circuit. Hope and Durbin appeared on the same bill with him in Cleveland at the Bandbox Theater, which turned out to be a fluke opportunity.

Norman Kendall, a local theatrical agent, needed an act to open for Arbuckle—someone to loosen up the audience.

Arbuckle had not been well received in some areas, even with the Virginia Rappe trial and a not-guilty verdict three years behind him.

The Volstead Act, outlawing alcoholic beverages, had become the law of the land. Women in packs were ready to shut down bootleggers, ladies of the evening, and the immoral likes of Fatty Arbuckle.

It is doubtful that Hope and Durbin did anything to increase Arbuckle's lagging popularity, but they caught the interest of the great man himself. He agreed to introduce them to a fellow over in Alliance, Ohio, who produced what were known as "tabloid shows."

The tabloids served the same purpose for entertainers that baseball farm teams do for future major league players. They were a proving ground for unknown talents. One such vaudeville outlet, the Gus Sun Circuit, had spawned Al Jolson and Eddie Cantor.

Hope and Durbin were signed at $40 per week each to go on the road with a show called "Jolly Follies" in the fall of 1924. "We opened," Hope says, "in East Palestine, Ohio, and went from there to Ottawa, Ohio. That's where I asked what time the rehearsal started and the theater manager said 5:30 P.M., because the butcher shop didn't close until 5:15 P.M. That didn't make much sense to me but when I finally pried it out of the manager the explanation was that the fiddle player worked at the butcher shop."

In Huntington, West Virginia, the Hope/Durbin duo died, or rather, part of it did. Lloyd Durbin ate some homemade coconut cream pie and became violently ill in the middle of their skit. Hope accompanied him back to Cleveland where he lived three days in the hospital, with his partner at his side most of the time, before expiring—not from food poisoning, but from tuberculosis.

Hope quickly replaced him with George Byrne, a young fellow from Columbus, Ohio. Byrne turned out to be the right choice. He and Hope continued on with the show for two more years.

Hope learned one lesson from his tour with Jolly Follies:

along the "Bible belt," mores were strict. Off-color actors quickly found themselves persona non grata at the local Bijous if their skits were even slightly "blue." Fundamentalists had thin skins and did not trust show people. Stories, mostly founded on rumor, of lecherous actors kidnapping young ladies along the tour route and ruining their lives, were rampant. When a vaudeville show came into a small town they found lawn signs reading, "Dogs and Actors Stay Off the Grass."

Despite such precautions, young girls and boys, bitten by the show business bug, did run off with road shows and circuses and that alarmed the local gentry.

Theater owners and managers, tuned in to the tastes of their audiences, posted notices backstage delineating in great detail any and all phrases which, if used on stage, would ban the violator from the theater for life.

Bob Hope almost never used offensive language or jokes. He kept very close to the fringe, but never plunged into vulgarity. He often said, "I would never do a skit my mother wouldn't enjoy."

There were also rules about fraternization with members of the opposite sex. Certain hotels would not rent to show people because of the "orgies" that went on in the rooms they occupied. Hope once faced an irate hotel manager, who found him alone in the room with a female member of the troupe. He found Hope shirtless and assumed the worst. It took a great deal of explaining that she was merely giving him a hot camphorated oil treatment for an upper respiratory infection.

George Byrne and Les became close friends, and later in-laws when George's sister married Hope's youngest brother, George.

Hope had more in common with Byrne than with his previous partner and they developed a sort of mental telepathy both off- and on-stage. Their timing as a dance team brought them favorable notices from the most severe critics along the circuit.

The *Times-Herald* in Newport News, Virginia, gave them a rave revue, which Hope clipped and kept, as he did all of his notices:

But for the premier honors of the entire bill, Hope and Byrne came through with flying colors in the eccentric dance. Friends, it was a regular knockout. There has never been anything better in this house of this kind. They easily take first place without a contest. They tore the house down and came back for more and they got it.

Les quickly dispatched copies of the review home to every member of his family.

During this tour he became smitten with a young Irish lass, Kathleen O'Shea, featured in a piano number, and he wooed her with gusto. The consummate Romeo, Hope knew how to charm girls. His mother never approved of these liaisons and when he would come home between tours she interrogated him about his activities on the road. No girl would ever be good enough for her Leslie.

Kathleen O'Shea dropped out of the show later to open a dress shop in Morgantown, West Virginia. For a long time Hope kept in touch and often acted as a scout for her store.

"If I saw an item I thought she could sell in West Virginia, I would buy one and send it to her along with the address of the manufacturer," he mused, "and I think she did profit from that. I sure hope so. She was some kind of beauty."

Chapter 3

Les and George set up temporary headquarters in Cleveland and worked diligently to improve their act. Once satisfied that they had enough new material to sustain a tour, the two hoofers decided the time had come once again to abandon Cleveland.

An agent in Detroit named Ted Snow, having heard through the grapevine that the act might be available, contacted them and asked if they'd like to be booked into Detroit's State Theater at $175 a week. Indeed they would. Through Snow, the duo also picked up an additional $75 for a nightclub gig at the Oriole Terrace.

Their arrangement, not unusual today, presented a strict schedule of timing. They would complete the last show on stage at the State Theater, then grab a streetcar to the Oriole Terrace in time to do a show there. Neither of them had ever made so much money.

With cash in their pockets, Hope and Byrne caught another streetcar, returning downtown where Hope gambled away his week's earnings.

The act hung around Detroit for more than a month following their first gig at the State Theater, playing first one club and then another. Their popularity in the Detroit area grew rapidly and by popular demand they returned for a second stint at the State where they were billed as "Hope & Byrne—Dancing Demons."

While in Detroit, the team also accepted a booking into the Stanley Theater in Pittsburgh. Pittsburgh, a stop on several vaudeville circuits, had become a proving ground for numerous acts bound for Broadway. Hope aspired to New York, but whether he might be destined for Broadway remained to be determined.

Hope always had confidence that the next date would be bigger and better than the last, and another rung up the ladder to New York City and the big time.

Many times he has told the story of how he and Byrne prepared for Pittsburgh. Over the years, Hope has become a genuine skinflint with his money, but in those early days he personally scouted every act, every magazine, and every trade publication in order to be not only fashionable but the "Beau Brummel" of stand-up comedy.

Against Byrne's judgment, Hope coerced his partner into joining him on a pre-Pittsburgh trip to Chicago to have photographs made by Maurice Seymour, the best photographer west of New York City. They wore their new outfits—white spats, high-waisted trousers, Peter Pan collars, smart Eton jackets. Accessories included black high hats and black canes, tipped white. A new "traveling trunk" completed their wardrobe.

Hope understood the power of publicity and appearance. Their publicity packets were the classiest in the business. Hope told his partner not to worry so much about the cost. "Once I'm a star, I'll promote all of this. It won't cost me a dime."

They opened their Pittsburgh stand at the Stanley Theater with a soft shoe number, wearing the jazzy dress clothes purchased in Chicago. Then they changed into a more comedic costume consisting of papier-maché fire helmets and pseudo fire-fighting regalia. To the fast movement of "If You Knew Susie," George and Les pranced around the stage, one with a hatchet, while the other dragged a hose with a bulb full of water hidden inside his fireman's jacket.

At the end of the number, Hope reached inside his jacket

and damn near drowned the entire brass section of the orchestra. The audience loved it, but the sax players were not impressed.

After Pittsburgh, Hope was ready for Broadway. "It's the Palace for me, man," he told George. "You coming?"

Of course he was coming.

They arrived in New York in the fall of 1926, looking for immediate bookings. Both were disappointed to discover that nobody knew who they were and nobody cared.

They might have been just another pair of hayseeds from the provinces if Hope hadn't had the foresight to insist on the expensive publicity portfolios they put together in Chicago.

Hope had personally dropped off a publicity package at the William Morris booking agency when they first arrived in New York. A smart agent by the name of Abe Lastfogel liked their pictures and sent for them. He was the same Abe Lastfogel who would later move his operation to Hollywood and help establish the most powerful theatrical agency on the West Coast.

Lastfogel sent them out in a package on the Keith circuit, along with eighteen-year-old Siamese twins from England named Daisy and Violet Hilton. The twins were the freak stars—physical oddities were commonplace in vaudeville— while Hope and Byrne played second bananas, or "deuces." The twins did their thing—dancing, singing, talking, and provoking curiosity. Hope and Byrne did a bit with them and then took second place on the bill in their own spot with the routine they'd brought from Pittsburgh. Both acts joined in a rousing finale, which brought the house down.

Their unit played the East Coast and near midwest from Baltimore to Youngstown, ending up in Providence, Rhode Island. During a six months' period they played every town with anything resembling a theater, often using a CocaCola case as a step up to the stage. They were stars in their own minds, especially in Hope's.

Critics, he said, never bothered him. He would tell Byrne, "The audiences love me. What do critics know?" But deep down inside, he resented anyone saying or writing that his act wasn't the best in the business.

Hope had become so certain of his greatness and appeal that

in Providence, at the end of the tour, he convinced Byrne that
they were worth a lot more money the next time around and
demanded a big raise from the show's producers.

The money men laughed and in very demeaning language
told them to grow up. No raise, no show. Hope and Byrne quit
the show in Providence and didn't sign up for the next run.
Instead, they returned to New York, "where," Hope quickly
reminded Byrne, "the big money is."

They moved out of the Lincoln Hotel into a smaller place
called the Somerset which catered to a lot of the acts from
The Palace Theater, just next door, when they were "between
shows," which really meant unemployed.

Unable to find theater work, the two dancers found gigs in
small clubs in and around New York City. These, plus their
savings from the tour, kept them fed, clothed, and sheltered.

They finally were called to audition for a new Ruby Keeler
show, *Sidewalks of New York.* Expecting big parts, they rushed
over to try out. Their parts were small—chorus boys, as a
matter of fact—but they were able to dance and slip in a little
comedy. After the show tried out at the Garrick in Philadelphia,
it would be moving on to Broadway where the boys would be
seen by "important show business people."

Hope, not liking being without a woman, wired Barbara, his
girlfriend from Morgantown, West Virginia, to come up to
Philadelphia for the September 5 opening. She promised to be
right up, but did not arrive for several days. Hope found out
that during that interval she had been in New York seeing a
piano player at a different hotel.

Before packing her off, back to the coal mines, he invited
her to a party at the Maidstone Hotel where most members of
the cast were lodged. During the night, with prohibition-banned
rum, whiskey, and gin flowing freely, two of the male cast
members decided it would be funny to arrive in full drag, and
they did—along with a number of similarly-clad male friends.

By the time the police arrived in answer to numerous complaints, the pranksters had long since evacuated the premises
for greener pastures.

After tryouts in Philadelphia and Atlantic City, *The Sidewalks of New York* opened on Monday, October 3, 1927, at New York's Knickerbocker Theater. New York was having one of its most glittering seasons. Ruby Keeler was a smashing success and the show a solid hit.

The opening bit by Hope and Byrne became so insignificant they were given notice and found themselves once again close to Broadway, but not close enough.

Milt Lewis, an agent who would later become important as talent director for Paramount Pictures, searched around trying to find them work and actually secured a second spot with an eight-act vaudeville troupe at a theater which showcased road acts. In his own mind, Hope already knew everything worth knowing, and decided he would use his one Broadway credit to bully his way into a better situation.

Instead of a dance act, he and Byrne worked up a couple of jokes which brought them to the attention of super agent Johnny Hyde, later known as the agent who "laid and played Marilyn Monroe into stardom." Hyde would not, however, go out of his way to see them at the theater where they were working. He'd already heard about their jokes and wasn't interested.

Devastated but ever the optimist about his future, Hope decided that the money might not be in New York after all, but in Chicago, so he and George packed their bags and headed back to the sticks. Sticks or not, they had to eat, so Hope humbled himself to work for $50 a night in New Castle as third act on the bill. They were booked in for three days, earning $150 each for the run.

On the last night, Hope started kidding around at the end of the show, hyping the incoming shows as "the good shows" which brought some laughs from the audience. He warmed to laughter and before he was done for the evening, he had them begging for more.

By the time George and Les arrived by bus at the depot in Columbus, Ohio, the team had been dissolved because Les wanted to try a solo act as an emcee. In some ways he would never look back, yet he could never forget the humiliation of being fired from a Broadway hit show and being forced to play rinky-dink towns in order to eat. His life and career were finally resting on a firm foundation, even if he didn't know it. And if he didn't, he soon would, because nobody had more faith in Les Hope than Les Hope. He declared himself to be as good or better than the headliners of 1927 and he didn't care if he happened to be the only one who knew that. In his mind, everybody would know—sooner, rather than later.

Chapter 4

Hope tried a couple of skits in blackface, and considered himself at least equal to Al Jolson, but he was confused as to the direction he would take next. His ego would not allow him to bare himself before the public as anything but a handsome, slick, suave, and sophisticated ladies' man.

He hung around his mother's house for a while, but his ambitions and goals were in the theater. He'd merely have to tack his course. That course led him to Chicago—again. Broke, with no visible means of support and no prospects of gainful employment, he landed in Chicago in the middle of winter. January in Chicago is neither the time nor the place to be broke and stranded. But where there's Hope . . .

Chicago in 1928 had already begun the transition from strictly vaudeville in its theaters to a combination of vaudeville acts and silent films. A new era in show business, just around the corner, would change public entertainment forever and begin vaudeville's death knell.

By 1929 Warner Brothers would release *The Jazz Singer,* the first talking motion picture. The silents, shortly thereafter, were relegated to two-bit, rat-infested theaters in less desirable neighborhoods. But in the late spring of 1928, that possibility wasn't even thought of.

Without a partner Les Hope seemed, even to himself, something of a failure. He expected to be working regularly as a freelancer. However, as the theatrical metamorphosis moved into place, so did organization and big money. The RKO circuit controlled theaters and vaudeville acts and, since leaving New York, Hope had no inside connections. He scraped about for independent agency gigs but got nowhere.

Theaters had their own orchestras, announcers, and emcees and had it not been for a chance encounter with an old vaudeville friend who was working with the Loew Agency, he might have admitted defeat and returned to Cleveland. Charlie Cooley introduced him to an independent agent/producer by the name of Charles Hogan. As a favor to Cooley, Hogan tried Hope out as an afternoon Decoration Day act in West Englewood as a replacement for the master of ceremonies. He received $25. Hope would have done it for nothing.

If a moment comes which changes a life forever, this had to be it for Hope. Both the theater manager and Hogan liked him and decided to try him out at another theater. Again he replaced a regular emcee, this time at the Stratford, a neighborhood theater.

A one-day tryout turned into two weeks and then four, and eventually led to six months' work at a starting salary of $200 per week. With his confidence riding high again, he made another name change. "Lester" had been too academic and "Les" too casual. During his appearance at the Stratford he changed his name to Bob Hope.

Bob began to diversify his act. Not only did he perform the routine comedy stuff, he began to schmooze with his audiences and they loved it. He sang a little, stole jokes and rewrote them to fit his own sense of timing, made himself the butt of jokes, and began to lose his feeling of being a handsome leading man. He had finally found the fertile ground for a brand of comedy that would eventually build him an empire, both artistically and financially.

He made new friends, some of whom would be a part of his

show business organization throughout their own careers. He had the opportunity to hone and sharpen his material. If something didn't work one night, he'd try something else the next. With a long run, he could do that. His audience at the Stratford knew his capabilities and they let him know when he got it right. He had a thing with audiences. He would say, for instance, "That's the last joke I'll buy from that guy." The audiences ate it up. They weren't used to hearing entertainers speak so frankly.

Off stage he began to look more like some of the roles he would later portray in films—Beau Brummell, or New York's debonair mayor, Jimmy Walker. He dressed in dapper fashion, got his own apartment, and hired a lovely young apprentice secretary who was somewhat stage-struck. Louise Troxell went against the admonitions of her devout Catholic parents and joined Bob as a female foil when he took his new act on the road during the fall season of 1928.

Bob and Louise worked up the same kind of routines that were serving George Burns and Gracie Allen, Jack Benny and Mary Livingston, and any number of other husband-and-wife teams. Bob emulated husband-and-wife teams in other ways, too. He quickly nested with his numerous partners and with the exception of a very important item, a marriage license, he and his female partners set up housekeeping. Throughout his career Bob surrounded himself with beautiful women, many of them Hollywood's most glamorous starlets, and some well-known screen sirens.

Hope and Louise were signed by the Keith-Western Time Circuit which, to Broadway, was like Boston, New Haven, and Philadelphia—just a stair step below the big time. The Keith Circuit, like all the other big vaudeville organizations, searched the country for new faces. The new stars came from the "farm clubs," the circuit cities. Scouts covered hundreds of acts around the country and reported back to the big producers. They searched for that one-in-a-thousand act or personality which could be integrated into a Broadway production with the possibility of becoming a genuine star attraction.

No comedian ever worked rapid-fire dialogue with a foil

better than Hope. He didn't need long, involved jokes. Henny
Youngman did it alone, but Hope did better by bouncing off
a beautiful young girl, always making himself the butt of the
joke. For instance, with Louise, a skit that always garnered
great laughs:

Louise would walk on stage carrying a brown paper sack.

LOUISE: How do you do?
BOB: What have you got in your little bag?
LOUISE: Mustard.
BOB: Mustard? What's the idea?
LOUISE: You can never tell when you're going to meet
    a ham.

It was pure corn and played well in the corn belt, across the
plains in middle America.

In Kansas City he did one bit alone. He'd come out on the
stage and start singing a popular song of the day. After every
other phrase he would look at his wristwatch. At one point he
stopped, excused himself, and took out a bottle of medicine
from his coat pocket, then swallowed a couple of spoonfuls.
He put the cap back on the bottle, pocketed it, and continued
his song. By then the audience was both amused and puzzled.
His body would begin to quiver and shake. As the laughter
subsided, he would quip, "I forgot to shake the bottle." The
crowd roared its delight.

One of Bob and Louise's first outings came in St. Paul,
Minnesota. The audiences liked them, but didn't go overboard
with enthusiasm, which didn't please Hope very much.
Throughout his entire career he always shared his mother's
opinion of himself: he was better than anyone else and one day
the world would know it.

Their next engagement brought them to South Bend, Indiana,
and the heart of Catholicism—Notre Dame University. Hope
always claimed he didn't know that Notre Dame was a Catholic
university, but most people thought he had his tongue high up
in his cheek when he said that. It is altogether possible, however,
that he wasn't familiar with one of the most popular politicians

in the country. During the 1920s Bob Hope was too self-involved to be concerned with American politics. Only after he became a radio star did he begin to make jokes about politicians, finally seeing what a tremendous success Will Rogers had become, partially because of his biting political wit.

Hope stepped out onto the stage in South Bend to a roaring welcome. He wore the brown derby and had his new fad, a big cigar, shoved into the side of his mouth. He told one of his jokes that hadn't done that well in St. Paul and this time, the audience clapped, cheered, and stamped their feet.

He later found out that Al Smith, a great Irish Catholic politician running for president against Herbert Hoover, used the cigar and derby as his trademarks. Also, when Al Smith, the Democratic Party candidate, lost the race to Republican Herbert Hoover in 1928, Bob got a real dose of American prejudice against Catholics. He never forgot it.

South Bend became a classic example of a joke being "time warped." Many years later he returned there, came out on stage with the same wardrobe and same shtick, and went nowhere. The newer, hipper audience didn't get the joke.

On that same tour he and Louise hopscotched across Texas, which had a number of vaudeville theaters. In Fort Worth he repeated the same routines as he had previously in Chicago to appreciative audiences.

He walked out on stage, full of himself after South Bend, working his usually one-liners, actually almost stepping on his own lines at times to speed up the pace. Some years later, recalling the event during an interview, he said, "I was telling the audience, 'You've got to get my stuff fast because that's the way I sell it.' "

He and Louise were billed next to the final act which is a prime place to be—some say the best spot on the ticket. In vaudeville it is usually a boffo comedy situation. On opening night they performed before an almost totally silent audience. When he came off stage, he slammed his derby onto the floor and refused to be a part of the finale, telling the unit manager, "Get me the hell out of here on the first train. I want to go back to the United States."

Bob O'Donnell, an unpretentious guy who seemed to hang around the wings while the acts were performing, came back to the dressing room and asked Hope, "Hey, fancy pants, what's the problem?"

"If I wanted to play to foreigners I'd go to Africa. I'm not for these people. *That's* what's the matter!"

O'Donnell laughed out loud. "Son," he said, "you're in Texas. Don't talk so fast. These folks can't understand a word you say. Relax. It's summertime. Ain't nobody goin' anywhere. So take your time. You'll be all right."

Hope responded sarcastically, "Thanks too, too much."

After O'Donnell left the room, Bob asked the unit manager, "Who the hell is that jerk? Does he know who I am?"

"Oh, he knows who you are. You don't know who he is."

"So, who is he?" Bob asked again.

Shaking his head in disbelief, the unit manager said, "Only the head of the International Vaudeville Circuit. That's who he is."

Although Hope doubted the guy's logic, once he learned his identity, he had second thoughts. O'Donnell taught him a very critical lesson in comedy. "Know your audience. Sometimes it don't pay to rush things. Don't be in such a hurry," he said. "Let the audience catch up with you."

Afterward, when he had what he used to call "a slow audience," he would pause if the audience didn't get the joke at first, and say, "Take your time. I've got all night." They loved it in Fort Worth during the second show and by the end of the day, Hope said, "I was almost a hit." His ego assuaged, he decided to continue the Texas tour.

Unknown to Hope, O'Donnell did more than teach him a lesson. He liked Hope's quick wit and style so much he wired the Keith main office in New York to alert them to be sure and catch Bob's act. Also, unknown to O'Donnell, Bob had been in contact with a New York agency, Morris and Feil, sending them his pictures and background. They in turn sent him form letters which essentially asked him to stop by when he was in New York and they'd take a look.

Hope, who couldn't recognize a form letter from Tolstoy,

bragged to Louise that this would be their big chance. "Why, they'll have us featured in Flo Ziegfeld's Follies." If O'Donnell thought he was good, Bob thought himself superior.

He arrived in New York to a rude awakening. In the Morris and Feil outer offices the receptionist asked, "Who are you?", which he found somewhat insulting.

As he stood before the agents, one of them again asked, "Who are you exactly? Do we know you?"

Indignant, he answered, "I'm Bob Hope. I'm the Hope who's been writing to you."

"What do you do?"

"You don't know what I do, and you wrote me all those letters? Just give me back my pictures." They did. On his way out of their office, he yelled back over his shoulder, "B. F. Keith knows who I am!" And they did.

Lee Stewart, one of the Keith agents, told Bob, "Keith wants to see your act."

"Tell me where." Bob said.

"At the Jefferson over on 14th Street."

Bob knew the Jefferson. It had a reputation for beer-drinking brawlers, quicker to hurl a rotten egg than toss a rose at a performer.

"You don't think I'm going to perform in that dump?"

Bob suggested uptown at the Hamilton, Riverside, or Coliseum. He didn't intend to be swatted down again, and was still smarting over his reception by Morris and Feil. Stewart thought he ought to audition for Keith at the Jefferson.

"Look," Hope said, "I've been in touch with both the William Morris Agency and the Publix Circuit. They're all interested. So don't try to con me with some two-bit joint like the Jefferson."

He left the Keith office with mixed emotions and butterflies in his stomach. "I figured," he said, "that when the stakes are high, you gotta play high."

It paid off. Less than a week later the Keith office had found him a spot at Proctor's Eighty-Sixth Street Theater on the same bill with Leatrice Joy, a motion picture star who was touring the country, plugging her new picture. Hope would follow her.

Stewart warned him, "There won't be much money."

"I don't want any money."

"Are you crazy?"

"Like a fox. I just want them to see me. That's all. I got other people chasing me, too. But I'd like Keith to see my act. If they don't like me or the act, okay. I don't need money." It was the biggest bluff of his life.

In the meantime, he acted as though he really didn't need the money. He contacted an old friend, Charlie Yates, and asked him to find someplace where he could warm up his act. "Anywhere will do," he said. "Out in the bushes will be just fine."

It turned out to be the Dyker in Brooklyn for three days, which would be fine with Hope. He only wanted to brush up a couple of routines. He didn't give a damn about the house. He'd never play there again. For his three days he received twenty-five dollars.

Lee Stewart took time to see one of his shows at the Dyker and warned him, "Proctor's is a pretty big theater."

"Is that so? Well, if I don't score there we'll never talk to each other again. Okay?"

The day he opened at Proctor's he asked the doorman, "How's the audience here?"

"The toughest in New York, kid."

In the wings, waiting for Leatrice Loy to complete her talk, he remembered that she and her current husband, film idol John Gilbert, were having all kinds of problems in their marriage.

He came sailing out with his derby and cigar in place, outlandish plaid pants, and a big smile. He stopped at center stage and faced the audience. For a moment he remained silent. The audience tittered. Then, pretending to focus on a woman in the audience, he quipped, "No lady, this is not John Gilbert." The audience roared its delight. Beatrice Loy was not amused, but Hope could not have cared less about movie stars. He aimed to be the toast of Broadway.

Backstage, after the show, a joyous Lee Stewart greeted him. "I knew you had it . . . how about that audience?"

"What about the way I bombed at Dyker?" Bob asked.

"That's no theater."

The William Morris Agency also had a representative call on Bob backstage, after the first show, wanting him to come down to their offices the following day.

"Talk to me later," Hope said, "after the eleven o'clock show," which was the last show of the night.

When the Morris agent came back a second time, Hope smugly told him, "I can't do it."

"What can't you do?"

"Come down to the Morris office tomorrow."

"Why not?"

"I've signed with Keith."

He didn't tell the guy that he'd tipped Lee Stewart about his first visit and that Stewart got in touch with Keith and after the second show he offered Bob a three-year contract at $400 per week. Bob negotiated him up to $450 and closed the deal before the last show. He could have held the Keith people at bay while he checked out other offers that might have been more lucrative, but because Keith booked the Palace Theater in New York, every vaudevillian's goal, Bob took the deal without any regrets.

More puffed up than usual, Hope did the third show with the confidence of a seasoned professional, opening his act with a very self-assured, "Now that the amateurs are finished . . ."

Having signed with one of the biggest circuits in the business, Hope had to constantly come up with new material—and it would have to be topical. He hired his first professional comedy writer, Al Boesberg.

Chapter 5

Broadway! Broadway! Broadway! But not yet the Palace. And besides, Broadway would soon be assaulted with the same financial woes that would devastate the rest of the country and the world as well. In the United States, unemployment would reach a staggering twenty-five percent.

Fortunately for Bob Hope, he signed his contract a week or two before the financial world collapsed. Nevertheless, signing with B. F. Keith put Hope aboard his rocket to becoming an American treasure—a world-wide icon. Now that he had a term contract with a major vaudeville agency with assurance of making a living for three years come hell or high water, he needed only to worry about the next level of his career.

Having been accepted by the greatest theatrical agency in the country, Bob became a more responsible employer. Contrary to what his audiences might have thought, he and Louise did not have a joint contract. She worked for him.

He'd been paying her $50 a week for a long time and she expected to get a raise along with Hope's three-year contract with the Keith Circuit.

He doubled her salary to $100 a week, leaving him with $350 to spend on whatever he wanted or needed. Earmarking

$50 a week for his mother back in Ohio, he still had $300 clear. His contract gave him freedom beyond his wildest imagination. Deciding that he needed a car suitable to his new station in life, he considered two very popular models, a Packard and the classy-looking Pierce Arrow.

While deciding, he ran into Al Lloyd, who had given up theatrical agenting for a more secure occupation—selling insurance. He suggested to Bob that he think about his old age. "Why not invest some money in your future? You can't go wrong with insurance."

"I can't drive an insurance policy," Bob said.

In the end, he remembered something John D. Rockefeller had once said about not trusting anybody. Hope construed that to mean, "Look out for yourself." He put Al Lloyd and John D. Rockefeller together and opted for insurance. It was a downpayment on what would become a half-billion dollar empire.

Just prior to their first Keith engagement at Brooklyn's Albee Theater, Wall Street crashed. On October 29, the show business Bible, *Variety,* made its most famous announcement of all times: WALL STREET LAYS AN EGG.

Wall Street bombed, but Hope's act got better reviews—especially the part played by Louise. Moving from the Albee to Proctor's, again, on November 5, 1929, *Variety* took note of the Keith Circuit's new find:

> Hope, assisted by an unbilled girl . . . clever at handling comedy lines . . . If some material, especially where old gags are found, could be changed, chances are this would double strength . . . Next to closing . . . had no trouble handling spot . . ."

The Hope ego had trouble dealing with Louise getting special attention. He was the star. He couldn't handle any upstaging by an underling. After reading the review, the girl he claimed to be in love with demanded a solo spot in the act. This infuriated Hope, immediately diminishing his affection.

Instead of taking the position that what was good for the act would be good for him, he fired off a telegram to Mildred

Rosequist, asking her to join him when he played Cleveland the following week. Louise could go take a hike. To sweeten the deal, he proposed marriage to Mildred, who proved to be just as independent as Louise: she promptly rejected both offers. Adding to the insult, she announced her forthcoming marriage to another man.

Having made a fool of himself, he had to eat some crow and keep Louise in the act. She withdrew her demands and when the couple arrived in Cleveland he proudly announced their engagement. Mildred wasn't fooled, but she let him save face by keeping her mouth shut.

Although he still hadn't made it to the Palace in New York City, Bob had become pretty much a headliner in vaudeville. The folks back in Cleveland considered him the biggest star on Broadway. So it came as no surprise to anyone that, after his fiasco with Mildred and the announcement to his family of his engagement to Louise, he arrived in Cleveland to perform at the Orpheum Theater to great fanfare.

His mother hadn't seen him on stage since he'd taken off to the big time. By the time it came to go to the theater on opening night, she was so nervous she refused to go with the rest of the family. However, after the *Cleveland Press* gave him a four-star review, she agreed to attend the matinee on the following day.

Bob's brother Jim often repeated the story of accompanying his mother to see the hometown boy making good on stage. "My mother," he said, "trembled from head to toe, just sitting there beside me in her seat, tears running down her face, her fingernails digging into my palms."

When Bob came on stage she stiffened, relaxing only after the audience had given him a long and rousing ovation. About midway through his act he sighted his mother and stopped. "There she is, folks! That's Mahm! The one with the lilies of the valley on her hat. There she is. Way back there. Stand up and let these folks see you, Mahm!"

His family threw a party at the family home on Euclid Avenue after the evening show. Bob hadn't been home in a while so there was a lot of family gossip to catch up with and, of course, they eyed Louise with skepticism.

Each of his brothers had gone into some sort of business, and part of the evening's conversation centered on the Wall Street crash and the effect it would have on Bob's career. He assured them that he had a three-year contract with a guaranteed income. "Besides," he said, "stocks go up and stocks go down. You think those big shots on Wall Street are going to let the economy go down the drain?"

Never one to miss a golden opportunity, Bob scanned the real estate section of the papers and found that the cost of houses had dropped significantly. It was time for his mother to have a decent house, he thought, in a decent neighborhood, so he purchased a house at 3323 Yorkshire Road in the exclusive Cleveland Heights district.

He didn't bother to notify his mother about his new purchase and blithely announced that he was throwing out her old furniture. Avis thought he'd lost his mind. Ignoring her protests, he swept her up in his arms and physically carried her out to the car, where Fred was already behind the wheel with the motor running. The two of them delivered her to the new house. Two items of furniture did go with her—her sewing machine and her piano.

Bob had more than one reason for buying Avis a new house. Although he didn't discuss the matter with his mother, one of his brothers had called him aside the day he arrived in Cleveland to tell him the bad news: Mahm had cervical cancer. Her doctor had advised surgery as quick as possible, but she wasn't about to upset "Lester" with her problems, afraid it might interfere with his performance. No, she'd wait to make that decision.

One of the first houses Bob and Louise played under his new contract with the Keith Circuit was the Palace Theater in Chicago, home of gangland's most notorious bootlegger, Al Capone. Capone ran Chicago. He handed down orders and city officials jumped. Half the city's hierarchy were on his payroll. The other half profited indirectly.

Unadvisedly, Bob decided to do a skit with Louise in which he used Al Capone's notoriety to make a point:

LOUISE: You're very attractive.

BOB: Yes, I come from a very brave family. My brother slapped Al Capone in the face.

LOUISE: Your brother slapped Al Capone in the face?

BOB: Yes.

LOUISE: I'd like to shake his hand.

BOB: We're not going to dig him up just for that.

After the show the theater manager approached Bob. "Mr. Hope," he said somewhat nervously, "I think you ought to get rid of that joke while you're in Chicago."

"Why?"

"Some of Al's boys catch our Saturday night shows and we don't want to offend anyone, if you know what I mean."

Bob ignored his advice and kept the skit in the show and, just as the manager had warned him, the boys showed up and were not remotely amused.

Early Sunday morning a sleepy Bob received a phone call.

"You Bob Hope?" the gravel-voiced caller asked.

"Yeah, why?"

"You doin' a joke about Al Capone?"

"Sure. It's part of my act. Anyway, what business is it of yours?"

"Just don't do it anymore. Okay?"

"Who is this?"

"I'm just one of the boys. Get rid of it."

Bob finally got the guy's point. "Yes sir," he said, "it's out."

During the matinee, Al Capone became Jack Dempsey, heavyweight boxing champion of the world. Bob never heard from Capone's boys again—not even a promised thank you—and he didn't want to. Comedian Joe E. Lewis got his throat slashed because he chose to ignore warnings from gangsters.

Al Boasberg kept wiring new jokes to Hope during his first Keith tour, which was limited to the United States and only as far west as Chicago, where the Orpheum Circuit picked up and went all the way to the West Coast, with Canadian stops along the way. Bob and Louise played Winnipeg, Calgary, and Vancouver and then down the West Coast, hitting Seattle, Portland, San Francisco, Los Angeles, San Diego, and back to New York via Salt Lake City, Denver, Omaha, Kansas City, and St. Louis.

He did not do as well on the Orpheum Circuit as he had with Keith. On the other hand, he didn't bomb either.

Al Boasberg, a bear of a man whose size accommodated an unbelievable intake of food, thought up most of his comedy material while sitting in a bathtub of scorching-hot water. He and Bob did not have any formal contract. He wrote the jokes and Bob sent him a check.

The two of them would sit down at a Chinese restaurant in New York and work on jokes together over chop suey and green tea. Boasberg knew that if Bob wanted to be successful over the long haul he'd have to develop some sort of format and Al, a student of the American entertainment scene, knew how public taste changed from day to day.

So Al worked up a revue format which served Hope well when he and Louise made their first cross-country tour. Boasberg has also been credited with arranging Bob's first screen test—long before he became famous on radio.

Bill Perlberg, a good friend of Al's, happened also to be an agent with the William Morris office in Hollywood. During a conversation on the telephone, Boasberg alerted his friend that Hope would be playing the Hill Street Theater in Los Angeles and if nothing else, he should catch Bob's act. "I think this kid has movie potential," Al advised.

Bob and Louise were well received at the Hill Street and after the show on opening night, he received a phone call from Perlberg, who explained who he was and that Al had suggested he get in touch.

"What makes you think I'd give up vaudeville for films?" Hope asked.

"Al says you're good."

Bob laughed. "That's only because he writes some of my material."

"I've never seen you work, but Al has a pretty good eye for talent. Anyway, the studios are hiring a lot of New York talent, and what's the harm in doing a screen test? Why don't you come over and let's see what you've got?"

"Well, I might work it in," Bob said with his usual show of self-possession.

"Okay, report to the Pathé Film Studios the morning after you close downtown."

Meanwhile, Bob made a tour of Hollywood Studios and saw the big sound stages and all the activity. He managed to visit the set of *The King of Jazz,* bandleader Paul Whiteman's life story. All the activity and professionalism impressed him. Bing Crosby was part of the Rhythm Boys, a singing group with Paul Whiteman's band. Bob and Bing had yet to meet, but we now know that was an inevitability. Bob had just become interested in golf and, incidentally, had almost passed up the screen test to play a few rounds while waiting to move on to San Diego for his last West Coast appearance of the tour.

On a Thursday morning Bob and Louise arrived promptly at Pathé as scheduled, and were taken immediately to make-up. The director dropped by to say hello and Bob asked to see his script.

"No script, kid. Just do your vaudeville act and we'll shoot it."

"Just like that?" Bob asked.

"Just like that, kid. This is Hollywood."

The revue that Al Boasberg cooked up for Bob and Louise was called *Antics of 1930,* not unlike the Olsen and Johnson shows that would later storm Broadway. They did some of those routines for the film test. The director yelled "Action," and the duo went into their act, which included one of Hope's most famous routines:

"It's very exciting at my hotel . . . the other day a lady guest came down to the lobby and demanded to see the manager. She said, 'Something terrible is happening.

There's a bat in my room,' and the desk clerk said, 'Don't get excited, lady. We'll send up a ball.' Another guest walked into the lobby and asked, 'Is there a Katz in the hotel?' and the clerk said, 'No, there's no Katz here.' The man said, 'Well, if one comes in, send him up. The mice are eating my shoes.' "

Another skit used in the screen test:

HOPE: I was standing out in the lobby when a lady came up to me and asked if I could tell her where she could find the rest room. So I told her it was just around the corner.

LADY: Don't give me that Herbert Hoover talk—I'm in a hurry to go.

Full of himself, Bob left the studio assured in his own mind that he'd be in demand by every studio in town by Monday morning. He left his number with Perlberg and headed for Agua Caliente in Mexico to do some gambling before opening in San Diego.

Monday came and went without any word from Perlberg. Finally, unable to stand the suspense, Bob phoned him. "Hey, Bill, how'd it go? I guess you've been busy or you would have called me, right? When can I see the test?"

"You really want to see it?" Perlberg asked, seeming surprised.

"I don't want to be the only one who hasn't seen it when the offers start coming in," Bob responded.

"I'm sure Pathé will be happy to let you see it. I'll set it up."

"But," Bob queried, "how did *you* like it?"

"Go see it and then we'll talk," Perlberg said.

Bob and Louise sat alone in projection room 8 as the test results lit up the screen. At the end, the projectionist called down, "Mr. Hope, would you like me to run it again?"

"No, thanks," Bob said. He would later confess that it had been "the worst twenty minutes of my life." What worked on a vaudeville stage definitely did not work on a sound stage with a camera. Bob had no sense of camera angles or presenting himself in the most flattering manner. His nose seemed longer than Pinocchio's. "I wanted to crawl out of the studio," he lamented.

As soon as he could get out of California, he and Louise climbed aboard the train to Salt Lake City. He'd had enough of movies. "Broadway," he told Louise, "that's where I belong."

Although Broadway beckoned, so did the golf course in Salt Lake City. At their hotel he got on the bus with some members of the show who were toting golf bags. He'd done pretty well on small practice courses, and decided to try driving. He rented clubs and played a full eighteen holes for the first time. Pleased with his ability, he immediately went out and bought a set of clubs. By the time they arrived back in Manhattan, he'd played courses in every city along the way. Most important to Bob, he'd broken 100.

Chapter 6

Having conquered the greens, Hope wanted some greener pastures—like the Palace Theater on Broadway. He had lunch at Lindy's with Lee Stewart and confronted him. "I think I'm ready for the Palace. It's a Keith theater, and I'm under contract to Keith. I've had rave reviews all across the country. So when do I play the Palace?"

"In time, Bob. All in due time."

"I haven't got time. I want to get on with my career and until I open at the Palace . . ."

"We're working on it, Bob. Meanwhile, I'd like you to do another tour. By the time you get back I hope I'll have big news for you," Stewart told him. "Take some time off while I line up some tour dates. Go visit your folks in Cleveland. You've been working hard. You deserve some time off."

Bob reluctantly agreed. He and Louise departed, he for Cleveland and Louise to Chicago to visit her father. As usual, his mother had an angle to protect another of her brood. Bob's younger brother, George, seemed to Avis to be on the verge of taking the wrong course in life. To prevent a family catastrophe she wheedled at Bob to find something for George to do. "Make him a part of your act," she suggested.

"Mahm," Bob pleaded, "I've already got an act."

She persisted. "Les, I'm sure if you put on your thinking cap you'll come up with something. I know you can do it."

In order to please his mother, Bob figured out a way to use George as sort of a plant in the audience—a stooge. In other words, while Bob performed on stage, George would needle him from the audience and they'd do a bit of bantering back and forth.

The idea couldn't have come at a better time. Bob had been thinking for some time of putting together a unit of his own— a show in which he would be the star attraction. At 20, George would come cheap. Meanwhile, he'd be able to keep an eye on his kid brother. Everybody would be happy, especially his mother. He knew that in her present physical condition, stress over one of her children was the last thing she needed. He returned to New York with George in tow, both happy as larks.

Lee Stewart booked Bob's act into the Coliseum Theater, a somewhat impressive movie house that featured vaudeville acts between screenings. With the onset of the Depression, every agent had to fight for his clients. On Wednesday afternoons the Keith executives met in their conference room at the Palace Theater. The sessions were often raucous.

Although the world financial crisis had not as yet done any great damage to vaudeville, the Keith managers, agents, and bookers around the country were fully aware that their business would eventually be affected. It became a "numbers crunching" game long before economists picked up the expression.

The Coliseum had a reputation for class and the furthering of acts which appeared there. Stewart's idea of booking Hope into the Coliseum had a two-fold purpose. First, he wanted to keep his star client busy and happy. Secondly, if he kept him booked in and around the New York City area, there would be the advantageous local publicity. The Keith bosses read the columns and reviews and were always looking for acts to bolster ticket sales for their crown jewel, the Palace.

A near disaster, which no one could have foreseen, came close to destroying any chance of Bob's getting into the Palace. A film delineating the horrors of World War I, directed by

Lewis Milestone and starring a very young Lew Ayres, just happened to be playing at the Coliseum along with Bob's act.

The film depicted such a depressing picture about war and its ravages, from a young German soldier's point of view, that it left audiences devoid of any sense of the comedic. As the final credits rolled and THE END appeared on the screen, Bob came bouncing out on the stage full of adrenaline and found himself faced with an audience in mourning. Bob's routines actually annoyed the theatergoers. How dare the management treat such a serious movie with so little respect?

Not one audible laugh came from the crowd, and many patrons fled the theater in tears during George's debut as a heckler. Devastated, Bob threw a tantrum backstage similar to his earlier outrageous behavior in Fort Worth, Texas.

He later admitted that he'd reacted badly. "I should have known it couldn't possibly work. The audience was still in shock. Had he told them that he was just doing his job, he went on, ". . . they might have understood." Instead, he stormed off stage and declared that he would not go back on as long as that picture played. Lee Stewart convinced him to hang in. "It would be a very bad thing for you to do. Not only will you not play the Palace in the future, you might just get yourself kicked out of vaudeville."

Bob's ruffled feathers finally smoothed down. It was only a four-day engagement and he'd faced worse, although he couldn't remember when. Once the gig had been completed, Stewart quickly sent him out on another tour of the Orpheum Circuit, with Louise and George.

The Coliseum fiasco brought Bob to the conclusion that if he wanted to continue as a headliner in vaudeville, he would have to compete with movies. In order to do that, he'd have to have an act as good or better. He had no doubt that "talkies" meant that motion pictures were here to stay and would soon be moving into the forefront for the entertainment dollar.

Despite the Keith Organization's efforts to put on a happy face, their showplace, the Palace, had been losing money. In an attempt to stem the tide they converted from what had been a very successful two shows a day to five. The change devastated vaudevillians.

Despite that drastic move to shore up their losses, by the end of 1931 the Palace went into the red to the tune of $200,000 per year. The Depression had finally made it to Broadway. Show business impresarios were pulling out what hair they had left and eyeing the ledges of New York's skyscrapers just in case.

In February, 1931, Bob, Louise, and George closed their Orpheum tour in Cleveland. In his dressing room, removing his make-up at the end of their Cleveland appearance, Bob had ambivalent feelings about leaving town. He knew his mother's health had deteriorated. Fearful that he might never see his beloved Mahm again, he almost hoped that he wouldn't have another engagement right away.

The cold, dreary winter weather matched his mood. In addition to his mother's weakened condition, he had Louise to contend with. To be sure that she continued to warm his bed, he'd made promises he had no intention of keeping. Louise, on the other hand, had diamond engagement and wedding rings on her mind.

There could not have been a better tonic for Bob when Lee Stewart burst into the dressing room, his face aglow despite the freezing temperatures outside.

Bob looked up, "What the hell . . ."

"We did it! We did it!" Lee announced.

"Did what?" Bob asked.

"The Palace."

A skeptical Bob Hope asked, "Yeah? When? 1935?"

Lee laughed and clapped his hand on Bob's shoulder. "Right now—1931. In fact, you're opening with Bea Lillie next Monday—for two weeks."

"You're serious?"

"Absolutely! So get your butt back to New York. You got work to do, my friend."

It had always been his dream. "I've got to tell Mahm," he said. "She needs to know this right now."

The news did seem to perk Avis up. It had always been her dream, too. "I told everybody you were better than Frank Fay. Now the whole world will know it."

Despite the knowledge that his mother was slipping away, Bob had to laugh. She hadn't lost her spirit.

Some years later, Lee Stewart would recall his opinion of Bob's reaction to the good news.

"Bob was on the verge of a breakdown. I've never seen him so nervous. But in spite of his nervousness, his brain was clicking. He knew he was going into fast company, that he was following the best in the business."

Bea Lillie headlined the show, held over for a second week. Her sharp English wit went over big with savvy New Yorkers. The bill also featured singer Vivian Segal, who'd just arrived from the West Coast, as well as humorist Harry Hershfield.

Hope, Louise, George, and Lee Stewart put their heads together and came up with a stunt to get the public to pay attention to Bob's act.

Bob contacted Milt Lewis—who would became head of talent at Paramount Pictures, where Bob would spend most of his movie career—and asked him to round up unemployed Broadway actors to pretend to picket Bob's run at the Palace. They were to carry signs complaining about Bob's treatment of George and Louise. Some of the signs read: BOB HOPE IS UNFAIR TO STOOGES, LOCAL 711 or BOB HOPE IS UNFAIR TO DISORGANIZED STOOGES, REFUSES TO PAY FOR THEIR LUMPS, BUMPS, DOCTORS AND HOS-PITAL BILLS.

Though it got him the intended attention, it also backfired. With so many actors and theatrical people out of work along Broadway, many people sympathized with the bogus "stooges" and wouldn't cross the picket lines. Elmer Rogers quickly ordered Bob to call off the troops.

Bob didn't care that the New York press gave him tepid reviews or that the audiences came to see Bea Lillie, not Bob Hope and his *Antics of 1931*. He'd made it to the top—the big time—*the Palace!* But one critic annoyed the hell out of him.

Jerry Wald, writing for the old *New York Graphic,* gave Bob one of the worst zingers in his career.

"They say," Wald wrote, "that Bob Hope is the sensation of the midwest. If that's so, why doesn't he go back there?"

With all the acts on Broadway, Hope couldn't understand why he had been singled out for such a vicious barb. It wouldn't be the first or the last time a critic looked upon his abilities with disdain, but he never got used to it. His mother had instilled in him a high sense of self-importance. She never looked kindly on anyone who doubted or besmirched her adorable "Les."

When recounting the incident over the years, Bob Hope never mentioned Jerry Wald's name, nor did he ever forgive him, despite the fact that Wald became a very influential writer and producer in Hollywood.

Hope's run at the Palace had some stiff competition up and down the Great White Way: George and Ira Gershwin's *Of Thee I Sing* (the first musical comedy to be awarded a Pulitzer Prize); Noel Coward, co-starring with Gertrude Lawrence in *Private Lives; The Wonder Bar* starring Al Jolson; and *The Band Wagon,* starring the current (and sensational) song and dance brother and sister, Fred and Adele Astaire.

He'd reached vaudeville's glittering summit—and it took him some time to realize just how far he had actually come.

Opening night found him a nervous wreck, his timing woefully off. Once again, his insecurities overtook him. After the first show he told Lee Stewart that he might not yet be ready for the Palace.

Lee laughed nervously. He didn't want to upset his star. He knew that Bob's time had come and he didn't intend to let Hope spook himself. "You're doing just fine. It's just first-night jitters. What the hell, it's the Palace. You know how many hoofers would trade places with you tonight?"

Stewart urged Harry Hershfield, who knew how to calm a stomach filled with butterflies, to talk to Bob. Harry's encouragement helped get Bob and his group back on track.

Sunday nights at the Palace were famous as "celebrity nights" and assured a packed house. With theaters dark, other actors and vaudevillians had an opportunity to check out the

Palace talent while, at the same time, seeing and being seen by their peers.

Elmer Rogers, who managed the Palace, wanted to give Hope a lift, so he prevailed upon him to emcee the first Sunday Celebrity Night during his appearance, assuring the nervous comedian that the house would be "packed with Broadway stars."

Hope thought, "Damned if you do and damned if you don't." He once told Ernie Kovacs that he "felt something like a minor league ballplayer suddenly being thrust into the big leagues, coming up at bat in the ninth inning with the game tied and the winning run on third."

The object of emceeing Celebrity Night was to tell some good jokes, introduce celebrities from the audience, and, if possible, get them up on stage in impromptu situations. Old-timers tell of shows that went on long into the night because once on stage, stars became hams and went out of their way to upstage one another. There was no animosity, just entertainers doing what jazz musicians had been doing for years—jamming for fun.

Bob got off to a terrible start, due mostly to shattered nerves. Many in the audience were familiar with Hope's growing reputation and understood his predicament. Most of them had been there before, and on more than one occasion.

Help came from unexpected sources. Sitting close to the front, where they could be heard well both on stage and in the theater, Eddie Cantor, Al Jolson, Ken Murray, Ted Healy, and a dozen other big Broadway names were enjoying the night off from their own shows.

Bob told his Herbert Hoover joke about prosperity being right around the corner, a chicken in every pot, and two cars in every garage. His very hip audience knew the joke by heart, many of them having already filched it from Bob and incorporated thinly disguised versions into their own acts. So they felt some obligation to the new kid on the block.

Ken Murray got out of his fifth row seat and ran down the aisle toward the orchestra pit, demanding that Hope let him tell a joke.

"I've already heard it," Hope snapped, and the audience roared.

One after another, the famous and notorious got into the act with Bob. What ensued left professional sensibilities thoroughly sated and the rest of the crowd with an unusually enjoyable evening in which they could forget their hunger, unemployment, and Depression blues. It also brought attention to Bob from his peers, important producers, directors, and powerful members of the Broadway press corps.

Always quick to pick up on some small bit that could be expanded into a good skit, Bob's brain seemed to be computerized to capture and record the most insignificant little nothing if it seemed to please the audience. He had one such skit that came about quite by accident.

One of his stooges, Toots Murdock (along with Bob's brother George), would play to him from the balconies of theaters. Toots, as Bob recalled somewhat sentimentally, "had the same problem as my father. He drank too much." Toots was a working alcoholic. Sometimes that created a problem.

While playing the Palace, Bob would place Toots in the left balcony and George in the right balcony. Johnny Peters, another of Bob's stooges, would come on stage with a megaphone and do a take on Rudy Vallee, the most popular male singer of the day, while Bob stood to one side and made faces to the audience.

In the middle of the skit, George would yell across the balcony to Toots, "Hey Herman!"

Bob would give him a withering look and George would slump back in his seat in an endeavor to become invisible. Back to Johnny and his megaphone. "My time is your time . . ."

GEORGE: Hey Herman!
TOOTS: Whadda you want?
GEORGE: What time does the show start?
BOB(from the stage): Wait a minute! Do you realize what you're doing? You're upsetting my act.
GEORGE: This is an act?

In one instance Toots, with one too many nips from his bottle of spirits, hung so far over the balcony railing that Bob thought he was going to land in the lap of someone on the floor below.

Bob quickly attempted to soothe the audience and distract them from the severity of the situation. "You can tell my friend in the box is destined for greatness. Nothing can stop him. Not even his talent."

This went on for several shows even though Hope gave Toots a dressing-down between shows and even threatened to fire him. All to no avail. Expecting him to have sobered up somewhat before the next show, Bob opened the show as always and waited for the cross-dialogue between George and Toots. Apparently Toots had totally ignored Bob's admonishments and had, in fact, really loaded up after the last show.

Enraged, Bob could only think that after the show he'd fire Toots on the spot. To his utter surprise, a drunk Toots Murdock went over big with the audience. They had no idea that the stooge was blotto. They were convinced that his antics were all part of the act. Never one to go against audience tastes, Hope never mentioned the matter again.

Having survived another obstacle in his struggle to reach the top of the heap, Hope acquired his first real evidence of wealth by treating himself to a new Single Six Packard, with a 3.9 litre six-cylinder engine purring comfortably under a long blue bonnet. A status symbol par excellence, the new vehicle attracted women—beautiful women. Hope may have stammered a little on opening night at the Palace, but he never stammered where women were concerned. He'd become an expert in bringing willing damsels into his boudoir, and if his new Packard became a conveyance, all the better.

Louise, who dropped hints to friends that she would soon become Mrs. Bob Hope, was not amused. Whenever the subject of marriage came up, Bob would divert the conversation into other areas. Louise's frustration and Bob's reluctance would eventually reach a boiling point. In the meantime, Bob had other plans.

Chapter 7

Tired of touring, Bob wanted to get into something more stable—something that would allow him to stay in one place longer. He did not envision marriage as an option. Factually, he had devised a plan to get rid of Louise and her nagging about Holy Matrimony. At the end of a tour in the spring of 1932, he made a decision he hoped would help him shed some of his problems, Louise in particular. He wanted to be a solo star, not part of an ensemble. His decision would temporarily cost him a slice of his weekly income, now over nine hundred dollars a week. During the early thirties, that would be comparable to what our top stars of today make—without the onerous income taxes.

Economically, he had everything planned out. Although he never discussed it, he always worried that Louise would find some way to cut deeper into his income.

While Hope's star seemed to be on the rise, other big names of the day were beginning to slip into the past, along with full employment and fat paychecks.

The Palace Theater had peaked and would soon see the beginning of its decline. Some Broadway actors were looking toward Hollywood and "talkies." Silent film stars, some of whom did not understand the use of dialogue, were destined to the ash bin. Many of the "he-man" screen idols spoke with effeminate lisps, sounding more like Betty Boop than swashbuckling pirates.

Popular actresses of silent films like Clara Bow and Theda Bara were suddenly relegated to retirement.

New York voice coaches found gold in the Hollywood hills. Those thespians who bridged the treacherous waters separating silents and talkies spent long hours and thousands of dollars learning to speak for the new motion pictures. Grown men practiced roaring like lions in order to deepen their voices for the screen. For some, it worked. For others, it provided serious sore throats.

In this precarious environment, Hope returned to the Palace with *Antics of 1932*. His reviews were nervously conservative. *Variety* reviewed his latest act with watered-down generosity:

> Just a so-so lineup on tap here this week, with Bob Hope playing the role of lifesaver. It took this funster to finally wake them up to a degree. After he got under way he had them howling at his comedic reactions and great comedy material. Hope is a pippin performer, and ad-libbing helps tremendously to get many extra laughs from the supporting company and the musicians in the pit as well as the audience.

A new revue, *Ballyhoo of 1932,* was being put together during Bob's latest stint at the Palace. The producers, consisting of Bobby Connelly, Norman Anthony, Russell Patterson, and Lou Gensler, had already cast a number of popular comedy names for the revue. Al Jolson's manager, having seen Hope at the Palace, suggested that Bob be brought on board.

Such a move would reduce his salary from $1000 a week to $600. Although many of his cronies teased that he accepted the offer in order to have his pick of the gorgeous girls in the show, Bob truly wanted the change of pace which the revue would give him.

After rehearsing throughout the long, hot summer, while

politics and political conventions monopolized the headlines, *Ballyhoo* opened to a disastrous first night in August 1932 at the Nixon Theater on Atlantic City's Steel Pier. The chorus girls missed their opening cue and the electricity disappeared momentarily as the orchestra played the overture in the dark.

When Bob hesitated to go out on stage, tell a few jokes, and generally warm the audience up until the show could get back on track, Lee Shubert—one of the show's backers—snapped at him, "Don't be so hard to work with. Get out there and do your thing!"

Bob's bouncy personality actually calmed down the restless opening night audience. He received such a warm response from the crowd that Shubert suggested he go out and ad-lib like that to open the show every night. Hope agreed only on condition that he be allowed to slip in some of his own funny bits.

In one instance a vendor walks up and down the aisle pitching his wares while Hope is in the middle of a routine.

VENDOR

PEANUTS . . . POPCORN . . . CRACKERJACKS.

HOPE

(OFFENDED)

JUST A MINUTE. WHAT'S THE IDEA OF SELLING PEANUTS AND POPCORN DURING MY ACT?

VENDOR

I HAVE TO DO THIS TO MAKE A LIVING. I ONLY MADE A HUNDRED DOLLARS THIS WEEK.

HOPE

(JUMPS DOWN INTO THE AISLE)

HOW MUCH DID YOU SAY YOU MAKE DOING THIS?

VENDOR

A HUNDRED A WEEK . . .

HOPE

(SNATCHES THE BASKET FROM VENDOR)

GIVE ME THAT BASKET. YOU GET UP THERE ON THE STAGE.

The show opened on Broadway at the 44th Street Theater on September 7, 1932, and took a lathering from the tough New York critics. The *New York Times* theater critic said, ''The chief things that *Ballyhoo* lacks are charm, distinction, and any kind of theatrical allure.''

It closed in slightly less than four months. However, Bob Hope profited because of the additional exposure and having saved the show with his patter in front of the curtain. It didn't hurt him economically that he still had a valid contract with Keith, which immediately booked him into Broadway's Capitol Theater.

A young singer, formerly one of The Rhythm Boys out of the Paul Whiteman Orchestra, had left ''Pop'' 's big band to carve his own niche by challenging another crooner, Russ Columbo. Bing Crosby and Russ Columbo had voices so much alike that unless a song had already been closely associated to one or the other, heated arguments arose over whose voice was crooning the love songs. Had Columbo not suffered an untimely gunshot wound to the head in September of 1934, the already-boiling feud between the two singers might have exploded into violence.

By the summer of 1932, while Bob Hope rehearsed *Ballyhoo,* Crosby, now an established star, had settled into Hollywood after signing a contract with Paramount Publix (before it became Paramount Pictures) and toured nationally to promote his first full-length movie, *The Big Broadcast of 1932,* based somewhat loosely on the hit Broadway show, *Wild Waves.*

When Bing arrived in New York to head the bill at the Capitol Theater, along with his guitarist Eddie Lang, his current salary of $4000 a week amounted to about four times that of Bob Hope. Crosby's status impressed Bob, and when he found out that they would be on the same bill, he personally greeted Bing when the crooner arrived in New York.

Bing had been brought to New York to host a radio show sponsored by Chesterfield cigarettes starting in January of 1933. While preparing for the show, his brother Everett Crosby managed to get him a booking at the Capitol.

Thus the twain indeed met—Crosby from Washington State and Hope from England by way of Cleveland.

Bing considered himself the top talent in the world and made no secret of it. He considered Bob Hope to be just a country boy compared to his own status as "America's singing heart-throb." Consequently, Bing bored easily. Many who worked with him over the years learned that his sharp responses and cold persona were not personal assaults. It was just the Crosby personality.

The show opened on December 2, 1932. Bing often invented gimmicks to spice up his work. Listening to some of the out-takes of songs he recorded with the Andrews Sisters and many others, one can quickly pick up on his sense of the magic moment. He thought it made no sense at all to come out on the stage, sing, and then return to his dressing room until the next show.

Bob and Bing discovered a common interest in O'Reilly's Bar, directly across the street from the Capitol, where the two retired between shows for a bit of refreshment.

Prohibition had barely come to an end and O'Reilly's was one of the first bars in New York to offer legalized booze. During one of their drinking bouts the two created their on-stage banter, although a great deal of ad-libbing took place. The two men were naturals.

For instance, Hope would strut out on the stage and open the show:

HOPE

AH, GOOD EVENING, LADIES AND GENTS. I'M AFRAID WE'LL HAVE TO DO WITHOUT MY PARTNER TONIGHT— SOME CAD LOCKED HIM IN THE WASHROOM.

The crowd, sensing some nonsense in the making, started to laugh. Before the laughter had completely faded, out would walk Crosby, holding a brass doorknob attached to a piece of splintered wood.

CROSBY

GOOD EVENING, LADIES AND GENTLEMEN. I FEEL I MUST
APOLOGIZE. YOU'LL HAVE TO FORGIVE ME FOR WORKING
ALONE TONIGHT — MY PARTNER HAS AN UPSET STOM-
ACH . . .

HOPE
(INTERRUPTING)
. . . NOW WAIT A MINUTE! I DON'T HAVE AN UPSET
STOMACH.

CROSBY
(WAVING THE DOORKNOB IN HOPE'S FACE)
YOU WILL AFTER YOU SWALLOW THIS.

Theirs was a match made by the gods of show business.
When they weren't boozing it up at O'Reilly's, they played
billiards at the Friars Club. Bob, of course, had been a pretty
good amateur pool player back in Cleveland as a teenager, and
his skills came in handy at the Friars—for higher stakes.

Crosby always said that "If Hope hadn't lucked into show
business, he'd have still become a millionaire shooting pool.
He suckered them all in, and won every bet."

One of Crosby's early biographers, Barry Ulanov, in *The
Incredible Crosby* (published in 1948) said of the bonding
between Crosby and Hope:

> They never did settle upon which was the straight man
> and which the comic. It's that moot point which has
> served so well for so many years as the base of the Hope-
> Crosby comedy—a suggestion of rivalry, an intimation
> of sword's-point differences always successful as a pat-
> tern of comedy, particularly meaningful in the United
> States where feigned anger, vigorous physical attack, and
> vituperative verbal abuse so often veil attachments
> between friends, especially when the friends are men and
> don't want to be mistaken for anything else.

Contrary to statements made over the years by both men and
by publicity hype, they were not really close friends in their

private lives. Hope would have enjoyed a close relationship, but Crosby had few real friends outside his family, and kept it that way throughout his life.

Bob and Bing worked up routines that would eventually pair them in the now famous "Road" pictures with Dorothy Lamour. Meanwhile, the show went well. The *New York Times* treated the pair with kindness, gushing that "Bing Crosby pours out his heart to the strains of several sentimental ditties. Bob Hope pops in and out of the show as master of ceremonies, bringing with him some amusing chatter on the political situation." (Hoover and Roosevelt provided plenty of material for political satire—the real seeding of Bob's famous take-offs on political figures.)

The year 1932, momentous for Hope, brought about certain confusions for his biographers, one of which has never been properly ironed out. In his "authorized" biography of Hope, William Faith—who handled the comedian's publicity for a number of years—states that Bob and Louise "had gone so far as to take out a marriage license in January 1932 . . ." but that "Louise was simply not in Hope's future plans . . ."

Hope himself swears that he's only been married once, to the former Dolores Reade, his wife for more than 60 years. According to Bob, he and Dolores were married in Erie, Pennsylvania, on February 19, 1934.

In his The Secret Life of Bob Hope, published in 1993, Arthur Marx presents a somewhat different scenario. Marx states that the marriage bureau in Erie has no record of Bob Hope marrying Dolores there on February 19, 1934, or on any other date. Marx goes even further: "According to documents, he did marry his former vaudeville partner and live-in girlfriend, Grace Louise Troxell, in Erie, Pennsylvania, on January 25, 1933, more than a year before he claims to have married Dolores there."

On a marriage certificate referred to by Marx, "Hope gave his name as Leslie T. Hope, occupation 'salesman,' and his home address as 3323 Yorkshire Road, Cleveland, Ohio. Grace Louise listed her occupation as 'secretary' and her home address as 642 West 64th Street, Chicago, Illinois."

The addresses were indeed the home addresses of Bob's parents and Louise's father, respectively.

The records further indicate that Alderman Eugene P. Alberstadt performed the ceremony, witnessed by William M. Dill, "Clerk of the Orphans Court."

According to a notice in the *New York Herald Tribune,* Louise and Bob appeared together as partners in July 1934, which would mean that even after Bob and Dolores were husband and wife, something was going on between Bob and Louise, professional or otherwise.

Louise later married a Chicago gambler and bookmaker who serviced a good number of entertainers. There is no known record of a divorce to dissolve her marriage to Bob. Rational thinking would bring one to the conclusion that a divorce was quietly arranged, perhaps even out of the country. Otherwise, wouldn't it seem logical that Louise might have cashed in on Hope's fame later on?

Add one more ingredient to the mix, one that theoretically might have oiled the waters. After her marriage to Mr. Halper, a daughter was born to Grace. Under California law if a woman is married to a man and has a baby, that child is considered to be the offspring of her husband.

If Marx is to be believed, and no one in the Hope camp has disputed him, Grace's daughter received a monthly support check from one of the Hope enterprises for years. Arthur cites William Faith as being "... aware of Hope's first marriage" and that he also knew of Grace Louise's subsequent marriage to Halper and the birth of her child, but "was forced to suppress the information in exchange for Hope's cooperation in giving him access to some of his business files and personal papers."

And so, the mystery remains unsolved.

Most of us think of the 1939 World's Fair as the advent of television. Bob Hope first appeared on television in 1932. CBS station W2XAB had gone on the air in New York City in 1931. By the time Hope worked with Bing Crosby and the Capitol Theater in Manhattan, television was already talked about as a medium of the future. Bob, along with other members of *Ballyhoo,* Willie Howard and Lulu McConnell, performed on CBS television in a series of celebrity galas.

Lighting, transmission, and other early glitches left Bob with the impression that television would never replace vaudeville. By the same token, he didn't give much credence to the future of radio. Many years later, he'd regret that he hadn't seen his own potential as a radio comedian, which is strange, because Bob had always had a sense of things coming in his direction. Even stranger is why, after appearing several times as a guest on Rudy Vallee's show, he hadn't appreciated the magnitude of Vallee's 24 million radio listeners.

Rudy Vallee's radio guests—some well-known celebrities, others on their way to being famous—were what made his show so popular. In addition to Hope, a litany of show business talent joined him for his weekly hour of fun and music: Fanny Brice as "Baby Snooks," Milton Berle, Red Skelton, Lou Holtz, Alice Faye, Dorothy Lamour, Frances Langford, and the Mills Brothers. Vallee also introduced the great popular music from Tin Pan Alley, songs that withstood the new waves of music and survived to become standards.

Many of the young singers and entertainers Bob Hope met while in vaudeville and guesting on those early radio shows would become lifelong friends and part of his show business circle. Two in particular, Dorothy Lamour and Frances Langford, were relatively unknown at the time. Dorothy Lamour probably hadn't yet changed her name from Dorothy Peterson (when she sang with Herbie Kay's big band). Langford became an integral part of the Bob Hope USO tours and Lamour, of course, teamed with Crosby and Hope for the popular Paramount Pictures "Road" films.

Hope, in retrospect, believed that perhaps two things distracted him during those early excursions into radio broadcasts. "For one thing, I felt uncomfortable talking into a microphone in a studio, and secondly, I'd always performed before a live audience on the stage. Vallee did his show in a studio without an audience, except for the technicians."

Bob had been so nervous during those early shows that he "... kept kicking the microphone stand after each joke."

The national political campaigns of 1932 pitted incumbent Republican President Herbert Hoover against the popular Democratic Governor of New York, Franklin Delano Roosevelt. The country, in the throes of the Depression, could not have found a more suitable metaphor for overcoming adversity than FDR, a man who had risen from a near-fatal illness—poliomyelitis—to emerge a hero against seemingly unbeatable odds.

Although unable to stand alone, much less walk, FDR refused to be beaten down. He could have rested on his laurels for the rest of his life merely for having been elected Governor of New York.

President Hoover, on the other hand, had many good programs designed to bring the suffering nation out of its financial collapse, but he hesitated and hesitated. Roosevelt, once he became president, incorporated many of his predecessor's ideas into what became known as the New Deal.

Humorist and movie star Will Rogers became one of the first nationally known entertainers to make fun of politics, politicians, and political chicanery. He poked fun at his own political party by declaring that "I am not a member of any organized political party. I am a Democrat." Long after Rogers is forgotten, people will repeat his statement—and perhaps never know who said it.

Bob Hope jumped on the bandwagon during the Hoover-Roosevelt campaign. Taking potshots at presidents and other world leaders became a part of his routines from vaudeville to television, adding further to his type of comedy which is indelibly imprinted on the 20th Century.

1933 began with a new president and his New Deal, a devastating dust bowl across the Great Plains, and unbelievable unemployment lines. Broadway's Great White Way's street corners were inhabited by beggars, Apple Annies, and pencil salesmen. Some of these had, only a couple of years earlier, been part of the hellbent, bootlegging, speakeasy-laden Roaring Twenties.

Riding high on his way to the top of the heap, Hope had no such worries. He expected the new year to be all fireworks and popping champagne corks as he worked his way more and more into the American psyche.

With his life and career moving so fast, he didn't have time to think about the negatives, but he would—and soon.

Chapter 8

Despite his success and promising future, Bob could do nothing to improve his beloved Mahm's health. The new year opened bleak and dreary. His mother's condition had worsened and the best doctors he could find gave him the same sad prognosis. Avis's days on earth were numbered in weeks, months, or perhaps a year at best. Her cancer had progressed rapidly.

His mother's health so concerned him that he had a private line installed by her bed so they could communicate daily. She had total access to his time when he wasn't on stage. She read the reviews and dispensed motherly advice to him from her sickbed in Cleveland. He spoke to his father only when necessary because Harry, as he always did when troubles arose, found a bottle in which to drown his sorrows.

Bob greatly respected motherhood, yet he did a skit as a part of his routine which always made a big hit with the audiences. He would sing a little ditty about mom, aptly entitled, "My Mom." The lyrics were warm and sentimental. After the first verse a little old gray-haired woman would come out on stage, walk up to Bob, and tug his elbow. He would then give a cue for the music to stop and turn to address her:

HOPE

HOW MANY TIMES HAVE I TOLD YOU NOT TO BOTHER ME HERE?

OLD WOMAN

SON, GIMME A LITTLE MONEY TO HAVE MY TEETH FIXED.

HOPE

WHAT DID YOU DO WITH THE TWO DOLLARS I GAVE YOU LAST MONTH?

OLD WOMAN

PLEASE, SON, I HAVEN'T EATEN FOR DAYS.

HOPE

IF YOU AREN'T EATING WHAT DO YOU NEED TEETH FOR?

OLD WOMAN

PLEASE, SON . . .

HOPE

MOM, HOW'D YOU GET OVER THE WALL? I THOUGHT YOU WERE HAPPY THERE. I SENT YOU THAT SHAWL . . .

(He signals for stagehands to help her off stage as he continues the final line of the song).

He included the skit in his routine at the Capitol Theater at the end of 1932. Major Edward Bowes, the man who created the Original Amateur Hour on radio (later succeeded by Ted Mack), hosted the Capitol Family Hour radio show and had tremendous influence in theatrical circles. He called Bob on the carpet and requested that he drop that particular skit from his act.

Not wanting to upset the Major, Bob innocently asked, "But why? It gets great laughs."

A stern Bowes reminded Bob that he was not performing in a burlesque house. To emphasize his point, he asked Bob if he, too, didn't have a mother and would he like to see her portrayed in such a manner.

Hope had never even thought of such a comparison and, embarrassed, immediately dropped the skit without a word to anyone as to why.

As the Palace Theater and vaudeville began to slip over the horizon into oblivion, Bob Hope's star continued to rise.

Therefore, in early 1933, it came as no surprise that the Palace would want him back as the headliner. Despite the hard times which were befalling vaudeville and its grand showcase in particular, Bob could never resist "playing the Palace." Thus he found himself on stage during a matinee while out in the audience Max Gordon, a major Broadway producer, had slipped quietly into the theater to see what new acts were in the offing.

It just so happened that he was already in production with the Jerome Kern-Otto Harbach musical comedy, *Gowns by Roberta,* which would turn out to be Kern's next-to-last Broadway production. They had not as yet cast anyone for the role of Huckleberry Haines, a quick-witted, fast-with-the-one-liner orchestra leader.

As far as Kern and Harbach were concerned, one might as well have suggested a vaudeville clown. Neither wanted any part of anyone from that vulgar "vaudeville." Not to be put off so easily, Gordon persuaded the two musical giants to come and spend a few minutes watching Hope at the Palace, which they reluctantly did.

They caught Hope on an afternoon when his repartee had a particular tang and with the aid of hecklers in the audience he sent out one zinger after another. He brought the house down that day, and the three showmen left the theater ready to go into rehearsals. They had their Huckleberry Haines.

Broadway musicals were eons away from vaudeville. Most vaudevillians had difficulty making the transition to the Broadway stage. Those who did were and are memorable. Not counting Bob Hope, the cast included singing star Fay Templeton, who was returning from retirement in order to play the aging Madame Roberta. George Murphy had been signed as the college fullback, quickly replaced by Ray Middleton, who could both act and sing and had the physique of a football star—and who also went on to great stardom in Broadway musicals. They kept Murphy on to play a lesser role as Huckleberry Haines's manager. Almost total unknowns, at the time, were signed for lesser roles: Sydney Greenstreet, Imogene Coca, Fred MacMurray. Playing drums with the pit orchestra was Gene Krupa. He spent most of his evenings learning to read music under the tutelage of the great Glenn Miller, who had not yet found his niche as the most loved big band leader of all times. Tamara, a Broadway chanteuse, played the dress designer, née Russian princess.

Hope immediately clashed with Otto Harbach and the director over his lines. He thought Harbach too old-fashioned and not up on current comedy. He'd insert a joke from his own files and Harbach would say, "No! Not in my show!" Their seesaw arguments distracted everyone involved. Hope had comedic sense enough to know if a joke would lay an egg and he became more and more convinced throughout rehearsals that they would need a nest in which to place all the "eggs" that Harbach wanted in the show.

The story involved an American college fullback who inherits a fashionable dress salon in Paris upon the death of an aunt. He goes to Paris, takes over the operation of the fashion house, and quickly falls in love with the chief designer who, as the plot thickens, is discovered to be a genuine Russian princess. Hope played the proverbial sidekick. The fullback (Ray Middleton) must decide who will win him in the war of romance— his sweetheart from college or the newfound Russian princess.

One of the standards from Tin Pan Alley, "Smoke Gets In Your Eyes," was written by Kern for the show.

The show opened in Philadelphia, the title changed simply to *Roberta,* to a sour reception. The critics panned it. Max Gordon knew something was wrong, and it had nothing to do with costumes or sets. Close to $120,000 had been spent to produce a class musical, but with all its glamour, it lacked luster.

If Bob Hope had battles with Harbach, he had another personal war he couldn't possibly win. Every letter and phone call from Cleveland reminded him that Avis would soon be a memory—gone forever. It became almost more than he could stand. His mother had always been there when others were not.

The New York opening was just around the corner. Kern didn't want to take the show to Broadway in its current state, so he and Max Gordon decided to bring in a seasoned director from New York. Hassard Short agreed to take the next train to Philadelphia with one proviso: he wanted everyone, including Gordon, Kern, and Harbach, to leave him alone and let him repair the production. They had no choice but to accept.

Hassard Short arrived at the theater the following morning, a mink-lined coat tossed casually over his shoulder, and immediately took command, ordering assistants in every direction to do his bidding.

He came up with all kinds of new ideas to prepare the show for Broadway. He, in fact, redid most of the show to suit himself. He redesigned sets, ordered new wardrobe, and gave Bob Hope leave to do "whatever you can to get laughs."

Hope, pleasantly shocked, still went to Jerome Kern and asked his permission before inserting the line that had so angered Harbach. He explained the situation to Kern, whose response was, "Sure, why not? It couldn't hurt."

Roberta opened on Broadway at the Amsterdam Theater on November 18, 1933—a Saturday night—with the Hope line intact. Although the show received no smash reviews, the critics were much kinder than they had been in Philadelphia. Despite the lukewarm reception, the Jerome Kern songs brought the public out, and by word of mouth the show's popularity increased.

Robert Garland, writing for the *World-Telegram,* barbed: "There's no tune you can whistle when you leave the theater. I tried to pucker on the one about smoke getting in your eyes, but it turned out to be 'The Last Roundup' before I reached the sidewalk."

Hope received kudos from two of Broadway's most prestigious critics, Brooks Atkinson of the *New York Times,* who could be brutal and often destroyed the careers of those he disliked, and Percy Hammond from the *Herald Tribune.* Atkinson's acerbic pen spared Hope:

"The humors of *Roberta* are no great shakes, and
most of them are smugly declaimed by Bob Hope, who
insists on being the life of the party and who
would be more amusing if he were Fred Allen."

* * *

Hammond, complimenting the comedian on his first Broadway appearance said:

> "Mr. Bob Hope is a quizzical cut-up. He's an airy sort of chap who says things like, 'Long dresses don't bother me—I have a good memory,' and 'Love is like hash; you have to have confidence in it to enjoy it.' "

Impressed with his "almost rave" reviews, and having received such a strong response from the audience at his "hash" joke, Bob began slipping in little ad-libs that were not in the script—all to the amusement of a receptive audience.

William Harbach, Otto's son, who became a television producer, told biographer Arthur Marx that Bob Hope had ". . . met a fellow named Billy Reade, who'd hang around the stage door to sell him one-liners for ten and twenty bucks a crack . . . then Bob would stop in the middle of a scene during a performance to turn to the audience and try out one of the jokes he'd bought. Corny jokes like 'Did you hear about the farmer's daughter who wouldn't go to bed with the traveling salesman? . . . Well, you won't because it hasn't happened,' or something like that. Well, this was a book show, and my father would hit the ceiling every time Hope would try to throw in one of those vaudeville jokes that had nothing to do with the plot. But Hope wouldn't stop until my father finally had Billy Reade barred from the stage door."

Roberta became the second-longest-running show of the season. It took a final curtain on July 14, 1934, having run for eight months. Not bad for depressed times. Better than that—and not counting the wonderful Jerome Kern songs that remain popular today—three Hollywood legends were spawned from *Roberta:* George Murphy, Fred MacMurray, and Bob Hope (although Hope's Hollywood star would not shine for a few more years). The two songs most remembered from *Roberta* were "Smoke Gets In Your Eyes" and "You're Devastating."

George Murphy always credited Bob Hope with making *Roberta* a successful show.

Nevertheless, George was a song and dance man and his competitive spirit caused him to see Hope as a threat during the run. He later admitted that "He's a great and wonderful man, but when we were both young and on Broadway in the same show, he was my competition."

Later that year, Broadway's Paramount Theater marquee emblazoned:

CLAUDETTE COLBERT IN "THE GILDED LILY"
with
Fred MacMurray

MacMurray had been signed by Paramount Pictures during the run of *Roberta* and was back on Broadway—as a movie star!

An interesting aside, attested to by George Murphy in his autobiography, *Say... Didn't You Used to be George Murphy?,* is that the male members of *Roberta,* for the most part, went on to greater things. Besides Hope, MacMurray, and Murphy, Robert Middleton became one of Broadway's brightest leading men. Not so lucky were the women of *Roberta.* Fay Templeton had a heart attack, Lyda Roberti committed suicide, and Tamara was killed in a plane crash on her way to entertain American troops in Europe during World War II. George Murphy and Cary Grant were scheduled to accompany Tamara on the USO tour, but through a fluke were sent out on a different plane.

Hope should have been sitting on top of the world. He not only conquered vaudeville, but he had also transcended the stigma (in the minds of serious Broadway producers) of being a vaudevillian who went on to stardom on the legitimate stage. Yet, his personal life did not reflect the glory of stardom. He found himself without a female roommate for the first time in years. Although it was his own doing, the loss of Louise created an emptiness in his everyday life. Even more depressing,

Mahm's cancer had spread rapidly and he almost dreaded answering the phone lest his worst fears become reality.

Due to his success in *Roberta,* he purchased a brand new Pierce-Arrow automobile and once or twice a month made the long drive from Broadway to Cleveland and back to spend as much time with his mother as possible.

Faced with a lost lover and a dying mother, he had to confront another professional crisis. Richy Craig, his joke writer, was dying from tuberculosis. A lot has been said over the years about the big hearts of show people, but seldom was it more evident than when Richy Craig finally succumbed to his disease.

He and Hope had been enjoying a running gag at the expense of Milton Berle, who had the reputation of "borrowing" comedy material from his competitors. He'd done it to Richy Craig once too often, so Hope and Craig cooked up a scheme to teach him a lesson. They'd take Berle's material and perform it at benefits and fund-raisers where Berle was also appearing. They would arrange to get on stage early, ahead of Berle, do his jokes, scoot out quickly, and go on to the next benefit. When Berle performed he couldn't understand why his jokes weren't getting any laughs.

Finally somebody tipped Berle off, so one night he caught up with Hope and Craig, came on stage, and lambasted them. All the comedians in New York were laughing it up, which angered Berle all the more.

However, just as the feuding reached equatorial temperatures, Craig suddenly fell ill in his dressing room at the Palace, spewing blood from his ruptured lungs. Berle found him, then went out on stage and performed in his place. When Richy Craig died a short time later, Milton Berle and Bob Hope got more than forty top Broadway stars to perform at a benefit for Craig's widow.

The gesture so touched Mrs. Craig that she presented Bob Hope with her husband's complete joke books.

Years later, in Hollywood, when Lou Costello's one-year-old son drowned in the family swimming pool on an afternoon just prior to Abbott and Costello's weekly radio show, half of Hollywood volunteered to fill in for the grieving father. Lou thanked them all, but keeping a promise to his son, went on despite his grief. Not until after the show did the studio audience, and the world, learn of the great comedian's personal tragedy.

Show people, despite their fierce competitiveness, often reveal hearts larger than their oversized egos when tragedy befalls one of their own.

Although dark clouds hung heavily over Bob Hope's personal life, at least one of them contained the proverbial silver lining. In Bob's case the lining turned out to be platinum.

Chapter 9

On December 21, 1933, Bob's fellow cast member in *Roberta,* George Murphy, and his wife Julie were invited to hear a new singer named Dolores Reade. She was appearing at the Club Richman on West 56th Street, not far from the theater. Familiar with Hope's situation, Murphy, trying to cheer him up, asked Bob to join them for a drink after the show.

In his autobiography, George Murphy claims to have been responsible for bringing Bob and Dolores together. Several slightly differing recollections exist as to the way the two met. Bill Faith, in his biography of Hope, claims that the Murphy party, which included Bobby Maxwell, a friend of the Murphys, walked into the Vogue Club on 57th Street and that Bob's first sight and sound of the future Mrs. Hope came as Dolores sang, "It's Only a Paper Moon."

At first glance, Bob's heart practically jumped for joy. Murphy said, "Bob couldn't take his eyes off Dolores, who sang enchantingly that night. Later all of us, including Dolores, went on to John Perona's and then Reuben's."

The following day all Bob could talk about was that "wonderful Dolores Reade." Within days they were dating regularly, states Murphy.

After ten years of marriage Dolores, in an interview with *Modern Screen,* a popular filmland magazine, gave her version of their first meeting.

"I hadn't caught his name and wasn't the least interested." She did ask him if he wanted to dance and he declined, which she found rather odd since she assumed he was in the chorus of *Roberta.* After all, she thought, if he was a friend of Murphy's he must be dancing in the chorus.

George and Julie returned to their table, said Dolores, and "George asked me to dance. We'd danced around the room just once when Bob cut in, saying, 'I've changed my mind.' I was so astonished that for the first time I took a good look at him. I saw a very young, and at that moment, a very serious, fellow. But then and there, I knew I liked him."

The 29-year-old singer went home in the wee hours of the morning and told her mother, "I've met my future husband." When her mother asked who he was, Dolores turned to her and said, "Oh, I don't know. Probably just a chorus boy." Her mother didn't give it a second thought.

Dolores went to see *Roberta* and slipped out of the theater after the show without going backstage to congratulate Bob. When he didn't hear from her he went to the Vogue to find out if he'd done something wrong or insulted her in some way. He couldn't figure out why she distanced herself from him.

She explained how embarrassed she'd been, assuming him to be just a chorus boy when he had such an important role in the play. "I should have known better," she said.

Both had to work on New Year's Eve, but met afterward and watched the dawning of 1934 on the doorstep of the small Ninth Avenue apartment she shared with her mother, Theresa Kelly DeFina (DeFina was Dolores's birth name).

Theresa DeFina, a no-nonsense, devout Irish Catholic mother, did not approve of her daughters, Dolores and Mildred, dating men who were not good, hard-working Irish Catholics. Bob Hope, in addition to being English, did not openly embrace any religious faith, which immediately put a damper on his future with Dolores in Mrs. DeFina's eyes.

Defying her mother's wishes and opinions, Dolores spent

every possible free moment with Bob. They were rapidly becoming an item along Broadway. As luck would have it, or so Mrs. DeFina hoped, Dolores accepted a singing engagement at the Embassy Club in Miami, opening in mid-January. From Theresa's point of view the good Lord himself couldn't have done her a greater favor. Certain that all of her Masses and prayers were not in vain, she accompanied her daughter to Miami.

Bob and Dolores consumed a nice chunk of their salaries on long distance phone calls, talking for hours, and eventually got around to the subject of marriage. Dolores had fallen head over heels for this serious young man.

Their long distance plans were suddenly interrupted when, on Sunday, January 22, 1934, Mahm, at last found freedom from pain. Bob had lost his best friend, his most devout fan and supporter, and toughest critic. He went directly to Cleveland to make funeral arrangements, picking up the tab himself, not wanting to further burden his saddened family.

He returned to New York immediately after the funeral. It would be a long time before he could return to Cleveland and not feel saddened by the absence of his beloved mother.

Bob knew he couldn't handle this kind of grief alone, and had already made up his mind to marry Dolores. She'd told him several times that she would break her engagement in Miami if he just said the word. He figured the time to settle down had finally arrived. Back in New York, the first thing he did was phone Dolores. "Come home, I need you."

They were on the phone every day, sometimes two and three times, until she returned to New York on February 13. Mrs. DeFina still disapproved of Dolores getting married at the time, and certainly not to Bob Hope—"that Protestant!"

Dolores knew the words by heart, having heard them over and over at weddings, ". . . and forsaking all others . . ." and in this instance her heart overruled her mother's dominance.

Some of the hate-mongers, who never seem satisfied to see two people in love, sowed some seeds of dissension, intimating in roundabout ways that Bob and Louise were still involved. But the innuendo caused Dolores slight worry because she

knew that Bob Hope loved only one woman and that woman
was Dolores Reade.

Here again, the stories vary. Bill Faith, who certainly had
access to all of the Hopes' official records, states in his biography of Bob that the two lovebirds eloped to Erie, Pennsylvania,
where they were married on February 19, 1934.

The New York *Herald Tribune* carried an item on August
4, 1934, which read as follows, according to another biographer:

BOB HOPE TO WED MISS READE

Bob Hope, who played a comedy lead in *Roberta* last
season, and Miss Dolores Reade, a nightclub singer,
announced their engagement yesterday. They will be married about Thanksgiving. Both are appearing in the stage
show at the Capitol Theater. Mr. Hope also has appeared
in *Ballyhoo of 1932* and in vaudeville.

Sixty-odd years later, who cares? Bob and Dolores have
climbed every peak, traveled every valley, through good and
bad times together.

The new Mrs. Hope, a woman of sound judgment and financial savvy, not only took great pride in turning their three-room
apartment into a home, but also became very involved in her
husband's professional and business affairs. She gave her seal
of approval to his choice of Louis Shurr as his agent. Shurr,
who later moved on to Hollywood, bringing along his New
York nickname, "Doc," was one of the most highly respected
agents in the business and Hope continued to be his number
one client until the agent died a few years ago.

Shurr had great foresight. He knew that the action would
move to Hollywood and that with moving picture houses spring-
ing up all across the country, in one day more people could
see a star on the screen than during the entire run of a Broadway
show.

He angled to have Hope play Huckleberry Haines in the
upcoming movie of *Roberta*. The studio didn't want Hope and
gave the role to Fred Astaire. Paramount offered him a co-
starring part with Jack Oakie and Ginger Rogers in *Sitting*

Pretty, with a four-week contract worth $8,000. The screen test, done in New York, had the same effect on both Bob and Dolores as his earlier Pathé test in Hollywood had on him. Some say the studio didn't like the test and nixed Hope. Jack Oakie once told me that Bob Hope didn't want to do the picture because "in those days he didn't think a Broadway star ought to be in the movies. He still thought the live audience was the only way to go."

Oakie seemed to be somewhat on the right track. Although Hope made dozens of movies during his long film career, he always preferred a live audience. With the advent of World War II and the USO tours, he finally found the best of all worlds. He could make movies and be seen by millions, and he could perform live before thousands of servicemen in every corner of the globe.

During the late spring of 1934 Bob did agree to do a two-reeler with actress Leah Ray for Educational Pictures, shot at the old Astoria Studios on Long Island. Originally titled *Jumping Beans,* it later became *Going Spanish.* Bob wished it had been sunk on the Spanish Main. When Walter Winchell asked him what he thought of his film debut, he said, "When they catch Dillinger, they're going to make him sit through it."

Winchell, being the good reporter, printed Hope's exact words in his column, which was a show business Bible in New York. The studio head called Shurr and yelled in his ear, "We're having enough trouble selling that guy without him knocking the picture. He's fired!"

Bob pleaded with Winchell to print a retraction, but he should have known better. Winchell wasn't known for his retractions. As a matter of fact, if you complained about a Winchell item, you might be demolished in his next column—and he had the power to do just that. In New York he had the same power that Louella Parsons and Hedda Hopper later developed in the motion picture business.

Warner Brothers saw something in Hope and signed him for six two-reelers, which he made over a period of three years, some of which were as bad or worse than the ones before. Bob pocketed the $2,500 per three days work on each film and gave very little thought, at the time, to a career in films.

The first two-reeler under the Warner Brothers contract, *Paree, Paree,* was the film version of Cole Porter's Broadway musical, *Fifty Million Frenchmen.* Once again Bob's singing stole the show, just as it had in *Roberta,* although few producers considered him a singer of any promise. When he sang Porter's "You Do Something To Me" to his costar, Dorothy Stone, he added another facet to his ever-increasing brilliance as a performer.

His real screen talent wouldn't be recognized until 1938, when he finally got a decent picture on the West Coast.

A month before *Roberta* closed, in June of 1934, Shurr arranged a second appearance for Bob on the Rudy Vallee radio show. This time he received some important print space in *Variety.*

His easygoing, underplayed style is as likeable on the air as upon the rostrum of a variety or legit house. His jokes are aged, but his delivery and general approach to humor is modern.

Seems no reason why Hope could not do well on a regular commercial assignment. Perhaps it may be argued he has no catch phrases or distinctive identification, and this may be valid cause for caution up to a point.

But he wears well, his knack of self-joshing and unabashed realization of his own daring is calculated to please where more perspiring methods of getting laughs exhaust and enervate.

When *Roberta* closed, Bob fell back on his old-reliable, vaudeville, and took off on a ten-week tour, with Dolores replacing Louise in his act. Dolores hadn't done vaudeville, but her love for and confidence in her new husband allayed whatever fears she might have had. In a 1953 story in *Woman's Home Companion* she recalled that East Coast tour:

That was an exciting and challenging experience. What he expected was perfection. He never let down for a moment on stage and heaven help me if I did! I simply had to go out there every show and pitch. Hard. We did six and seven shows a day. Sometimes my mind would wander and that was fatal. Bob would get very angry and right there on stage in the middle of the act, he'd crack, "What's the matter with you, tired?"

Dolores's voice had a quality that caused her to be compared to the famous torch- and blues-singer, Libby Holman, but without the latter's sad quality, that of a woman unlucky in love. Dolores had no such problems. She was very much in love. She possessed a very caressing voice and when she sang a love song you knew she believed in love.

Delighted to have Dolores with him on the tour, Bob seemed to be enjoying himself as they traveled, all the while hoping that Doc Shurr would find him the lead in a new Broadway show. After all, he'd been a star on Broadway in a play that had a very successful run. He expected that some producer would want him right away, but that's not the way it happened. Out on the road he began to get antsy. He'd tasted success on Broadway—and liked it.

Shurr interrupted Bob's tour when he called him back to New York. Harry Richman wanted Hope for his new Broadway musical, *Say When*. Harry Richman, no slouch in his day, sang and danced and had been a major vaudeville star when vaudeville was "the thing." Now, neither vaudeville nor Richman had a lot to brag about. Hollywood and radio were invading the entertainment business in a big way.

Harry Richman, anxious to get back on top, actually invested $50,000 of his own money in the show. His somewhat silent partner and primary money man turned out to be Mr. Charles Luciano, better known in Mafia circles as "Lucky" Luciano, one of the most notorious gangsters in the history of organized crime.

From the Roaring Twenties until only recently, celebrities

hobnobbed with known mobsters. One need go no farther back than to Frank Sinatra and Phyllis McGuire and their close associations with Sam Giancana, one of Chicago's true gang-lords, so it came as no surprise to anyone that Luciano might be involved with celebrities.

Say When failed from the outset. Being in a Broadway show more or less broke up Bob and Dolores's act. Richman only wanted Hope, and got him. Another problem arose during the out-of-town tryout in Boston as the producers tried to put a Band-Aid on what was already being compared to the *Titanic*.

With no role for Dolores, Bob tried to help her put together a one-woman act in Boston while his show attempted to work out its many quirks. She accepted a straight songstress booking at Loew's State in Boston in order to be close to her husband with no concept of what was required to be on a theater stage alone. Used to singing with orchestras or to intimate groups in cocktail lounges and clubs, she simply didn't know how to put an act together and Bob, even though he tried to be helpful, became preoccupied with the serious problems plaguing his own show.

Dolores's audiences diminished after the first day. To her credit she sincerely tried to keep her own career going, but knew that compared to Bob's future, she had no career but to be what she really wanted to be: Mrs. Bob Hope.

Despite the misgivings of Hope, Richman, and others involved with the production had about *Say When,* the reviews were a delightful surprise.

Brooks Atkinson of the *New York Times,* notorious for his hatchet-jobs, said of *Say When*'s opening at the Imperial The-ater, ''. . . a lively show made-to-order for the itinerant trade of the Great White Way.''

Robert Benchley: ''. . . a real musical comedy.''

Even Walter Winchell praised it as ''the merriest laugh, song, and girl show in town.''

It came as no surprise to those in the know why *Say When* flopped. Harry Richman. It had to be his way or no way. Since he controlled the finances, he doomed the show by holding it hostage to his demands. He did not delude Bob Hope. "Bob," he confided, "if I can't be happy, this show is doomed." An unhappy Harry Richman prophesied the musical's demise on his own terms.

When *Say When* closed after a short run, Dolores retired from show business and devoted her life to Bob, his career, and their home on Central Park West.

Bob's income of five grand a week kept the couple off the relief rolls. The economy of the era made for some pretty strange bedfellows. John Dillinger, Alvin Karpis, "Pretty Boy" Floyd, Clyde Barrow, and the Barker Brothers (Ma Barker's boys) were earning a living at gunpoint, robbing banks, grocery stores, and filling stations, leaving a trail of blood in their wake. President Roosevelt, in quite a successful effort to salvage capitalism, was being hanged in effigy by the Wall Street barons he sought to rescue from oblivion.

American labor unions, some quite openly affiliated with Bolshevik groups, were demanding a decent living wage for their members. Organized crime quickly joined in the effort, raking in high "agency" fees for the muscle it provided.

General labor strikes were rampant in the United States during the summer and fall of 1934. From the corporate point of view, all labor unions were "communist" or "subversive." A great drought covered the breadbasket of the country and laborers, when they could find work, were putting in ten- and twelve-hour days, six days a week. Child labor laws were largely ignored due to the need to feed families. The minimum wage of twenty-five cents an hour did not exist until 1938.

The analogy is important. While Bob Hope earned $5,000 per week, the average worker with a wife and four kids made perhaps as much as $1,200 a year—if he was lucky. Had it not been for another rising star, the ratio between celebrities and ordinary workers might have remained exactly the same.

While Bob Hope argued with Doc Shurr for another Broadway musical, ongoing events in Europe would fashion and mold a most important facet of Hope's career. Adolph Hitler became Chancellor of Germany in 1933 and by 1934 his plans, which led to World War II, were well underway. It seems amazing that a comedian and a dictator's lives could be so intertwined.

Chapter 10

During the latter part of 1934, still looking for another Broadway show for Bob Hope, an executive from the Bromo-Seltzer Company approached Louis Shurr with the idea of sponsoring a new radio show to star Jane Froman, a popular chanteuse, James Melton (a highbrow singer), and Al Goodman's orchestra. Would Bob Hope like to emcee the show?

Shurr approached Bob with the idea. Hope did not give him an immediate response. He not only discussed it with Dolores, but went a step further. He called Harry Richman, now one of Bob's closest professional as well as personal friends, based on the manner in which Harry had handled the closing of *Say When* with him. Harry Richman, for all his ego and demands, was fair to his friends. He allowed Bob the opportunity to seek other employment once he'd made up his mind to let *Say When* close—and Bob never forgot that.

So when he went to Harry and expressed his concern about the material he'd been using and asked if Richman thought it would be too stale for radio, Harry responded as the friend he had always been.

"Bob, how'd you like to take a drive with me?"

"Sure, Harry. Where are we going?"

"Just for a drive."

"Okay."

The two men drove along in silence for the most part, only occasionally commenting on the scenery. The trip took them to Harry Richman's upstate New York estate, which was somewhat of a surprise to Bob, who had no idea where Harry might be taking him or what he had in mind.

Over drinks, Harry confided to Hope that he could see the handwriting on the wall. "My thing has always been vaudeville—and vaudeville, whether I like it or not, is finished. Now, I've got a wealth of jokes and routines that I've assembled over the years and I got a hunch you can take that material and adapt it to radio."

The old vet simply gave Bob Hope a lifetime of comedy material he no longer needed. Bob Hope had a bonanza literally laid in his lap to be used as he chose.

After agreeing to audition for the radio show, Bob went to work browsing through the great mass of material and worked up what he thought to be a presentable monologue.

More than just presentable, Bob's audition delighted the Bromo-Seltzer people, who immediately signed him as their emcee.

When the show debuted on January 4, 1935, *Variety* had very little, if anything, good to say about it. However, Bob Hope had been excluded from their negative criticism. The reviewer thought Hope to be "intermittently very funny," and added that "Hope is easy to take, but hard to remember."

Far from dissatisfied with the critical reception of his official debut into radio, Bob hired two writers, Lester White and Fred Molina, to polish his monologues. On one particular show he honored Walter Winchell, to whom he owed nothing, by doing a rapid-fire Winchell-like delivery of a take-off on the famous columnist:

"Flash . . . Newport, Rhode Island . . . Box of matches goes off in Reginald Dipster's hip pocket . . . Not permanent . . . just a flash in the pants . . ."

He then turned to a boy-girl routine reminiscent of his dialogues with Louise in vaudeville. He discovered a fresh new talent, Patricia Wilder, who quickly became known as "Honey Chile." Honey Chile had blond hair and a figure better suited to television than radio. But these were radio days and television had not as yet become a fixture in American living rooms.

"That's exactly how I became a part of Bob Hope's act," Miss Wilder explained to Arthur Marx when he interviewed her for *The Secret Life of Bob Hope.* Hope, incidentally, dismissed the book as a "pack of lies," while at the same time admitting that he hadn't bothered to read it.

Patricia Wilder, a true southern belle, came from Macon, Georgia—about as southern as you can get. She'd run off to New York, where she hoped to become famous and wealthy as an actress. After all, she reckoned, that's where actresses went to become famous. She expected to get her share of fame, fortune, and anything else due a sweet southern girl.

Honey Chile Wilder's recollections of how she became a part of Hope's show further complicates the exact date of Louise's departure from Bob's vaudeville act. It has been documented by Dolores Hope herself that she did the eastern seaboard vaudeville tour with Bob before he returned to New York to appear in *Say When,* and one would assume that Louise would have by then been long gone. Yet, Miss Wilder, in an interview with Arthur Marx, states that she was sixteen years old in 1935 when she arrived in New York, and having lunch at Dinty Moore's restaurant on 46th Street one day when a young man from Doc Shurr's office approached her and offered to get her into motion pictures.

Her uncle, Fred Ryan, said absolutely not. "She's going right back to Macon, Georgia, on the next Greyhound bus." He escorted her to a taxi, gave the driver instructions to deliver the teenager to the bus station, and bade her farewell. En route she changed the destination. "I want to go to the offices of Mr. Louis Shurr, the movie agent."

While being interviewed by Shurr, Bob Hope came into the office. Wilder says, "I could tell by the way he looked me over that he liked me."

Hope smiled and asked, "Do you want to go on the stage?"

"Sure," she replied.

According to Honey Chile, Hope arranged for her to come to the Capitol Theater to catch his act because Louise planned to leave the show. Afterward he asked her, "Do you think you can do it?"

"Sure," she said. "And you know," she told Marx, "I'd never been on a stage in my life." So his writers wrote her into the show, which led to her becoming his female foil on the Bromo-Seltzer radio show.

From the moment she opened her mouth on the air and asked, "Pardon me, Mistah Hope, does the Greyhound bus stop heah?" she'd found her place in show business.

Hope's writers, Lester White and Fred Molina, immediately began to put together new routines for the duo. One early skit between Hope and Honey Chile went like this:

HOPE: You know, Honey Chile, there are a lot of comedians on the air. Why did you pick me as your partner?

HONEY CHILE: 'Cause ah had a fight with mah folks and ah want to do something to disgrace 'em.

HOPE: Uh-huh. Well, you picked the right partner.

HONEY CHILE: You know, Mr. Hope, ah've got two brothers at home that ah'm sure would be a big hit on the radio.

HOPE: What's their names?

HONEY CHILE: The oldest is Ed.

HOPE: What's the young one's name?

HONEY CHILE: Ed.

HOPE: Two boys in one family by the name of Ed?

HONEY CHILE: Yes, Father always said that two Eds were better than one.

Although Hope and Honey Chile were big hits with radio audiences, Bromo-Seltzer did not live up to its name. The show turned out to be a big headache and folded with its broadcast of April 5, 1935.

So Bob, Dolores, and Honey Chile hit the road again. There were few really big vaudeville houses left and Bob Hope and his troupe were welcome additions to their stages. However, vaudeville served as little more than a filler between bigger and better movies. Hollywood had begun to create its own legends, many of whom did not originate on Broadway. The celluloid kids were growing into giants. Some minor actors in films were better known than major legitimate stage stars.

Although Florenz Ziegfeld died in 1932, four editions of the *Ziegfeld Follies* followed. The 1934 and 1936 *Follies* were more or less coproduced by Billie Burke, Ziegfeld's widow, and the Shubert Brothers, with Burke taking top billing as producer. Starring in a *Ziegfeld Follies* was, along Broadway, as prestigious, if not more so, as playing the Palace Theater. Bob Hope had never been in a Ziegfeld production. A lot of effort and pre-production went into the 1936 *Follies,* since it would be the last Broadway appearance of its star, Fanny Brice, before she departed the stage to become a major radio star as "Baby Snooks." She continued to star in that role until her sudden death of a cerebral hemorrhage on May 29, 1951.

Louis Shurr secured the lead male comedy role for Bob, who delighted in playing opposite the great Fanny Brice. In addition to Brice and Hope, the show lauded famed director John Murray Anderson. The cast included such present and future megastars as Ken Murray, Gertrude Niesen, Josephine Baker, Eve Arden, Judy Canova, Edgar Bergen and Charlie McCarthy, Cherry and June Preisser, Hugh O'Connell, the Nicholas Brothers, and Stan Kavanagh.

Vincente Minelli, who became a great director in Hollywood as well as husband to Judy Garland and father of Liza Minelli, designed the show. George Balanchine, in his debut, became an overnight sensation thanks to his brilliant choreography.

Vernon Duke created the music, with Ira Gershwin's lyrics,

and additional material by Ogden Nash, Billy Rose, and Dave Freedman.

The show gave Bob Hope an opportunity to shine as never before. In every scene he had the opportunity to joke, laugh, dance, and sing with Fanny Brice, Gertrude Niesen, and Eve Arden, with whom he shared the show-stopping "I Can't Get Started With You." Eve Arden went on to greater heights in movies and television, and became most famous for "Our Miss Brooks." Prior to the *Ziegfeld Follies of 1936* she'd been just another unknown, except for an appearance in *New Faces of 1935 (New Faces* would be little known off Broadway until Eartha Kitt put it on the map in the 1952 version with her hissing rendition of "Monotonous").

The show presented all kinds of pre-production problems and delays due to casting problems, illness, and other snags. Rehearsals were scheduled to begin in August, but did not start until mid-October 1935. Bob wasn't the least bit upset at the delays. In November, during the rehearsals for *Follies,* he signed to emcee another radio show, "Atlantic White Flash Program" for sixteen weeks with Honey Chile Wilder. When *Follies* opened in Boston, the sponsors sent Honey Chile along to be sure that she appeared on the radio with Bob in every episode.

At the Boston Opera House opening on Christmas night, Anderson and Lee Shubert were both concerned with its lopsidedness.

Fanny Brice felt that, as the star, she should have been given the best lines and brightest scenes. Instead, the show leaned more toward the male comedians, so changes were made to accommodate her—which improved the show.

Ken Murray, like Harry Richman, had his own ideas about what he should and shouldn't do. Unlike Harry, he had no interest as a backer so when push came to shove he either had to give in to the producers or get out. Always known for his "blue material," he made no exceptions when he wanted to use it in a show.

In Boston, Lee Shubert watched the show from the audience, incensed with Murray's deliberate disobedience. He couldn't wait until the curtain came down so he could get backstage to give Murray a piece of his mind.

Murray and Shubert were at odds from the beginning. Ken made it clear to everyone that he greatly resented Bob Hope being billed above him. Interestingly, Doc Shurr represented both men and sold them each as "lead comics." Shubert and Anderson both believed Hope to be the better attraction. His innuendos were sometimes bordering on "blue", but never grossly so.

In Murray's Boston dressing room, Lee Shubert lit into Murray and demanded that he "get rid of all that dirty stuff in your act. I don't like it. The public won't like it."

A combination of not getting what he considered proper billing and disagreements over his material caused Murray to finally leave the show, eliminating one of Fanny Brice's complaints that there were too many men, not enough Brice.

During the second week of their Philadelphia run, Fanny Brice developed a bad cold for which the doctor gave her some medication. He also prescribed sleeping pills because she had been having insomnia due to "personal difficulties." According to Bob Hope, her marriage to the legendary Billy Rose seemed to be on the rocks. Toward the end of the show one evening, Fanny began to lose it on stage, repeating the beginning of her song several times, seemingly lost in a fog. Finally Freddie DeCordova, the stage manager, brought down the curtain and they helped the befuddled star to her dressing room. (Freddie went on to become a successful Hollywood producer and director and for years was the producer of "The Tonight Show," starring Johnny Carson.)

Nobody ever knew for sure whether Brice took the sleeping pills on purpose or mistook them for cold pills, but throughout the show everybody worried about Fanny.

Fortunately for Bob, when the show opened at the Winter Garden in New York at the end of January 1936, no one topped his performance in the eyes of the audiences. The critics especially crowed about his "I Can't Get Started With You" sequence with Eve Arden, a tall, gorgeous redhead tailor-made for his suggestive type of comedy. The scene featured Miss

Arden, in a curve-caressing evening gown by Balenciaga, and Hope in a tux, attempting to seduce her on a street corner. In the beginning, Arden is cool to his advances but by the end of the skit she succumbs as the stage goes to black.

Fanny's acute depression, coupled with arthritis, became such a problem that finally in the spring of 1936 Billie Burke and Lee Shubert decided to put the show on hiatus during the summer to reopen in the fall.

Despite her marital problems and physical frailties, Fanny Brice managed to make an outstanding appearance in May 1936 to celebrate the thirty-fifth anniversary of the Shuberts of Broadway along with the *crème de la crème* of Broadway theater stardom: Al Jolson, Lou Holtz, the Howard Brothers, Sophie Tucker, Jack Benny, Bert Lahr, Ethel Barrymore, Helen Hayes, and Katharine Cornell, among others. Bob Hope shared the emcee duties of the evening.

Hit that he had become in the *Ziegfeld Follies of 1936,* Bob Hope would not return when the show reopened. He still had the weekly comedy radio show, the name having been changed to ''Atlantic Family,'' and a new female foil, another southern girl named Margaret Johnson, from Dallas, with a master's degree from Baylor University, but did not have the same charisma as Honey Chile Wilder, who quit the radio show after signing a contract to make movies for RKO Pictures in Hollywood.

Thanks to the generosity and sound advice of showmen like Harry Richman and Richy Craig, Bob accumulated and categorized more than 80,000 jokes, skits, and gags which served him well in radio and in the dozens of benefits in which he performed for the publicity value. Dolores made sure he included appearances on behalf of her Catholic causes.

Nonetheless, he employed no less than three or four writers, who met with him in his apartment on Monday mornings to go over his script for the weekly radio show. If Hope wasn't happy with the material, he'd work with the writers around the clock until it worked for him.

The completed script, delivered to the sponsors on Wednesday morning, came back to Hope that same evening with an

"OK" or "Not OK." If okayed, Bob let his writers go on about their work for the following week. If rejected by the sponsors, Bob and the writers wrote and rewrote right through Saturday's rehearsal for that night's show.

Bob's delivery always seemed so simple, but there never existed a harder taskmaster—and harder on himself than anyone else. Unlike comedian Jackie Gleason who did not like rehearsals and rarely attended them, Hope did not have a photographic memory. So he rehearsed along with the rest of the cast.

When Frank Parker, the singing star of "Atlantic Family," left the show in June of 1936 to join the Paul Whiteman radio show, "Atlantic," for all intents and purposes, became "The Bob Hope Show," and he agreed to stay on as the star.

He'd finally received more serious notice in Hollywood. Director Mitch Leisen and producer Harlan Thompson saw Hope in the *Follies* and thought he'd be right for a picture they had in mind for Paramount (originally to be called *The Big Broadcast of 1936*, it was later changed to *The Big Broadcast of 1938* because it didn't get made in time).

In the interim, due to the publicity resulting from the three Broadway shows in which he'd appeared, Doc Shurr had no difficulty finding another musical for Hope. Since his radio show, despite the mediocre and sometimes corny material, had better ratings than the popular "Fibber McGee" and "Jimmy Durante" shows, it was expected that Bob Hope would do radio shows emanating from New York City and look forward to a prestigious future as a star of Broadway musicals.

It surprised no one when Hope signed to costar with Ethel Merman and Jimmy Durante in a new Cole Porter show, *Red, Hot and Blue*.

The Hopes were on the verge of a new kind of notoriety, embarking on a social career which Dolores managed (and still does) like the CEO of a major corporation.

Thanks to Bob's accelerated income, the Hopes were able to entertain, and before long Dolores became one of the most popular hostesses in New York. Their apartment had been remodeled to suit Dolores's impeccable taste. While Bob rehearsed, performed, played golf, and worked out at a local gym, she planned their Saturday night parties, which attracted luminaries from New York as well as visiting Hollywood stars, producers, and directors.

The festivities were always designed to enhance Bob's career. Dolores liked bridge; Bob became adept at bridge. Bob loved golf; Dolores learned to play. They were a couple in love in the truest sense of the word, giving to and doing for one another.

Red, Hot and Blue was an apt title for the new show. Monumental egos were involved from day one. The cast included Jimmy Durante, Ethel Merman, and William Gaxton (replaced by Bob Hope)—all of whom went over the scripts and rewrites with a fine-tooth comb, raising the roof if one actor got an extra word more than the other.

William Gaxton, a big name on Broadway, went to the mat with Ethel Merman, a lady known for her temperament. As a matter of fact, the Susan Hayward role in the film *Valley of the Dolls,* from Jacqueline Susann's best-selling book, was pretty well known to be a take-off on Merman, and to make it more apparent, Ethel blew her cork when she read the book and again when she saw the movie.

During rehearsals in late summer, a fight broke out between Ethel Merman and Jimmy Durante over billing. Cole Porter finally calmed the two headliners by suggesting that their names be crisscrossed on the marquee in the fashion of an ''X'', so that each had one of their names as top billing. The crisscross was reversed weekly. Bill Gaxton stomped out during rehearsals, believing that Merman had been given a larger role, and never returned. Again, Porter solved the problem. He'd become an admirer of Hope and asked the director to talk to Louis Shurr and, if available, to sign Bob for the role of Merman's lawyer.

Porter played peacemaker for everybody else, but had problems of his own with the producer, Vinton Freedley, over the score. During the Boston tryouts, Porter decided that he'd had it with Freedley, so he left the show and returned to New York in a major snit. By the time the show got to New Haven, he changed his mind and agreed to return and fine-tune the score.

Bob Hope enjoyed the distinction of being the only important player in the show who didn't raise a ruckus. Hope, a great admirer of Jimmy Durante, deemed it an honor to be on the same stage with the great "Schnozzola."

Again, a song helped Bob shine. He dueted with Ethel Merman on one of Porter's all-time hits, "It's DeLovely," later released by Liberty Records as a 78 RPM solo by Hope, backed by Merman singing "Down In The Depths," becoming the first of Bob's numerous record releases.

The show finally opened at the Alvin Theater in New York on October 29, 1936, in a display of glitz and celebrity better shown today at Hollywood premieres. America's sweetheart, Mary Pickford, and Merle Oberon (already one of Hollywood's most glamorous movie stars) delighted the photographers as they arrived in the company of Cole Porter.

Walter Winchell, never one to forget a difference of opinion and still smarting from Hope's request that he retract a negative direct quote from the comedian about his first two-reeler, backhanded Bob by indicting the show's material. Said Winchell:

> "He's a clever comedian when the material is better than it is at the Alvin."

The New York Journal-American's critic John Anderson:

> "Mr. Hope is, as usual, urbane, sleek and nimble of accent. He knows a poor joke when he hides it, and he can outstare most of them."

The most devastating critique came from John Mason Brown, who may have paraphrased the famous Jerry Wald's earlier dismissal of Hope:

> "Hope as a comedian is a cultivated taste, which I must admit I have never been able to cultivate."

Bob Hope's great acclaim throughout his long and varied career came from the audiences, not the critics. He managed to touch the ordinary man's heart and push the funnybone button of Joe Six-pack's sense of humor.

The glamor of New York and Bob Hope's considerable success in vaudeville and musicals had a downside. Within a three-year period, while appearing in major shows on Broadway with stars he'd always looked up to, he lost both his parents. First his mother in January 1934, and then, in 1937, just prior to *Red, Hot and Blue* taking to the road, his father, Harry, died in Cleveland at sixty-six.

Perhaps Bob was getting tired of vaudeville and Broadway. Whatever the reason, *Red, Hot and Blue* ended his Broadway career.

Chapter 11

Too much of a good thing is too much, but too much of two good things can be good fortune, as Bob came to find out. The Woodbury Soap Company decided to sponsor a new radio show on NBC featuring the popular big band, Shep Fields and his Rippling Rhythm. The show was to be called "The Rippling Rhythm Revue."

Woodbury wanted Bob Hope to be their emcee. When Shurr notified him, Bob agreed immediately. The show, set to run thirteen weeks, would be renewed for an additional thirteen weeks if the ratings were good. Bob brought along Lester White and Fred Molina to script his monologues, which were crisp and delivered with rapidity.

"The Woodbury Hour" clearly established Bob Hope as an equal to Jack Benny, Burns and Allen, Fred Allen, Joe Penner, and any number of former vaudeville comedians who jumped aboard the radio lifeboats as the good ship vaudeville began its final list into the murkiness of nostalgia.

Hope seemed to have an eye and ear for aspiring young southern actresses who used him as a stepping stone to enhance their future aspirations. With Honey Chile now working before the cameras in Hollywood, and Margaret Johnson having left

radio because she looked and sounded so much like Judy
Canova and about to join Honey Chile in Hollywood, Hope
had no female partner.

Although the show exhibited some early technical problems
and so-so reviews from most of the critics, in its May 12, 1937,
issue, *Variety* did not find his material burdensome:

> Bob Hope's addition to "Rippling Rhythm Revue" . . .
> appears just what the doctor ordered . . . Fashion in
> which Hope maneuvers the program, glibly filling in gaps
> and introducing members, definitely sets him up . . . one
> of the swiftest-moving "Rippling" stanzas in many
> weeks . . ."

Long before the end of the first thirteen weeks, Woodbury
decided to renew the show—and Bob's contract—for another
thirteen weeks. About the same time Paramount, unable to
obtain Jack Benny, whom they originally wanted, opted for
Bob Hope, who accepted without even thinking how a movie
might interfere with his Woodbury show.

He had another dilemma, which involved Louis Shurr, who
at that time was not a Hollywood agent. His expertise centered
on Broadway shows and vaudeville. When Bob approached
him with the idea of getting another agent to represent him in
motion pictures, Shurr said no, but okayed Bob's having a
different agent for radio provided he received a small commission. Bob saw no problem with that. After all, Shurr could have
demanded a full agent's percentage.

Another young agent became acquainted with Bob and they
seemed to have a lot in common. Jimmy Saphier knew and
appreciated Hope's talent. He'd seen his vaudeville act and the
musicals in which he'd appeared. Saphier had also heard him
on the radio. Some years later he told an interviewer, "I thought
it a shame the home listeners weren't getting the best of him.
Radio simply wasn't using his talents properly." Saphier
thought Bob should be doing monologue without a partner.

Saphier, of course proved to be correct and Bob, who always
kept the faith with those who led him in the right direction,

remained faithful to Jimmy Saphier until Saphier's death in 1974. They originally agreed to a one-year tryout, so to speak, to see if they really did like each other and were the right combination. They did and they were.

Hope decided that he should have a press agent. During his time on the Woodbury Hour he'd come to think highly of Mack Millar, who handled publicity for Shep Fields. Millar had good connections. He knew Walter Winchell, Ed Sullivan, and Damon Runyon among other prominent columnists and writers who covered the show business scene on both coasts.

Millar maintained his home base in New York and seemed hesitant to give up Manhattan for Hollywood. Since Shep Fields and his band were also on board for *The Big Broadcast,* Bob's first Paramount picture, it meant that Mack Millar would be accompanying him to the coast for a limited time.

Mack arranged for Bob to be interviewed by Sam Kaufman of *The New York Sun.* Bob wanted to be the first to go public with his idea (and Saphier's) that a comedian's future success in radio would be based on the monologue.

The New York Sun ran Kaufman's interview with Bob on August 5, 1937, part of which went as follows:

KAUFMAN: I'm curious about your monologue prediction . . .

HOPE: . . . Will Rogers certainly clicked with it on the air many years ago. But the monologue is now showing definite signs of being a main comedy trend . . . my solo bits are patterned after my stage style . . . I attempt to make my topics newsy and seasonal . . . the microphone has certain limitations . . . I can't make humorous references to such headline events as child marriages and coronations . . . I've always approached it like I would the stage. And you can't . . . when I auditioned I was ghastly . . . went too fast . . . the lines . . . became just a blur . . . I . . . had to slow down . . . Winchell said that he would tell me to stop that god-awful 'hmmm-ha-ha-hmmm' noise that I made at the end of each joke . . . on the air it sounds as if I'd eaten too many green apples . . . I've cut out the moans, coughs, and grunts . . .''

KAUFMAN: What about all this controversy about live studio audiences?

HOPE: . . . I've had some doubts . . . It's not difficult to get laughs from your studio audience . . . you can influence them by your physical personality . . . I'm not sure . . . the listener is having the same hilarious time . . . I worry about the listener. I work best with an audience . . . comedy and laughs go together . . . studio laughter can be just as important to the faraway listener as it is to the comedian . . . the home listener gets a far greater kick out of a joke when he has company . . . he gets the point quicker when he hears the studio audience reaction . . . The critics . . . say we clown for the studio audience . . . and the home audience is missing the gag . . . from an entertainer's viewpoint, it's important to . . . feel audience response while on the air . . . If I fail to hesitate at just the right moment, the point of a joke might slip by . . .

KAUFMAN: . . . What got you into radio in the first place?

HOPE: . . . the more I got into it I saw the way it was going . . . it's the hot thing of the future—and I really liked the money.

In the thirties and forties, celebrities arriving from New York took one of the express train sleepers, usually stopping to pick up passengers in Chicago. It was considered chic and proper to depart the train in Pasadena, where a studio limousine stood by while the photographers and reporters crowded around the stars and did their business. Then they were swept away to Hollywood hotels or studios which, incidentally, were scattered around Los Angeles—not just Hollywood.

Bob and Dolores Hope, with their menagerie of two dogs, and Bob's agent, Doc Shurr, arrived in Pasadena aboard the Santa Fe Railroad's Super Chief on September 9, 1937, to begin their life in Hollywood under less than auspicious circumstances. Their welcome to California made page 13 of the *Los*

Angeles Morning News the following morning with a small caption reading: A COMEDIAN AND HIS WIFE. It went on to say that "Mr. Hope has never appeared in a major screen feature."

Neither Bob nor Dolores was amused by their press reception. New York actors, writers, and directors who came to Hollywood during the thirties looked down on motion pictures in the same manner that legitimate theater looked down on vaudeville. They came west for the money and hoped to grab as much as they could and slip out in the middle of the night back to New York—without any fanfare whatsoever.

However, most of them, once there, stayed. Everyone with any kind of Broadway success usually received the standard seven-year contract, which always gave the studio so many outs it might as well have been a sieve. Arthur Marx, in his unauthorized biography of Hope, said:

> "Just about anyone who'd originally made a mark in the legitimate theater . . . looked down on Hollywood as a place of uncultured, money-making heathens. Its product was considered mostly trash, turned out by uneducated former junk dealers, song-pluggers, and glove makers. More specifically, Louis B. Mayer, Harry Cohn, and Sam Goldwyn. The last couldn't speak straight English but his publicity-man-generated malapropisms were internationally famous."

Dorothy Parker dismissed the movie capital in her usual caustic fashion: "No matter how hot it gets in Hollywood during the day, there's never anything to do at night."

Broadway producer George Kaufman, upon being advised that in Hollywood the streets were "paved with gold," quickly responded, "You mean you have to bend down to pick it up?"

But dour-faced Fred Allen delivered the most direct hit. "Hollywood," he said, "is a great place to live if you're an orange!"

Hope did not bend over. Paramount paid him $20,000 a week for each picture in which they might decide to cast him. Such was the case for the expected ten weeks of shooting on *The Big Broadcast of 1938*. Not only did he have a substantial weekly salary coming in, he also had more than $300,000 stashed away in annuities which, compared to Bing Crosby, amounted to peanuts for the elephants down at the local zoo. According to Don Shepherd and Robert Slatzer in their comprehensive biography of Bing, by the time Hope got to Hollywood der Bingle's take at Paramount amounted to $1,000,000 for three pictures, plus all the other ventures he dabbled in, which did not include his enormous royalties from Decca Records. Many think Hope eventually ended up with more money than Crosby for the simple reason that he outlived him.

Anyway, once their bags were safely stowed in their Beverly Wilshire Hotel suite, Bob left Dolores to unpack while he rushed over to Paramount to meet the director, get his dressing room assignment, and prepare for shooting, which began on the following Monday. He'd already read the script.

Whether he knew about it, liked it, or didn't even care, Bob Hope's reputation (as much rumor as fact) preceded him. He'd said so many disparaging things over the years about the movie business—based mostly on his disastrous screen test several years earlier at Pathé—that film people thought him to be just another New York snob, something like broken-down southern aristocracy following the Civil War.

That's not to say he didn't have a celebrity's ego. He did. He was perceived to be vain, always checking himself out in the mirror. I've talked to a number of people who knew Hope in those early days, and one old-timer at Paramount explained it to me thusly: "I think he'd seen himself in all those silly two-reel things he did in New York and didn't like what he saw. His nose, which later became sort of a trademark, looked like Pinocchio's after someone hit him across the face with a baseball bat, which didn't make Bob a candidate for the industry's greatest leading man. He was self-conscious of his looks, always afraid he'd put on an innertube around the middle. Remember, he wasn't a youngster when he started his film career. Up in his thirties, I think." Actually, almost 36.

Dolores did not like Hollywood, being used to the sophistication of Manhattan, where her husband enjoyed major star status. In Hollywood, nobody knew Bob Hope nor did they seem to want to know him. Even her new hairdresser merely shrugged her shoulders when Dolores said, "I am Mrs. Bob Hope."

When Bob returned from the studio he brought with him a transcription of a song he would be singing with Shirley Ross.

"I thought you were supposed to have a solo," Dolores said, becoming ever more skeptical about any career her husband might have in California.

"You're gonna love this song, Dolores."

"What's it called?"

" 'Thanks for the Memory.' I want you to listen to it." She did, but didn't think it would go anywhere.

The song almost didn't go to Bob and Shirley, although it had been written expressly for them by Leo Robin and Ralph Rainger. Upon hearing it for the first time, Dorothy Lamour (also a member of the cast) told director Mitch Leisen, "That song will be a hit." Leisen knew that Dorothy had been a pretty good band singer in New York and knew something about music.

"If you feel that strongly about it, Dorothy, you can sing it. I'll find something else for Bob and Shirley."

"Oh, no," she responded. "I wouldn't do that to Bob. We were friends in New York. No, I want him to sing it." Dorothy, somewhat naive for Hollywood, never tried to upstage other actors or pull rank. Once she got into the "Road" pictures with Hope and Crosby, she found out what it meant to be betrayed by those you trust too much.

In her autobiography *My Side of the Road,* she remembers clearly the making of *The Big Broadcast of 1938* and her role in getting Paramount to keep Hope on the studio's contract player roster:

> ". . . I was surprised to hear that the front office thought
> Bob was too much like Jack Benny; they might not pick
> up his next option. I told them if they would *please* take
> up his option and put him into a few pictures—the *right*
> ones—they would have another big star who someday

would be an institution ... I got so carried away that I even offered to let them cut my salary in half and give it to Bob ..."

Film historians tend to forget that Dorothy Lamour was a star several years before Bob Hope found his way to Hollywood.

NBC arranged to do Bob's part of the Woodbury radio show via transcontinental wire from their studios at the corner of Vine Street and Sunset Boulevard. He hired a writer, Wilkie Mahoney, to help him write his monologue. The two men spent the first Saturday ironing out all the flaws before the Sunday airing. In those days all radio shows were broadcast live.

Late Sunday afternoon, about an hour and a half before air time, Bob discovered he would not have a live audience in the studio with him. He went through the roof. "Why didn't somebody tell me there wouldn't be an audience? I'd have gone out and brought one in." Adamant, he insisted that he have people in the studio when he did his monologue.

"But, Bob," the NBC executive handling the Hollywood remote said, "even if we wanted to, it's too late. We're too close to air time."

True to his ingenuity and ability to see a way out while others wrung their hands in despair, Bob asked who the line outside Studio "A" was for. Informed that they were waiting to get into the Edger Bergen-Charlie McCarthy Show, which aired at 5:30, Hope got an idea. He rushed over to Studio "A," where Edgar Bergen's rehearsal was going on, and called Bergen aside. He explained that he didn't like to go on the air in a dead studio.

"Look, Ed," he asked, "would you loan me your audience and I'll return them before your show goes on?"

Hope and Bergen had worked in New York at the same time and knew one another, so Edgar said, "Sure, why not?"

And so the audience, expecting Edgar Bergen and Charlie McCarthy, were ushered into Studio "B" first to see Bob Hope and then shuttled back into Studio "A" to see Edgar and Charlie.

The show turned out to be such a success that Woodbury agreed to allow a live audience for Bob Hope's monologue from Hollywood.

Bob's radio remote went just fine, but he ran into "first picture" problems. The studio technicians, make-up people, wardrobe, and miscellaneous studio executives and their flunkies always pounced on a "new fish." They'd all worked on many pictures and went about trying to tell Bob Hope how to be Bob Hope. They couldn't found into a more reluctant candidate.

Bob, by his own admission, arrived in Hollywood with a chip on his shoulder. It may have been more obvious to the House of Westmore, and to make-up artist Wally Westmore, who thought Bob should have his nose reshaped for the movies. Bob flatly refused.

"But," insisted Westmore, "movies aren't like the stage. In film we have close-ups. Your nose is just a bit of a problem . . ."

Hope interrupted, "I'll let you know."

When he asked Dolores about Westmore's suggestion, she shook her head. "No. You're not a leading man, you're a comedian. Your nose gets laughs. I like it just the way it is." And that ended Bob's film career as a serious leading man— to the betterment of everyone involved, especially his millions of fans around the world.

His director took him to lunch and gave him some advice about acting on film, explaining that the eyes say more on film than on the stage and that he shouldn't be waiting for laughs after each joke. Laughs were reserved for the theater audiences, not the crew.

Leisen, remembering that Dorothy Lamour had seen stardom for Hope all along, did something else unusual to get more spontaneity from his actor. Normally songs are pre-recorded and lip-synched on film. Knowing how much Bob preferred doing it "live," Leisen set up the bar scene where Hope and Shirley Ross do their duet of "Thanks for the Memory," and instead of a soundtrack, the director brought the full Paramount orchestra onto the set and let the couple do the scene live.

Researching material for this book, I watched *Big Broadcast* four or five times and there *is* a difference in that scene. It projects itself, even in black and white, as an intimate eavesdropping on something very special between two people in love.

"Thanks for the Memory" had a lot to do with Hope's career and he adopted it as his signature theme song for life. During his USO tours and overseas trips to entertain the troops, he phrased the lyrics to suit the locale and situations. I doubt anyone has counted the many verses Bob and his writers composed.

The Big Broadcast of 1938 had the silliest plot, dominated by W. C. Fields as the ship's captain. He changed his dialogue as it pleased him, depending on how much, and of what vintage, he had imbibed on that particular day. His antics alone were enough to deep-six the entire effort. Only Bob and Shirley's duet saved the picture.

Columnist Damon Runyon, often caustic in his reviews of Hollywood musicals (when he deigned even to notice them), raved about Bob Hope:

> "What a delivery, what a song, what an audience reception."

Okay, he had one film, one rave review, one option renewed. What next? He worried about Mack Millar going back to New York. Mack had been immensely helpful to him while making *Big Broadcast.* Paramount had a number of publicity flacks on salary as part of an enormous publicity department. They also had a roster of stars, all of whom were known names, not just some newcomer with Broadway experience and a radio show.

He didn't want to fall between the cracks. During a conversation with Millar, Mack let it be known that his wife wanted to relocate to the West Coast and perhaps he might be convinced to stay on with Hope. He'd need two hundred dollars a week. Bob countered with an offer of one-fifty and future upgrades. They shook hands and Hope hired a publicist—and a highly regarded one, to boot.

Hooray for Hollywood!

Chapter 12

The actors and executives at Paramount jostled for attention just as the studios themselves competed for the public's entertainment dollars. Metro-Goldwyn-Mayer liked to say it had more stars than there are in heaven. Paramount had Mount Olympus covered. During the thirties and forties, signing a long-term commitment to a studio meant giving up most of one's civil rights. The studio moguls ran Hollywood the way Al Capone ran Chicago—with an iron hand. A contract player didn't make a personal, much less professional, move without the studio's okay. "Image" belonged to the studio, not the actor. One slip and a studio could, and sometimes did, blackball a star.

Yet, dozens of actors clawed and scratched their way into long-term bondage. Paramount's "slave" list included: W. C. Fields, Gracie Allen, Benny Baker, Jack Benny, Ben Blue, Bob Burns, Charles Butterworth, Bill Frawley, Russell Hayden, Roscoe Karns, Bea Lillie, Harold Lloyd, Martha Raye, Charlie Ruggles, Mae West, Edward Arnold, Lew Ayres, Charles Bickford, William Boyd, Gary Cooper, Bing Crosby, Robert Cummings, Marlene Dietrich, Frances Farmer, Gabby Hayes, Marsha Hunt, Dorothy Lamour, Carole Lombard, Ida

Lupino, Fred MacMurray, Ray Milland, Lloyd Nolan, Anthony Quinn, George Raft, Shirley Ross, and Randolph Scott.

Hope survived all these legends. Bob had been drafted into the major leagues of show business where they eat rookies alive.

During the thirties, as the country's economy began to emerge from the swamp of depression, studios ground out movies as fast as Henry Ford produced automobiles. Major films were great, but cost a lot of money, so the cash cow became what were known as ''B'' movies—somewhat similar to an ''A'' record with a ''B'' flipside. Usually the ''A'' number became the hit. Occasionally the reverse was true. For instance, a new trio from Milwaukee, The Andrews Sisters, had recorded ''Nice Work If You Can Get It'' for Decca Records. That was supposed to be the hit. Reversal of fortunes interfered and an old Yiddish tune, ''Bei Mir Bist du Schoen,'' became a runaway best-seller and established the Andrews Sisters as major recording stars.

Paramount's boilerplate formula involved lots of songs, big names, and press hype. And the cash flowed. Bob's next picture, *College Swing,* was already in the can by the time Paramount released *The Big Broadcast of 1938* (January 1938). In *College Swing,* as with *Broadcast,* Bob got the part because it had been declined by another actor. This time the studio asked for Jack Oakie, but Oakie didn't want to be swallowed up by all the major stars set to appear in the film. He would not get top billing and after reading the script he thought even less of the picture.

With an insignificant role and few lines, Hope decided to have a conversation with the producer, Lew Gensler, who produced *Ballyhoo of 1932* and owed Hope some back salary, a subject that did not come up during their meeting. Lew agreed to beef up the part for Bob so that, without saying, whatever debt he owed the comedian would be considered paid in full.

College Swing featured a galaxy of Paramount's big names, including, besides Hope, George Burns and Gracie Allen, Edward Everett Horton, Martha Raye, Ben Blue, Jackie Coogan, Betty Grable, John Payne, Jerry Colonna, and Robert Cummings.

Paramount expected that a production number with Bob and Martha Raye singing Frank Loesser and Burton Lane's "How'd Ya Like to Love Me?" would carry the picture just as "Thanks for the Memory" did for *The Big Broadcast of 1938*. It didn't. Bob did not have the same chemistry on the screen with Martha as he had with Shirley Ross. The Hollywood variety film is practically non-existent today, but in the thirties the studios mimicked the very format they made fun of at cocktail parties—vaudeville.

Some in the industry thought it a waste of talent to cram so many big names into "nothing" pictures. Yet, during the studio system when stars were signed to long-term contracts and drawing weekly paychecks, the moguls wanted to be sure they got their money's worth. Stars like Fred MacMurray, Dorothy Lamour, Paulette Goddard, and Carole Lombard might be working on one sound stage in the morning and on another in the afternoon—in two different pictures at the same time.

Truthfully, it involved more than just keeping the hired hands busy. During the thirties Hollywood had a basic-training mentality. During no period of time in film history did so many great names get as much valuable training as they did during those few years preceding World War II. While the motion picture industry geared up for the future, rumblings of discontent stirred along the Asian side of the Pacific rim and in Central Europe. Bob Hope and his fellow workers would play a larger part in America's future than few, if any of them, might imagine.

Bob, as he always did when something didn't come off the way he expected it to, became fidgety and his old doubts about Hollywood lingered nearby. Dolores, only waiting for the word, would have had their bags packed and reservations made one-way to New York in a hot minute. She simply did not like Hollywood and considered the Hollywood cadre a poor second fiddle to Broadway.

Tired of hotels, she wanted a home and children, ideally in

one of New York's fashionable suburbs. A social animal, she loved the atmosphere of New York and its environs.

To keep busy, Bob accepted any and all requests to appear at benefits if they were being covered by reporters, columnists, and photographers. He knew from his years on Broadway that publicity contributes heavily to an actor's popularity and staying power.

He appeared at the racetrack with Bing Crosby, kibitzing the singer about his "nags." Crosby loved horses and horse racing and owned, over the years, some very valuable horseflesh, which won him more money than he liked to admit.

Paramount milked the Crosby-Hope antics and encouraged the tongue-in-cheek public rivalry. During this period Bob made friends with Jerry Colonna, who would later become his side-kick in radio and television, and on USO tours.

His publicity agent, Mack Millar, kept up a flow of copy and photos to the dailies and the all-important fan magazines. The United Press wires hummed on October 15, 1937, with the following release:

> On Sunday, Crosby and Bob Hope, who just arrived from Broadway to work in pictures, will play for the dubious title of "Golf Champion of the Entertainment World." The loser will work for one day as extra in the other's current picture.

Hope lost by a score of 84 to Crosby's 72 and was "humili-ated" at having to play an extra for one day in *Doctor Rhythm*, Crosby's next picture at Paramount. The whole thing, done to focus media attention on Bob Hope (Paramount and Crosby were much better known names) brought the press out in force. Their studio treated them with all the hors d'oeuvres and good-ies with which the media is, and always has been, bribed in return for favorable coverage. Bob loved it. "Just spell the name right, kid," Hope told a young Hearst reporter named Patte Barham, who giggled a polite, "Yes sir, Mr. Hope." Bob didn't know it, but her father, Frank Barham, the publisher of Hearst's evening newspaper, *The Herald Express,* happened to be a close personal friend of William Randolph Hearst, an international media giant.

Patte Barham went on to establish herself as a prizewinning journalist covering the Korean War for the Hearst Syndicate and her recent biography of Marilyn Monroe, *Marilyn, the Last Take* became a runaway best-seller.

Bob Hope read the trade papers daily, knew every new radio show that might be in the planning stages, who the sponsors were and the probable format. He had an uncanny ability to pick up tidbits that were often overlooked by his agents.

He made it his business to know if Paramount hired a new director, writer, or actor from New York, what pictures were being planned, and how he might fit into any of them. It did not delight him that Paramount wanted to cast him in nonsensical roles until he "got the feel of Hollywood." He'd already felt Hollywood and it didn't feel all that good.

Dolores had more than a feel. She'd had it up to her ears and almost convinced Bob on more than one occasion that by hanging around in Hollywood to become a movie star he'd be wasting his time. Yet, something compelled him to stay on.

When not pestering Doc Shurr about pictures and road tours, he would either be on the phone or meeting with Jimmy Saphier, working out schemes to get his own coast-to-coast radio show.

Doc Shurr called Bob one day to let him know he would be paired again with Martha Raye in a picture called *Give Me A Sailor*. He didn't relish being typecast as Martha Raye's foil, but he agreed to do the film. With a contract to honor, he hadn't built up enough clout to "renegotiate" as major stars often did.

Both he and Martha were comedy stars and he preferred being the sole comedian playing against straight characters. But he hardly had a choice in the matter. If he didn't do the picture, he might be suspended or fired. He grumbled to Doc and Dolores, but never complained at the studio. Most directors found him to be the consummate professional on the set, in contrast to some of the more famous names with whom he worked.

With Christmas rapidly approaching, he and Dolores decided

that after the holidays they'd look for a house and put hotel living behind them. Dolores wanted a Christmas tree and the comforts of home and they could well afford them. So why not let this be their last Christmas cramped up in a hotel suite? Bob agreed, but for the moment other things needed attending to.

Jimmy Saphier brought him an offer he couldn't think of turning down. Dick Powell—at the time better known for his crooning than as the actor and director he later became—along with Rosemary Lane (one of the three Lane sisters who each, in her own right, became stars of radio, films and Broadway), were costarring in a variety show, broadcast coast-to-coast. Sponsored by Lucky Strike cigarettes "Your Hollywood Parade" aired one hour a week in prime time.

The producers offered Bob two consecutive weekly spots with the caveat that if the audiences liked him he'd be given the comedy spot on a permanent basis. Saphier explained to Hope that this would allow him to develop his monologues since he'd have a seven-minute spot on each show.

Bob didn't blink an eye. "Where do I sign up?"

Lucky Strike approved of Bob's two appearances and it looked as if he would be a voice on radio indefinitely.

He debuted on "Your Hollywood Parade" December 29, 1937. Still shooting *College Swing* (*Give Me A Sailor* hadn't as yet gone into production), he and his writers worked around the clock to be sure he had a crisp, timely, and topical monologue. He thought correctly that any takeoff on Hollywood or politics would be considered funny to a nation beginning to rise up from the depths of depression. He pushed every funny button in radio's vast audience and assured himself that the second broadcast would merely be a warm-up for an assured sustaining spot on the show.

He made jokes about Crosby and his horses, Washington politicians, Paulette Goddard and her then-husband, Charlie Chaplin, and numerous other heretofore sacred icons. The public loved him and the columnists who covered radio and hadn't always thought his material to be so good, praised him as if paying penance for their earlier lack of confidence.

Once the second show aired he once again went after Saphier to find him his own show. "If they don't know I can carry a show by myself by now," he complained, "they never will know."

The Lucky Strike executives liked him so much they let it be leaked that they'd prefer Bob over Dick Powell to headline the show. Powell took immediate umbrage and quickly let the producers know that if they tried to violate his iron-clad contract, they'd be faced with a hefty lawsuit. As a result of Powell's resistance, Bob did not become the star of the show and the courtesy between the two men throughout the run of the show became strictly professional. Off the air, Dick Powell had little to do with his show's comedy star.

On March 23, 1938, "Your Hollywood Parade" aired for the last time, once again leaving Hope without a radio gig. *The Big Broadcast of 1938* went into general release nationally to warm reviews for Bob Hope and "Thanks for the Memory." *College Swing* would soon be in general release, with the production of *Give Me A Sailor* nearing an end.

True to their commitment to one another, Bob and Dolores leased a house in the San Fernando Valley from Rhea Gable, Clark's first wife, early in the new year. His option with Paramount had been picked up after the completion of *College Swing*, and the Bob Hopes began to slip into the Hollywood scene like a foot into a comfortable shoe.

The best was yet to come—and it would be grand.

Chapter 13

If anyone doubts the old adage about one hand washing the other, Bob Hope's career turns would put their doubts to rest. In 1938, Hope couldn't have been more unhappy with the direction in which his motion picture career seemed to be heading. Paramount continued pairing him with Martha Raye and, much to his further displeasure, some of Hollywood's "A" group (oh, yes—they've always had a caste system in Glitterville, but it took four decades before *Los Angeles Times* columnist Joyce Haber gave it a tag) were whispering that Bob and Martha had become the poor man's Burns and Allen.

Several events occurred almost simultaneously. Dolores decided that they ought to buy or build a home of their own. She wanted a place that could become the family homestead. Very interested in golf, and the publicity value it offered, especially with Paramount's exploitation of the competitiveness between Bob Hope and Bing Crosby, he and Dolores found three acres in the Toluca Lake area of the San Fernando Valley on the edge of the Lakeside Country Club.

They purchased the property for $6,000 and added another three acres several years later at three times their original purchase price. "Hope's place out in the Valley," as it became known in the industry, is now worth millions.

By the end of the year they were comfortably ensconced in their new abode, with all the "good china" and furnishings which had previously been in storage. Up until the time that they actually moved in, Dolores hadn't been certain that they wouldn't pack their bags suddenly and move back to New York.

Meanwhile, things were starting to pop for Bob in radio land. Without the knowledge of anyone in the Louis Shurr office, he and Jimmy Saphier had quietly been negotiating for Bob to host his own coast-to-coast radio show in prime time on NBC.

Pepsodent Toothpaste had, for many years, sponsored radio's "Amos and Andy" show. Amos and Andy, two white men, Freeman Gosden and Charles Correll respectively, parodied blacks as Step'n'fetchit stereotypes. Ironically, the show enjoyed one of the highest ratings among the numerous radio comedy shows on the air during the thirties. They were especially popular among America's white blue-collar workers. The show would decrease in popularity as America entered World War II when thousands of black men went into the military to fight for their country. American mores were changing ever so subtly, although much of the country remained segregated.

Pepsodent executives were looking for something different. Saphier knew Tom MacAvity, West Coast representative of Lord & Thomas, the advertising agency handling the Pepsodent account.

A bug in MacAvity's ear, a phone call to the agency's New York office, and the wheels began to turn in Bob's favor as the replacement for Amos and Andy. In the end, Saphier set a deal that gave Bob his own half-hour weekly radio show on NBC, sponsored by Pepsodent at $3,000 per show. Over the six years, an escalation clause would increase his weekly stipend to five grand per week.

Although Bob's radio material rarely could be called "offensively risqué", the CEO of Pepsodent expected a family show. Bob had been known, on occasion, to do double-entendre jokes in vaudeville. Lord & Thomas wanted it clearly understood that there would be no funny business, else the morals clause would be imposed, and immediately. Bob Hope never made a deal that didn't have his fingerprints on a "must have" clause. In exchange for promising to be a nice young man on the air, they gave the comedian "full production control." Such concessions were rarely granted, a sure indication that Bob Hope had something special to offer both the sponsor and its audience.

Could Bob Hope sell toothpaste? He sold the hell out of Pepsodent and his monologue signature on radio became, "This is Bob 'Pepsodent' Hope . . ."

The show would first air in September 1938 on NBC from 7:00 to 7:30 P.M. on Tuesday evening, sandwiched between two other top-rated comedy shows: "Fibber McGee and Molly" and "The Red Skelton Show." Bob Hope's position in radio had been signed, sealed, and delivered.

"Amos and Andy" found a new home at CBS radio.

Paramount decided to renew Hope's option, but didn't notify Louis Shurr right away because certain executives in the front office kept dragging their feet. Others pushed to complete the deal, fearing that since Bob was not too keen on the pictures he'd been given, he might jump ship in favor of radio while the studio took its time completing the proposed renewal. So they continued to dally.

By the time Y. Frank Freeman, Paramount's head of production, got around to reading all the glowing reviews of *Big Broadcast* and numerous other favorable articles about his client that Mack Millar assembled and delivered to Freeman's office, Doc Shurr had closed a deal with producer Edwin Lester for Bob to reprise his Huckleberry Haines role in the West Coast premiere of *Roberta*.

Roberta opened on June 6 and ran through June 21, 1938, at the Philharmonic Auditorium (Los Angeles' answer to New York's Carnegie Hall).

A delighted Bob Hope invited everyone he knew in Hollywood to come and see him as a "real actor" and not as some ham shooting and reshooting bad scripts. Beautiful, blond, and tragic Carole Landis, a Hollywood newcomer, played Sophie in the

Los Angeles production of *Roberta*. Miss Landis, suffering from depression and other personal problems, committed suicide several years later, at the peak of her career.

On the day of *Roberta's* opening at the Philharmonic, Y. Frank Freeman notified Louis Shurr that Paramount would be exercising its option on Hope's services and, to frost the cake, would bring him back together with Shirley Ross, since they'd been so successful in the *Big Broadcast* as a team. Freeman, knowing how Hope felt about another match-up with Martha Raye, thought Bob would be delighted to know that Paramount thought him worthy of such an offer.

"Not so fast," Shurr demurred. "First of all, Bob's already signed to do a vaudeville tour, leaving immediately after the final curtain comes down on *Roberta*. You'll have to wait your turn.

Shurr, still smarting over Bob and Saphier keeping the Pepsodent deal such a secret, decided to flex his own muscles. Aware that he'd been caught without an apt response, Freeman agreed to all of Shurr's conditions and so Paramount and Bob Hope "renewed their vows" and began a long and mutually lucrative association, a marriage (with the exception of one long suspension) that would clearly establish Bob Hope as a major movie star.

Two days after *Roberta* closed at the Philharmonic, Bob, with Dolores as his girl singer and former child star Jackie Coogan (married to Betty Grable), opened at Loews State on Broadway to great fanfare and lots of press coverage. New Yorkers love it when one of their own comes home from Hollywood.

In its review of June 29, 1938, *Variety* praised not only the show, but singled out Bob and Dolores:

> An especially pleasant and rich torcheroo is projected by Dolores Reade (Mrs. Hope), who knows how. Tone quality is individual. Diction good, too.
>
> For a show closer, Hope returns to paraphrase "Thanks for the Memory" to celebrate, half-facetious, half-nostalgic, the forgotten delights of vaudeville. Kidding or not, there's a heart tug in that routine for anybody who dotes upon the theater and rues its sorry defeat

at the hands of mechanization. Hope, with the typical coloration of a true trouper, would probably swap Pepsodent, his new sponsor, for the old Palace any day.

When a *New York World-Telegram* reporter inquired as to why Bob liked California, considering how he had bad-mouthed it for so long, Hope responded with a typical Hope quip: "Why not? They're giving me better parts. And I can play golf with Dad—Crosby, that is—all year round, and go to quiet parties."

Most of the New York press corps thought of Hollywood as swinging wilder than Chicago in the Roaring Twenties. It never occurred to them that making three and four and sometimes five motion pictures in one year took a tremendous amount of energy—learning lines, being on the set at five in the morning, and often working late into the night. Such energy could not be wasted on parties. Hollywood nightlife was reserved for tourists, people who didn't take their work too seriously, or stars taking a breather between films.

On Broadway, the routine, once learned, becomes rote. Entertainers performed their evening show, then had an opportunity to make the late rounds and sleep until noon if they pleased. Movie people, unlike Broadway show people, did not (and do not) sleep until noon except on film or between pictures. The cocktail hour is a Manhattan original.

Bob found himself defending the town and industry he had not so long ago condemned as being unfit for a real actor. Hollywood had replaced Cleveland and New York as his hometown. To his surprise, both he and Dolores missed California—and the prospect of moving into their new neighborhood where, in due time, a magnificent permanent home would became the largest estate on Moorpark Street with Lakeside Country Club as their front yard.

He and Dolores bade all their New York friends farewell at a series of cocktail and dinner parties. Both knew, as did their hosts, that Bob's wonderful New York had been replaced by California.

Back in Los Angeles, over after-dinner drinks one evening, he said, "Honey, everything is moving so fast that it's becoming difficult to keep up. You're trying to balance too much and my schedule is getting to the point that I can't manage it without help.''

Dolores, always perceptive of her husband's moods, interrupted him. ''What you're trying to tell me is that you want one of your brothers to come out to California and help out. Isn't that right?''

Bob did miss his family. He'd always been very close to his siblings in the past, but in California that became more difficult. ''Well,'' he said, ''I do need someone I can trust. I sure as hell don't trust many people out here.''

''How about your brother Jack?''

As if reading his mind, she'd picked up his thoughts. Bob had already decided to send for Jack, who was recently divorced.

''I think you're right,'' he said, smiling to himself at how easily he'd gotten Dolores to come on board with the idea.

''So it's settled.'' She, too, smiled.

Dolores had other reasons to smile. She knew that men in the motion picture business were judged a great deal by the kind of women they married. All too many male stars let lust guide their marital decisions, marrying starlets and chorus girls with great legs, ample breasts, and a vacuum beneath their bleached and hennaed locks. Such marriages generally ended in an early divorce once the novelty of the women's youthful bodies wore off.

Dolores picked and chose her husband's friends as though selecting the menu for a state dinner. She wanted him to be surrounded by the most respected and influential men and women in the business and set out to accomplish just that.

They counted among their neighbors in Toluca Lake the Bing Crosbys, W. C. Fields, Broderick Crawford, the Humphrey Bogarts, Mary Astor, Ozzie and Harriet Nelson, Forrest Tucker, James Cagney, Ruby Keeler, and the William Holdens. Holden, also a new face under contract at Paramount, and his wife became close friends with the Hopes, often alternating dinner at each other's homes. The friendship continued throughout the years and, when Bob and Dolores built a house in Palm Springs some years later, the Holdens were in residence nearby.

Dolores nourished the friendships she cultivated in Toluca Lake and thanks to those connections, she and Bob met many important producers and studio executives, all of whom served to increase their prestige in the acting community.

In due time their neighbors profited as much from the relationship as did Bob and Dolores. Bob always extended his hand to help a friend in need, whether it be a phone call or a loan (contrary to his reputation for stinginess in other areas).

Interestingly enough, California in the thirties didn't differ much in its segregation policies from other parts of the country. Country clubs had restrictive clauses against blacks, Jews, and other ethnic groups. The Hopes had no black neighbors. Excluding Jews from celebrity neighborhoods was difficult, since most of the studios were controlled by brilliant Jewish men, transposed from New York, bringing with them their motion picture expertise from the studios they had founded on Long Island and in Manhattan.

Lakeside Country Club had restrictions in both race and religious beliefs. If Bob had any objection to those exclusions, he never voiced them, nor did he let it deter him from becoming a member.

Hope remained a member of Lakeside all his life, despite later criticism as civil rights emerged from the ashes of segregation. Crosby eventually succumbed to public pressure and joined Bel Air Country Club, where race and religion were openly tolerated.

Jack Hope, operating a meat market in Akron, Ohio, ached to move to California and hang out with his famous brother. He'd always aspired to becoming a songwriter and often voiced his belief that "songwriters don't get published in Ohio—you got to go to New York or California." He preferred California, and why not? It had movie stars, sunshine, sandy beaches, and thousands of beautiful women.

Yet, he seemed surprised when Bob called and asked if he'd like to join him on the West Coast. Bob wanted him to help manage his affairs, which were expanding at such a rapid rate that Dolores couldn't keep up with them and still maintain any kind of social life which both she and Bob considered important to his career.

Jack jumped at the opportunity. He didn't exactly know what Bob had in mind, but California beat Ohio any day of the week. Besides, he reasoned, he'd have lots of movie star stories to tell the folks back in Ohio on visits and in letters.

So he abandoned the meat market, packed his belongings and tossed them into his 1937 Pontiac, and headed west. He did not stop until he pulled up to the main gate at Paramount Studios and announced his arrival to a suspicious security guard. Jack looked the part of a man who had driven nearly three thousand miles nonstop; hair disheveled, clothes dirty and wrinkled, smelling more of the road than eau de cologne.

"I'm here to see Bob Hope," he announced to the gateman when asked his business.

"And who, may I ask," inquired the leery guard, skepticism apparent in his voice, "is calling on Mr. Hope?"

"I'm his older brother. Just got in from Ohio."

Jack Hope and Bob Hope didn't look anything like brothers. They were built differently and whereas Bob had dark hair and brown eyes, Jack was a blue-eyed blond. Only after the guard talked personally on the phone with Bob did he permit Jack onto the lot, directing him to Bob's dressing room.

Bob had plenty of plans for Jack—and, eventually, other members of his Cleveland family. Mahm had told him to look out for his brothers and, whatever Mahm said received attention throughout Bob's life, long after she was gone.

The Hopes of California would become as important and prominent in the entertainment business as the Browns would in California politics. Two kinds of first families, but still first families.

Chapter 14

Bob, a workaholic all his life, welcomed his new schedule. He never walked onto a set unprepared, always knew his lines and marks. He would arrive at the studio, having studied his lines the night before, and often would be going over material for his radio show while sitting in the make-up chair.

His hang-loose attitude did not deter his professionalism, although certain directors were driven to distraction by his antics during rehearsals. A classic example occurred during rehearsals for his new picture at Paramount with Shirley Ross, which changed names a couple of times before emerging as *Thanks for the Memory*, to capitalize on the success of their famous duet.

Bob decided not to take the film too seriously. He'd be a professional, but he didn't intend to allow the picture to interfere with his preparations for the Pepsodent radio show. He'd made his brother Jack the producer in order to put him on salary and to use him as a conduit through whom he could receive gossip and send down orders. Bob now understood that despite earlier misgivings, radio—not motion pictures—would establish his identity in the minds of American audiences.

Once the Pepsodent show got off to a healthy start, people

would flock to the movies to see the Bob Hope who lifted their spirits and made them laugh on Tuesday nights. To his credit, once he understood the ramifications of radio on the public psyche, he never again uttered a disrespectful remark about the medium.

George Archinbaud directed *Thanks for the Memory,* and from the outset he let it be known that he did not like cut-ups on his pictures, that making movies was a serious business, and that he would tolerate no funny business on the set. It became an open invitation for Bob and Shirley Ross to have some fun at the director's expense.

Bob hadn't forgotten a relaxing technique that Andy Devine cooked up with Martha Raye while they were filming *Never Say Die.* Andy wanted Bob to take the afternoon off and go with him to play golf. Bob, still fairly new at the Hollywood game, didn't want to get in trouble.

"I don't think we'll escape from this chain gang today," Bob said.

"I think we can. Watch me."

So Andy spends part of the morning convincing Martha Raye that the studio is working her too hard.

"What do you mean?" she asked.

"I mean, these producers just get all they can out of you while you're hot. They don't care what happens to you, and you're working all the time and they're beating your brains out and they're getting the money, and it drains your energy and you ought to watch yourself."

After a couple of more workings-over, Andy had Martha believing that maybe she should take the afternoon off. So following lunch when they were setting up the next scene, Martha promptly collapsed on cue and the director called out loudly, "That's all for today, boys."

Bob spent the afternoon playing golf with the devious Andy Devine—beating him, of course. Andy Devine taught him a lesson. Nothing is so important that one should let it dominate. "You gotta have some fun once in a while," he told Bob.

* * *

So, from the beginning of shooting on *Thanks for the Memory,* Bob decided that rehearsals could be a drag if he allowed it and Shirley Ross, a willing co-conspirator, agreed.

Neither of the stars meant any disrespect toward their director, but they were working once again with a silly script and once again the pivotal scene involved their singing a duet which became the brightest spot in an otherwise dull picture. The song, "Two Sleepy People," enjoyed great popularity, went on to become a standard, and is to this day a favorite in cocktail lounges and piano bars.

During rehearsals, Shirley and Bob chewed gum constantly. It nearly drove Archinbaud crazy. He complained they were interfering with his thought processes, that he couldn't get a proper camera angle if they kept it up. His complaints and appeals fell on deaf ears. The pair would make up lyrics as they went along during rehearsals, adding gag lines to a very serious song about two people in love, sleepy, and smoking cigarettes.

In no time at all, the entire Paramount lot knew that some mischief might be taking place on the *Thanks for the Memory* set. By the time the director shot the scene, the sound stage had filled to capacity with other actors, grips, carpenters, electricians, wardrobe people, and hairdressers. Nobody loves a gag better than film people. They are the biggest gossips in the world, which is why there are more than a dozen versions of what happened that day, on that particular set.

When the director said, "This will be a take," the two quickly stashed their gum inside the arms of their chairs and Bob, loving an audience and seeing how many people were on the set, nearly broke Shirley up when he whispered, "I thought we'd draw a better house than this."

The director swore he'd never make another picture with such idiots, but he did—just once more. The following year he again directed Bob and Shirley from another stupid script entitled *Rhythm Romance.*

Bob had four pictures released in 1938, all of them duds. Their only redeeming quality involved the songs that he warbled to a female interest. Of one thing, however, he was certain: his radio show would have the best format and the best jokes and there would be no stale scripts.

In order to accomplish that, he hired the best young writers available and worked with them, sometimes around the clock, until the shows glistened like fifty-dollar gold pieces. He lured Melville Shavelson and Hilt Josefsberg from the East Coast and added a couple of more young Hollywood guys who were lean and hungry and put together the nucleus of a writing team that would serve him throughout his show business career.

Shavelson remembered those early days on the Pepsodent show. ''If you make the fellas whose jobs depended on their not laughing, laugh, then Bob would check off the joke and that went into the show. That's when I developed my first ulcer!''

Bob took nothing for granted. The Pepsodent show, his own show, had been the vehicle he'd yearned for ever since he woke up and discovered the power of radio and how many people could hear his voice at the same time.

He wanted topical subjects, things the ordinary guy had on his mind. Politics ranked high as did snobbery, Hollywood, and New York's society blue bloods. But did he love to needle the high and mighty. He found the perfect format for his kind of humor in radio and he would go for broke. He'd either be loved or dismissed by audiences. Willing to take that risk, he went on the air for the first time on September 27, 1938, with a full complement of writers, having added Al and Sherwood Schwartz, Jack Douglas, Rene Duplessis, Norman Sullivan, Norman Panama, Melvin Frank, and Dr. Sam Kurtzman. With such an array of talented scribes (most of their names are now legend), he had to be the best comedian in the business because he had the best team.

Arthur Marx, in his biography, *The Secret Life of Bob Hope,* says of Hope's writers:

''Those who served Hope had to be on call twenty-four hours a day. Since there was still massive unemployment in America in 1938, it wasn't that difficult to find talented young men, just out of college, who were willing to give up their lives for fifty or seventy-five dollars a week.''

Comedians were tough on their writers. Most tried to get the best for the least amount of money. Bob Hope had a system he might have picked up from his pals Edgar Bergen and Rudy Vallee, both of whom were known to want writers on the cheap for long hours and brilliant minds. In the thirties there were no unions to protect the writers from their voracious employers, and so the word "slavery" became part of a writer's vocabulary.

Bob Hope's attorney, Martin Gang, who later became a famous show business divorce and contract expert, created the contracts for Bob's writers. They were employer/employee contracts that, not unlike landlord/tenant agreements, always came down on the side of the employer. These contracts included an option clause for the next radio season that the employer (Hope) didn't have to exercise until two months after the end of the current season.

It was like deciding which fish to take out as the lake went dry. Most of the comedians picked up their good writers' options before the season ended, insuring them some security for the next year. Bob waited until it was too late for his writers to be signed by another important show. In so doing, he insured that he would get them at his price and on his conditions. In later years, the writers finally got tired of being treated badly and formed a union to protect themselves. He also had a clause that, like today's "work for hire" contracts, gave him ownership of all material the writers wrote for him which precluded their using any of their own material elsewhere. The Writers Guild of America protects today's writers from such skullduggery.

During that first season Hope could be excused for not paying his writers more. Pepsodent provided only a $3,000 budget for each weekly episode, out of which came Bob's own salary. An old-timer from the NBC radio days told me that during the early part of his first season on the radio for Pepsodent, with all the expenses of producing the show, Hope's salary came to practically zero and that he was so dedicated he would probably have spent part of his Paramount salary to make sure he stayed on the air.

Maybe.

Two of his bright youngsters, Melvin Frank and Norman Panama, came from Chicago to write for Milton Berle. When Hope found them they were pounding the pavement and knocking on the doors of Fields, Cantor, and Jolson—knocking on doors that did not open.

They'd come on the lot at Paramount when Bob was working with Martha Raye and Andy Devine on *Never Say Die,* which the studio slipped in after *Thanks For The Memory.*

In an interview with Charles Thompson, Mel Frank recalls meeting Hope as though it were yesterday:

"It was the first time either of us had been inside a major studio and there was this incredibly handsome guy, in make-up, sitting in a little cubbyhole. He just looked up at us and said, 'I've been enjoying you guys all night!' Well, at that time, all he had to do was look and . . . wham . . . we melted. If he wanted to, at that moment, he could—for $12—have signed us for life . . ."

Their first assignment came when Bob's radio guest was to be Groucho Marx. After spending three hours with Groucho, who strummed a guitar on his living room floor, they came away with several pages of usable dialogue for Groucho's spot on the show.

"Some of those jokes," Mel recalled, were Groucho's and they were good, but some of them were ours and they were also good."

Bob liked the material and complimented the two young men on their accomplishment. The show went well, got lots of laughs, but Groucho, as he was wont to do, upstaged Hope at the end of his bit. "I'd like to sell you an old suit of clothes," he said to Hope, "but I see you've already got one . . ."

The audience went wild, so Bob used a lot of Panama and Frank's material for guest stars.

For that first show everyone had a case of opening night jitters. In those days there was no such thing as doing the show at 7:30 on the East Coast to be rebroadcast at 7:30 on the West Coast. It didn't work that way. Both shows had to be broadcast live. From Hollywood that meant doing a remote at 4:30 in the afternoon for 7:30 consumption in the east and then doing the whole thing all over again live, before a second audience, at 7:30 for the folks out west. Often the changes made between shows created great differences in what went out over the airwaves in the second show.

An immediate difference between Bob and his sponsors came about over the show's signature song. In the George Gershwin musical, *Of Thee I Sing,* he had written a novelty tune entitled, "Wintergreen for President." Pepsodent wanted to use the tune but change the words for the show's opening to "Here's Bob Hope for Pepsodent."

Taking advantage of his contract, which gave him full control of the show, Bob said absolutely not. He wanted "Thanks for the Memory," and "Thanks for the Memory" he got—well, sort of. Both sides compromised. Pepsodent got its rousing opening music, but most significantly, Bob closed the show with a warm and tender "Thanks for the Memory." On his first show he had no Honey Chile, no girl to bounce his jokes off. He knew that Jack Benny had lots of fun with Eddie "Rochester" Anderson and that worked. But Pepsodent had dropped "Amos and Andy," who imitated being black. So he picked Jerry Colonna, who'd worked with him in *College Swing.* He'd also been made aware of Colonna's ability to do many other things. He felt he could use Colonna, known for his wide-ranging mustache and high-pitched voice which could sustain a note as long as an opera star, in many comedic situations.

He picked Bill Goodwin as the show's announcer, a man with experience and the ability to deliver comedy lines with the smoothness of wet glass.

Skinnay Ennis, having left Ray Noble, came on board with his new band. To complete the musical element, Bob hired a group consisting of Marvin Bailey, Pauline Byrnes, Vin Degan, Howard Hudson, Mac McLean, Jerry Preshaw, and Bill Seckler, dubbed "Six Hits and a Miss."

His first celebrity guest was to be actress Constance Bennett, whose roles in film were straight out of the New York society that Hope loved to target with his wittiest barbs.

The first script would be overly long—perhaps an hour or an hour and a half—the object being to select the best jokes and file the rest away to be used or revised for later use.

Before a live audience on Sunday evening at NBC's West Coast studios on the northeast corner of Sunset Boulevard and Vine Street, the show was transcribed (recorded on disc). The following day Bob and his writers would play and replay the transcription until they'd culled out all but the finest material for the half-hour show on Tuesday which, in fact, did not add up to thirty minutes due to time allocated for commercial announcements.

Those Sunday night shows had a two-fold purpose. They gave him a chance to do just about anything he wanted. Equally important, his audiences were mostly out-of-towners come to Hollywood to see movie stars and line up for live radio broadcasts. Then, on Tuesday, they might be somewhere listening to the radio with friends and relatives, explaining how it was all done and retelling the jokes that never made it on the air.

Bob's first show went well. He had a good lead-in from "Fibber McGee and Molly." He introduced himself, "How do you do, ladies and gentlemen ... this is Bob Hope ..." and the show took off and never stopped through 1952. He turned the mike over to Bill Goodwin, who announced, "Connie Bennett, Jerry Colonna, Skinnay Ennis, and his orchestra, and Six Hits and a Miss."

Bob then launched into a seven-minute monologue in which he took aim at his announcer Bill Goodwin, Paramount Studios, a Texas Legionnaire, women in general, and it soon became clear that nothing was sacred to Mr. Hope. He did a clever routine with Connie Bennett and Bill Goodwin about a baseball game between "the Brooklyn Debutantes and the Dead-End Girlies," in which he poked some fun at America's first lady, Eleanor Roosevelt, known to be a globetrotter as the eyes and ears of her husband, President Franklin D. Roosevelt.

GOODWIN: "Look at that woman going around and around without stopping. Who is it?"

HOPE: "Oh, that's Mrs. Roosevelt."

Ennis's band played, the group sang, and Colonna did his thing, beginning with a long, drawn-out opening to "Ah, Sweet Mystery of Life," for which he became famous. The audience roared.

Hollywood critics had the same attitude toward radio as Broadway showmen had had earlier on toward vaudeville. They simply looked down their noses. The Hollywood columnists wanted to write about movies and glamorous film stars with their new wives, husbands, and lovers—or whatever else they could find to whet the always-avaricious appetite of film buffs. Radio couldn't compete for their column space.

One radio columnist, in an overnight review, gave Hope's show short shrift: "None of the opinions of the new Hope show seemed to jibe." But Bob and his sponsors liked it and the American listening audience liked it. As Harry Truman once said when all the pollsters and political columnists were badmouthing his presidency, "The only people who like me are the voters." In Bob's case it was the audience, and they were the ones that really counted.

Despite certain critics, *Variety* reviewed the show on the eve of his second week and gave "hope" to Hope:

That small speck going over the center-field fence is the four-bagger Bob Hope whammed out his first time at bat for Pepsodent. If he can keep up the pace he'll get as much word of mouth for 1938-39 as Edgar Bergen got for 1937-38. He sounded like success all the way.

But it's his particular gift not to seem to be trying. And that's a great psychological aid. It suggests wearing. Or, maybe we're neglecting the writers. However he or them is/are, house rules allow an extra bow.

The Sunday night live audience run-throughs were so popular even insiders often couldn't get in. The fans started lining up hours before showtime because nobody knew what Bob would do. As a matter of caution, NBC had a censor (known as a "continuity man") in the studio and after each Sunday night session, he'd delineate all the material Bob had used which the network or sponsor disapproved of and warn him, "You can't use that on the air."

Walter Bunker, an NBC executive in the control room on Bob's shows, remembered that Bob would argue his side of the material and declare that "I'm going to use it anyway." Bunker had instructions that if the continuity man wanted something blooped, then he, Bunker, would do exactly that. Hope tested the rulings to the limit but finally gave in, knowing that he was defeating his own goal: having a sustaining family radio show. He should have known better anyway. It hadn't been that long since Mae West had been banned from radio for a very off-color "Adam and Eve" joke.

Thanks to a great start and the subsequent word of mouth, which travels as fast as the speed of sound in Hollywood, major stars lined up to guest on the Bob Hope show. During his first few months he boasted such stellar personalities as Madeleine Carroll, Shirley Ross, Groucho Marx, Joan Bennett, Pat O'Brien, Rosalind Russell, Paulette Goddard, and a very teen-aged Judy Garland, America's new singing sweetheart. Her appearance brought such high ratings that Bob signed her to be his vocalist for the following season.

"The Bob Hope Show" ended the season in a respectable fourth place in the ratings. Only Jack Benny, Fred Allen, and Edgar Bergen bested him in audience appeal.

Chapter one, verse one, of the Bob Hope Pepsodent half-hour had been written, delivered, and was now published.

Now one of America's most popular radio comedians, adored by millions of fans, he hoped next to do something about his situation at Paramount.

Another matter, probably more important than either radio shows or motion pictures, would soon take priority over all others. Both he and Dolores wanted a family—and that presented some complications that required resolution.

Chapter 15

Dolores, brought up in a strict Catholic home, expected a marriage with a houseful of children. Not only had she been influenced by church and family, she also possessed natural mothering instincts which, along with her great beauty, Bob found attractive from the start.

Bob and Dolores have always been reserved when discussing their reasons for adopting children. It would be a logical assumption that one or the other had problems that precluded conception.

Robert Slatzer, a coworker and close friend of Hope's younger brother, George, says that the problem did not rest in Bob's camp. Slatzer, as quoted in Arthur Marx's unauthorized biography of Bob Hope, repeated the story to me in a recent interview:

"I became very friendly with George Hope. Bob recruited him away from Cleveland to come out to Hollywood and involve himself in Hope's various business activities. George and I had much in common, both being from Ohio. When I first met him, I was a publicist at Paramount, having given up my job at the *Columbus*

Dispatch and moved to California to work in the film industry. Hope, Crosby, and Lamour had already made several of their "Road" pictures and Bob pretty much had his way at the studio.

"Bob and Dolores had previously begun adopting kids and I asked George one day why they didn't have any kids of their own. Didn't Dolores want to carry a baby, or what? He laughed and said, 'I can tell you one thing, it sure wasn't Bob's fault. He told me that when he worked in vaudeville a lot of girls pointed a finger at him as being the father of their children. That's how he learned to use protection."

Marx says that Lillian Kramer, wife of Nathan Kramer (they owned the Edison Hotel in Manhattan), told a friend of his that Dolores confessed to her that due to a secret abortion, she'd been damaged in a way that prevented her ever having children. Abortions of any kind were illegal at the time and subjected the woman to immediate ex-communication from the Catholic Church.

Marx also alleged in his biography of Hope that in the spring of 1936 Rita Canzoneri, wife of lightweight boxing champion Tony Canzoneri, gave birth to a daughter named Denise. The Canzoneris were neighbors of the Hopes when they lived on Central Park West in New York. Dolores and Rita, according to Marx, spent a lot of time together.

On one particular visit to Rita's apartment, Dolores is reputed to have asked Rita, "Why don't you give me your baby?"

"Are you kidding?" Rita said.

"No, I'm not kidding," Dolores responded sadly. "You see, I can't have a baby. You can have all you want."

The most Dolores has ever said for the record is that she couldn't have children.

Be that as it may, the Hopes eventually became the parents of four fine and healthy adopted children.

George and Gracie Burns recommended a foundling home in Evanston, Illinois, called "The Cradle." Bob and Dolores got in touch with the home's director, Mrs. Florence Walrath, and told her they were interested in a son. Dolores felt it only proper that Bob have an heir. The director assured them that she saw no problem with their request but that it would probably take some time. To this day, baby boys remain in short supply through adoption agencies.

Paramount seemed determined to keep Bob on the lot just to play around with his head, giving him innocuous assignments in order to keep him busy and get their money's worth. In early 1939 the studio put him back in harness with Shirley Ross and George Archinbaud in a silly bit of nothing called, *Some Like It Hot* (not to be confused with the Tony Curtis/Jack Lemmon/ Marilyn Monroe classic). Paramount released the picture as *Rhythm Romance,* probably due to the fact that it featured Gene Krupa and his orchestra and another blockbuster song, ''The Lady's In Love with You,'' which would be recorded by and included in the repertoire of dozens of top singers. And so another Hit Parade standard came out of a Bob Hope picture.

Bob had been so well received by radio audiences, Paramount brass began ever so slowly to see potential picture audiences in his Tuesday night listeners which numbered in the millions. Bob's studio seemed last to recognize the obvious. Hope already knew that if he had a future in pictures it would be because of his radio popularity. Over the years his premonition proved to be right because no other radio comedian had as much success in motion pictures.

Fred Allen tried and flopped, as did Jack Benny, Burns and Allen, and Edgar Bergen. George Burns did not become a movie star until he teamed up with Walter Matthau in *The Sunshine Boys.* Milton Berle never did well in movies. He didn't make another public splash, after radio, until he emerged in the early fifties as ''Mr. Television.'' Only Red Skelton among Hope's contemporaries could match him in films before making the transition to television. It must be noted that monologues seem to have been the key to those few comedians who stood out in all three mediums.

Bob Hope became ever more in demand as a public speaker. All of those charity events he'd done just to gain recognition began to pay off, not only in big bucks but in fame of a different genre.

Frank Capra, a director who became president of the Motion Picture Academy, hosted the 1939 Academy Awards presentations for the best film categories of movies actually released in 1938 and tapped Hope to be a presenter of the "Short Subjects" awards. An ecstatic Bob Hope showed up at the Los Angeles Biltmore Hotel's Banquet Room on the evening of February 23, 1939, with some advance knowledge from Capra that if he did well he'd be glad to turn the hosting job over to the comedian the following year.

An interesting event occurred that night just prior to Hope coming out on the stage. George Fisher, whose name became legendary as a journalist and radio personality covering the Hollywood scene, had surreptitiously planted a microphone in the back of the Banquet Room in his press cubicle.

The Academy had absolutely forbidden any live radio coverage of the event, but the innovative Fisher broadcast the ceremony live from the scene over KNX radio (CBS) for several minutes before someone alerted NBC, whose local executives crawled all over the Academy for pulling a dirty trick by giving KNX an exclusive.

By the time hotel and Academy security discovered the source, Fisher, even as fire axes chopped into the door of his booth, signed off the air. They found him innocently taking notes for the story he would later file about the winners.

Bob came on stage to do his thing just as George's broadcast abruptly came to an end, so his sharp quips missed the airwaves. Hope, at his best, *is* the best. That night he rode high, his theme song, "Thanks for the Memory," having already won an Oscar as "Best Song of the Year." Hope sharpened his knives and wit with relish as he took on the large celebrity audience.

Gazing out over the largest single gathering of motion picture talent ever in one place at the same time, he took one look at all the Oscars amassed on a table and launched his first barb of the evening. "Looks like Bette Davis's garage," he quipped. The star-studded audience roared its delight, none more so than Bette Davis (a perennial best picture nominee and nominated that night for *Jezebel),* and her male entourage, which included the man on whose arm she had arrived, director William Wyler, whose ex-wife Margaret Sullavan was also in attendance as a nominee for best actress (she lost out to Bette Davis).

Hope's prestigious debut did not escape the notice of Adolph Zukor, the most powerful man at Paramount and one of the most influential men in motion pictures. Hope had been a star in vaudeville, on Broadway, in radio, and in the eyes of the public. Yet it took an appearance at the film industry's own awards to cause the studio to focus seriously on Hope's film career.

Charlie Chaplin had always been Hope's idol, even as a kid. Paramount had Chaplin's current wife, Paulette Goddard, under contract. When Adolph Zukor personally ordered the studio to cast Hope and Paulette Goddard in *The Cat and the Canary,* Bob said yes without even reading the script. Once he'd seen what a great part it would be, he said yes again.

Production on *The Cat and the Canary* began in April, shortly after the Academy Awards, and was completed toward the latter part of May. Bob had a surprise for Dolores. She'd always wanted to visit Paris but somehow there had never been an opportunity to get away because of her husband's exhaustive work schedule. One evening, during the filming of *The Cat and the Canary,* he said, "How would you like to take a trip?"

Her first thought was that he'd heard from Mrs. Walrath that a baby boy had become available. He shook his head. "No, that comes later. Where would you really like to go just for a vacation?"

She didn't believe he was serious. Bob Hope take a vacation? "Well," she said and hesitated, "I've always had this great yearning to visit Paris."

"You got it!"

Dolores still didn't know exactly what her husband had in mind. He'd had a recent letter from a relative in England, his Aunt Lucy, who thought it might be nice if he sent her an autographed picture to show to her friends who were always asking if her famous American nephew was old Harry's boy.

Bob outlined the scenario. They would visit his old hometown in Wales, which would also give him a chance to visit his ninety-six-year-old grandfather. "You know," said Bob, shaking his head in amazement, "the old man still rides his bicycle every day. Imagine being so active at that age." The world would one day express the same wonderment about Bob Hope being "so active" as he approached the century mark.

"Go on," she said.

"The Pepsodent show goes on summer hiatus June 20, so we could do a little vaudeville in New York and then sail for England. Just relax and have a good time."

Dolores didn't understand what any of this had to do with Paris.

"Oh, I forgot to tell you," Bob said, as though he'd forgotten part of the story, "after England comes Paris."

Dolores insisted that he get a vaudeville booking in Chicago along the way. She wanted to visit The Cradle and have a talk with Mrs. Walrath.

He said that could also be arranged.

He'd been so involved with work and career, Hope suddenly realized that in many ways he had neglected his wife. Their entire marriage had been focused on Bob Hope. Feeling a sense of guilt, he decided it was time to do something for Dolores, so Evanston and Paris would be her reward.

Both Bob and Dolores were extremely nervous when they presented themselves to Mrs. Walrath at The Cradle. Neither of them was used to interrogations; celebrities, in particular, were gone over with a fine tooth comb by top-flight foundling homes. Mrs. Walrath wanted to be sure that her charges were placed in well-established, loving homes.

Mrs. Walrath received glowing letters of testimony from the film colony as to Bob and Dolores's integrity and stability. The Cradle's director found them acceptable, but they would still have to wait awhile.

The CEO of Pepsodent lived in Chicago and while there Bob and Dolores accepted an invitation, along with advertising executive Albert Lasker, to come on board the Smiths' two-hundred-foot yacht for a dinner party and cruise on Lake Michigan.

As the launch approached Mr. Smith's yacht anchored off shore, Albert Lasker swept his arms wide to encompass the looming yacht and said, "Remember one thing, Bob, Amos and Andy built that boat."

With just the proper pause, while his face hardened into the soberest expression Dolores had ever seen on her husband, Bob replied, "When I finish with Pepsodent, Smith will use that," pointing to the yacht, "as a dinghy." Then his smile returned.

Bob and Dolores had a grand time and Dolores charmed both the men and their wives with her elegance and grace. Pleased that his star could not only sell toothpaste, but had a class act off the air, Smith couldn't have been more delighted. As he escorted the couple to the gangplank that would return them to Chicago and their Drake Hotel suite, he handed Bob a big, fat envelope.

"Enjoy Europe," he said, and winked. Bob slipped the envelope into his coat pocket. In their hotel room he opened the envelope. It contained a $2,500 letter of credit on a London bank and two first class, round-trip tickets—outbound on the luxurious French liner, the *S.S. Normandie,* and returning on the elite British passenger liner, the *Queen Mary.*

Bob must have slept well that night, satisfied that he had begun to secure a portion of the pie large enough to accommodate his talent and ego.

Chapter 16

Bob and Dolores, both filled with anxiety and looking forward to their European cruise, arrived in Cleveland en route to New York and were met by his three brothers, Sid, Fred, and Ivor, and their respective wives, Dorothy, LaRue, and Gertrude.

While in Cleveland, Bob and Ivor put together the plan to form Hope Metal Products, a company that Bob would essentially back, but Ivor would operate. With George, Jack, and Jim in California, it turned out to be only half a family reunion. Jim, the black sheep of the family, was never expected to attend any function hosted by his famous brother. He had preceded Bob to California, appearing in a number of low budget films, but had never really made it as an actor. Apparently his failure and Bob's enormous success created a chasm between the two brothers that would never be breeched.

As family gatherings go, this brief reunion had none of the flavor they'd all enjoyed before Mahm died. Bob may have been the celebrated member of the family, but she had made and enforced the rules. She would have been very unhappy that any of her children had become alienated from another. No excuse would have been acceptable.

Bob and Dolores played Atlantic City before opening at New York's Paramount Theater for a twelve-day run prior to embarking on their European cruise.

The New York World's Fair of 1939 was in full swing when the Hopes played the Paramount. Bob went to the fair, where he saw a lot of new electronic inventions on display, including the introduction of television—which he saw as a "silly box that will never catch on."

There had been a time when Bob would have appeared anywhere, anytime, just for the press coverage. Bob now would not visit the World's Fair in Flushing Meadow, Queens, until the management agreed to declare "Bob Hope Day at the Fair." He and Dolores would ride in an open car through the fair, accompanied by New York's "Little Flower," Mayor Fiorello LaGuardia. Bob Hope had become an important man.

Whether he realized the scientific and historic nature of the fair, Hope became a part of history since the 1939-1940 New York World's Fair represented the end of the Great Depression and the beginning of the modern world of tomorrow. But that world would have to wait while the present one engulfed itself in a conflagration to complete what had been started in World War I. By the end of August, World War II would begin with Adolph Hitler's Nazi invasion of Poland.

Bob Hope had his day at the fair and looked forward to sailing for England on the *Normandie* a couple of days later. Many notables would be traveling companions with the Hopes. Some of them would be making their last trip until after the war. Others would make their next voyage in uniform.

The Hollywood contingent included Charles Boyer, Norma Shearer, Madeleine Carroll, George Raft, Roland Young, and Edward G. Robinson as well as Ben and Bebe Lyons. Washington had its representatives on board, some of whom should have been able to read the immediate future—Henry Morgenthau, Jr., the U.S. Secretary of the Treasury, for instance.

When asked about the winds of war being generated in Hitler's Germany, Bob, in one of his typical off-the-cuff remarks, dismissed the question. "There won't be a war," he said as flippantly as though he had been asked if a cloudless sky held rain. He might have further elucidated his point, except for the interruption of an entourage with police escort speeding up to the loading area. Out of a black limousine stepped the first lady of the land, Mrs. Eleanor Roosevelt, who had come to bid goodbye to a relative.

This was the first real vacation Bob and Dolores had taken since their marriage and they intended to enjoy it and not worry about political intrigue, domestic or foreign.

And enjoy it they did. In England they saw all the new West End shows, shopped on Bond Street, and played golf at every opportunity.

During the second week of their London visit, they visited Bob's birthplace at 44 Craighton Road in Eltham, just outside London. They visited Bob's 96-year-old grandfather in Hitchin, where Bob hosted a party in honor of the family patriarch. Hoping to impress his British relatives with one of his famous American monologues, Bob fell flat on his face. He couldn't understand what the hell was going on. He'd been upstaged by Eleanor Roosevelt in New York and when his grandfather told him to sit down and pay attention, the old man got up and went into his own routine, whistling and dancing and joking, and got a great round of applause. Hope had been bested on both ends of the trip.

His grandfather told him not to feel badly. "You're just a tourist," he said. "You've forgotten your native sense of humor."

Of course the event was covered by the publicity department of Paramount Pictures out of their London office. Photographs of Hope, his relatives, and especially his remarkable grandfather, James Hope, were presented to Bob.

They finally bade goodbye to the Hope clan and made their way to Dover, where they took the boat train to Paris, a city already caught up in the grip of the festering crisis that would soon spread like burning oil around the world.

The Hollywood studios were making telephone calls, sending out cables, and doing everything possible to round up their stars throughout Europe. Paramount and NBC bosses urged Hope to get out of Europe as quickly as possible.

So certain was the Hearst Newspaper Empire that another world war would soon erupt, they allowed Louella Parsons to lead her column off as follows on August 25, 1939:

> With war imminent, Hollywood yesterday realized how many of its important stars are still in Europe. Tyrone Power and Annabella . . . Charles Boyer . . . Robert Montgomery . . . Maureen O'Sullivan . . . Bob Hope, who planned a European holiday, is cutting his visit short to hurry home.

When the *Queen Mary* sailed from England on August 30, 1939, it would be its last civilian voyage for a long time to come. Later that day, Hitler's hordes invaded Poland. Fortunately, Bob and Dolores had decided not to wait until mid-September to return home. It seemed that every American in Europe tried to get on board the August 30 sailing.

Three days later, with the liner still en route to the United States, France and England declared war on Germany and German U-boats, already a threat in the Atlantic waters off the coast of Europe, now became a real menace to passenger liners between England and the United States. Would Hitler make a big opening statement by sinking the luxurious passenger liner? Nobody knew, but everyone on board prayed their own personal prayers.

For the first time, Bob Hope displayed a courage and understanding that no one truly expected from the comedian. He gave one of the great performances of his life for the passengers and crew of the *Queen Mary* and for a short spell took everyone's mind off the awful specter hovering about them.

He wrote a parody to "Thanks for the Memory" on the afternoon the news of war reached the ship, singing it during his performance that evening. It so impressed the ship's captain that he had a copy made for every passenger. Here is the ditty that appeared in a box on *Variety*'s front page, hand delivered by Mack Millar after the ship docked in New York:

Thanks for the Memory, Of this great ocean trip, On England's finest ship, Though they packed 'em to the rafters, They never made a slip. Ah! Thank you so much. Thanks for the memory, Some folks slept on the floor, Some in the corridor, But I was more exclusive, My room had "Gents" above the door Ah! Thank you so much.

Whether he knew it or not, Bob Hope had already played his first USO show—so to speak.

They did not tarry in New York, but instead took a train to Chicago to see Mrs. Walrath. Dolores fell head over heels in love with the little eight-week-old girl the director showed them.

Dolores thought the baby was beautiful; Bob thought she was "okay."

She wanted to take the baby home with them right then, but The Cradle's director hesitated, wishing to be sure that Bob would come to feel the same way Dolores did about the "girl baby." So she sent them home empty-handed.

Not long after they returned to California, Dolores, at Mrs. Walrath's request, returned alone to Evanston and brought the Hope's first child home. They named her Linda Theresa.

While Dolores busied herself with motherhood, Bob worked on his first show of the second season for Pepsodent on NBC. He had a rock-solid lineup of regulars with the addition of the very popular Judy Garland, whose recent film *The Wizard of Oz* seemed destined for all kinds of awards. Hope also brought in Brenda and Cobina, two characters played by Elvia Allman and Blanche Stewart as not-so-thinly-disguised caricatures of two spoiled New York debutantes, Brenda Frazier and Cobina Wright, Jr.

Remembering an old friend, Bob used Honey Chile on his radio show whenever he could. Her promised career at RKO and the Fred Astaire picture never panned out. Hollywood had, in fact, done what it often does to hopefuls—dumped Honey Chile.

With a full season behind him, Bob felt more flexible opening his second year on the air for Pepsodent. Due to his popularity, superseded only by Jack Benny and Edgar Bergen, he took more risks, broke new ground, became more outrageous, and discovered that poking fun at celebrity and making himself the butt of jokes hit the funnybone of his radio audience. People thought of Bob Hope as being "one of us" because he ridiculed the same things they found fault with. Punching holes in the puffery of the high and mighty became a Hope trademark. He'd done nothing more than "do" Will Rogers, updating him for a new generation.

Bob's ratings for the second season continued to rise along with his popularity. America loved Bob Hope. The timing could not have been better when *The Cat and the Canary* hit the screens in November 1939. Thanks to the popularity of his radio show, Bob Hope fans jammed the theaters. America's favorite comedian paired with the gorgeous Paulette Goddard, a master of comedic timing in her own right, created the ideal marquee and box office magic. The Bob Hope juggernaut seemed invincible. Like Midas, everything he touched turned to gold. Even the New York critics, who had never really considered him a serious film commodity, tipped their hats to his screen presence.

The *New York Times* movie critic, Frank Nugent, gave an honest appraisal of the film, through which can be seen the emergence of Hope's substantial improvement as a screen personality:

> Streamlined, screamlined and played to the hilt for comedy, [it] is more harebrained than hair-raising, which is as it should be. Panels slide as menacingly as ever; Paulette Goddard's screams would part a traffic snarl in Times Square; the lights dim and an eerie wail rises when the hopeful legatees assemble in the manse in the bayous for the reading of Uncle Cyrus's will. Over them all broods Bob Hope, with a chin for a forehead and a gag line for every occasion.

Nugent liked some of Hope's lines but took issue with others ("Let's drink scotch and make wry faces"). He describes Mr. Hope's trick of delivering his jests timidly, "with the air of a man who sees no good in them. . . . When they click, he can cut a little caper and pretend he is surprised and delighted too. It's not cricket, but it is fun . . ."

Other critics lauded the pairing of Hope and Goddard as well. Bob always credited *The Cat and the Canary* with establishing him as a film star. He called it "the turning point in my film career."

No higher compliment could have been paid him either personally or professionally than one given by the master comic himself, Charlie Chaplin. During the production of *The Cat and the Canary,* Bob attended a celebrity event at Santa Anita racetrack, just outside Los Angeles, where he ran into Paulette and Charlie.

"You know Charles, don't you, Bob?" she said by way of introducing her husband to her costar.

Bob had never met the great Chaplin, and felt subdued before his idol. After a few words about working with Paulette and an expression of how much he enjoyed all of Chaplin's work, especially the film, *Modern Times,* Bob was stunned by Chaplin's unsolicited appraisal.

"Young man," Chaplin said, waxing serious, "I've been watching the rushes of *The Cat and the Canary* every night. I want you to know that you have some of the best comic timing I have ever seen."

Overwhelmed by such a compliment from the greatest comic of all times, Bob could barely mumble his thanks.

As Hope's stock rose with the Paramount brass, the studio began to build on the "feud" between him and Crosby. They'd been taking potshots at one another on Broadway and as they found themselves guesting on the same radio show, and later on each other's shows, the ribbing took on a genuine Hatfield and McCoy flavor. There were times, in fact, when the two disagreed during the filming of their many "Road" pictures when the thrusts became more than jest, because they never were "buddies," in the true sense of the word. Most of their back and forth tongue-lashings were for money and publicity, whether in movies, on radio, or on the golf course. Each seemed hell-bent for leather to amass more worldly goods than the other.

Complimented by Chaplin, a peer of Crosby, getting in and out of Europe in time to avoid the opening of World War II, and arriving safely back in California as a new father of a baby daughter gave Bob Hope all any normal guy could ever want or need. The bonus? He had Dolores. No man could have done better than that.

What else could there be? Plenty—and it was all just around the corner.

Chapter 17

By the time Paramount came up with the "Road" pictures, Dorothy Lamour had already attained major stardom with fifteen films to her credit. She'd costarred with some of the most sought-after male hunks in the business, including John Barrymore, Ray Milland, Jon Hall, Henry Fonda, George Raft, and Robert Preston.

Bing Crosby had done nothing of consequence that didn't feature his crooning, and Bob Hope's career consisted mostly of "B" pictures until *The Cat and the Canary.*

There are almost as many versions of how Paramount came to do the first "Road" picture as there have been "Road" pictures. In her autobiography, *My Side of the Road,* Dorothy Lamour gave the following account:

> I remember I had just finished lunch with Pauline Kessinger in the Paramount commissary, and on the way out stopped at a table where Bob and Bing were carrying on so that I nearly choked from laughing. Leaving the commissary, I was still laughing when I bumped into two writer friends. "What's so funny?" they asked. I told them that I had just been joking with Hope and Crosby,

and that if they could only come up with a story involving two crazy guys and a "gal in the middle," I would love to play her.

Those two writers have forgotten our brief conversation that day, but soon after, the first "Road" story was turned in to the front office and I got my wish—Hope, Crosby, and I were set to star in it.

In his biography of Hope, *Portrait of a Superstar*, Charles Thompson says that Paramount's staff screenwriters, Frank Butler and Don Hartman, had to come up with a finale for a lucrative series of frothy South Sea Island films, most of which had starred Dorothy Lamour in her famous sarong.

According to Thompson, a previously shelved "B" story, *Beach of Dreams,* was dusted off, hokeyed up, and retitled *Road to Mandalay.*

The writers, Butler and Hartman, didn't like "Mandalay" because "it didn't sound treacherous enough," Don Hartman said.

"You can take a piece of used chewing gum and flip it at a map, and wherever it sticks you can lay a "Road" picture, so long as the people who live there are the kind of jokers who cook and eat strangers. If they're nasty and menacing, it'll be a good "Road" picture. The key to the whole thing is menace offsetting the humor."

Arthur Marx says nothing about any title except *Road to Mandalay.* However, all seem to agree that the idea of teaming Hope, Crosby, and Lamour did not occur to anyone until after Fred MacMurray and Jack Oakie had declined (with no female star considered as yet). Paramount even considered using George Burns and Gracie Allen with a third party to be named later, but the writers, both top-notch comedy scripters, felt it would require an entirely new concept. George Burns once told this writer he and Gracie had been offered the picture and turned it down because "Gracie thought the whole thing was silly."

Bob Hope and Bing Crosby saw plenty of potential. They could ham it up as con artists on the lam, traveling the world, having a hell of a lot of fun. Dorothy Lamour, a proven figure in a sarong, would add spice and sex to the potpourri.

Neither Bob nor Bing liked taking direction, whereas Dorothy Lamour had strict work rules. She said, "I have always listened to my directors and memorized the lines of my costars as well as my own." Anyone who ever worked with Lamour knew that she might be fun between takes, but on the set it was all business.

Hope and Crosby's shenanigans on the set were well known. It took a commanding director to control them. Victor Schertzinger, the director assigned to steer *The Road to Singapore,* had a background in musicals and looked forward, in particular, to working with Bing Crosby. Crosby had a great sense of what would and wouldn't work with a song. His recording sessions were usually flawless. A stickler for accuracy, he did not need to do a dozen takes to get a song right. When there were foulups, it was not usually Bing's fault. There were, of course, exceptions. Some of the outtakes of his recordings with the Andrews Sisters were hilarious due to Bing's deliberate adlibbing, and several of their hit recordings together contain Bing's unscheduled insertions.

Neither Crosby nor Hope paid the least bit of attention to the scriptwriters or director during the filming of *Road to Singapore.* They made up lines as they went along and poor Dorothy Lamour seems at times in the completed picture to be in a constant state of bewilderment—which happened to be the truth. She would study her lines, and the cue lines from either Hope or Crosby and when she should have been speaking; then she waited, and waited and waited, for the cue, which never came.

The set began to resemble monkeys unleashed from the jungle, despite the weeping and wailing of writers, the director, Lamour, and other members of the cast and crew.

One day when Bing and Bob were tossing asides at one another like baseballs around a sandlot, they completely forgot that Dorothy was even there. She had to yell out right in the middle of a scene, "Hey fellas, I'm here, too. Remember?"

Crosby was completely broken up and yelled right back, "If you see an opening—say something!"

Schwertzinger threw up his hands in despair and yelled, "Cut," and called off shooting until his actors "could pull themselves together."

Lamour also threw in the towel. "After the first few days, I decided it was ridiculous to waste time learning the script. I would read over the next day's work to get an idea of what was happening. What I really needed was a good night's sleep to be in shape for the next morning's ad-libs. This method provided some very interesting results on the screen."

Bob and Bing became Paramount's answer to Universal's Abbott and Costello.

A handsome young Latin boy, who started in the business by hiring himself out to private parties for two bucks a night doing imitations of Crosby, Louis Armstrong, and Maurice Chevalier, played the heavy in a supporting role in *The Road to Singapore*. His pictures and awards would eventually number in the dozens. His name? Anthony Quinn.

Arthur Marx quotes Quinn's recollection of two incidents on the set:

"I remember once, Bing was supposed to take a swing at me in a scene and hit me hard on the chin. He wasn't supposed to actually hit me, but somehow he mistimed his swing during the take and landed a pretty hard blow to my jaw. I just stood there and looked at him, but didn't go down. Suddenly Hope turned to him and cracked, 'You can't hit very hard, can you, Bing?'

"In another scene, I was dancing with Dottie in a big production number. There must have been a hundred extras in the scene as well as Bing and Bob. I was supposed to be holding Dottie very close to me in the dance. Now Dottie is a very tough broad. Suddenly she put her hands on my shoulders and shoved me away fiercely, which wasn't in the script. This brought Victor Schertzinger, the director, to his feet. 'What's wrong, honey?' he yelled out. 'Why'd you do that?'

" 'I can't dance with trim,' screamed Dottie. 'The son of a bitch has a hard-on!'

"The silence was deafening. Suddenly Bing yelled out, 'You should be happy you can give someone a hard-on, Dottie!'

"Everyone on the set roared, except Dottie."

Quinn worked so well with Crosby and Hope the studio featured him as an Arab Sheik two years later in *The Road to Morocco*. Quinn swears that the "Road" pictures made so much money they created opportunities for him he might otherwise not have had.

Lamour had a few tricks up her sleeve also. She withstood unbelievable harassment from both Bob and Bing. One day she'd just about had it with the two men hogging a scene and said, "How about a line for me?"

Bob said, "Quiet, honey. All we want you to do is to look beautiful and twirl your sarong."

The following day she showed up on the set with all her teeth blacked out and refused to do anything about it until she'd been assured that all of her lines would be included in the scene they were shooting.

Bing Crosby rarely, if ever, appeared without a hat unless he had on his "rug." In one scene in *The Road to Singapore*, Bing and Bob were in bed and were required to remove their hats and replace them with skull doilies. Bing said, "Absolutely not." A very vain man about his bald head, he felt it detracted from his manhood.

Once in bed, Bob said, "Bing, we're going to take off our hats when we're in the sack, aren't we?"

"No," Bing said, adamantly. "We sleep with our hats on."

The director, not at all amused, yelled out, "Take those goddamn hats off. You're in bed!"

Having fun at Crosby's expense, Bob said sheepishily in a little-boy voice, "I can't. Bing won't let me."

The director stopped the scene and called for the producer

to deal with Bing. Being a very important star, Bing could get away with breaking the rules where others couldn't. But this was not a matter of rules—this scene required "no hats."

Whenever a director had problems with Crosby on any of his pictures, he simply called in the producer because he is the money man and doesn't like unnecessary delays. Of course, all of that changes when the star is the producer—about which there will be more later on.

After hours of cajoling, threatening, and begging, Bing and the producer reached a compromise in Bing's favor. The hats remained on.

When *The Road to Singapore,* premiered at New York's Paramount Theater on April 13, 1940, no one, including the studio executives, the stars, or the press (which gave the picture excellent reviews), had the slightest notion that what might make a splash with the public would turn into a tidal wave.

Bob Hope told Pete Martin in a *Saturday Evening Post* article:

> "There was no thought, however, that the first "Road" picture would develop into a series. It became a series when a writer named Sy Bartlett came in with a story about two fellows who were trekking through the jungles of Madagascar. The catch was that a movie named *Stanley and Livingston* had just been released and was so similar to Bartlett's that it ruined it. Bartlett's story was a highly dramatic one, but Don Hartman took it, gagged it up, and named it *The Road to Zanzibar*.

So *The Road to Zanzibar* became the second "Road" picture.

The *Road to Singapore* went into general release nine days after its New York premiere and became an instant smash hit, packing theaters and causing the cash registers at Paramount Pictures to overflow with profits.

All was forgiven. Even Dorothy Lamour, who had suffered outrageous behavior on the part of her costars, could not complain. Success heals all wounds in Hollywood and *The Road to Singapore* was "boffo," as they say in the trades.

Hope personally did his bit to promote *The Road to Singapore* prior to its release. He had his writers create two skits for his Pepsodent radio show about the picture, one in February and the other in April, hyping the public in advance.

In the interim, Hope had been prepping himself for his official duties as emcee of the 1940 Academy Awards, which had moved from the Biltmore Hotel to the Coconut Grove of the Ambassador Hotel in Los Angeles. It was a year in which Darryl F. Zanuck, head of 20th Century-Fox Pictures, made six presentations (probably a record) while his studio won only one award, special effects for *The Rains Came.*

As Paramount prepared the release of *The Road to Singapore,* Bob began filming a second picture with Paulette Goddard, based on the success of *The Cat and the Canary.* The new picture was called *The Ghost Breakers,* which producer Arthur Hornblow, Jr took from a 1922 remake of a 1915 silent movie. The plot had cast Bob in the role of a radio commentator comically involved with a murder and a castle in Cuba overrun with ghosts. Of course, he falls in love with Paulette Goddard in the process.

In the middle of all this success Bob made his first appearance as the official host of the Academy Awards. What a grand year in which to debut! As Bob came on the scene, Frank Capra had not only turned over the emceeing job to him, but also relinquished his position as president of the Academy to producer Walter Wanger, introducing him as "a fearless liberal." Alfred Hitchcock, sitting at the Wanger table, slept through Wanger's acceptance speech.

Wanger then introduced Bob Hope as the "Rhett Butler of the airwaves." Hope responded, "What a wonderful thing, this benefit for David Selznick," since it had already been leaked by the *Los Angeles Times* that *Gone With the Wind,* a Selznick picture, would take away the lion's share of the golden statuettes. There was such a furor over the *Times'* reneging on a promise kept by other news organizations that it became the last year the awards were decided in advance. The following year, the firm of Price Waterhouse collected and tabulated the ballots and winners were not known until they were announced from the stage. This process worked so well it has been in place every year since.

The previous year, Bob had looked at the table holding the statuettes and made his famous comment about Bette Davis's garage. This year he moved the comment to her living room. Of the four top awards, three of which went to *Gone With the Wind,* only Clark Gable did not win in the best actor category for his portray of Rhett Butler. Most Americans resented Robert Donat winning for *Goodbye, Mr. Chips,* especially since he did not even show up to receive his award. It so upset Gable that he told his wife, actress Carole Lombard, "If I can't win with this picture, I'll never win. I'm through going to these things."

He did return to be a presenter, but never won the coveted award—and wasn't even nominated for his role in *The Misfits,* considered by many film critics to be one of his greatest performances in a long career.

Chapter 18

Bob took his last five Pepsodent broadcasts of the season on the road. He wanted to be able to go back to his vaudeville roots at the different theaters still presenting stage shows between films. His show had replaced Jack Benny's as the number one radio comedy show and he was in such demand that theater owners were delighted to pay him $12,500 per week.

During this tour he began to understand, for the first time, his own popularity. In an interview for the February 1972 issue of *Nation's Business,* he was asked, "What made you realize you were a household name?"

His spontaneous response:

> "We opened at the Chicago Theater and we were mobbed. People were lined up around the block, standing in the rain, waiting to get in."

The theater manager came back to his dressing room and said, "Mr. Hope, you've broken the house record."

Bob immediately got on the phone to Louis Shurr in New York City and said, "Louie, do you want to come here and take a look at something, because if you don't, I can get the Morris Agency to do it.'' The William Morris agency, which had once insulted him by asking him to audition, would now very much like to have Bob Hope under contract.

Shurr took the next flight out to Chicago, where he saw for himself the mobs that were coming to see Bob Hope. Bob, who always had one eye on the cash register, instructed Shurr to tell Paramount Pictures ''that we want a little more money, about $50,000 a picture.''

He had his contract changed to give him fifty percent of all money grossed over fifty grand per week during the tour in addition to his guaranteed salary. He had been doing five shows a day and still the line of those unable to get in reached around the block. He wanted the theater manager to cancel the movie and just have short intermissions between his shows, but the manager wouldn't do that. He had contracts with the studios to play the picture or there would be no picture the following week. The studios controlled all distribution and could cut a theater off cold if anyone played games with them.

So Hope added two more shows per day by having the newsreels, cartoons, and coming attractions cut to bare bones, and still the throngs lined up. The theater's grosses went up to $73,000 that week, causing Hope to pocket better than $20,000 rather than the $12,500 under his old contract. The man certainly read Dickens' *A Christmas Carol*. Old Scrooge must have danced in his grave when he learned that someone was carrying on his old tradition.

Hope went on to Cleveland, where he continued breaking house records and also continued pressuring Shurr to get Paramount to up his per picture deal to $50,000 despite his contract, which clearly stipulated $20,000 with four pictures to go. Not only that, had Bob reneged on re-signing with Paramount, he could have well been blackballed by the studio and would not then have been making pictures with any studio in town. Independents and ''B'' studios would be afraid to touch him because the majors controlled all distribution since they owned the vast majority of the theaters. Those they didn't own they coerced into seeing things their way. No cooperation—no product.

But occasionally purses opened and contracts were renegotiated to include "bonuses," which became a quid quo pro deal that satisfied both parties but left the studio moguls controlling the contracts and lives of the actors.

It so happened that Sam Goldwyn desperately wanted Bob Hope for a picture. Louis Shurr explained that Bob still had a four-picture deal under his current option with Paramount and they were not likely to loan him out.

Goldwyn, something of a simpleminded genius, told Shurr, "I just got Gary Cooper from Paramount and I think they'll let me have Hope, too. See what you can do."

Much to Shurr's surprise, Paramount agreed to let Bob do a picture for Goldwyn. Shurr always thought there had been some sort of deal made behind his back. When he related the good news to Goldwyn, Sam seemed not at all surprised and said, "That's great and I'll tell you something else. I don't want to take advantage of this situation. I'll pay Bob the same as he gets for a picture at Paramount."

Shurr, quickly onto the back-room poker game involved, in effect told Goldwyn to go fly a kite.

Goldwyn, still playing coy, pretended not to understand. "What," he asked, almost too naively, "does Mr. Hope want?"

"One hundred grand," said Shurr.

Goldwyn said that in that case there's no deal, and for all intents and purposes the situation seemed forgotten. But foxy Goldwyn never forgot anything. He had some other ideas, as did Paramount and just about everybody else involved in what would soon become a real horse trading session.

The picture for which Cooper had been borrowed by Goldwyn, *The Westerner,* was to be premiered at the same time in Dallas and Fort Worth, some 28 miles apart. Out of the clear blue sky, Paramount asked Bob if he would go down to Texas to emcee the event. It involved his making a total of eight appearances on behalf of the film, four in each of the two cities. Just before his last appearance at the Will Rogers Coliseum in Fort Worth, Goldwyn conveniently placed himself in the wings as Bob came out of his dressing room and prepared to go on stage. Goldwyn shook his hand and as an aside said, "You know, my boy, I still want to do that picture with you. Why don't you tell your agent to lower his price and I think we make a deal, eh?"

Hope knew how to play poker as well as Goldwyn, so in the finale of their pre-film demonstration on stage, everyone of importance to the picture was brought out on stage, one by one, to be introduced to the packed assemblage. When it came time for Hope to introduce Sam Goldwyn, he said, "Ladies and gentlemen, I now want you to meet one of the truly great men in our business, Mr. Sam Goldwyn."

The crowd applauded, Goldwyn glowed in the limelight for a few seconds, and then he said, "I haven't made a comedy since Eddie Cantor left me. I never found a comedian who I thought could do as well, until now. I finally found one in Bob Hope." Thinking he had Bob pinned to the mat, he turned to his emcee and asked, "How about it, Bob?"

Expecting something of this sort, Bob quickly responded, "Okay, Sam, let's talk money."

Goldwyn's face flushed and in a barely audible voice, he said, "Not now, Bob."

"Right now," Hope said, standing his ground. "Let's just lie down here on the stage and talk deal until we arrive at something."

Grabbing the startled studio head by the lapels, he pulled him down to the stage floor, microphone in hand, and said loud enough to be heard in the theater without a mike, "I want a hundred grand!"

"Too much," Goldwyn said, his voice gaining some control. "I only pay Cooper . . ."

Hope interrupted him. "Who cares what you pay that drugstore cowboy?"

The audience, thinking this was all part of a script, was in stitches. Both men then really began getting into their act for the audience and finally settled on $75,000.

The picture, as yet untitled—actually unscripted—would not be made until after the United States entered the war, and would costar Hope and another Paramount contract player, his cohort in the "Road" films, Dorothy Lamour.

Just another one of the vagaries of Hollywood.

In July of 1940, baby Linda reached her first birthday. Bob and Dolores had already agreed that when Linda was one year old it would be time to adopt again—this time a boy to be named Anthony. Thanks to the manipulation with Sam Goldwyn, Louis Shurr managed to get Paramount to up Bob's fee per picture to $75,000. Bob still had two more pictures for Paramount that year, so by the end of 1940 his total income hit $500,000, putting him among the top moneymakers in the industry.

Bob went alone to The Cradle in Chicago this time to pick out their new baby son, Anthony, who quickly became simply "Tony." After the selection was made, Dolores went to Chicago to join Bob and Tony and the three flew back to Hollywood together.

Dolores decided it was time to buy some more property. This time she wanted a place complete with a home. Bob purchased three more acres adjacent to the six acres they already owned. The new acreage on Moorpark Street in Toluca Lake offered a white-brick, fifteen-room English farmhouse. Crosby lived within walking distance.

The house leaked like a sieve and during the first rains the living room resembled a swimming pool. But with a new roof and considerable remodeling, the house was ideal for Bob, Dolores, and their children. Today he has personal living quarters, a separate building for his secretaries and business activities, and a one-hole golf course plus Lakeside Country Club in his backyard.

With the fall season's radio show for Pepsodent already in preparation, he had to find a new singer to replace Judy Garland, who had been pulled off the show by Louis B. Mayer in a fit of paranoia. Judy was under contract to Metro-Goldwyn-Mayer, over which Mayer ruled with an iron hand, so she had no voice in the decision.

Paramount immediately put Bob back before the cameras, filming *The Road to Zanzibar*. In addition to the three regulars, Paramount added Una Merkel and Eric Blore to the cast. To direct the picture, the studio again selected Victor Schertzinger; Don Hartman and Frank Butler (more or less posing as writers) were on board to reprise the script. Their lines were outrageously rewritten by Bob and Bing as the cameras rolled. Dorothy had become very adept at mind-reading because she had to have instantaneous responses, which she, too, began to do off the top of her head. There simply was no way to know when the two cut-ups would read the lines written by the writers.

They stayed with the proven formula. This time around, Una and Dorothy were performers stranded in darkest Africa looking for a way out. Bob and Bing played stuntmen barnstorming Africa—also seeking an escape back to civilization.

While filming *The Road to Zanzibar* Bob stumbled upon a great revelation. In his *Portrait of a Superstar*, Charles Thompson grasps exactly where Bob Hope's future in films would have the greatest impact:

> "Zanzibar also firmly set the seal on the comic character
> Bob had been gradually building over the years; from now
> on he would portray himself as the egotistic, excitable,
> fumbling, cowardly romantic who inevitably loses the
> girl . . . He became the butt of the biggest jokes and the
> world loved him for it . . ."

In the "Road" pictures, Bing would always get the girl and that's the way it would be. Bing and Bob got the laughs, but Dorothy managed to snatch a share of the spotlight. The Hollywood cameramen voted her the "Best Undressed Woman" on the screen. Censors kept their scissors sharpened. She had one scene in which she appeared to be wearing nothing but the fern behind which she stood. In a nude bathing scene, wild animals steal her sarong and she appears to be totally nude. The flesh-colored bathing suit revealed more than it hid.

Outside of comedy, such a scene would not have been allowed by the censorship committee.

Dorothy Lamour always contended that had they filmed the off-camera antics on the sets of the "Road" films, they would have made more money than the pictures did.

Bing told the complaining writers, "Look, if it works, what the hell are you crying about? And by the way, if you hear one of your lines, just yell 'bingo!' "

Bob's rationale was that both men had extremely popular radio shows, they created a feud over the airwaves, and when people came into the theater "they wanted to see the same thing on the screen. That's all we did—re-create our battling radio personas on film."

Neither of the two men gave a damn about writers or directors. The only thing they took seriously when working together was having fun and picking up fat paychecks. Outside of that, making motion pictures became something to do until they could get out on the golf course—usually different courses, rarely with one another except for charitable events, which put extra money in their respective pockets.

Frances Langford replaced Judy Garland on Bob's Pepsodent show and remained with him for many years, becoming a mainstay on his USO tours.

Bill Goodwin became such a popular announcer, Bob began to feel that the audience might be giving more attention to Bill's lines than Bob's jokes. Bob replaced him for the 1940-41 season with Ben Gage, which very graphically points out the opinion held by most of Hope's competitors: he simply was not a team player. He had to be the star. Only two people were ever able to hold him at bay—Bing Crosby and, later on, Lucille Ball. Those two were simply too big for Bob to upstage.

Crosby had all kinds of hangups about his manhood, which is somewhat a surprise considering all the kids he fathered. He resented any reference to his balding pate. Of course, Hope loved to get little digs in about that, but never went so far as to really anger Crosby.

In *Edith Head's Hollywood*, by Edith Head and Paddy Calistro, there is a terrific insight into a basic difference regarding Crosby and Hope and their masculinities:

"As she fitted the dress on the comedian, she probably reflected on the days when she had dressed Bob Hope and Bing Crosby in their famous series of 'Road' pictures. In the true spirit of comedy, Hope loved to dress up in women's clothes, but Crosby never agreed to be seen in drag . . ."

Hope had no such inhibitions. He joins a great host of comedians who delight in wearing women's wear, including Jack Benny, Phil Silvers, and Milton Berle—to name but a few.

Miss Head had a few barbs for one of Hope's costars, Paulette Goddard:

"Paulette often carried cigar boxes filled with jewels, precious jewels that Chaplin had given her. She would open the cigar box, pass it around temptingly for all the seamstresses to see but no, don't touch, they're not cigars, they're precious gems, jerks. That was her attitude. I think she was actually much better known for her jewels than her acting, at least at Paramount. I designed her wardrobe for *The Cat and the Canary* (1939) and *The Ghost Breakers* (1940), both with Bob Hope, but I don't remember her clothes at all. I just remember her tormenting my staff with that damn cigar box full of jewels."

According to Edith Head, the fun really began with Bob, Bing, and Dorothy teamed up for the "Road" pictures. She'd known all three since they made their debuts at Paramount and dressed each for their first pictures.

"We all grew up together at Paramount, but Hope was the baby. My most vivid memory of his first film is Hope singing a duet of 'Thanks for the Memory' with Shirley

Ross, who was dressed in a silly black hat and leopard-skin vest and muff I designed for her. By then Bing was a well-established star and Dorothy Lamour was one of the top pinup girls and box office attractions . . . audiences went mad for them as they chased one another . . . The story didn't matter; everybody came to see the latest gags . . . I didn't have to worry about authenticity. If somebody wrote and said, 'Edith . . . they don't wear headdresses like that,' I didn't give a damn. If Bob Hope wanted to wear it because it was funny, he wore it.''

Once Edith had a sketchy idea of the script—it didn't take her long to discover that lines didn't mean anything to Hope and Crosby—she'd send an assistant over to Western Costume to bring back some samples and got to work designing turbans and other items for the actors. She had no problem with Dorothy's sarongs, having designed her first one for *Jungle Princess* several years earlier.

Again, she understood the difference between Bob and Bing. Hope loved to dress up. Crosby was Crosby.

''Bing loathed dressing up. I don't think Bing really cared about playing any character but himself. His movie roles were usually variations of Crosby the Crooner . . . he preferred simple clothes . . . It pained him to put on any headgear more exotic than a Panama hat or a golf cap . . . He couldn't really have the fun with his getups that Bob had . . . I always noticed . . . Bing's aversion to costumes . . . Bob has a special place in my heart for what he did for my costumes in the 'Road' pictures . . . There were chaotic plots and gags and lavish sets and great music, but Bob Hope pulled it all together . . .''

As 1940 came to an end it became ever more obvious to Bob Hope that the United States would eventually be drawn into the war in Europe. He had no more idea of a forthcoming bloody Pacific war than anyone else. Although an American, England was his mother country. He had relatives ''over there'' and feared for their safety along with thousands of other Englishmen who had adopted the United States as their home.

He began, as he would later say, "somewhere in the back of my mind to figure out my role in the event of a shooting war in which my adopted country might become involved."

He had a lot of thinking to do.

Chapter 19

Following *The Road to Zanzibar,* Paramount released three more Bob Hope films in 1941. The first, *Caught in the Draft,* costarred Dorothy Lamour. Congress passed, and President Roosevelt signed, the Selective Service Act, commonly known as "the Draft", in 1940, preparing for our eventual active participation, if necessary, in the conflict raging in Europe.

Hollywood, sensing the inevitable, began turning out pictures relating to the involuntary conscription of ordinary young American men into the armed forces. The highly successful combination of Abbott and Costello and the Andrews Sisters in *Buck Privates* was released in February 1941, about the same time Paramount went into production on *Caught in the Draft* (released in June 1941).

Hope played an egotistical, self-centered film star who had no intention of going into any man's army. Lamour, in the role of a colonel's daughter, is Hope's love interest. In order to prove to Dorothy that he is not a draft dodger, he fakes an enlistment into the Army. The fake turns out to be the real thing and Bob ends up as a buck private in hot water throughout the picture.

For the first time in many moons, Dorothy Lamour did not

wear her famous sarong. Edith Head designed twenty-two gorgeous black-and-white outfits that highlighted her every curve.

The picture, shot on location at the Paramount ranch north of Los Angeles, premiered at Fort Ord Army base in Monterey, California. The studio transported a dozen of its biggest stars for the event, including Bing Crosby, Madeleine Carroll, Pat O'Brien, Ellen Drew, Frances Farmer, Paulette Goddard, Joel McCrea, Patricia Morison, Melvyn Douglas, Betty Field, Susanna Foster and, of course, Bob and Dorothy.

The Paramount brass knew what they were up to. The two "Road" pictures were the biggest grossers in the studio's history at the time, so Crosby, Hope, and Lamour were the cream of the crop on the junket. Everyone else became added attractions.

Time magazine reviewed the picture thusly in July 1941:

> "The process of making a corporal out of Rookie Hope (to prove that he is man enough to merit the colonel's daughter) consists of enrolling the comedian in each new attack outfit (tank corps, parachute troops, etc.) as it is formed and letting the gags fall where they may. Some of them get up and walk, but many just lie there. Hope's view of it, after running a tank into the colonel's car: 'Me trying to be a corporal! I'll be lucky if they don't try to take away my citizenship.'
>
> "Grade-A Hopeism, after the tank accident: 'Terribly sorry about the car, sir. I hope you haven't kept up the payments'."

During the filming of *Caught in the Draft,* Bob started to throw his weight around in a manner not appreciated by his director, David Butler. They were on location in Malibu Canyon off the Pacific Coast Highway, north of Los Angeles. Shooting had been held up several days due to bad weather. The first day the sun came out the director wanted to shoot as early as possible before the California weather betrayed him.

The morning shots were completed and he asked Bob to be on the second location in Malibu Canyon for an early afternoon shoot. Bob, taking along his and Lamour's make-up man, Harry

Ray, set out toward the location site, but decided to look into some real estate in the area. By the time he eventually made it to the Paramount ranch they were losing daylight. Being a big star, Hope got away with costing the studio a lot of money. And the land he purchased that day increased its value to millions of dollars and created a major financial scandal for Hope years later.

Hope already had a reputation among members of the fourth estate as "a hard man with a dollar." Crosby introduced him to the "ponies," where he made a few bucks the first time out. Once he lost on a race, he decided horses were not to be trusted. "There are," he told Bing, "better ways to build a fortune." Jokes and gags were highly profitable for Bob and, at the time, his were locked up in a vault and insured for $25,000—not exactly peanuts in 1941.

The men who wrote those jokes and gags, dialogue for his films and radio shows, referred to Bob Hope as "Scrooge." One payday Hope stood on a chair with their checks. He fashioned them into paper planes, then sent them sailing out to the waiting scribes. Hope considered it a gag; the writers didn't. To them it was just another way in which he let them know that he was Bob Hope and they merely his underlings.

He kept them on call 24 hours a day, holidays included, and it was not unusual for a writer's Thanksgiving or Christmas dinner to be interrupted by a summons from Hope. They were always subject to his whims and if they expected to get paid, they treated every call from Bob as a command performance, because it was. If any writer objected, he could be, and often was, replaced without sentiment or severance.

Yet writers waited in line to write for Bob Hope. Once a writer worked for him, he had no trouble finding work elsewhere.

In February 1941, Academy President Walter Wanger hosted the Oscar ceremonies at the Biltmore Hotel. President Roosevelt had asked for and been granted the privilege of delivering a six-minute radio message at 8:45 P.M. to open the evening's ceremonies. Roosevelt thanked the Hollywood community for supporting his Lend-Lease Bill to assist England in its war against the Axis, for helping to raise defense funds through personal appearances around the country, and for promoting "the American way of life."

The president received thunderous applause from the Academy audience. Bette Davis responded, "Mr. President, I have followed your leadership for years with pleasure, but to follow you on tonight's program is not an easy task. I never dreamed I would be on the same bill as the president of the United States."

Judy Garland added to the plaudits for Roosevelt by singing "America" to the president. Her boyfriend and future husband, David Rose, listened at a table with her employer, Louis B. Mayer (an ardent Republican who hated FDR).

Darryl Zanuck, head of 20th Century-Fox Studios, was introduced as "Lieutenant Colonel." Wanger introduced "Private" Bob Hope as emcee for the evening.

Hope, eyeing the Oscars, quipped, "What's the matter, did Selznick bring them back?"

He couldn't miss the opportunity to capitalize on his earlier Bette Davis jabs. He looked out at her table and added, "Bette drops in at these affairs every year for a cup of coffee and another Oscar."

He seemed completely befuddled, however, when in the middle of speaking, Wanger came out on the stage and interrupted him with a presentation of his own.

"It gives me a real pleasure to give a humanitarian award to Bob Hope in recognition of his unselfish services for the motion picture industry, a special plaque honoring him as the man who did the most for charity in 1940."

After kissing the plaque, Hope quickly introduced B.G. DeSylva, the current head of Paramount. "He's just loaned me to Sam Goldwyn for one picture. Sort of a lend-louse bill."

The audience roared at vintage Hope.

The following morning, the *Los Angeles Mirror* complained that the Academy prevented the morning papers from meeting their deadlines by allowing radio to broadcast the awards live. Their complaints fell on deaf ears. The public and the studios liked the suspense created by secret ballots and sealing the results with Price Waterhouse until the actual presentations. Also, not knowing who the winners would be, nominees made every effort to be on hand as did all the others who wanted to be seen with them.

Hope just had fun being emcee.

After *Caught in the Draft,* Bob went directly into *Nothing But the Truth* with Paulette Goddard. It would be his third picture to be released in 1941. Three down and one to go.

Bosley Crowther, the satiric film critic of the *New York Times,* actually liked the picture, giving Hope a better than decent review:

> ". . . here is an ancient farce comedy, already seen twice in films, which derives from an idea so obvious that it no longer supports a parlor game. Yet Paramount, plus director Elliot Nugent, plus the ever entangled Mr. Hope, kick it around so blithely and with such a candid application of hokum, that you can't help but find it amusing."

Bob Hope has always admitted that he had difficulty being lured away from vaudeville and Broadway into any other medium of entertainment. He'd had a horrible experience at Pathé shortly after motion pictures began the transition from silents to talkies, and his half dozen or so two-reelers did nothing either to enhance his career or boost his confidence as a film actor.

Fortunately, he had agents like Louis Shurr and James Saphier who saw his potential in radio and pictures. Saphier guided him adeptly into radio when he absolutely thought it was a waste of his valuable Broadway time. The same thing happened with Louis Shurr and motion pictures.

By 1941 he had become an established radio and motion picture star, sitting on top of the heap with few genuine comedic peers. He knew about the draft, lend-lease and the war in

Europe, but he somehow didn't quite get it when asked to do his radio show from a military base.

He'd just come out of a session with his radio show writers in the NBC studios at Sunset and Vine and was about to get into his Cadillac and drive out to his home in Toluca Lake. As he opened the car door a Pepsodent scout called out, "Hey Bob, wait up a minute. I'd like to talk to you about something."

Bob recognized Al Capstaff, one of the guys who watch-dogged Pepsodent's interests in Hollywood. "What's up?" he asked.

"The New York office thinks it might be a good idea if you did one of your radio shows live from March Field." The Air Force did not become autonomous until after World War II, so at the time it was the Army Air Corps, part of the United States Army—just another army base to Hope.

Bob didn't get it. "What are you talking about? You want me to take the entire group out to Riverside to do a show for some flyboys?"

"Pepsodent wants you to do it."

"But why?" Bob persisted.

"Well, you know they have the war going on in Europe and we're sure to get into it eventually. It'd be a patriotic gesture, plus great publicity for you."

Half joking, Bob said, "I'm already popular." They both laughed. "Why don't they just bring the Air Corps down to NBC?"

"You know how many guys there are out there? Over two thousand," Capstaff said.

That got Bob's attention. He always enjoyed live audiences, and the larger the better. It reminded him of the glory days at the Palace and on the vaudeville circuit. Also, he performed better in front of large audiences, plus there were more of them to laugh—and that sounded good on radio.

"Two thousand, you say?"

"Yeah. Two thousand."

He scratched his chin for a moment, thinking about all the new material he could use on servicemen—jokes about the

brass, the local watering holes, and the lack of women in nearby
towns.

"All right," he said. "Let's do it."

Again he had to be persuaded to do something that would
have a strong impact on his life and career. However, he had
never made a more momentous decision. Not only would this
first trip to March Field open up a new chapter in his career,
but would cause him to touch and be touched by more people
in the years ahead than he could ever have imagined in his
wildest dreams. This move would etch his name in the annals
of military and civilian morale forever.

Chapter 20

On Tuesday, March 6, 1941, Bob and his entire radio cast traveled out to March Field near Riverside to do the Pepsodent show in a base hangar. The entourage included announcer Bill Goodwin, Jerry Colonna, Vera Vague, Frances Langford, Skinnay Ennis and the band, and a number of technicians. Bob arrived by Cadillac, the others by bus.

Although base personnel had been advised not to "swamp Mr. Hope with requests for autographs," and to "wait for the show," that evening, it didn't stop the dozens of GI's who ignored the base commander's request and surrounded Hope as he exited his car. They did the same with the bus carrying the other entertainers and the band.

Bob's show that evening was totally oriented toward the military, the soldiers' gripes, and local color. After the orchestra warm-up, Bill Goodwin opened the radio show and then came Hope. Bob strutted out on the stage to thunderous applause. When the applause let up, he said, "How do you do, ladies and gentlemen, this is Bob 'March Field' Hope ..." which became his signature announcement to tell the radio world that he was on location and not sitting in some comfortable radio studio where the air-conditioning and heat worked properly.

He told a few jokes about his reception at the base, each of which pictured him as a sort of "Sad Sack Hope," always in trouble. For instance, he told the March Field airmen, "As soon as I got in the camp they gave me a ten-gun salute," adding after a proper pause, ". . . that's what they told me on the operating table."

The Commanding General at March Field later said that Bob Hope had given his men a painless shot in the arm that only a letter from home could supersede. "He lifted the morale of these men beyond anything I've ever seen."

Bob enjoyed doing the show, especially the audience reception he received. However, he preferred doing his show at NBC studios where, if anything went wrong, it could be quickly corrected in the control room. He always feared some disaster like a power failure that would cost him his national audience for any period of time.

Despite all of the hoopla about performing before so many soldiers and being able to exploit the strict rules under which they lived—actually just being "one of the guys"—Hope did not think broadcasting from a military base would do anything more than make him look like a road edition of a Broadway show.

"We'll do the show in the studio next week," he told his writers. "Let's get started on our material."

And that was that.

The following week the Pepsodent show emanated from home base at NBC's Hollywood studio at Sunset and Vine. After March Field, the show went over like flat champagne. It came as a shock to Bob Hope. By the time the show came to a close, he understood that there had been a major change in his own personality in the week since doing his show from a military base. Something about those boys being away from home and genuinely appreciating the fact that a celebrity of Hope's stature would take time out of his busy schedule to care about them affected him in a way he didn't totally understand. Patriotism alone couldn't possibly be the reason. He'd never been much of a patriot. Hope thought more often as a businessman, providing a product or service to satisfied customers and receiving remuneration for his efforts—remuneration in multiple seven-figure segments annually.

So business played an important role in the shift of operations he would soon be making. Being patriotic wouldn't hurt the box office—yet, there lingered in the man a sensitivity to the loneliness of young men (who should be having the time of their lives dancing to Glenn Miller and Benny Goodman's music at the neighborhood malt shops) being deprived of their youth because they cared enough about everyone's right to enjoy the things they were giving up.

An enormous obligation crept into Bob's sense of being "Bob Hope," an obligation that had nothing to do with the importance of being a star. He once told a magazine writer, "It overwhelmed the hell out of me."

His May 20 show was broadcast from the San Diego Naval Station. He brought along luscious blonde Priscilla Lane to add sexual impact to the show.

After his usual, "Good evening, ladies and gentlemen, this is Bob, 'San Diego Naval Base' Hope," he went into his usual routine of demeaning everyone from lieutenants to admirals and at one point Vera Vague, a Lily Tomlin of the thirties and forties, went into a skit in which a man-hungry spinster says to a sailor who had made a pass at her, "If you get fresh with me I'm going to go to the head of the Navy ..." The rest of the script, "He's a dear friend of mine," couldn't even be heard on the radio, drowned out completely by the explosion of laughter from the swabbies.

No one bothered to tell the civilian writers that in Navy lingo, the toilet is known as "the head." Hope stood befuddled, and someone had to explain to Bob "Navy Base" Hope the purpose of a "head" in the Navy.

Acceptance of his show in San Diego was no less enthusiastic than it had been at March Field.

The following week found him doing his show for the U.S. Marines at San Luis Obispo and the week after that he brought *Caught in the Draft* director David Butler and Broadway musical star Mary Martin along to Camp Callan, where he previewed *Caught in the Draft* for the guys in khaki.

He gained an even greater radio audience around the country by mentioning the names of different servicemen at the bases he broadcast from. It was "Hi, Mom," apple pie, and "How are dem bums in Brooklyn doin'?" America loved it—and they loved Bob Hope.

Bob Hope and the United States Military Forces became so synonymous that from his second appearance in the summer of 1941 until June of 1948, rarely were Hope's Pepsodent shows not broadcast from a military installation. On only a few occasions did he alter that format. When he could not leave Los Angeles due to necessary medical treatments, he did two broadcasts from NBC's Sunset and Vine studios.

During these early travels out to military bases, he took time off to play golf at Lakeside, sometimes with Bing—more often with others because Crosby always beat him—and on one occasion he complained about the *Time* Magazine article that made him out to be such a money-hungry skinflint. Crosby had not read the article, but after listening to Hope complain about it throughout the entire golf game, he went home and dictated a letter to *Time* which read:

"My friend Bob Hope is anything but cheap. He does an average of two benefits a week. His price for a personal appearance would be about $10,000, so he gives away $20,000 every week of his life. Is that cheap?"

The magazine lost little "time" responding to Bing's assault:

"*Time* agrees with Bing; however, Bob from time to time has been known to put undue pressure on a nickel."

Even though it's obvious that Bob Hope didn't become a zillionaire by giving away his money, he and Bing both, despite their enormous wealth, made personal considerations that benefitted others.

As Bob's show became acclimated to a military background in mid-1941, London was undergoing around-the-clock blitzing by Hitler's Nazi Luftwaffe bombers. In the midst of so much destruction, Londoners came out in droves to see constant showings of *Caught in the Draft,* while in the Midlands a bomb-wrecked Coventry Cathedral became an open-air cinema for the city's homeless to come and watch Hope's latest comedy. Bob learned of his impact on Britain during those early years of the war many years later. "I had no idea," he said, "but it makes me feel good to have brought a little laughter, because they had more than their share of grief and tears, I'll tell you."

With Bob's last Pepsodent show of the season in the books, he went back to Paramount to do some dubbing on *Nothing but the Truth,* after which he flew into New York for a conference with Vic Hunter of Pepsodent and John McPherrin of Lord and Thomas, Pepsodent's ad agency.

Pesodent had for some time expressed an interest in running some sort of contest along with Bob's radio show in order to hype their product. Bob didn't like radio contests. It reminded him too much of the Depression days when theaters gave away dishes and bags of groceries on Saturday nights to struggling families who happened to have the lucky tickets. He had a much better idea.

Bob listened to the pitches made by the ad agency and grey-suited Pepsodent representatives. When they were finished and waiting for his response, he spoke.

"I have a better idea," he said. "If I am so popular, why don't I write a book? You know, sort of a comedian's autobiography. I can fill it with jokes, laugh at myself—just like I do on the radio. You could give the book away."

"I don't know," one of the men from Lord and Thomas said.

The Pepsodent executive's face brightened. "Go on, Bob," he said.

"Nobody knows what my fans want better than I. I've got scouts all over the country who report in to me regularly. I can tell you what goes over in New York or in Miami or Mississippi. I get more fan mail than you can imagine. You know what they want? They want pictures and information—information about Bob Hope, who he is, what he does, inside stuff. What do you think that adds up to? My autobiography. It doesn't have to be a long book and it doesn't have to have a hardcover. Just paperback which would be very cheap to produce.

"I can write the book. I also have a picture, *Nothing but the Truth,* to be released in October or November, and with the help of my writers I can whip up a book in no time."

One of the men asked, "How can a book, toothpaste, and a movie, tied together, help our client? Won't Pepsodent be lost in the shuffle?"

Bob laughed. "I suggest you talk to Paramount. We might even call the book *Nothing but the Truth.*"

After coast-to-coast consultations between Paramount and Pepsodent, a deal was consummated in which Bob Hope couldn't possibly lose. It became one of the greatest publicity stunts of the year. The book would sell for ten cents and a Pepsodent Toothpaste boxtop.

Lord and Thomas came up with a proposal to have every available star in Hollywood have his or her picture taken while supposedly reading Bob's book.

Nothing but the Truth established Hope in another venue—that of author. Numerous other books bearing Hope's name would follow in the years to come, most of which were written by ghosts or his hired writing staff.

The book had a real New York "literary tea" at Sherman Billingsley's Stork Club, to which celebrities and reporters were invited. Pepsodent began counting Christmas blessings.

Bob now had influence in Washington, D. C., because of his interest in the military and raising money to help England in its fight against Hitler and the Italian dictator, Mussolini. Defense contracts were out there for the grabbing, so Bob, while on the East Coast, and his brother Ivor got some of the defense contracts for their jointly owned company in Cleveland, Hope Metal Products. It was all very legitimate because the company had the know-how to produce the products needed for war.

He returned to Hollywood where Paramount immediately had him on a sound stage in its film version of the hit Broadway musical, *Louisiana Purchase,* in which he would costar with Vera Zorina. It turned out to be a nothing picture, which both

Bob and Miss Zorina would just as soon forget. The actors were not the problem. What had been a great Broadway show, with songs by Irving Berlin, turned out to be a parody of Louisiana during the reign of political boss Huey Long and if it made money at all it was due to the Hope name. Vera Zorina had only appeared in three previous Hollywood films, and was relatively unknown to American moviegoers. She came across as a rather cold personality on the big screen and never reached genuine stardom.

Hope premiered his 1941-42 Pepsodent show in Chicago on September 23. Frances Langford, now a regular on the show, had a long list of Decca recordings to her credit, many of those duets with Tony Martin—big hits in a country crazy for "Victrolas," which were cranked up and used either steel point or finely honed wooden needles to produce sound. The 78 RPM records had to be played separately and the player cranked before each playing. Jukeboxes were the thing in bars and at drive-in restaurants, but electronic record players had not as yet come into homes in great quantity.

Back in Hollywood, Hope resumed broadcasting from Sunset and Vine with the addition of Frances Langford and Ben Gage. Jerry Colonna and Skinnay Ennis were still aboard. However, Brenda and Cobina had taken off on a long vaudeville tour.

Since Bob's film, *Nothing but the Truth,* was in release, his first guest back in Hollywood was Paulette Goddard, his co-star.

Pepsodent had printed two million copies of the 95-page *Nothing but the Truth.* They were selling almost faster than they could be printed and bound. One columnist commented that "Bob Hope is doing more to assure that Junior brushes his teeth than all the dentists in the land. The American Dental Association ought to sue him for interfering with their right to earn a living."

Hope hadn't a worry in the world. His family and bank account were both healthy. As one of the most respected men in America, he was asked to be part of the Hollywood Chamber's annual Santa Claus Lane parade—riding a horse. Not much of an equestrian, he agreed only if the horse was "one of those broken-down brewery plugs that would be too tired to get fresh with me.''

Preceding him in the parade line-up that Saturday night, December 6, 1941, a large banner announced BING CROSBY'S FASTEST RACEHORSE. Bob received an ovation along the parade route down Hollywood Boulevard, second only to that of Santa Claus.

He'd had a very busy day and looked forward to sleeping late the following day. The year was nearing an end and he needed a vacation. However, he was completing *My Favorite Blonde* with Madeleine Carroll at Paramount, and he had his radio show to think of and . . . well, a vacation would have to wait. But there was nothing to keep him from getting a good night's sleep, which is exactly what he would do.

Little did he know that by the same time the next day he would be gearing up to go without sleep many nights in the next four or five years.

Bing Crosby had given him a pre-Christmas present by appearing as a walk-on in *My Favorite Blonde.* Hope especially liked that. The film idea came from a 1935 Alfred Hitchcock picture, *The 39 Steps,* which had starred Robert Donat and Madeleine Carroll. The script by Frank Butler and Don Hartman was adapted from a story concocted by two of Hope's former radio writers, Melvin Frank and Norman Panama, who had the idea of doing a comedy version of the serious Hitchcock shocker. A trained penguin was brought on board with which Bob would sing a revamped version of "Thanks for the Memory."

They needed a bit actor to play the role of a truck driver who speaks one line of dialogue. Bob suggested Crosby, hoping that the crooner would allow him to get even for the time he lost the golf bet and had to appear in a Crosby film as an extra.

Buddy DeSylva, Paramount's head of production, said, "You know Crosby wouldn't do that."

Hope said, "Let's see. I think he will."

Bob got Crosby on the phone and invited him to come over to the set that afternoon. Crosby agreed, not knowing what Bob might have up his sleeve—but certain there must be a trick in it. His curiosity drove him to accept Hope's invitation.

"And by the way," Hope added, "put on a leather jacket."

Once on the set, Crosby thought it would be a kick to play a truck driver with his back to the camera as Bob, playing an unknown vaudevillian, asked the guy leaning against a truck the way to a picnic ground. The driver asked Hope for a match. As he brought the match to his face, he turned and faced the camera, then walked away.

Pretending shock and disbelief, Hope half-mumbled to himself, "No, it couldn't be!" as he gave the camera the famous Hope "askance" stare.

Crosby, unbilled in the film, became the first major motion picture star to do a walk-on, originating the "cameo" role.

Hope went directly home after the parade and straight to bed. He planned to play golf at Lakeside the next day and he wanted to be fresh and wide awake.

AMERICA GOES TO WAR

"Hope Follows"

Chapter 21

At approximately 3 A.M., December 7, 1941, a Japanese Lieutenant Commander Ono sat in the radio room of the aircraft carrier *Okagi*. The *Okagi* headed up the task force comprised of 353 planes on 6 carriers, escorted by 34 submarines. The ship quietly slipped through the blue Pacific while Ono listened to KGMB, Honolulu's all-night music station, as the voice of Bing Crosby crooned the lyrics of "Sweet Leilani."

Between songs, the announcer gave the weather report: "Partly cloudy, ceiling thirty-five hundred feet, visibility good." Ono had heard all he needed to know.

The aircraft carriers, fast battleships, two heavy cruisers, a light cruiser, eight destroyers, and a train of three oilers and a supply ship comprised the Japanese armada at the ready 250 miles away, hidden under a cloud bank, having crossed the Pacific Ocean from Japan undetected.

Several days earlier the commander of the Japanese fleet received orders from Tokyo: CLIMB MOUNT NITAKA 1208, which meant: ATTACK AS PLANNED ON DECEMBER 8 (SUNDAY, DECEMBER 7, 1941, PEARL HARBOR TIME).

At 7:53 A.M., while Bob Hope relaxed at home in Toluca Lake, the Japanese flight commander radioed Admiral Nagumo,

"Tore, Tora, Tora," meaning "Tiger" and "We have succeeded in surprise attack." Two minutes later, Japanese torpedo bombers began diving on Battleship Row, where the U.S. battleships, *Utah, Nevada, Arizona, Tennessee, West Virginia, Maryland, Oklahoma,* and *California* lay at anchor. The *Pennsylvania* was docked at Cassin Downes, undergoing repairs. Having first destroyed the airfields, the attack planes were free from any real defense which allowed them to incur the enormous damage they did to our fleet—and, they hoped, to our morale.

The U.S.S. Battleship *Nevada's* band was playing "The Star Spangled Banner" on the ship's deck when the first wave of Japanese planes swept out of the skies to lay their eggs of destruction. Even as the U.S.S. *Arizona,* resting next to the *Nevada* in the harbor, went quickly to the bottom of the crystal clear waters of Pearl Harbor with almost two thousand of its sailors and marines, the band played on. The bandleader later admitted that "It never occurred to me that I could stop the national anthem once it was started."

World War II had begun for the United States of America.

Bob Hope had been awakened near noon (Pacific Coast Time) that Sunday morning by Dolores, who brought him some coffee and the morning papers.

The *Los Angeles Times' This Week* magazine supplement carried an article about Bob's latest picture, *Louisiana Purchase.* In the article, Bob discovered a paragraph that brought him fully awake. The writer had given out very detailed and personal information regarding his financial condition:

"The comedian's gross income during 1940, from radio, movies, and personal appearances, totaled $464,161.78. Even after business deductions, Bob paid, for 1940, federal and state income taxes totaling $142,047.66. His 1941 gross income will probably rise to $575,000, but considering the defense rates Congress has approved, he may remind himself of his favorite joke about Crosby: 'Bing doesn't pay a regular income tax. He just calls up

Secretary Morganthau each year and asks, 'How much do you boys need?' "

Bob Hope's writers were probably also amazed with the contents of the article—not because they feared someone might try to kidnap Bob's kids due to his great wealth, but because if he had so much loot, how come he played so cheap and chintzy when it came to paying the men whose jokes and gags made him so famous and wealthy?

Writers and Bob's income would evaporate in the events that would soon follow. Bob relaxed in his bed, listening to a football game on the radio, while Dolores listened to Arthur Rubinstein playing with the New York Philharmonic.

Three thousand miles away, First Lady Eleanor Roosevelt, in the midst of hosting a luncheon for 35 guests, awaited President Roosevelt, who had promised to join them. At the very last moment he sent word that he would be unable to attend, sending regrets. He'd just been advised of the Japanese sneak attack on Pearl Harbor, where the crown jewels of America's naval forces lay at anchor.

Within a short time radio programs throughout the United States were interrupted with the flash bulletin:

"JAPANESE WAR PLANES ATTACK PEARL HARBOR"

Bob never forgot that morning. Dolores came rushing into the room and said, "The Japanese have attacked Pearl Harbor." Bob laughed at her, waiting for the punch line which never came. It didn't take long until his football game was interrupted with a war bulletin.

He recalled in his book, *Don't Shoot, It's Only Me:* "That afternoon I went to a football game at Gilmore Field, the Hollywood Stars' stadium. There was a big crowd until halftime, when orders came over the public address system for all men in uniform to report to their units immediately . . . half the men in the stands got up and left."

As Secretary of State Cordell Hull prepared to meet with

the Japanese envoys in Washington, the attack took place, which made the insult to the national honor of the United States all the more grievous.

While President Roosevelt met with his cabinet and military advisors, Bob Hope ordered his brother Jack to get ready to drive him and Dolores to the Long Beach Naval Base, where he was previewing his Tuesday night show.

"It ought to be one hell of a show, let me tell you," he said, mostly to himself.

The devastation at Pearl Harbor was unbelievable. Many of our battleships, the backbone of the American Navy, were either crippled and inoperative or sunk in the bottom of Pearl Harbor. Thousands of military personnel and civilians were killed and an equal number were wounded.

The radio carried as many rumors as facts. Chaos on the airways would not be an understatement. Unconfirmed rumors spread that San Francisco had been bombed and the fires were reported to be greater than those of the 1906 earthquake that destroyed the city.

All up and down the West Coast the stories were the same. Only the truth need be told. The truth would be enough.

The following day President Roosevelt went before a joint session of Congress and made his famous "date that will live in infamy" speech to initiate the United States into "a hot war against Japan." Within a few days we found ourselves also in the war against Germany and Italy. The sides were chosen. The Allies versus the Axis.

Meanwhile, Hope had a radio show to do Tuesday evening, a show that did not air. President Roosevelt, aware of Hope's 23 million listeners, asked Pepsodent to relinquish the Hope time slot to give his second declaration of war speech to the American populace.

President Roosevelt's voice was somber but reassuring:

"My fellow Americans," the president began, "I must report to you tonight that many American soldiers and sailors have been killed by enemy action. American ships have been sunk. American planes have been destroyed.

"The Congress and the people of the United States have accepted that challenge.

"We are going to win the war and we are going to win the peace that follows, so help me God."

The following week, Hope's show returned to the air from the NBC Studios in Hollywood without any intro of "Thanks for the Memory." He went directly into a speech which reflected his feelings about the war and his hopes that all citizens would get involved in the national emergency. He also gave Pepsodent the privilege of being the first toothpaste to endorse America going to war. He said, in part:

"Good evening, ladies and gentlemen, this is Bob Hope, and I just want to take a moment to say that last Tuesday night at this time I was sitting out there with you listening to our president as he asked all Americans to stand together in this emergency. We feel that in times like these, more than ever before, we need a moment of relaxation. All of us on the Pepsodent show will do our best to bring it to you. We think this is not a question of keeping up morale . . . There is no need to tell a nation to keep smiling when it's never stopped. It's that ability to laugh that makes us the great people we are—Americans! All of us in this studio feel that if we can bring into your homes a little of this laughter each Tuesday night we are helping to do our part. Thank you . . ."

Having done his patriotic duty, Hope felt a need to get back to his job—making people laugh and loosen up in the face of adversity—and he did. For instance, he poked fun at California's nervous state:

"Well, Los Angeles had its first blackout the other day. Every electric light in the city went out. I saw one guy standing in the street and laughing like anything. I said, 'What are you so happy about?' and he said, 'At least I'm not alone. Look—this month nobody paid their

bills . . .' There's nothing to worry about, though. California alone could beat Japan. After all, how long could the
Rising Sun hold out against the Drifting Fog?''

Hollywood, as stunned as the rest of the country, took some
time to get oriented to being at war. Within a few days they
discovered rationing. Gasoline, shoes, food, tires, and that precious commodity, silk stockings (and later nylons) made ration
stamps as popular as defense savings stamps and bonds.

Bob Hope's December would have been all glory had it not
been for the Japanese attack on Pearl Harbor. During the month
his picture had appeared on the front page of all the newspapers
astride the horse he rode in the Santa Claus Lane Parade the
night before. On December 19, he had been voted the ''Leading
Entertainer'' and ''Leading Comedian'' in America by the
nation's radio critics who also awarded him a commendation
as ''Champion of Champions,'' a most coveted honor. The
Hollywood Press Photographers honored him with their highest
award and *Motion Picture Herald* announced the day after
Christmas that due to the enormous financial success of *Caught
in the Draft,* Hope was now a member of the elite few at the
top of the heap as a box office attraction—which meant more
to him than anything else. That honor meant better contracts,
more endorsements, more money per film, and more money
for personal appearances.

As Bob Hope thought of his awards and the financial advan-
tages they would give him, one of his ''Road'' costars had
already begun the process that would make her the number one
war bonds salesperson in the motion picture industry.

Dorothy Lamour, a natural born patriot, remembered another
war. During World War I, Dorothy's mother had dressed her
up like a Red Cross nurse and sent her out to sell thrift stamps.
If she could sell thrift stamps to help out in World War I, why
couldn't she sell bonds to help finance this new war?

She recalled being a guest at the Roosevelt White House a
couple of times and remembered that the president offered her
the use of his summer White House in Warm Springs, Georgia,
to do one of her South Sea Islands pictures. Roosevelt had

become a fan of Lamour's after screening an advance print of *The Hurricane.*

On December 11, 1941, before President Roosevelt preempted Hope's evening show that Tuesday night, Dorothy Lamour had a long conversation on the telephone with Secretary of the Treasury Henry Morganthau, talking a mile a minute about her plan to sell war bonds. She later said, "I expected him to hang up on me. I didn't speak so rapidly because of nerves. I just had so much to say and I didn't want to take up too much of his valuable time."

Morganthau never mentioned her rapid-fire presentation. He said, "Miss Lamour, what can we do to help you and when can you start?"

"I'm packing now," she said. "I have just a few retakes on *The Fleet's In,* the picture I'm completing at Paramount, and then I'll be off and running."

Within days Dorothy, taking heavy doses of sulfa drugs for an infection she'd picked up from a member of the crew, stood in front of a large crowd of important bankers in New York City. She presented herself before the nation's financial wizards in a long-sleeved black dress with a high neckline, hat, and gloves—not only to appear as a dignified salesperson, but mostly to cover up as much of her body as possible. An allergic reaction to the sulfa had caused her entire body to break out in a rash.

One elderly banker, who seemed to reek of old money and AAA-rated bonds, rose to thank her for wearing such conservative attire instead of a sarong. She gave all the credit to her mother, who had raised her to behave like a lady.

The White House press office gave her a rather stiff and formal speech to read, which might have been good for a politician, but it did not fit Dorothy Lamour. Abandoning her notes, she spoke from the heart. She convinced the stodgy bankers that they should ante up and they did, big time.

Moving over to New York City College, where the kids were more "hip," she spoke in a manner more in tune with their situation and sold them $10,000 in savings stamps that afternoon. Many of the students used their lunch money to buy them. Dorothy Lamour could be very convincing. Of course, from the back of the auditorium there came a cry of, "Hey, Dottie, take it off."

Another popular film actress, Carole Lombard, had already begun selling war bonds. She'd just completed what would turn out to be her last film, *To Be or Not to Be,* with Ernst Lubitsch directing. There'd been no hitches on the picture, which called for a small end-of-film celebration. After December 7, 1941, Hollywood began to frown on lavish parties. It didn't look good for movie stars to be cavorting around in nightclubs while America's youth died on the world's battle-fields.

Howard Dietz, drafted by Secretary of the Treasury Morgan-thau to organize a "Hollywood Victory Caravan," asked Carole to join the first tour along with more than 20 other stars. She begged Clark Gable to come with her, telling him that it would be an opportunity for them to "have a little time together" before he accepted a commission being urged on him by Washington. He declined, having already made plans to visit the Pentagon to discuss his options. Studio press representative Otto Winkler and Carole's mother, Bessie, accompanied the star on the important bond tour.

Dietz had insisted that no one fly, that all must take the train because of the many stops along the way. He went out of his way to warn Carole Lombard about flying because everyone knew she hated spending even one day more than she had to away from her husband. Gable and Lombard epitomized the fabled Hollywood romance that lasts "until death do us part."

When Gable returned from Washington to begin shooting *Somewhere I'll Find You* for MGM with Lana Turner, he found a buxom blond dummy on his bed with a note from Carole: "So you won't be lonely."

While in Indianapolis, Carole sold over two million dollars in bonds, signed autographs, and shook thousands of hands. The trip had been successful beyond anyone's imagination. Anxious to get back to Clark Gable, she refused to take the train back to Hollywood. A *Life* magazine writer suggested she take the train and get some rest on the way back to the coast.

"I hate choo-choos," she told the reporter. "I'll have plenty of time to rest in my own bed long before the train arrives in California."

Taking off from Indianapolis at four A.M., the flight to California was scheduled to take 17 hours, interrupted only for refueling stops.

As plans for a welcome home party were overseen by Clark Gable and a few of the couple's close friends, Larry Barbier, waiting in the Burbank terminal for Carole and her mother's plane to arrive, was handed the following message:

> "On January 16, 1942, at 7:20 P.M. (PST), Mrs. Gable was killed, along with her mother, Otto Winkler, and nineteen others when the TWA twin-engine DC-3 in which she was a passenger crashed into a vertical rock cliff near the top of Potosi Mountain, thirteen minutes after leaving Las Vegas, Nevada."

Carole Lombard became the first of dozens of Hollywood celebrities, in both civilian and military capacities, to die in defense of their country in World War II.

At the beginning some Hollywood producers did not entirely support the war. Movie moguls were not interested in having their production schedules thrown out of kilter so that their money-making male idols could go off to war. What happened to Clark Gable is not a rare example of how the studios placed obstacles in the way of their stars going to war.

Lieutenant General H. H. "Hap" Arnold, Chief of the Army Air Forces, sent the following message to Clark Gable on January 23, 1942, a week after his wife's funeral:

> "CAPTAIN SY BARTLETT, WHOM YOU KNOW, HAS JUST BEEN TRANSFERRED TO THE ARMY AIR FORCES. HE INFORMS ME THAT YOU WISH TO JOIN THE AIR FORCES. IF WE DO NOT, REPEAT NOT, CONFLICT WITH YOUR STUDIO'S FUTURE

PLANS FOR YOU, I BELIEVE IN MY CAPACITY
AS CHIEF OF THE ARMY AIR FORCES, THAT WE
HAVE SPECIFIC AND HIGHLY IMPORTANT
ASSIGNMENT FOR YOU. CAPTAIN BARTLETT
WILL BE IN CALIFORNIA WITHIN A FORTNIGHT
AND WILL DISCUSS MY PLANS WITH YOU."

Howard Strickling, publicity director for MGM, on direct
orders from Louis B. Mayer, wired Sy Bartlett that he did not
notify Gable of the message, nor should he, and he wished to
meet with Bartlett personally to discuss the matter. Strickling
would later rationalize his decision by stating that he didn't
believe Gable was in any emotional condition to make such a
commitment so shortly after the death of his wife.

On August 12, 1942, Gable, having never recovered from
his loss, went down to the local recruiting station in Los Angeles
and enlisted as an ordinary soldier "for the duration of the war
plus six months."

Upon learning of Gable's actions, Strickling fired off a wire
to the War Department, stating, "Clark appreciated arrangements you made." Gable had no idea about any arrangements,
just as he was never told that Carole Lombard had been decapi-
tated in the plane crash—although one fails to see any analogy
in that.

Meanwhile, the Bob Hope show did not play another military
base until January 27, 1942, when his troupe descended on the
San Diego Naval Base, where his show was welcomed with
open arms with one exception. Guest star Robert Young did not
receive the enthusiastic cheers reserved for gorgeous blondes.

"Dammit," Bob said. "These guys don't want men—they
want beautiful women!" He decided not to make that same
mistake again.

In order to placate the Navy guys he ad-libbed jokes about
women. "I really don't think there are enough girls around
this base," he said, adding, "Today I saw twenty-six sailors
standing in line to buy tickets to see a hula dancer tattooed on
a guy's chest."

Chapter 22

Bob Hope expected once again to emcee the Oscars in February of 1942, but thanks to World War II the Oscar extravaganza became nothing more than a dinner without fanfare. Turning thirty-nine in May of that year, Hope missed being drafted. The cut-off age at the beginning of the war was 35. He could have enlisted along with Henry Fonda, Clark Gable, Tyrone Power, and others, but chose rather to go the United Service Organization route—USO, where he did more for the morale of American service men and women than all the bombs dropped on Japan.

He continued to make big dollars. In January of 1942 he completed shooting *My Favorite Blonde* and immediately set off with Bing Crosby in February on a series of golf matches to raise money for war relief. They kicked off the tour at the Western Open Golf Tournament at a course in Phoenix, Arizona, then over to Texas where they hopscotched across the state from San Antonio up to Dallas/Fort Worth, then on down to Houston and Corpus Christi in southeastern Texas. The tour, so comic that Hope auctioned off his shorts to the person making the largest single donation, ended up back in California for a Red Cross Benefit Match in Sacramento.

Both men were worn out. Each had his radio show and other commitments in addition to the efforts they were extending toward the war effort. Their return to Paramount to familiar scenes and faces became more a vacation from the road than working for those terrible studio chieftains.

Teamed again with Dorothy Lamour, with David Butler directing, and Anthony Quinn as a very unpleasant Arab Sheik, Bob and Bing began prepping for a new "Road" picture, *The Road to Morocco*. Frank Butler and Don Hartman, both of whom knew full well that Bob and Bing would ignore the script, were given the "writing assignment" for whatever that term might mean to two actors who would rather have fun than act.

Bob Hope had one scene in which he was supposed to kiss a camel. The camel spat in his face with the cameras rolling. It is without a doubt one of the funniest scenes in film history.

Part of *Road to Morocco,* shot on the 20th Century-Fox back lot (now occupied by Century City, an adjunct to greater Los Angeles,) included a scene involving stampeding horses. Hope and Crosby, caught unprepared in a narrow alley as the horses were turned loose, were lucky not to be trampled to death. The director thought the scene hysterically funny. Hope and Crosby were not amused.

Broadcasting from military bases kept Bob Hope's Pepsodent show number one in the ratings. He had become the most popular entertainer in America, thanks to the responses from the guys and gals he entertained.

In late April of 1942, he flew into Washington, D. C. with Colonna and Frances Langford to join the Hollywood Victory Caravan on its two-week, cross-country tour to raise money for the Army and Navy Relief Fund. Joan Bennett, James Cagney, Olivia de Havilland, Bert Lahr, Ray Middleton, Eleanor Powell, Spencer Tracy, Desi Arnaz, Rise Stevens, Joan Blondell, Frank McHugh, Laurel and Hardy, Charles Boyer, Groucho Marx, Bing Crosby, Cary Grant, and Claudette Colbert were already in the nation's capital rehearsing their various songs and dances, skits, and routines for the pending tour.

Tin Pan Alley and Broadway threw in a contingency of

playwrights and songwriters—Moss Hart, George Kaufman, Johnny Mercer, Jerome Kern, and Frank Loesser. Hope, of course, would be the emcee. It turned out to be an Oscar event sans awards.

First Lady Eleanor Roosevelt threw a gigantic lawn party for the celebrities. Daily *Variety* dubbed the event Bob Hope's Victory Caravan, explaining that:

> ". . . as long as Hope was on stage the show had zest and lift . . ."

The show played to SRO audiences in Washington, Boston, Philadelphia, Cleveland, Detroit, Chicago, St. Louis, St. Paul, Des Moines, Houston, and Dallas, raising thousands of dollars.

In Houston, Bob emceed the Caravan in the Coliseum, then went directly to Ellington Field to do his Tuesday night Pepsodent radio show, garnering double publicity and again assuring the nation that Pepsodent was the fighting man's toothpaste.

Bob loved to join Bing and some of the other guys on the tour in barbershop quartet sessions at night after the shows whenever he wasn't off doing a benefit or broadcasting from a military base. "One night," Groucho Marx said, "we were in a restaurant and the three of us, Crosby, Hope, and I, started singing barbershop style again. But we needed a fourth to make it a quartet, so Bing went from table to table trying to recruit a bass. Everyone turned him down. I've often thought how ironic it was that the most famous singer in the world had to plead with customers to sing along with him. Perhaps they didn't recognize him—without his toupee."

Arthur Marx tells a story related to him by one of Hope's writers, Sherwood Schwartz. "One night while everyone, including Hope and Crosby, was in the lounge car reminiscing about vaudeville experiences, the phone in the lounge car rang.

" 'Hello?' said the porter who picked up the receiver. He suddenly got a puzzled expression, then asked, 'Bing who?' "

On another occasion during the tour Bing, known to down a bottle in record time himself, became so fed up with Pat O'Brien's carrying on that he angrily accosted the actor: "Listen, Pat, you've got to stop acting like Father Flanagan all day and Sherman Billingsley at night.'' He referred, of course to the Father Flanagan of Boys Town, whom Pat played on the screen, and Billingsley, a one-time bootlegger and owner of the very popular Stork Club in New York City.

By the end of the tour the celebrities had performed in 65 shows plus all the side events that the various stars managed to squeeze in along the way. They sold over one billion dollars in War Bonds. Hollywood had truly gone to war and ''General Hope'' led the charge.

Sam Goldwyn finally nailed Hope for the promised picture during the summer of 1942. The picture, *They Got Me Covered,* shot at Goldwyn's Santa Monica Boulevard studio in Hollywood, would not be released until 1943, but it might as well have been shot at Paramount. The usual crew worked together—Hope, Lamour, and David Butler in the director's chair.

The film—typical Hope—cast Bob as a bumbling foreign correspondent brought back to the United States due to his failure to cover Hitler's invasion of Russia. In the end, Hope and Lamour break another big story and all is forgiven—and he gets his job back. End of picture.

Bob lost Skinnay Ennis and his band to the Army, so when he decided to do an Alaskan tour in the fall, he took along guitarist Tony Romano as Skinnay's replacement. Jon Hall, recently wed to Frances Langford, had to be convinced that she was more essential to the war effort than to home and hearth before he would allow her to accompany Hope, Romano, and Colonna on the trip.

Hope entertained the troops, but took his meals with the brass at the Officers' Club in the company of Major General Simon Buckner, the Alaskan Military Commander. Hope was touched by what he saw in the far northern reaches of America's armed forces. In his book, *Don't Shoot, It's Only Me,* he says:

''The soldiers in Alaska were the loneliest guys in the world. Also the coldest. They didn't even have enemy troops close by to pump up the adrenaline and keep them warm. Only in the farthest islands of the Aleutians had the Japanese made landings. On an island called Umnak we did a show for a bunch of fliers who had just come back from a bombing mission in dense fog. We never found out whom they had been bombing. I'm not sure they knew, either ... Frances ... was the first white woman ever to visit Umnak ...''

As Langford sang, "Isn't it Romantic?", Hope said he looked down in the audience and saw one airman with his arms around his buddy, who was crying. "It was a sight I was to get used to ... seeing a pretty girl ... hearing her voice ... brought the war home, and home to the war ...''

The trip to Alaska did something to Bob and it seemed somewhat ironic that he later said, "How could I stay safely home in the U.S. putting on shows when all those casualty reports ... were in the daily newspapers? There was something wrong about sending boys overseas to their possible deaths while the entertainers were working at Sunset and Vine and eating dinner at the Brown Derby. You had to go overseas, where the danger was, to be truly appreciated. And I was determined to be appreciated, even if it killed me.''

Ordinary people were already asking why so many of Hollywood's big stars were not in the service. How could they get deferments when the youth of America was dying for them? Hope often ran into that question—and he had no answer. Fan magazine writers and columnists took potshots at entertainers making big bucks while GI's were sloshing around in the mud and dying for $21 a month.

In defense of Bob's doing his bit for the war by entertaining, Ed Sullivan wrote in his *New York Daily News* column, "Here's something interesting—and it indicates how smart is John Q. Public: Nearly everyone says that Bob Hope, married and father of two adopted children, should be deferred.''

Bob, anxious to go overseas and entertain, where he would be appreciated by men and women hungry for anything from the states, had the support of Pepsodent but just as MGM had tried to keep Clark Gable out of the service, Paramount did not want Bob to go into the war zones. He had picture commitments and the studio wanted them kept.

There were other reasons for Bob not to go overseas at the time. His family and friends were worried about his health. His doctor had warned him to slow down. And Dolores fretted that he didn't spend enough time with Linda and Tony. She didn't want them to grow up knowing their father from fan magazines, movies, or as "that man on the radio."

All normal activities, however, were put on hold. Never before had the nation come together in such a common cause nor has it since—and perhaps it never will again.

The Armed Forces Radio Services opened up a Hollywood office. Ronald Reagan became an Army captain assigned to the AIRS Hollywood site. Hope loves to tell the story of the day Captain Reagan served as Officer of the Day. One of Bob's writers, disguising his voice, called the good captain and said, "Captain Reagan? This is Lieutenant Colonel Whitney of the Fifty-fourth, on secret orders from General McNair. I have a company of one hundred men en route to Camp Roberts and we're running late. Can you provide bivouac?"

As the story goes, Reagan quickly looked up "bivouac" in the military dictionary, and responded, "Yes, sir!" He then called Abbey Rents and asked them to deliver one hundred army cots to AFRS.

The prankster writer, having given Reagan time to make his arrangements, put in another call to AFRS. "Captain Reagan? Lieutenant Colonel Whitney here. Very sorry, I miscounted . . . our unit consists of one hundred and fifty men. Is that a problem?"

Reagan is reputed to have responded, "The impossible we do immediately." He then called the rental service back and asked them to provide fifty more cots.

Milking the joke to the utmost, the writer made a last call to AFRS. "Captain Reagan? You know, of course, the Fifty-fourth is a cavalry unit. Be sure to have enough hay."

Although Captain Reagan never again heard from "Lieutenant Colonel Whitney," Warner Brothers sent over enough straw to accommodate an international square dance.

Meanwhile, Hope, back at Paramount, began preparations to start shooting *Let's Face It,* a Broadway musical comedy written by Herbert and Dorothy Fields, with Cole Porter's music.

Having received $100,000 from Sam Goldwyn for *They Got Me Covered,* Bob felt it was beneath his dignity to work for less. He therefore insisted that Louis Shurr and his partner, Al Melnick, force Paramount to upgrade his salary. The studio had no choice but to succumb to Bob's demands because he had become their top moneymaker and the most popular movie star in the country.

Let's Face It featured Bob in his usual state of confusion this time in a wartime setting—a hipster who isn't hip, a smarty who outsmarts himself. The writers deep-sixed any semblance of the Broadway show, opting for "the Bob Hope formula." Actually, very few of Hope's pictures were beyond a "B" rating, even with big name costars. Perhaps three or four could be called "A" films—the ones he made with Lucille Ball and his almost-ignored, next-to-last feature film, released in 1969, *How to Commit Marriage,* in which he costarred with Jackie Gleason and Jane Wyman. Throughout his career he was never nominated for an Oscar. He once responded angrily when asked if he felt bad about being ignored, despite his great popularity at the box office: "I should say not. I got the money . . . It's work and I got the money."

The Road to Morocco, already in release, received rave reviews. Once again, the songs from a Bob Hope film made it to the Hit Parade—as did Crosby's recordings of the film's tunes.

Paramount, as well as the other studios, hammered out film after film that were nothing more than vaudeville/big band/short-on-story/long-on-talent extravaganzas. Two of them were *The Fleet's In* and *Star Spangled Rhythm,* with Bob Hope as emcee and featuring Bing Crosby, Ray Milland, Vera Zorina, Victor Moore, Mary Martin, Veronica Lake, Fred MacMurray, Dorothy Lamour, Dick Powell, Alan Ladd, Franchot Tone, and Paulette Goddard.

These pictures were geared toward America at war. In each, the troops were being entertained and propagandized in one manner or another.

The war in Europe raged on with no end in sight throughout 1942, while Japan had so prepared for the Pacific conflict that every major island and port, including the Philippines, fell to them quickly. Americans and their allies would have to scratch, claw, die, and leave every square foot of coral and rock soaked in blood before any victory could be claimed.

Bob Hope, Martha Raye, Jack Benny, and dozens of other Hollywood names filled every open moment in their busy schedules with visits to stateside camps, air corps bases, and military hospitals which were filling up daily with the maimed and dying from wherever American servicemen and women were in battle.

Christmas of 1942 in the United States was a glum one. More and more gold stars were being displayed in the windows of homes and shops around the country to signify the loss of a family member. Everyday life changed. Lucky Strike, Chesterfields, Camels, Old Golds, Philip Morris, Kools—all well-known brand cigarettes—sponsored many of the most popular radio shows: Lucky Strike led the way with ''Your Lucky Strike Hit Parade''; Glenn Miller, sponsored by Chesterfields, reminded radio audiences, as his orchestra played ''Moonlight Serenade'' softly in the background, that ''They satisfy . . . them that smokes 'em, likes 'em''; we walked a mile for a Camel and Johnny asked us to ''Come in and call for Phillip Morris,'' while the Packard Motor Car Company told us to ''Ask the man who owns one.'' But few Americans were buying new automobiles.

We were told that ''Lucky Strike Green has gone to war'' and L/S/M/F/T or ''Lucky Strike Means Fine Tobacco.'' It took getting used to buying Luckies in a white package. GI's created new words—''Gizmo,'' ''Snafu,'' ''Kilroy,'' ''Luke the Spook.'' We learned that ''A slip of the lip can sink a ship.'' Spies lurked in every corner to do us in, ''sabotage'' became the watchword in defense plants. Many of these new wartime expressions were turned, by clever tunesmiths, into popular songs of the day. Women went to work in unheard-of numbers: ''Rosie the Riveter'' became a symbol for women in the defense industry, as well as a very popular song. American women on the job in defense plants were immortalized by Ann Sothern in her film role as *Swing Shift Maisie.*

As a country at war, America soaked up any kind of entertainment in order to find some relief from the daily casualty lists.

Chapter 23

Having accepted the prospect of a long war, Hollywood's industry made an attempt in 1943 to return to some semblance of normalcy. One of the first steps in that direction was to reinstate the glamor and glitter of the Academy Awards.

Bob Hope returned as host for the third time. It was a year of patriotic nominations. The ceremonies began at 8:30 P.M. on March 4, 1943, in the Coconut Grove of the Ambassador Hotel. Among the pictures nominated were *Mrs. Miniver,* a story of war-torn England and a family's struggle to survive, *Wake Island,* about war against the Japanese in the Pacific, and *Yankee Doodle Dandy,* the George M. Cohan musical about World War I.

To open the ceremonies, Jeanette MacDonald sang two verses of "The Star Spangled Banner," which most guests found excessive. Marine Corps Private Tyrone Power and Army Private Alan Ladd brought forth a flag with the names of more than 27,000 members of the Hollywood community who were in the service of their country.

A message from President Roosevelt, read by actor Robert Donat, thanked the film industry for "turning the tremendous power of the motion picture into an effective war instrument without the slightest resort to the totalitarian methods of our enemies.''

When Bob Hope stepped up to the microphone, he set the tone for the evening. ''The leading-man shortage is so great, pretty soon we'll see Hedy Lamarr waiting to be kissed while they put a heating pad on Lewis Stone.''

Hope's friend Crosby got a big boost when he sang Irving Berlin's song, ''White Christmas,'' in *Holiday Inn,* winning the best song award.

The government had placed limits on income and civilian purchasing, so when *Mrs. Miniver* received its fourth award of the evening, Hope quipped, ''If *Mrs. Miniver* keeps up like this, the government will put a ceiling on statuettes.''

Jimmy Cagney won best actor for *Yankee Doodle Dandy* while Greer Garson received an Oscar for best actress in the title role of *Mrs. Miniver,* which won best picture.

With the exception of Bob Hope's performance as emcee, the Oscar awards were pretty well trashed by the Hollywood trade journals.

With all due respect to the criticisms, prior to the attack on Pearl Harbor, Hollywood had been forbidden by the Neutrality Acts to go near the Nazi threat, since Germany was the most lucrative outlet for American films in Europe. Politics and high finance ignored ''Europe's war.'' There were a lot of isolationists in Hollywood and Washington, even as late as 1943.

At the Hollywood Canteen, which had opened its doors in October of 1942, there was no discrimination. Allies were welcome, one and all. Bob Hope, Martha Raye, and just about every star in Hollywood joined the canteen's cofounders, John Garfield and Bette Davis, washing dishes, waiting tables, and knocking themselves out to welcome the guys and gals in uniform.

Armed Forces Radio (out of Hollywood) continued to work around the clock getting music, comedy, and dramatic programs out to the troops in the field. Only one time throughout the war did AFRS broadcast publicly. On Christmas Eve of 1942 a ''Command Performance'' went public over the four American radio networks along with all independent stations at the same time. As a strict rule, the AFRS programs were dedicated, and beamed out, to men and women in uniform only.

Bob Hope emceed that particular program, opening with "How do you do, ladies and gentlemen. This is Bob 'Command Performance' Hope, telling all you soldiers, sailors, and marines that although Johnny Doughboy found a rose in Ireland, what he really wants is that stinkweed in Berlin . . ."

"Last week," he said, "my aunt gave her girdle to the scrap drive—now she's dreaming of a wide Christmas . . . These days wives are no longer backseat drivers. They sit up on the hood with a straw and siphon the gas of the cars in front of them."

The show featured an all-star cast performing before a live audience of several hundred military personnel. Other stars included the Andrews Sisters, Spike Jones and his City Slickers tearing "Jingle Bells" to bits, singer Ginny Simms and her husband, bandleader Kay Kyser, Red Skelton, and Bing Crosby.

Kibitzing with Crosby, Hope said, "Say, Bing, do you realize we're being heard by a billion people in over thirty countries?"

Crosby's quick response: "When you lay an egg tonight, Ski Nose, it's an international omelette, isn't it?"

In 1943 Rudolf Hess, one of Hitler's chief advisors, made his famous sneak visit to Scotland in an effort to persuade England to join Hitler in an attack on Russia. For his efforts he received 45 years in a British prison. American Forces had invaded French North Africa and with their allies had occupied Casablanca, Oran, and Algiers.

Bob finally got his chance to get into the hot war. He absolutely had to let everyone know he wasn't afraid when the War Department cleared him for a European USO tour to begin after his last Pepsodent show of the season aired from Camp Perry on Lake Erie, near Cleveland.

Bob and Dolores arrived in New York in mid-June, taking a suite at the Waldorf Astoria, awaiting what was a secret take-off time on a Pan Am Clipper from La Guardia Marine Terminal. Anxious to get started, Bob kept busy with briefings, overseas shots, and last-minute preparations. The troupe included Frances Langford, Jack Pepper (an old vaudeville friend), and Tony Romano with his guitar.

In the wee hours of June 25, 1943, Bob and Dolores lingered on the tarmac, saying their tearful goodbyes before Bob gave her one final hug and boarded the big Clipper.

After a rough flight due to bad weather, the plane landed at Foynes, Eire. The group flew in another plane to Bristol, England, then went on by train to London where, despite a shortage of bedroom space, they found rooms at Claridge's.

During a brief visit with his 99-year-old grandfather, Hope was admonished by the old man for not spending enough time with his family. Bob assured his grandfather that Dolores was doing a bang-up job while he took care of another job that needed to be done.

Dolores worried about Bob's health. He had developed some serious problems with his left eye, a hemorrhaging problem that plagued him constantly thereafter.

She kept herself busy with the children, the Catholic church, the American Women's Voluntary Services, and other charitable and wartime activities. "Work," she said, "keeps me from going crazy worrying where my husband is and if he is safe." She knew he would take chances—even in a war zone—because he'd always taken chances, but none so dangerous as the ones he now undertook.

After meetings with USO officials, having drivers assigned and mailing privileges established via the APO, Hope wanted to know, "When do we meet the troops?"

Within hours he was putting on his first European show at Eye Aerodrome, a bomber base, just prior to a departing mission over Germany.

Bob immediately made light of his draft status by saying that the draft board "don't even ask your age anymore. They just hand you a copy of *Esquire* and watch what page you turn to . . . I asked them what my classification was and they said 7L . . . coward . . . "

No GI who ever saw Hope perform in a combat zone ever doubted his courage. It was not until the Vietnam War that the amount of money he made from his televised shows from overseas came under scrutiny.

Hope was merely warming up:

> "I've just arrived from the States. You know . . . that's where Churchill lives . . . he doesn't live there . . . he just goes back to deliver Mrs. Roosevelt's laundry. You know, they're drafting all the leading men in Hollywood. But Crosby is still there. If they keep it up, most of the romantic heroes will be on the adrenaline side . . ."

While still in England performing at Burton-upon-Trent in Staffordshire, Hope's dying 99-year-old grandfather called out for his famous grandson. Bob rushed to his bedside, hoping that the old man would recognize him. Two days later James Hope died.

Bob's tour was backbreaking. The troupe put on more than 200 shows from England through Africa, Sicily, Tunis, Bizerta, Tripoli, Bone, Catania, and Palermo. Rickety old planes and bouncing jeeps jarred every part of their bodies. During a show before almost 20,000 GI's at Messina, they were surprised by a German air attack. Bob suffered a twisted knee diving into a deep ditch, which required him to use a cane throughout the rest of the tour.

Spending the night at the Excelsior Hotel in Palermo became a nightmare for Hope and his troupe. A Nazi air-raid caught them totally by surprise. The town and the hotel took a terrible beating from the dive bombers; he remembered it as "the most frightening experience of my life."

While rehearsing for a radio show in Algiers to be aired by transcription to the United States, one of the captains escorting Hope and his troupe interrupted the group, advising them that General Eisenhower would like to see them at his headquarters.

Hope decreed it to be the greatest thrill of the tour for him. "Meeting General Eisenhower in the midst of that deadly muddle was like a breath of fresh air. It quieted us all, brought us all back to our senses, and in every way paid us off for the whole trip."

Eisenhower told Hope that he'd heard of his close calls in Italy, but assured him that "You're perfectly safe here. We haven't had a bombing in three months."

Hope did his radio broadcast that night and returned to the Aletti Hotel for what he expected to be a good night's sleep. He certainly needed it, as did Frances and the rest of his group. He didn't get to bed until after midnight. Barely asleep, he was awakened and ordered into the bomb shelter. For almost two hours the German Luftwaffe gave Algiers one of the most severe poundings it had endured during the war. Bob felt genuine relief as he boarded a plane for England later that evening.

Back in London, Bob and his compatriots performed in Leicester Square for 5000 Allied servicemen.

John Steinbeck, on July 23, 1943, cabled his column to the New York *Herald Syndicate* from London:

"Probably the most difficult, the most tearing thing of all, is to be funny in a hospital . . . The time hangs very long. Letters, even if they came every day, would seem weeks apart. Everything that can be done is done, but medicine cannot get at the lonesomeness and the weakness of men who have been strong.

"And Bob Hope and his company must come into this quiet, inward, lonesome place, and gently pull the minds outward and catch the interest, and finally bring laughter up out of the black water.

"There is a job. It hurts many of the men to laugh, hurts knitting bones, strains at sutured incisions, and yet the laughter is a great medicine . . .

"Finally, it came time for Frances Langford to sing. The men asked for "As Time Goes By." She stood up beside the little G.I. piano and started to sing. She got through eight bars when a boy with a head wound began to cry. She stopped, and then went on, but her voice wouldn't work anymore, and she finished the song whispering and then she walked out, so no one could see her, and broke down. The ward was quiet and no one applauded . . ."

No entertainer ever wore his or her heart on their sleeve as much as Frances Langford. She felt the pain and suffering of each and every injured serviceman or woman to whom she sang. She and Martha Raye competed as to which was more motherly to the troops. Martha became one of the boys, more or less, and tried to hide her feelings. Frances had too much maternal instinct. They were all the boys next door to her.

Bob made the cover of *Time* magazine for the first time on September 20, 1943. Beneath his picture was one simple line: FIRST IN THE HEARTS OF THE SERVICEMEN, accompanied by a cover article aptly entitled, "Hope for Humanity." The story ended with a simple paragraph:

> "Inexhaustible, Hope piles job on job—work, which originally meant the path to glory, has become an end, a need, a form of excitement in itself. His camp tours, by putting him under incredible pressure, have given him an enormous lift. Pleased that he is first in the hearts of the servicemen, he can hardly wait to be off to the South Pacific. 'When the war ends,' Hope confesses freely, 'it'll be an awful letdown'."

Hope needn't have worried. He still had two and a half wars to go.

He came home to a hero's welcome, wherever he went—even to the jaded watering holes of Hollywood. For one of the few times in his life that hadn't involved the illness or death of a loved one, Bob suffered genuine humility. He had been so overwhelmed by what he saw on the tour that he made feeble attempts at one-liners, too overwhelmed to deal with his feelings. Dolores told her friends that he had "come home a sobered man," in the truest sense of the word.

Bob would later write of his first wartime tour with hindsight that contained a lot of insight into what it meant to be Bob Hope entertaining "home-hungry" troops in the field of battle:

> "I came back to find people exulting over the thousand plane raids over Germany ... Those people never

watched the face of a pilot as he read a bulletin board and saw his buddy marked up as missing. Those thousand plane raids are wonderful only because of the courage and spirit of the men who make them possible.

"We at home would understand all this better if every one of us could go through a few hospital wards, stop at a few emergency dressing stations, pray for our own courage in operating rooms as we watched twelve and eighteen teams of steel-fingered surgeons perform miracles of science on men who had performed miracles of courage."

Simon and Schuster approached Bob and asked him to write a book about his experiences in the war. Bob replied, "The war isn't over."

"Yes," the editor said, "but there'll be other tours of duty and other books. We think it would be good for the morale of the country."

However reluctant he might have been, Bob asked a writer friend, Carroll Carroll, if he would help him with a book that he wanted to call *I Never Left Home*.

"I've never written a book, Bob. I'm a gag writer," Carroll said.

He finally succumbed to Hope's persuasions and the book, when published, became a bestseller and opened up a writing career for the man who had done it all.

Bob wrote in the preface, "I saw your sons and your husbands, your brothers and your sweethearts . . . God knows I didn't do any fighting. But I had a worm's eye view of what war is . . . I did see your sons and daughters in the uniforms of the United States of America . . . fighting for the United States of America . . . I could ask for no more."

Chapter 24

Between 1938 and the fall of 1943, Bob Hope went from being a sub-title in *The Big Broadcast* to the best known entertainer in the world. He had the number one radio show in the country, was Paramount's biggest star and moneymaker (although Bing Crosby would have argued the money aspect), and in the mind of all Americans—military and civilian— he was the most beloved entertainer in the world.

From the beginning of World War II, Hope's efforts to entertain the troops were unparalleled. As his wartime activities increased, his motion picture career subsided. During 1944 only one Bob Hope picture made it to the screen—*The Princess and the Pirate,* costarring Virginia Mayo, a Goldwyn-RKO release.

Jack Benny hosted the Academy Awards on March 2, 1944. Busy with a dozen projects, Bob seemed not to mind at all. Anything to do with the military found him the first to sign up, whether it be broadcasting live from an army camp or doing benefits for the Gold Star Mothers.

Paramount had been trying for almost a year to line up a new "Road" picture. It was not until November that *The Road to Utopia,* went before the cameras. Norman Panama and Melvin Frank were assigned to write the script, a departure from the previous "Road" scripts written by Frank Butler and Don Hartman, and "departure" doesn't begin to describe the liberties taken by the writers.

Hope, Crosby, and Lamour each had script approval. They were the biggest moneymakers on the Paramount lot, so if any of the three objected to something, changes were made—especially when it came to Crosby and Hope.

The writers approached Crosby first, then Hope, and finally Lamour with their script ideas. Dorothy knew she would see the story outlines as well as the scripts after her two costars had seen them. There was one scene, for instance, that involved a live bear. Both Hope and Crosby had apprehensions about working with the animal, but caved in when the trainer convinced them that the bear was harmless. In the scene the trainer lost control of the bear and both Hope and Crosby were in jeopardy as the animal rampaged about the set. Once the bear had been secured, Hope and Crosby escaped to their dressing rooms, refusing any further scenes with the beast. The very next day the bear removed the arm of its trainer.

Gary Cooper, a great practical joker, walked onto the set one day and found Dorothy Lamour in a snit. Without telling her, Bob and Bing had decided to take the day off, to play in a charity golf match. She arrived at six A.M. for make-up and wardrobe. Sitting around all morning, she finally shed the cinched corset and formal gown for lunch. Thoroughly disgusted with Hope and Crosby, she had to be coaxed back into her costume when she returned to the set.

Having some fun, Cooper told Dorothy, "I wouldn't put up with that if I were you. You're just as big a star as those two galoots. Go take off all that garb and get the hell out of here."

Dorothy needed no urging. When Hope and Crosby finally wandered in, Lamour passed them on the way out. It took a lot of coaxing from Buddy De Sylva and apologies from both her mischievous costars before she got back into harness for an afternoon under the hot studio lights. Although usually a very good sport, Dorothy Lamour was a major star in her own right. Truthfully, however, neither of the men could have cared less what she thought—especially Crosby who, over the years, grew to resent most of his female costars. He had great respect for good female singers like Ella Fitzgerald and Rosemary Clooney, both of whom he admired for their professionalism, but actresses did not impress him much. When Dorothy Lamour and Captain Bill Howard were married in April 1943, Bing snubbed the newlyweds' reception in the Crystal Room of the Beverly Hills Hotel. Every major star from Paramount, as well as the brass (except those in service), came to wish Dottie and Bill good luck—except Crosby.

Something else happened on *Road to Utopia,* causing the censors to raise their eyebrows. Crosby usually got the girl at the end. This time, in a freak sequence, the three are scampering across an ice floe with the villains in hot pursuit. Suddenly a rift develops and the floe splits—leaving Hope and Lamour drifting in one direction and Crosby in the other. Years later, Crosby visits the long-wedded Bob and Dorothy. When their son presents himself, he is the spitting image of Crosby. Bob kept the scene from being cut out completely by ad-libbing, "We adopted." Audiences roared. Crosby had won again.

Arthur Marx says that the story wasn't too far from the truth. It was no secret that both men tasted wine, so to speak, from vineyards far from the family estates. Marx tells one interesting anecdote, which he says took place in the forties.

According to Marx, Crosby had his appendix removed and when Bob came to see him in the hospital, Bing remarked that a particular nurse had a lot to offer in the sack. "You ought to try her, Bob," Bing supposedly said.

Taking down her name and the floor she worked on, Hope thanked Bing. The following day he called Dr. Tom Hearn, his personal physician, and asked to be scheduled into St. John's Hospital in Santa Monica "for a rest." Hearn, always after Bob to take better care of his health, quickly agreed.

Bob insisted that he wanted the same floor, the same room if he could get it, that Crosby had occupied. He later told Bing that after a few rounds with the nurse, "I really did need a rest."

Like every other community in the country, Hollywood lived

by the marital double standard. Men would be men. Women knew their place. American men would be in for a great surprise once the war ended. Their spouses and sweethearts had worked in defense plants and discovered that the bedroom and kitchen weren't the only places a woman could shine.

The Road to Utopia, completed in March 1944, was not released until 1946. Whether or not the censors put the pressure on Paramount is unknown. The studio claimed a "backlog" of product. Crosby, Hope, and Lamour were never on the back burner—they were money in the bank and popular belief had it that Paramount was afraid to release the picture until after the war—too many men were separated from their families, and too many "Dear John" letters were arriving at the APO's on a daily basis.

Bob really wasn't interested in doing another picture. He had his Pepsodent radio show airing weekly from a different base—and he wanted to get back into a plane and head out to entertain the troops in the Pacific.

He was crazy about President Roosevelt, so when the planners of the annual Gridiron Dinner in Washington asked him to emcee their big shebang on March 11, he readily accepted when told that the president would be the guest of honor.

Roosevelt, having all kinds of problems with a reluctant Congress and even some of his closest advisors worried about his running for an unheard-of fourth term, enjoyed any kind of break from the political battlefields. Although an hour late for the event, Bob Hope came prepared to open up the president's laugh box.

Hope had met Churchill, Eisenhower, and Mrs. Roosevelt during his USO travels, but had never met the president. As it happened, a series of severe thunderstorms hovered over most of the Eastern seaboard and civilian planes were grounded. Air Corps General Arnold came to Hope's rescue and furnished a military transport plane with orders to "Get Hope to the dinner. I don't care what the weather is. Just get him to Washington in time for the Gridiron Dinner."

Because Hope arrived one hour late, Ed Gardner of "Duffy's Tavern" (another popular radio show) had taken over the emcee duties. Several acts had preceded Bob's arrival, but he brought along enough political confetti to make everyone, including President Roosevelt, forget that he had stood up the president of the United States for a full hour.

Bob came bouncing out onto the stage as though it had all been planned:

> "Good evening, Mr. President and distinguished guests . . . I'm delighted to be here . . . I was late getting here because we flew through mud all the way . . . I've always wanted to be invited to one of these dinners . . . and my invitation was a long time coming . . . I thought it had been vetoed by Barkley . . . Perhaps I shouldn't mention Alben here . . . it's too much like talking about Frank Sinatra to Bing Crosby.''

At first the crowd began to titter—then a loud blast came from the president's table as the great man threw back his head and roared his delight. With the president's approval, the entire house broke into uproarious laughter. If it was funny to FDR, then it was funny to the rest of the audience.

Having been given the okay from the chief himself, Hope took his political satire a bit further:

> "Trying to find a room in Washington is like trying to find 'My Day' (Mrs. Roosevelt's newspaper column) in the *Chicago Tribune* (owned by Colonel Robert McCormick, an arch-foe of Roosevelt and extreme right-wing Republican) . . . and did you know . . . speaking of the *Chicago Tribune* . . . that Fala, the president's little Scottie, is the only dog ever housebroken on that newspaper . . .''

The president laughed so long and so loud that those at his table swear tears were running down his cheeks. With the presidential seal of approval, Hope was soon being compared openly to the late Will Rogers. One newspaper columnist, Richard Wilson, in the March 12, 1944, issue of the *Des Moines Register* went so far as to say:

> "The gap left by the death of Will Rogers, as a comedian whose barbs at politics and politicians were particularly appreciated in Washington, has been filled.
>
> "Bob Hope has stepped into the shoes of Will Rogers in this respect, and from now on he will be sought in Washington to provide that extra touch at the capital's lavish public functions."

Bob did the Gridiron Dinner while suffering from a terrible cold which he couldn't seem to shake even after five days in the Florida sun before returning to California to keep his commitment at Goldwyn Studios to do *The Princess and the Pirate.* En route he did his Pepsodent radio show and during the week that followed managed to take the long way home by covering all the camps and bases he could in the Caribbean during the six days he should have been resting up in preparation for going before the cameras again. He made one quick stop at the Arizona-California border to entertain some soldiers at an out-of-the mainstream camp.

Dolores couldn't believe her eyes when she saw him. The man looked completely worn out. She insisted that he come with her to their Palm Springs home and get some rest. Wearily, he reported to Goldwyn Studios to keep his film commitment. With his energy at an all-time low, Hope romped through the film and appeared to be having the time of his life. Bosley Crowther, the tough film critic at the *New York Times* gave him plenty of credit:

> "Hope can literally keep a film alive, even when his retinue of writers rather obviously and languidly despair."

Happy to have the picture behind him, Bob had become somewhat obsessed with two things: entertaining the troops and adding to his rapidly growing financial empire.

For some time it looked as though he and Paramount might have come to a final parting of the ways. He wanted more money, while Paramount insisted he honor his current contract.

Bob hired one of the most powerful show business lawyers in Beverly Hills to represent him. Martin Gang represented a number of top film stars, directors, and producers. Consequently, he had more than a little clout with the studios.

Bill Faith quotes Hope as asking Martin Gang to show him how to hold on to some of the money he earned, instead of it all going to "finance B-17's and battleships."

Gang told him there was only one way to do that—"Form your own production company and make movies in partnership with Paramount."

Paramount Studio did not agree with Mr. Gang's idea. Hope proffered the idea, over lunch, to Y. Frank Freeman, insisting that he had to keep more of the income he earned.

Freeman told the actor, "If you insist, we'll suspend you."

Bob wouldn't budge. "Then suspend me."

So for the time being Bob Hope turned his back on Paramount Pictures. Having completed *The Princess and the Pirate* for Sam Goldwyn, he made arrangements with the USO to take a small group to the South Pacific to entertain American and Australian troops who, side by side, were fighting a bloody, island by island, battle against the Japanese warlords. He intended to take along his happy trio, Jerry Colonna, Frances Langford, and Tony Romano. On June 6, 1944, he broadcast his last Pepsodent radio show of the season which coincided with D-Day—the Allied Invasion of Europe. He opened his radio show thusly:

"Folks, this is Bob Hope speaking from a P-38 airfield near Van Nuys, California. We've looked forward to being with these men, and doing our regular show here, but of course nobody feels like getting up and being funny on a night like this. What happened during these last few hours none of us will ever forget. How could you forget?

Bob abandoned his monologue and delivered a very personal, heartfelt speech:

"You sat there and dawn began to sneak in, and you thought of the hundreds of thousands of kids you'd seen in camps the past two or three years ... the kids who scream and whistle when they hear a gag and a song. And now you could see all of them again ... in four thousand ships on the English Channel, tumbling out of thousands of planes over Normandy and the occupied coast ... in countless landing barges crashing the Nazi gate and going on through to do a job that's the job of all of us. The sun came up and you sat there looking at that huge black headline, that one great bright word with the exclamation point: INVASION! The one word that the whole world has waited for, that all of us have worked for.

"We knew we'd wake up one morning and have to meet it face-to-face, the word in which America has invested everything these thirty long months ... the effort of millions of Americans building planes and weapons ... the shipyards and the men who took the stuff across ... little kids buying War Stamps, and housewives straining bacon grease ... farmers working round the clock ... millions of young men sweating it out in camps, and fighting the battles that paved the way for this morning. Now the investment must pay—for this generation and all generations to come."

Frances Langford capped the evening by singing "Ave Maria."

Thirty-five million Americans tuning in had never seen nor heard this side of Bob Hope—the humanitarian who cared as much for those boys crossing the English Channel as he did for his own children and the boys who would fight in Korea and Vietnam later on. Now, he really wanted to get into the Pacific War. His speech was compared to the fireside chats for which Mr. Roosevelt was famous.

On June 22, 1944, Bob and his group of entertainers departed March Field near Riverside, California, aboard a C-54 litter plane headed for Saipan to pick up some wounded. The first stop was Hickham Field at Honolulu, gateway to the Pacific War.

Hope's troupe was destined for what became known as "The Pineapple Circuit," islands most Americans had never heard of. In addition to his regular crew, he was accompanied by Barney Dean and a sensational young dancer, Patty Thomas.

In Hawaii he did a show for the airmen at Hickham Field. General Douglas MacArthur provided his personal plane, a C-54 Liberator "Seventh Heaven," and his personal pilot, Captain Frank Orme, to transport Bob's troupe to tiny Christmas Island. A year earlier, Gary Cooper had been the only entertainer they'd seen until Hope arrived.

They then began to island-hop: Canton Island, Tarawa, Kwajalein, Saipan in the Marianas, Majuro, Bougainville, Munda, and Tulagi—names unknown at the time, now etched in the annals of American warfare.

Along the way, Bob was told about an island called Peleliu, a Japanese fortress in the Carolines north of New Guinea and east of the Philippines. Marines of the 1st Marine Division had been training for over six months on another tiny island, Pavuvu, in preparation for the invasion of Peleliu. These Marines were all but forgotten. No entertainers had ever stopped by to say hello.

Bob Hope changed that. He got his kids together and they flew in Piper Cubs, finding fifteen thousand anxious men waiting to give them the greatest ovation they received throughout the tour. Forty percent of those Marines did not make it back home. Bob said it was the most touching stop on the entire trip.

Worn out, Bob and his gang were persuaded to get some rest in Australia. They climbed aboard a Catalina PBY Flying Boat, which lost an engine and crash-landed in the middle of a shallow river. Natives from a village of six hundred came to their rescue. Hope and his troupe were so grateful they performed for the natives, who seemed to enjoy it very much, although they understood very little, if any, of the language.

Bob and his war-weary group traveled 30,000 miles, doing 160 shows before departing New Guinea on September 13 for the fifty-hour trip back to the United States, where they landed at Lockheed Airport in Burbank just around the corner from Bob's home in Toluca Lake.

On September 15 he broadcast his first Pepsodent show of the season from the Marine Air Station in Mojave, California.

Paramount Studios strictly enforced his suspension, denying Bob work for any other studio in any capacity. The moguls were a monopoly—a monopoly that wouldn't be broken until James Garner took on Warner Brothers in the early sixties, thumbing his nose at their suspension and breaking the back of the studio contract system.

Without films, Bob Hope felt free to devote more time to the troops, which he did right into the middle of 1945.

Chapter 25

Hollywood gossip columnists continued to chatter about the widening chasm between Bob Hope and Paramount Pictures. At one point someone suggested that the studio should ask Bing Crosby to use his influence as a mediator in the worsening situation between star and studio. Both Crosby and Hope denied any such effort. Louis Shurr, however, tried everything to patch up the rupture because Hope's suspension cost him a bundle.

Finally, responding to criticism and pointed questions, Hope made a statement:

> "We've both said our little sarcastic things, but I really suspended the studio. I'm not on salary. My contract calls for straight picture deals. The time out will be added on to my contract. And if someone will suspend the war I'll be happy to start another picture. As it is I'm booked with GI Joe, and besides, I'll give the country a nice rest. How often can people stand to look at my kisser?"

The self-serving statement contained at least two inaccuracies. First, Paramount definitely did the suspending and in doing so, took Bob off salary. Second, he declared that he was on a "straight picture deal," but failed to indicate whether or not the contract covered only a picture at a time or several pictures over a period of time.

He buttered his own bread by involving the war and GI Joe. How could Paramount respond? The studio would have appeared to be against servicemen. Hope had Paramount in the palm of his hand and he exploited the situation fully, always seeming to take his employer to the woodshed for injuries, real or imagined, imposed upon him.

So Bob Hope sat out the war with Paramount and did not return to the studio until after the Japanese surrender on September 2, 1945.

On March 15, 1945, Bob co-hosted the Academy Awards with John Cromwell at Grauman's Chinese Theater on Hollywood Boulevard.

With Hope on suspension and not allowed to make movies with any studio, his nemesis, Bing Crosby, moved into first place as the number one box-office attraction of the year. Additionally, Crosby had been nominated in the best actor category for his performance in *Going My Way,* which received a total of 10 nominations, as had its biggest competitor, David Selznick's war film set on the home front, *Since You Went Away.* Bette Davis received her seventh nomination and Greer Garson her fourth in as many years.

Right up to showtime, Bing Crosby was guzzling drinks in the clubhouse at Lakeside. He'd made up his mind not to attend the awards. Why give Hope fuel for jokes? Maybe. Maybe not. The Paramount studio hiearchy did not find Crosby's indifference amusing and prevailed upon his mother to insist that he attend—which she did. He arrived at the theater after the awards were underway.

Bob Hope launched into his monologue with enthusiasm. "This," he announced, "is the first time I knew this was a theater. I've always thought it was a place where Darryl Zanuck sent his laundry."

The Academy President, Walter Wanger, interrupted his monologue to present Hope with his second Special Award, a life membership in the Motion Picture Academy.

The comedian quickly quipped, "Now I know how President Roosevelt feels."

Hope later waited in the wings as Gary Cooper announced the Best Actor award, which went to Bing for *Going My Way.*

Crosby didn't hesitate to let Hope have one. "I couldn't be more surprised," he said, "if I won the Kentucky Derby. Can you imagine the jokes Hope's going to write about this in his radio show? This will give him twelve straight weeks of material for his radio program, talking about me."

And, indeed, Hope made immediate hay by slipping onto the stage behind the crooner. The crowd, sensing a gag, began to laugh. Crosby thought they were with *him,* so he continued, referring to the film's director, Leo McCarey, "This is a real land of opportunity when Leo can take a broken-down old crooner and make an Academy Award winner out of him."

Hope waited until presenter and presentee had left the stage before he took the opportunity to heckle Crosby. "Crosby's winning an Oscar is like hearing that Sam Goldwyn was lecturing at Oxford." The star-studded crowd roared its approval. Goldwyn, as everyone knew, rivaled Yogi Berra and Casey Stengel when it came to speech.

Milking the situation further, when Going My Way received the Best Picture award, which was accepted by Paramount boss Buddy DeSylva, Hope waited until DeSylva came out from the wings, then dropped to his knees as though begging forgiveness and began polishing the executive's shoes. Ingrid Bergman's Best Actress Oscar for *Gaslight,* seemed almost anti-climactic.

Three of the year's most popular (and eligible) movie songs were not even nominated: "Cow Cow Boogie," "Hit the Road to Dreamland," and "One For My Baby."

Little did anyone know that only three weeks later, Hope's beloved President Roosevelt would die suddenly of a cerebral hemorrhage on April 12 in his cottage at Warm Springs, Georgia, at the age of 63. All of Hope's FDR jokes were immediately placed in mothballs.

Hope took Roosevelt's death personally, as did most Americans. Roosevelt had guided the nation through the Great Depression and almost to the end of World War II and had become more of an icon than a national leader. He had provided Hope with so much humor for the Pepsodent radio show. More importantly, he was the first president to give Hope a political base in comedy. Bob always said that FDR was his greatest audience. No president thereafter, including those Republicans with whom Hope became closely linked, was spared Hope's political barbs.

Five days following the sudden demise of FDR, Hope opened his radio broadcast with some encouragement for the new president, Harry S. Truman:

> "This is Bob Hope, ladies and gentlemen. It was only last Tuesday that we were laughing and whooping it up with an audience of a thousand Marines. Only seven days ago tonight, but I want to tell you it feels like a thousand years. A few seconds ago we listened to the voice of Harry S. Truman, thirty-third president of the United States of America. No man on earth, today or all the way back through history, has faced so great a responsibility as president Truman. One hundred and thirty million Americans are serving notice that they will stand beside him to the completion of the task to which Franklin Roosevelt gave his life."

The war in Europe ended on May 8, 1945, just three weeks after the death of the man who, along with Winston Churchill, put together the grand design for victory.

Bob Hope wrote the following letter in his daily syndicated column:

Dear Fala,
    You probably don't remember me. But I knew you back in your kennel days when we were a couple of young pups—in fact, we chewed our first bone together, remember? In writing you this letter, I'm speaking for dogs throughout the world, for we are all deeply grieved

to hear of the death of your master. Your personal loss is felt by all of us. You know as well as I do that leading a dog's life is no bed of roses. But a dog's life is for dogs. Human beings shouldn't horn in on our territory. But lately a lot of men and women and kids have been leading a dog's life, and your master was one of the humans who didn't like to see that sort of thing happening. That's why we respected him—he wanted to keep human beings in their right place. And he did something about it. He made a lot of people see the light, or as we'd put it, he put them on the right scent. Let's hope they can keep their noses to the ground and work it out for themselves, even though his personal guidance has been taken away from them. With deepest sympathy,

Fido

Truman, grateful to Bob Hope for telling his millions of radio listeners to get behind the new president, quickly made arrangements to have Hope bring his show to Washington for a three-hour extravaganza to start up a new bond drive. The Seventh War Loan Drive brought in more than $2.5 million dollars. To acknowledge Hope's contributions to the war effort, Truman invited Bob, Frances Langford, Vera Vague, Tony Romano, Jerry Colonna, and Skinnay Ennis (now out of the military) to perform in the Gold Room at the White House.

Truman always felt close to the troops; he'd been an infantry captain in World War I. He asked Bob to perform the same exact show he'd been doing for the men in the trenches. After the show, President Truman, along with his wife and daughter, gave Bob and his Pepsodent cast and crew a personal tour of the White House.

Bob would later say of Harry Truman, ''I got to know him quite well and we became friends. I liked him because he always said exactly what he thought.''

Europe had settled for what peace there might be, following the dual suicide of Hitler and Eva Braun at the end of April. President Truman felt Bob Hope had something to contribute to post-war Europe, so he dispatched Bob and his entourage to England to do a series of shows for the American troops who were crowding into English ports, awaiting orders to return to their families in the United States.

On the Fourth of July 1945, Hope opened the tour, performing before over 10,000 troops at London's Albert Hall. By the time the tour was finished, they'd performed in Paris, Amiens, and Marseilles.

Although Hope may have been a Republican who loved Democratic presidents, he was not interested in a performer's politics. He respected talent. So, in Nice, during one of the last shows of the tour, he saw the French musical star Maurice Chevalier sitting in the audience.

Bob knew Chevalier when they'd had adjoining dressing rooms at Paramount and had great respect for the sophisticated Frenchman. So he asked the major in charge to go out into the audience and bring Chevalier up to the stage so he could introduce him.

The major said, "Oh, no, Mr. Hope. You mustn't introduce Chevalier. He's suspected of being a Nazi collaborator."

In a burst of spontaneous anger, Hope snapped at the major, "I'm not a judge and I'm not a jury. I'm just the emcee here and this guy is one hell of an entertainer."

He left the major openmouthed, and went to the edge of the stage, calling down to Chevalier, "Hey, Maurice, come on up!"

Dressed in a white turtleneck sweater and red pants, Chevalier was totally surprised when Hope asked him to sing before an audience of troops, most of whom were fresh from fighting the Nazis, and he seemed somewhat hesitant and unprepared. More than anyone else, he knew all the allegations and had fiercely denied them. However, to face such a large audience of allied servicemen . . . what if they rejected him outright? Bob didn't wait for his friend to say yes or no.

Hope's introduction was simple. "Ladies and gentlemen, Maurice Chevalier." The troops stood and applauded. When Chevalier completed "Louise," his theme song, the roar was thunderous as thousands of servicemen clapped, whistled, and

Publicity still from early Bob Hope NBC radio show, circa 1939–1940.

Bob Hope and Martha Raye clown around in a scene from *The Big Broadcast of 1938*, in which Hope and Shirley Ross sang "Thanks for the Memory," which became Bob's life-long theme song. The first of four films in which Paramount tried to pair Hope and Raye as a slapstick Burns and Allen without success.
(Paramount Pictures 1938)

Bob Hope, Dorothy Lamour, and Bing Crosby strut their stuff in *Road to Singapore*, the first of their seven money-making films. Hope and Crosby often made up the dialogue while the cameras were rolling. (Paramount Pictures 1940)

Bob Hope and Bing Crosby attempting to woo the ever-so-coy Dorothy Lamour along the *Road to Zanzibar*, the second of the successful "Road" series and their last pre-war picture together. (Paramount Pictures 1941)

Bob Hope joins Paulette Goddard as she checks out the not-so-dead body in *The Ghost Breakers*, their second co-starring film. At the time, Goddard was married to Charlie Chaplin, Bob's all-time comedy idol. (Paramount Pictures 1939)

Bob Hope and his trained penguin come to the rescue of gorgeous Madeleine Carroll, on the run from the Nazis in *My Favorite Blonde*. Bing Crosby appears in one of his famous cameos. (Paramount Pictures 1942)

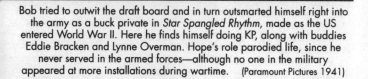

Bob tried to outwit the draft board and in turn outsmarted himself right into the army as a buck private in *Star Spangled Rhythm*, made as the US entered World War II. Here he finds himself doing KP, along with buddies Eddie Bracken and Lynne Overman. Hope's role parodied life, since he never served in the armed forces—although no one in the military appeared at more installations during wartime. (Paramount Pictures 1941)

Bob Hope and Vera Zorina recreate a scene in the film adaptation of the hit Broadway musical, *Louisiana Purchase*. The stars were hopelessly mismatched—Zorina lacked the comedy flair to serve as a foil for the spontaneous Hope, making this one of Bob's less-remembered films. (Paramount Pictures 1941)

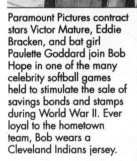

Paramount Pictures contract stars Victor Mature, Eddie Bracken, and bat girl Paulette Goddard join Bob Hope in one of the many celebrity softball games held to stimulate the sale of savings bonds and stamps during World War II. Ever loyal to the hometown team, Bob wears a Cleveland Indians jersey.

Bob Hope reluctantly does his first radio show from a military base at March Field, near Riverside, California, on May 6, 1941. Thereafter, almost all of his radio shows during World War II were broadcast from military installations.

Bob Hope and friends between shows on a USO tour to entertain the troops.

Bob Hope surrounded by Hollywood starlets in a studio publicity shot to promote *My Favorite Brunette*, in which he co-starred with Dorothy Lamour. (Paramount Pictures 1947)

Bob Hope referees a YMCA boxing match in North Hollywood, California, on November 28, 1948. An amateur boxer as a youth, Hope devoted a lot of time to underprivileged youngsters in the Los Angeles area, encouraging them to seek a better life and turn away from street gangs and juvenile delinquency.

Many comedians have some inner urge to appear in drag in their films and Bob Hope, rivaled only by Milton Berle and Jack Benny, is no exception in this still shot from *The Lemon Drop Kid*. This film marked the second time that Damon Runyon's saga of a racetrack bookie in trouble with the mob was brought to the screen, and was the first of several films in which Bob co-starred with blond beauty Marilyn Maxwell. This version featured "Silver Bells," which joined Crosby's "White Christmas" as a traditional holiday favorite.
Paramount Pictures 1951)

Six-shooters drawn, Bob Hope joins co-stars Jane Russell and Roy Rogers in *Son of Paleface*, sequel to *Paleface*, in which Miss Russell was also Hope's femme fatale.
(Paramount Pictures 1952)

Backstage at the 1954 Academy Awards, emcee Hope poses with Bette Davis, Marlon Brando (Best Actor for *On the Waterfront*), Grace Kelly (Best Actress for *The Country Girl*), and Edmond O'Brien, partially obscured on the right (Best Supporting Actor for *The Barefoot Contessa*). An unhappy Bette Davis had just taken Hope to task for some of the zingers he shot her way during his opening monologue.

Left: Bob Hope and Jimmy Cagney in a soft-shoe routine from *The Seven Little Foys*. Cagney reprised his former role as George M. Cohan in a rare cameo appearance.

Right: Bob Hope leads the Seven Little Foys into one of the famous Eddie Foy routines.

The Seven Little Foys chronicles the trials and tribulations in the life of Eddie Foy, one of Broadway's favorite vaudeville comedians. Many believe that Bob's courtroom speech in defense of keeping custody of his children was his best performance as an actor.   (Paramount Pictures 1955)

Professional golfer Arnold Palmer, a close friend of Hope's, joins him on the set of *Call Me Bwana*, a film which co-starred Anita Ekberg. Shot at Pinewood Studios near London because of internal strife in Kenya, this vintage Hope film casts its star as a bungling safari hunter sent into the jungle by inept bureaucrats to retrieve a misfired moon missile. (No one ever explains Arnold Palmer's presence.) (United Artists 1963)

Bob Hope and Lucille Ball play husband and wife in *Critic's Choice*, the fourth and final highly successful coupling of the two film favorites. Hope, as a tough New York theater critic, succumbs to Ball's insistent pleading that he review her first Broadway play. His devastating critique drives him to a psychiatrist, the bottle, and the arms of a willing and anxious ex-wife, Marilyn Maxwell.   (Warner Brothers 1963)

Bob Hope and Phyllis Diller co-starred for the second time in *Eight on the Lam*—neither film did well. Jonathan Winters and Jill St. John co-starred in this picture, made toward the end of Hope's film career. (United Artists 1967)

In his last starring role, Bob Hope was paired with Eva Marie Saint in *Cancel My Reservation*, and they should have done just that! Awkward cameos by Bing Crosby, John Wayne, and Flip Wilson. Based on Louis L'Amour's best-selling novel, *Broken Gun*, this picture went awry from script to casting to bad reviews.   (Warner Brothers 1972)

In *How to Commit Marriage*, Bob Hope and Jackie Gleason play off each other as bitter enemies confronted by the fact that their two children are headed down the aisle. Contrary to some of the reviews, Hope was doing mature comedy that worked. He and wife Jane Wyman complicate the plot as a couple divorcing after more than twenty years of married bliss. (Cinerama 1969)

Bob Hope hobnobbed with presidents from Franklin D. Roosevelt to Bill Clinton, but his favorites were Eisenhower, Reagan, and Bush. In this undated photograph, he and fellow ski-nose Richard Nixon were each receiving honorary degrees.

The troops were always Hope's greatest audience. He loved their appreciation and traveled far and wide to entertain them in war and peace. Here he uses a golf club as a prop during his monologue at Da Nang, Vietnam (1971).

Bob manages to corral three of his most glamorous co-stars from his motion picture days to appear in one of his many television specials. Clockwise from left: Jane Russell, with whom he made *Paleface* and *Son of Paleface*; Hope, Rhonda Fleming, his co-star in *The Great Lover* and *Alias Jesse James*; and Dorothy Lamour, with whom he frolicked through seven "Road" films, *Caught in the Draft, The Big Broadcast of 1938, They Got Me Covered*, and *My Favorite Brunette*.

Bob Hope and Georgie Jessel greet each other at the podium during the 42nd Annual Academy Awards prior to Hope's presenting his former co-star and USO buddy, Martha Raye, with the coveted Jean Hersholt Humanitarian Award. (1969)

During a Bob Hope television special on NBC in 1980, Dean Martin and Bob recap a 1974 Hope "roast."

Surrounded by Oscars at the 47th Annual Academy Awards, Bob Hope tells the audience, "This looks like Bette Davis's garage," referring to the many Oscars won by the famed dramatic actress. References to Davis and her many nominations were always part of his appearances on the Oscar stage.

Hope in familiar
monologue stance at
Utapao, Thailand. (1968)

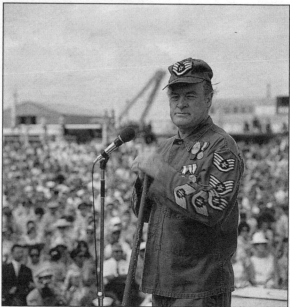

Bob Hope and his good friends, President and Mrs. Ronald Reagan (Nancy) at a formal affair. Reagan and Hope were old friends since their early Hollywood days.

Bob Hope and friends resting between shows during a bombing attack in Vietnam.

After the marriage of the Hopes' daughter, Nora, to Sam McCullagh in mid-August 1969. Left to right: older daughter Linda Hope Lande, Bob Hope, the newlyweds, Dolores Hope, and the altar girls.

Dolores Reade, a popular New York nightclub singer, just before she met Bob Hope, who was starring on Broadway with Ethel Merman and Jimmy Durante in the popular musical, *Roberta*.

Mrs. Delores Hope in the late 1990's after sixty-odd years of marriage to the famous comedian. At the time, she was performing in concerts with jazz singer Rosemary Clooney.

Bob, Dolores and their five dogs at a family Christmas Celebration in their Toluca Lake, California home.

Bob Hope at 94 still cutting ribbons, with his loving wife Dolores by his side, as always.

stamped their feet, giving the great French entertainer a standing ovation. He performed several encores, each of which was met with rousing applause. After all, he was Chevalier—a French treasure.

At a party later, Chevalier threw his arms about Hope and kissed him on both cheeks. "Thank you. Thank you. Thank you. I will never forget what you have done for me today."

After a brief rest, Hope finally got into occupied Germany, where he put on a show at General Ike Stadium, actually an athletic field near Bremen, for 8,000 members of the 29th Division, most of whom were recipients of the Purple Heart. Bob was introduced as "the only man in Germany who wears his hat on his unoccupied zone." The guys loved him.

While Hope entertained the troops in Germany, President Truman met Clement Attlee, Churchill's successor and Stalin at Potsdam to divide up Europe. During the Potsdam meeting, Truman received a cable from Washington: "Operated on this morning. Diagnosis not yet complete but results seem satisfactory and already exceed expectations."

The message, decoded, revealed that the first atom bomb had just created a massive crater somewhere in the western United States desert and was felt by gamblers at the tables in Las Vegas.

When Japan surrendered, Bob Hope was watching the GI Olympics in a rainstorm in Nuremberg Stadium. The games were interrupted for the announcement. Here is how Hope remembered that moment:

"It was a moment I'll never forget. That whole stadium full of guys seemed to rise twenty-five feet in the air. Nothing in my life had prepared me for that experience. The cheering, the shouting, even the crying. Thousands of men who knew at that one moment they were going to live. There were no questions, no doubts. A GI next to me hollered, 'Now I can go back to God's country—Flatbush!' "

* * *

Hope's career approached Mach one. His Pepsodent show held its number one position in the revered Hooper ratings. Lever Brothers, Pepsodent's parent company, signed him to a new ten-year contract at $10,000 per week. His total radio income, now estimated to be $1,000,000 per year, topped all others. By the fall of 1945, Paramount finally relented and permitted Bob Hope to form his own production company, Hope Enterprises, which enabled them to produce pictures in partnership. Hope Enterprises would later become the umbrella under which all of Hope's various ventures operated.

Producers and stars ever after owed Hope a debt of gratitude, just as they did James Garner, later on, for helping to break the studio system.

Paramount had been deluged with requests from moviegoers wanting to know when there would be another "Road" picture. According to Dorothy Lamour, the studio had received more than 75,000 letters demanding that the studio cast the trio again.

Paramount made all kinds of excuses as to why they couldn't get Hope, Lamour, and Crosby together at one time in order to do a proposed picture, *The Road Home*. The studio's excuses were only partly correct. Crosby and Lamour were available, but without Bob Hope, who was on suspension, there would be no audience. So *The Road Home* never materialized.

With the war over—between Hope and Paramount—Bob wanted to make a good picture when he returned to civilian life. *The Road to Utopia* awaited release after the first of the year, but behind that—nothing. It would be like starting all over again because Bob hadn't been before the cameras in almost two years.

In an effort to get Hope back in harness, Paramount could only come up with the remake of an old Valentino film from 1924, *Monsieur Beaucaire*. The producer didn't like the Panama and Frank script. A big argument ensued, involving the studio, Hope, two sets of writers, and the Writers Guild. Panama and

Frank prevailed, thanks to Bob Hope and George Marshall, who directed the "epic."

However, as sometimes happens, a funny script, good director, solid cast—and voilà—a hit film. Joan Caulfield and Bob Hope worked well together, as did all the actors, which included seasoned veterans Joseph Schildkraut, Patric Knowles, Cecil Kellaway and Reginald Owen.

Once the film wrapped, Hope seemed to become sullen and uncooperative. With his first picture in partnership with Paramount, he had something at stake, not previously on the table—his own money—a very important commodity to Bob Hope. Making it meant everything. Losing it was unthinkable.

The sneak preview at nearby Alhambra, California, left him doubtful. To Hope, the picture seemed flat in places, so he brought in comedy writer Frank Tashlin, who became a very successful writer/director at 20th Century Fox, to put together some new material.

"In the future," Bob declared, a Bob Hope picture will be letter perfect or it won't bear a Hope Enterprises label.

Despite anticipating a great career in producing, he would never abandon the boys and girls in uniform. Someone suggested to him that the war was over, so why not put his USO show in mothballs and get back to work?

Bob became very angry. "Look," he responded, "as long as there are servicemen and women somewhere out there keeping watch over America, I'm going to make damned certain they're entertained."

His radio show still originated from stateside bases. Arthur Marx quotes one of Hope's writers, Hal Goodman, on Hope, the military, and money:

"... He never gives anybody any money. He's one of the richest men in America, but he never gives anybody any money. He used to tell us writers, 'Crosby has more money than I have.' Well, Crosby never had as much money as Hope, because Hope worked at accumulating it. Crosby didn't ... You know why he never played Vegas ... he could have made $200,000 a week ... he didn't want money . . . he wanted them to buy his land in San Fernando Valley and give him land in Las Vegas in return . . . to trade up . . . not pay taxes . . . Vegas casino owners wouldn't go for that.''

As to entertaining the troops, Goodman continues:

". . . all those trips to play for the boys . . . the government paid for transportation, accommodations, etc., then he kept all the money that NBC gave him . . . so it didn't cost him anything, except the salaries of his cast . . . he made a huge profit . . . no overhead . . . he would end up with the special . . . the reruns, the film clips, the publicity, and all the other perks . . .''

Disgruntled writer? Or was it the truth regarding Hope's burgeoning financial empire and how it was acquired? Hope hired and fired writers as the checks payable to Hope Enterprises came more often in seven rather than six figures, all deposited to Hope "nest egg" accounts.

There is no law against making honest money any more than there is against being stupid . . . and no one has ever accused Bob Hope of being either dishonest or stupid. Some would say he is an opportunist who just happened to have made a lot of money by rolling up his sleeves and going to work when the opportunity arose.

Chapter 26

With the war over and his Paramount dispute settled, Bob had a chance to spend some time in Hollywood for the first time in years. Now, too, he had the opportunity to be with his children. He discovered that he really enjoyed being a family man. Dolores had kept the home fires burning while her vagabond husband signed on for the duration of the war. His presence in Toluca Lake became very much that of the war-weary soldier home from battle.

New Year's Day found Bob and Dolores leading the Rose Bowl Parade with Bob as Grand Marshal. On Pasadena's main street, Colorado Boulevard, one and a half million people watched the 58th Annual Tournament of Roses Parade pass into history.

Bob began 1946 the same way he always began a new year—determined to work harder and make more money than the year before. The new ten-year contract with Pepsodent raised his salary to $5,000 per half-hour segment.

January 2, 1946, found Bob on the job at Paramount Studios with Bing Crosby and Dorothy Lamour to begin filming *The Road to Rio*. Bing and Bob each had a one-third ownership in the picture, Paramount the other third. Lamour, cut out of the partnership, felt the sting of discrimination. The guys were ganging up on the girl—again. Ever the peacemaker, she made light of her situation. "I don't need all the hassle of being a producer," she said. Nobody believed that. Almost everyone knew that Bing and Bob had double-crossed her, but kept their mouths shut.

With the backlog of unreleased Hope films, *The Road to Rio* did not make it to the screen until 1948. In quick succession, Paramount released *Monsieur Beaucaire, Variety Girl,* and *My Favorite Brunette,* which co-starred Dorothy Lamour. It was a Hope Enterprises co-production with Paramount Pictures.

My Favorite Brunette received a full Hollywood premiere at the Los Angeles Paramount Theater with all proceeds allocated to the Damon Runyon Memorial Cancer Fund for Research. Television, in its commercial infancy, was just beginning to make inroads into American households. ABC's Pacific Coast network broadcast most of the premiere. Armed Forces Radio aired the festivities to the troops around the world, with Bob as emcee.

The entire Paramount "A" group showed up, as did dozens of other major celebrities, including Gene Kelly, Burns and Allen, the Andrews Sisters, Cary Grant, Edgar Bergen, Van Johnson, Frank Sinatra, Al Jolson, Jerry Colonna, Desi Arnaz, Betty Hutton, Dinah Shore, Jack Benny, Danny Kaye, Eddie Cantor, Jimmy Durante, Red Skelton, Benny Goodman and his sextette, and the Victor Young Orchestra.

Paramount hyped the film as Bob's funniest since his return to pictures, even arranging for Bob and Dorothy to record two songs from the film on Capitol Records, "My Favorite Brunette," backed by "Beside You," with popular singer Jo Stafford's husband, Paul Weston, conducting.

Crosby managed to intrude into Hope's picture. In the opening scene Bing plays the role of an executioner. Alan Ladd is a condemned man, already strapped into a chair in the state penitentiary's gas chamber when the governor issues a last minute stay of execution. From that point on, the picture became a Hope farce.

Variety Girl also premiered at the Los Angeles Paramount with all proceeds going to the Variety Club, an organization dedicated to kids. Hope and George Jessel were cohosts of the event and, again, every star from Paramount was in attendance with the exception of Betty Hutton who was busy having a baby. The event evolved into a slapstick fun fest, well covered by the media, with hundreds of fans seeking autographs.

On March 7, 1946, Bob Hope and James Stewart co-hosted the Academy Award ceremonies at Grauman's Chinese Theater. The night offered a first time event—the nominated songs had never been performed before.

As usual, Bing Crosby refused to appear at the awards, but other big name singers showed up to do their stuff: Frank Sinatra crooned "Aren't You Glad You're You?", "I Fall in Love too Easily," and "So in Love." Kathryn Grayson sang "Endlessly," "I'll Buy That Dream," "Linda," and "More and More." Dick Haymes performed "The Cat and the Canary," then "It Might As Well Be Spring" (from *State Fair,* in which he co-starred).

Dinah Shore wrapped up the warbling chores with "Sleighride in July," and "Some Sunday Morning." In the future, the awards would limit the number of songs performed by any one singer.

Jean Hersholt, by way of introducing Bob Hope, presented the comedian with a miniature Oscar. Hope took one look and quickly snapped, "I've heard of the *Look* Award, but this is the first time I ever knew the *Reader's Digest* was in this racket . . ."

Lost Weekend, the story of an alcoholic, for which Ray Milland won the Best Actor award, received a nod for Best Picture.

Joan Crawford, admitting she was "too frightened to show up because I'll just die if I lose—and I know I'll lose," stayed home feigning illness and expressed rehearsed surprise at winning Best Actress for her performance in *Mildred Pierce.* Crawford had no problem holding court in her bedroom once the awards were announced.

Although just another walk-through for the veteran Bob Hope, he couldn't exit without taking a dig at Crosby, who had been nominated for *The Bells of St. Mary's.* Referring to Crosby and Milland, he broke up the theater. "It's Four Roses against Old Grandad."

Bob had, over a very few years, accumulated a large encampment of "family" from Ohio. More and more he found himself dipping into his own funds to contribute to the welfare of relatives, but he didn't seem to mind. One writer complained that "Hope is robbing us to support these immigrants from Ohio." Along with his reputation as being very cheap with his writers, Hope also had it written into their contracts that once Hope had used the material no one else could ever use it again— not even the creator. The Writers Guild now protects writers in a much better fashion than when Hope was top banana in the comedy business.

The war ended and folks wanted to get away from thinking about guns and bombs and get on with the business of building toward the future. Even as people put the war behind them, eager to raise their families in the peace they'd fought to preserve, Hope continued to emphasize troop material in his radio scripts. Much to his surprise, he discovered that he had slipped in the ratings, finding his show in the number two slot behind Fibber McGee and Molly. Having been number one in radio for so long he couldn't imagine being anything else.

He promised the sponsors that he'd make changes in his format, but soon shelved that idea. By spring the Pepsodent show went back into first place anyway. People were buying Bob Hope, not formats.

His enormous financial outlay on family and investments caught him without enough cash to pay a whopping (for then) $62,000 tax bill. He took care of that minor matter, however, by pulling some rank in Washington for an extension. After all, he argued, "I did a hell of a lot for this country during the war and neglected to do anything for myself. I deserve a break." And he got it.

To rid himself of the tax bill, he proposed a personal appearance tour with a glitzy 40-person show. In Seattle a reporter for the *Post-Intelligencer* referred to Bob Hope as "a corporation."

Reporter Douglass Welch, after a confrontation with Louis Shurr who, refused to disclose any information on Bob's business ventures, wrote the following:

> "Wherever he goes, the whole board of directors ambles right along with him. They not only do all the things that the directors of any company normally do, but in addition they have been trained to laugh in the right places. 'Oh, that Hope! He kills us,' the directors say in chorus, laughing fit to kill and slapping their thighs. 'That's our boy over there making funnies. Yes, it is! That's our boy!' In public, Hope looks like a parade. Even when he goes to the gentlemen's retiring room he looks like a platoon. He is constantly surrounded with busy, worried, and preoccupied people, with briefcases, papers. and knitted brows."

It was the first time anyone had ever directly taken a potshot at Bob Hope on a personal level and he resented it.

He ran into some rather nasty business in Spokane which involved family—his black sheep older brother, James. Bob did not want to be upstaged by family. Jim and his wife, Wyn Swanson, were appearing at a theater in Spokane while Bob performed at a big stadium. For some reason, purposeful or otherwise, no one told Bob Hope that his brother had been booked into town concurrently.

Hope's brothers Jack, George, Sidney, Fred, and Ivor were all on Bob's payroll, either directly or through joint business ventures, mostly financed by Bob himself. But they were operating behind the scenes. When Bob found out about Jim and Wyn he blew a gasket. When a newspaper tried to get Bob and his older brother together for a photograph he told them to go to hell.

"He's got some nerve," Bob complained, "trying to compete with me."

During the tour Bob got a phone call from Fred advising him that his brother Sid was dying of cancer and wanted to see him. The United States Secretary of War, a guest in Hope's dressing room at the time, quickly arranged for a Navy plane to fly Bob to Ohio, where he would pick up his brother Fred in Columbus. Fred and Bob then motored to Sid's home in Ridgefield Corners, Ohio, where, after he visited his dying brother, another Navy plane was available to fly him out to do a show in Kansas City.

Bob Hope could request and receive that kind of service from the government whereas, with today's investigative mentality, the president of the United States must pay for personal trips in military aircraft. This all took place during the presidency of Harry S. Truman, a man who so respected his office that he purchased his own three-cent stamps for personal mail. Bob Hope had priority clout. Little wonder that he considered himself untouchable in the radio ratings.

Bob vowed to Sid that his wife and children would be provided for—that's all Sid wanted from his brother and felt Bob owed it to him. Bob agreed.

Hope's younger brother George explained Hope's indebtedness to Sid to Bob Slatzer. Sid owned some cottages, somewhat like a motel. He'd built a deluxe log cabin about four or five hundred feet away from the main cottages, set back from the road, surrounded by tall pine trees, sporting a small lake as well—very much like a Hollywood movie set—all for Bob's pleasure and comfort. Slatzer describes a typical scenario:

"Bob used to disappear from Hollywood, fly into Cleveland, and his brother Fred, who had the Ohio Provision Company—purveyors to hotels and country clubs— would pick Bob up and they'd drive down to Sid's where Bob would spend maybe a week driving golf balls out into the cornfields.

"Sid always covered for Bob when he imported girls from Hollywood to keep him company at the cabin. Bob never picked up his women on site. He always brought them in, eliminating any local scandals. So you see, Bob really was indebted to his younger brother."

The months in 1946 seemed to fly for the very busy Bob Hope. He made a flurry of quick films, none of serious consequence. In September his ninth season for Pepsodent got off to a rocky beginning with Carol Richards replacing Frances Langford and Desi Arnaz and his orchestra filling the Skinnay Ennis spot.

Bob took a beating in the trades as well as the dailies. *The Hollywood Reporter* ripped his show apart:

"Returning to NBC last night for the new season, Bob Hope was unable to overcome some of the worst material his show has ever been burdened with, and it's a safe bet that everybody connected with the offering will have heard from Charles Luckman at Lever Brothers by this time ... If this weren't the Hope show and if it were coming on the air for the first time, no reviewer in his right mind would give it more than thirteen weeks ..."

The Chicago Daily News headlined its review: TOOTH-PASTE BUT NO TEETH IN BOB HOPE'S OPENING SHOW.

From Hollywood to Chicago to New York, the story turned out to be pretty much the same. Even the *New York Times* turned against Hope:

"Bob Hope opened his ninth season on the air last Tuesday in the noble tradition of Jake Shubert's *The Student Prince*. You would enjoy it if you had not heard it the first, second, third, fourth, fifth, sixth, seventh, and eighth times. It was all there in this order: (1) Irium (2) Pallid

Patter (3) Irium (4) Joke about Bing Crosby (5) Jerry
Colonna arrives (6) Hope insults Colonna (7) Colonna
screams (8) Irium (9) Vera Vague arrives (10) Hope
insults Vera (11) Vera shrieks (12) Irium.''

The Hope ''brain trust'' could do little to squelch out-of-
town criticism. However, his clout in Hollywood meant that
he could do some manipulation with the trade papers and often
did.

Jane Gailbraith, while writing for *Daily Variety* in the late
1980s, wrote an honest but unflattering review of a Bob Hope
special.

Ms. Gailbraith had not been informed that editor Tom Pryor
had a rule that no disparaging remarks would be made about
the ''Pepsodent kid'' or his show. She presented her review in
Pryor's absence and it ran the following day.

A well-known press agent, Frank Lieberman, then employed
by any number of stars to make them look like gods in the
media, not only took issue with Ms. Gailbraith's review, but
personally paid a call on her at *Daily Variety*'s offices in Hollywood. When he finished his discussion with Jane he paid a
further visit to Tom Pryor, who, since the article appeared, had
returned from vacation. That very same day Jane presented
herself at her editor's office and, as she recalled the incident,
''. . . Pryor read me the riot act, and said that Hope employed
a lot of people and didn't deserve to be treated that way. He
was good for the business. And I retorted, 'Well, 20th Century-
Fox employs a lot more people, and you have no rules about
panning their product if it isn't any good.' ''

She was immediately transferred to a different beat where
she wouldn't be a fly in Bob Hope's ratings. A couple of days
later, *Variety* ran a full page of ''national reviews'' elevating
Bob Hope and his ''special'' to the status of stardom. Some
intelligent research on the part of Jane Gailbraith brought out
the fact that these were minor newspapers—one of which, *The
Chicago News,* did not even exist, nor did a certain reviewer
by the name of Sam Schwartz.

"Hope, or his publicity people," stated Gailbraith, "made up the whole thing."

The year did not end in a total bust for Hope and company. Dolores missed her mother and so, with some reservations on Bob's part, Theresa DeFina came to live with her daughter and son-in-law in California. Apparently Bob's success had caused his mother-in-law to overlook his non-Catholic status. By all reports, the two developed a fine mother and son relationship.

Theresa encouraged Bob and Dolores to adopt more children. She had been with them only a short time when they received a message from Mrs. Walrath notifying them that she'd found a baby girl, only two months old, whom she felt certain they'd love if they'd just come to Chicago and see her.

Bob and Dolores departed on the next available plane. As the Cradle's director had assured them, the baby girl fit the bill perfectly for a third addition to their growing family. While Bob and Dolores were oohing and cooing over their new child, Mrs. Walrath quickly introduced another baby into the equation—a three-month-old boy.

Love of children works strange miracles. The Hopes returned to Los Angeles the parents of four instead of the two they had when they'd departed.

Tony and Linda Hope's new siblings, sister Honora and brother Kelly, were quickly baptized in the font of St. Charles Borromeo Catholic Church only a few blocks from the Hope compound in Toluca Lake.

Bob returned to work and to the business of receiving more honors for his wartime devotion to the troops.

In October 1946 at a ceremony in San Francisco, the American Legion, in the presence of the legendary FBI Director, J. Edgar Hoover, Secretary of State Cordell Hull, and conscription czar General Hershey, presented Bob Hope the highest award the Legion had to offer: the Distinguished Service Medal.

He accepted the award with the promise that he would not stop entertaining the troops "until every hospitalized kid is on his feet again."

Later in the month, in Washington, D.C., he waited and listened as General Dwight D. Eisenhower, along with the top echelon of generals and admirals in the nation, lauded him and his efforts toward winning the war and then presented him with the highest civilian award given by the United States Government, the Medal of Merit.

Time magazine, in its November 18, 1946, issue, took on Bob Hope's financial empire and his ever-increasing compulsion to increase his vast worth.

> "Piqued by the small sale of *I Never Left Home,* Bob Hope has written another book. It is called *So This Is Peace,* and it deals, off the bottom of the deck, with Reconversion. . . . Published by the Hope Corporation."

The deal involved a three-way corporate parlay, according to *Time,* by which "Bob Hope expects to solve the No. 1 question of those in the million-a-year income bracket: how can they get around the enormous income taxes which would normally take all but $150,000 of that million?"

According to the article, Hope had, during the previous year, divided his numerous activities into a family of corporations: The Hope Corporation for books and Hope Records, Inc., for recordings, both of which were owned outright by Bob Hope. Hope Enterprises, on the other hand, boasted among its stockholders Bing Crosby and Director Leo McCarey (both of whom, along with Hope, were under contract to Paramount Pictures). This particular organization was tied to Hope's independent films and personal appearances for which he received compensation, often in the upper five figures.

As to *So This is Peace,* the Hope Corporation came up with $25,000 in front money in order to have the book printed, then financed the distribution through Simon and Schuster. *Time* magazine's figures revealed that even with *I Never Left Home* in print, the book made only $175,000. Hope donated the money to charity, which allowed him to deduct that amount under "charitable contributions" on his income tax return.

The magazine allowed that Hope should make a lot more on *So This Is Peace,* and "keep a big share of it."

In 1946 Hope grossed $500,000 in personal appearances and took in $10,000 a week from his radio broadcasts. It also was a year of speculative expense. More than a million dollars went into the production of *My Favorite Brunette.* Hope Records invested $25,000 on recordings of Hope's radio broadcasts (he owned them through certain contract clauses). In order to compete with Bing Crosby, who had bought into another baseball team, Hope invested in the Cleveland Indians. All of these ventures profited him personally and involved the personal income tax rate which, at the time, was extremely high. His corporate income bore a lower tax rate.

When asked if he intended to unload his corporations and pay only a 25% capital gains tax, Bob Hope had something to say. "We're not on the Big Board yet, but we're coming along. Pretty soon we ought to cut a lemon."

For all the criticism he'd received and continued to receive regarding the quality of his Pepsodent show, Hope had entertained more than 12,000,000 servicemen throughout the world. They were not just Americans, but men and women from all the Allied countries and, as Hope quipped, "I suspect a good many future Jap and German comedians are trying to steal my material."

Taking stock at the end of the year, Bob had many blessings for which he could be thankful: In Dolores he had the kind of wife of which most men merely dream—a woman of perseverance, tolerance, and understanding. He also now had four lovely children, two boys and two girls, a gorgeous home, a golf course and country club at his doorstep, and a career that produced money like the U.S. Mint. What more could he possibly want?

Asked that very question by Mike Connolly of the *Hollywood Reporter,* Hope, without so much as blinking an eyelid, responded, "I'll think of something."

GOODBYE TOOTHPASTE HELLO BERLIN

Chapter 27

Bob Hope and NBC nearly came to blows in April of 1947 because of radio censors. Just prior to that, however, Bob had his first real experience in television. Paramount Pictures opened up a small television facility on Melrose Avenue in Hollywood, adjacent to its film factory.

Bob Hope didn't think much of television in the beginning. The Paramount executives had other ideas. They knew of Bob's reluctance to chance both radio and motion pictures, and he had been wrong in his original assessment in both instances. The decision-makers at the studio saw Bob Hope as a natural in television. To bring this man into American living rooms would be to combine the Hope's voice from radio and his persona from motion pictures. Still, they didn't want television to diminish his movie appeal. Caught between an old tradition and an upstart new kid on the block, Paramount wanted to approach television cautiously.

The big studio decided on an experimental program sponsored by the Ford Motor Company's Lincoln Division. Many of the studio's major stars were assembled for the program, which Bob Hope emceed from a Mel Shavelson script.

Bob didn't want to do it, but his bosses at Paramount

insisted—as did his agent—that it wouldn't hurt to test the waters of the new entertainment medium. Bob told one of his writers, "It may be a new medium, but it's gonna get old pretty quick." He liked his image up on the big screen in movie houses. He couldn't envision millions of viewers, sitting at home watching a screen no bigger than a sheet of notebook paper, being entertained for any length of time.

"It's a bore and a bust," he declared.

During rehearsals he got no laughs and couldn't understand why. He complained to Shavelson. Mel told him, "Bob, it's the script. On television you can't be seen reading a script. It's like films—very visual."

"Yes, but in films I can blow a line and do a retake. What happens when I screw up and everybody sees it?"

"You'll have to learn to memorize your lines. That's what."

Shavelson had him throw away the script and later declared it to be "the biggest clambake of all time."

Bob opened the show this way:

"This is Bob 'First Commercial Television Broadcast' Hope telling you gals who have tuned me in—and I wanna make this emphatic—if my face isn't handsome and debonaire, it isn't me—it's the static . . .

"Here it is, 1947, and we're holding the first commercial television broadcast in the West. 'Commercial'—what a lovely word! Up 'til tonight I looked on television as something I might dabble in for a night or so . . . a week . . . maybe a month. But now it's gone commercial—meet the Yearling . . .

"Everybody wants me to go on television. I know they do. Anytime I hear somebody discuss my radio program, they always say 'I never could see that guy . . .' "

After the show he dismissed it as just another one-time gimmick. "What actor is going to give up his golf game to study a script?" He still had no idea what an important role he would play in helping to make television the entertainment of choice in millions of homes, bars and other places where people assembled.

Only a few days later another hassle with radio censors began. It started, innocently enough, with Fred Allen, one of Hope's perennial competitors on radio. Allen never cottoned to Hope's mild humor. He had one of the sharpest, most acerbic tongues in the business. David Sarnoff, who liked to be referred to as "Dr. Sarnoff," stood like a titan as head of NBC. Sarnoff strictly forbade any employee to speak disparagingly of NBC executives on the air.

Whether to intentionally flout authority or just poke fun at pompous network vice presidents, Allen referred to an unnamed NBC vice president as being "in charge of making molehills out of mountains."

Pipe organ music filled the airways as censors bleeped Allen off the air. A number of entertainers found it offensive that NBC had taken such action but did not have the fortitude to voice their objections.

Bob Hope had no such compunctions. A couple of weeks later, on his Tuesday night show, Hope's show went silent for several seconds as he began a defense of Allen. "If Allen's gag had been in poor taste or blue, I could see it . . ." Wham! Fade to silence. What his audience didn't hear, as he continued before the studio assemblage, was, "You know, in Las Vegas you get tanned and faded at the same time. Of course, Fred Allen can get faded any time . . ."

A succession of cut-offs followed as comedians, one after another, followed Hope's lead. Red Skelton, commenting on the NBC censorship of Allen, found himself axed for several seconds. The Gods of Radio atop Mount NBC were not amused.

A couple of broadcasts later, Hope had the audacity to tell his guest, Frank Sinatra, that he'd be joining him the next night on Frank's show (on CBS). It was taboo throughout radio for an entertainer to plug another network. During rehearsals he'd actually used "CBS." The network censors were so sure that he would do it again during the live broadcast that they cut him off at that point in the script—the second time they'd cut off the "king of radio comedians."

NBC, flooded with mail from outraged Bob Hope fans, issued a statement of apology about the Allen incident and as compensation made Allen, Hope, and Skelton "honorary vice presidents." Every comedian in the business began to take on network vice presidents in their monologues and continue to do so today. It all began when Bob Hope stood up for a fellow entertainer, knowing the old rule that if they do it to you today, they'll do it to me tomorrow—and they did. Sarnoff quickly learned the meaning of "backfire."

Just to make sure the network understood and would never again take on its top moneymaker, Bob Hope hosted a radio special sponsored by the Walgreen Drugstore chain. He did a skit with Groucho Marx, written by Manny Manheim and Charlie Isaacs, both well-known radio comedy writers.

Arthur Marx writes that according to Manheim and Isaacs, "It had barely started when it turned into a battle of off-color ad-libs between Groucho and Hope—some so off-color that much of the funniest material had to be edited out of the final transcription before it ever reached the radio listeners' ears."

The studio audience, however, got an earful as the scene opened with Bob, operating a small radio station in the desert, answering Groucho's knock on the door:

HOPE: Why, Groucho Marx! What are you doing out here in the desert?

GROUCHO: (ad-lib) Desert, hell! I've been sitting in the dressing room for forty minutes.

(BIG LAUGH)

HOPE: Seriously, Grouch.

GROUCHO: Seriously. I've been selling mink coats. Or selling mink coats seriously . . . Now here's a beauty for only forty dollars.

HOPE: Mink coats for only forty dollars! How can you sell them so cheap?

GROUCHO: I have no overhead . . . I don't advertise . . . I don't pay rent. And I steal the coats.

HOPE: Groucho, I know you don't steal those coats. Where do you get 'em?

GROUCHO: Very simple. I trap them with my big musical trap. I walk out into the woods and play seductive music on my zither. The little animals hear the music . . . do a striptease, and take off their furs.

HOPE: (ad-lib) Did I ever tell you about the two vultures who were plucking each other?

GROUCHO: (ad-lib) Well, it's hard to do without two.

(AUDIENCE GOES WILD AFTER HEARING
GROUCHO'S DOUBLE ENTENDRE)

HOPE: (also ad-lib, to the technicians in the booth) You can start editing the record now, fellas.

(BIG LAUGH)

. . . Oh, would we be faded!

GROUCHO: That'll be the biggest crap game in history.

(HOPE BREAKS UP WITH AUDIENCE, LOSES HIS
PLACE) I think it's your turn.

HOPE: I think so.

GROUCHO: Or do you want to quit right now? (*throws script down*)

HOPE: (ad-lib) I'm never going to feed you another line again.

GROUCHO: (ad-lib) Did I ever tell you about the two vultures who were plucking each other?

HOPE: You know we have a hook-up with Lea Frances (Hollywood's notorious madame).

GROUCHO: I'd like nothing better than to be hooked up with Lea Frances.

HOPE: (back to the script) But, Groucho, I don't need a mink coat. I'm an etching man myself.

GROUCHO: (picking up his script from the floor, blows something off it) You know this radio station has termites. You ought to send for an exterminator to get rid of them.

HOPE: If we don't get back into the script, Walgreen will get rid of us.

GROUCHO: Of course. Give me your last line again.

HOPE: I don't need a mink coat . . . I'm an etching man myself.

GROUCHO: Well, if you wear one of my mink coats you'll be etching.

(BIG LAUGH)

. . . Well, we can cut that, too, I guess.

HOPE: No . . .

GROUCHO: I fear the girls will be too warm in my mink coats out here in the desert.

HOPE: I always find the girls are warm when you promise them the coats. Once they get it on they cool off.

GROUCHO: Not these coats, Bob. These coats are all hot.

HOPE: I get it.

GROUCHO: This is some radio station here. What watts?

HOPE: What . . . what . . . what?

GROUCHO: Now look . . . you're not going to suck me into an Abbott and Costello routine . . . with me playing Abbott. Now, why have you got this place hidden out in the desert? I started out here last night trying to find it and it was like looking for a needle in a haystack.

HOPE: Well, where did you stay last night?

GROUCHO: In a haystack.

HOPE: Was it comfortable?

GROUCHO: No, I kept sitting on the needle. I found out one thing . . . a needle always points north.

After the show, John Guedel (creator and producer of "People Are Funny", starring Art Linkletter), approached Groucho and said, "Groucho, I think I know why you've been a failure on radio up until now."

"Yes!" growled Groucho, challenging the intruder.

"Yes. Up until now you've been restricted to doing script shows. What you do best, I'm convinced after tonight, is ad-lib. If I can come up with a show where you can use your ad-lib talent, would you be interested?"

And thus was born "You Bet Your Life," Groucho's radio/television show that ran two years on radio and another twelve years on the living room box. Groucho's ad-libs—most of which have never been aired—would play perfectly on cable today.

Bob tempted the censors on more than one occasion. During one of his Pepsodent shows he had Dorothy Lamour as a guest. In one scene he and Dorothy were to meet for a lover's tryst.

DOROTHY: I'll meet you in front of the pawnshop.
(Bob was supposed to reply "okay," but changed his mind.)
BOB: Okay, Dottie, and then you can kiss me under the balls.

Bob and Dorothy did another skit which caused eyebrows to lift and organs to pipe:

DOROTHY: Don't take me seriously, Bob. I was just pulling your leg.
BOB: (ad-libbing) Listen, Dottie, you can pull my right leg, and you can pull my left leg—but don't mess with Mr. In-Between.

NBC censors were livid, while the audience laughed so hard they rolled in the aisle. The following week the media had a field day at NBC's expense—sort of. Although the executives claimed to deplore the adverse publicity, they well knew that the ratings would shoot through the roof the following Tuesday.

During the summer of 1947 Bob took time away from personal appearances and radio broadcasts to take Dolores and the children on a two-week vacation to South America before launching a new film.

His former partner, Honey Chile Wilder, had married a wealthy Argentinian, Albert Cernadas. They lived in Monteviedo on a palatial estate and insisted that Bob and his family be their guests while in the Argentine. Unbeknownst to the Hopes, the Cernadas were conveniently in Europe enjoying their own vacation. It was widely assumed that the hot-blooded Latin, suspicious of what might have once been between Bob and Honey Chile, had swooped up his blond wife and removed her from the presence of "that North American Lothario."

After two weeks of touring, Bob, Dolores, Tony, and Linda

returned to the United States on a cruise ship. Bob overstayed his visits on the sundeck and sustained a sunburn so severe that it nearly turned into blood-poisoning. His face and legs were so burned that he ended up spending two days in a Chicago hospital after being removed from the Twentieth Century Limited en route to Los Angeles, where he was to begin work on a new picture with Jane Russell. The shooting schedule on *The Paleface* was delayed for a week while Bob recovered.

Howard Hughes boosted Russell's career through a wire mechanism to lift her breasts to overflowing for the super-hyped film *The Outlaw,* loosely based on the life of Billy the Kid. The mechanical fixture, modified, became known as the "uplift bra" that turned thousands of 32-inch busts into spectacular sights. Jane and Bob were naturals together. Bob's character as a correspondence course dentist, inept and bumbling, quickly succumbs to the obvious charms of Miss Russell.

Although *The Paleface* had little plot and even less acting, it nevertheless became Bob's biggest moneymaking film up to that time. "Buttons and Bows," the Livingston and Evans novelty love song he sang to Jane in the film, received a nomination for and won the Oscar as the best song from a motion picture at the Oscar awards the following spring. Whatever one thought of Hope's pictures, the songs were always Hit Parade material and often nominated for awards and, as in this instance, occasionally won them. Dinah Shore's single of "Buttons and Bows," (recorded on the last afternoon before the powerful James Petrillo, head of the musicians' union, pulled his members out of the recording studios), became one of her greatest hits, selling in the millions.

NBC converted the El Capitan theater on Vine Street into a showcase for Bob's radio show. It provided ample seating for the live audience he enjoyed. There were also other amenities to satisfy the king of comedy.

His first broadcast of the new season emanated from the El Capitan in late September to mixed reviews. *Variety* printed what most critics thought:

"Here's the epitome of radio's 'sad saga of sameness.' Apparently it's just too much to expect that Hope would veer an inch from his time-tested routine. His answer, it goes without saying, is: Why get out of the rut as long as there's pay dirt in it? And top pay dirt at that! By Hooper's count, too, Hope seems to be justified. His routine is apparently one of the things we fought the war for, like Ma's apple pie. Question simply is: who's going to outlive the other, Hope or the listening public?''

The London Times critic deigned to be kinder to England's self-exiled son in his review of *The Paleface:*

"Mr. Hope riots through the coloured West in the dangerous company of Miss Jane Russell . . . Mr. Hope is not one of those comedians who can rise above their material by the sheer force of genius and personality. No man is more perfect in his timing, more assured in his technique, more certain to squeeze the last virtue from a line, but he remains in the last analysis at the mercy of the 'gags' and situations with which he is supplied.''

Bob's friends, Paramount studio, Lever Brothers, and the NBC radio network executives had all been telling him to update his material. They were especially concerned that he seemed to behave like a little boy trying to get away with something. For instance, time and again his material had to be blue-lined because of the nature of his gags. If he found a way to slip in sexual innuendos, he did so—often before the censors could bleep them out.

He broadcast his first show from his new surroundings—surroundings remodeled to his taste—and almost immediately announced that he was taking his show back on the road. His decision infuriated the sponsors, who were not interested in laying out all the additional money required for a road show.

Additional rumors were spreading that Bob wanted to dump Lever Brothers to sign with Kraft Foods and the American

Broadcasting Company in a ploy that would pit him against Bing Crosby in the same time slot on a different network. Hope had nothing against the advertising agency that put him together with Lever Brothers. They could find him another sponsor and Kraft Foods would be just as good as any other. For some reason he turned sour on the Pepsodent executives, who always seemed to find something wrong with his show. Either it was too slanted toward a military no longer at war or so blue it caused their faces to turn red.

His worried friends and business associates continued monitoring his behavior. He normally snapped at his writers, but he began to find fault where there was none. Dolores, concerned about his health, urged him to have a physical checkup. He promised to do that.

On November 2 the Friars Club held a roast in his honor. He looked forward to that because those events were often real hell-raisers and what happened or was said remained behind closed doors.

Jack Benny, Georgie Jessel, Lou Holtz, Al Jolson, George Burns, and Danny Kaye gave him the going-over of his life. Nobody, however, could have stung him more than Bing Crosby, who refused to attend. His empty chair did more to demean Hope than all the barbs delivered from the podium.

For years members of the Friar's Club have told the story of the night Bing Crosby proved he wasn't anybody's friend— and certainly not Bob Hope's. Pressed by a reporter to comment on the snubbing of his good friend, Crosby flew into a rage. "My friendship for Bob," he said, his words clipped and sharp, "doesn't depend on appearing at testimonials."

The Shurr office knew why he hadn't bothered to honor his "friend." Al Melnick had begged him to come, even if he had to leave early, just to show Bob some respect. Crosby didn't just stand Hope up. Anyone who had cared to stop by Chasen's that night would have found Bing and a cute young actress upstairs in the celebrity room of the popular restaurant, while his wife, Dixie Lee, waited at home for him to return from the Hope roast.

England loved Bob Hope. When King George VI and Queen

Elizabeth invited him to attend the wedding of their eldest
daughter Elizabeth's wedding to Philip Mountbatten, and to
emcee a private Command Performance, it lifted his spirits. He
was so excited he threw a fabulous party aboard the *Queen
Mary* before sailing off to the land of his forefathers.

However, he left under a cloud. Lever Brothers, as obstinate
as their star, threatened to move his show from Tuesday evening
to a less desirable time. Covering all bases in case Lever Brothers actually carried through with their threats, Jimmy Saphier
began to sound out other potential sponsors. Everybody knew
and loved Bob Hope. Pepsodent could go to hell!

The Hopes had a fine time in London, enjoying the pageantry
of a royal wedding, the reception, the Command Performance,
and private moments with the Royal Family. Bob presented
Princess Margaret with an album of autographed celebrity photos, serrated around the edges like postage stamps. As he pointed
out some of the stars in the album, King George leaned over
his daughter's shoulder and pointed as Hope flipped through
the pages. "Look," said the King, "he's hurrying to get to his
own picture."

"Why not?" Hope quickly responded. "He's the prettiest."

The King asked, "Is Bing's autograph there, too?"

"Yes," quipped Hope, "but he doesn't write. He just makes
three x's."

"Why three?" The King asked.

"He had a middle name, of course," replied Bob.

The following day he had a long conversation with Secretary
of State George C. Marshall, who mentioned that with the war
over, the occupation troops seemed to have been forgotten.

Almost immediately Hope, Dolores, and a quick assemblage
of performers were entertaining the troops in West Germany,
much to the delight of the surprised servicemen and women.

He lost his voice toward the end of his whirlwind tour and
returned to London. Dolores and the Hope children were sent
home on the *Queen Mary* while Bob and three of his writers
flew back to New York.

During a change of planes in Shannon, Ireland, Hope
observed former First Lady Eleanor Roosevelt waiting to board

the plane that would bring Hope and his group back to New York.

Like a little boy, Bob tugged at the sleeve of one of his writers. "Go tell Mrs. Roosevelt I'd like to meet her."

"Why don't you go over and tell her yourself? I'm sure she remembers you from the Victory Caravan."

"I doubt it. She met so many stars. Now go do as I've told you. Tell her I'd like to meet her."

The First Lady beamed her delight. "Ohhh, Mr. Hope is one of the few comedians I don't mind meeting."

Upon his arrival in New York, Hope had to face the problems with Lever Brothers. During lunch with Charles Luckman, Bob promised to remain with Lever Brothers, but that didn't settle his differences with the Pepsodent branch of the worldwide corporation.

He surprised Dolores and the children by meeting them when the *Queen Mary* docked in New York. They returned to the West Coast together where Bob, looking tired and worn, kept his promise to Dolores. Dr. Tom Hearn gave Bob a thorough physical examination and warned him that he would have to cut back on his activities. "No man," he cautioned, "can continue at your pace without serious, even dire, consequences."

Bob immediately plunged into his next film, *Sorrowful Jones,* opposite Lucille Ball—one of his truly best friends. Lucille did not compete with Hope. She didn't have to. An institution in her own right, she had great respect for Hope and their work together meshed like magic.

At a press conference Hope went to great lengths to discuss the forthcoming movie and how much he looked forward to working with Lucy. However, the media wanted his impressions of the world's condition in the post-war era. He had, after all, traveled the world and had recently met with the Secretary of State. What did he think?

When the papers hit the streets the following day, *Sorrowful Jones* had become a footnote. Bob Hope the diplomat and authority on foreign affairs carried the day.

Despite prudes and jealous competitors, Bob Hope maintained his number-one rating in the hearts of his fans, who numbered in the millions, not only in the United States, but around the world.

Hope ended 1947 pretty much as the country did—tired and worn out from the Depression followed by a war that ravaged the world, but ready to take a deep breath and continue on the road to recovery.

Chapter 28

Honoring his commitment, Hope stayed with Lever Brothers but ceased advising his audience to brush with Pepsodent. In 1948 he asked them to lather up with Swan Soap—another of the British-owned Lever Brothers' products. Nonetheless, his future and popularity in radio were diminished due to the American public's ever-increasing interest in television.

As much as Broadway and radio fought Hollywood, all three united to withstand the invasion of television. A number of radio's most important stars made the transition to television—usually to their good fortune. Radio suffered the loss. During the late forties, radio began to segue into music, news, and commentary while the more popular dramatic shows merely made the move from "on air" to "live TV."

What Hope had refused to do for Pepsodent, he readily agreed to do for Swan. In September his new show debuted with some major cast changes as well as a revamped format. He went in more for political jokes, with much less military emphasis. Frances Langford left the show, replaced by Doris Day, "the girl next door" who had vaulted to popularity during the war thanks to her popular recording of "Sentimental Journey" while she was singing with Les Brown.

Doris, just beginning her screen career, had completed her first motion picture for Warner Brothers, *Romance on the High Seas,* in which the studio capitalized on her hit single, "It's Magic."

Doris, the exact opposite of Hope's previous girl singers, was very shy and hated performing before live audiences. She loved the recording studio because the only people around were the professionals she needed and respected. Also, Doris valued truth and honesty. It disgusted her to listen to the brownnosers who surrounded Hope, agreeing with his every word.

She immediately saw through Bob and his need to be praised. In her brutally honest autobiography, *Her Own Story,* Doris recalled the difficulties she had working with Bob:

"In between my first and second pictures at Warners, I put in a couple of tours of duty as a member of Bob Hope's concert and radio troupe ... Over a six-week period, the concert tour took us ... to a different city every night—and sometimes, when we played a matinee, to two cities in a single day. This was the winter of 1948 and we often flew through storms and turbulence that had me praying more than once ... An hour later I'd have to go out on the stage of whatever mammoth auditorium we were playing with my pipes in good condition and my personality bubbling ... By the time I finished my second fifteen-thousand-mile concert tour with Bob, I had developed a chronic fear of flying that haunts me to this day. ..."

She recalls their weekly radio show out of Hollywood and her aversion to live radio. After each broadcast, Bob's staff would circle around him and tell him what a dynamite show it was; but she knew that some of those shows were quite awful. "I couldn't believe that Bob, wise about show business as he is, didn't know it—but I guess it was easier for him to defer his judgment to the uncritical accolades of his aides."

Bob also dropped Jerry Colonna and Vera Vague from the

new show. He hired a few quality writers and got rid of the dozen or so he considered inferior. One of those new writers, Larry Gelbart (who truly stands tall among comedy writers), seemed to have a somewhat soothing effect on the Hope ego. Larry, honest to the core, would tell Bob when he felt something didn't work.

He learned that one kept his mouth shut about Bob's "other women," who included Marilyn Maxwell and Barbara Payton. Arthur Marx queried Gelbart about the open secret of Hope's dalliances: "I don't think any one of us was ever asked to perpetuate the faithful husband myth, but I think people were loath to puncture it. You figure the press has been looking the other way for years, so you say to yourself, 'Why should I be the one to blow the whistle on him?' Meanwhile he fooled around with anyone he could who was young and nubile who guest starred on the show."

Dagmar, famous for her hair and her breasts, led the parade of "guest stars."

Hope resented the untouchability of Doris Day, who, although married to Marty Melcher—not the most faithful of husbands—did not fall victim to Hope's enormous ego and sexual prowess. In retaliation, Hope referred to her as "Jut-Butt," a derogatory reference to her well-rounded bottom. Doris laughed it off but it could not have failed to hurt the very talented, extremely shy singer.

Milton Berle became a fly in Hope's radio "snake oil." Berle picked Tuesday, September 14, 1948, to inaugurate his television career—opposite the Hope Swan Soap Show. Bob did not find Berle's decision palatable, but tried to brush it aside as just another one of Berle's tricks.

Uncle Miltie knew exactly why he chose that particular time slot. Tuesday night had been known as "comedy night" on radio for many years. So why not take advantage of the publicity by taking on the competition—live—in living black and white? And it worked. The media loved the interplay between the two comedians.

When the Associated Press reporter Bob Thomas, one of the more reliable celebrity biographers, paid a visit to Bob's home to inquire about his being upstaged by Berle, Hope shrugged it off. As a matter of fact, he confided, "Hope Enterprises is already working on a few video ideas . . . including a new show for me."

He decried any thought of a weekly show, declaring that "people could get tired of you that often." He worried that when an audience could see his performance, he wouldn't be able to get away with the sound gags. He worried about having to "remember all those lines," a problem which would eventually be solved through the use of cue cards.

Hope reserved some of his sharpest barbs for Berle. "He's doing both a radio show and the Tuesday night television show for Texaco. And I understand he took a sizable cut in pay to do television. He must be nuts . . . They tell me that Berle's entire budget for the Texaco show is $15,000. Is he working for free?"

Thomas touched a seemingly sore spot when he asked Bob if it was true that General Motors wanted to star him in a television show. "That's right," he snapped, "but I don't have any time."

Asked if his sponsor, the network, or Paramount were putting the screws on him, Hope sputtered a few words and finally declared, ". . . I'm free to do anything I want! . . ."

President Harry Truman's upset victory over the odds-on favorite, Republican candidate Thomas E. Dewey, provided Bob Hope with plenty of political jokes during the winter of 1948-49. Truman loved Hope's take-offs—even when he wore the goat horns. Hope showed his thanks to the president upon his re-election by sending a telegram which read: "UNPACK."

The Tuesday following the 1948 presidential election, Hope went on the air with the following comment:

> ". . . Yessir, the Democrats did so well in that election, they're even coming out with a few new products named after the president . . . they've got a thing called the 'Harry Truman Popsicle' . . . It's a frozen Republican on a stick . . ."

During the period from April 1 to July 1, 1948, the Soviet Union sealed off all entrances to Berlin, attempting to force the other three allies—France, England, and the United States—out of the city. In order to provide food and fuel to the beleaguered city, President Truman (in conjunction with our allies) inaugurated the Berlin Airlift, dubbed "Operation Vittles," the most ambitious effort of its kind in history.

Secretary of the Air Force Stuart Symington, at the request of President Truman, asked Bob to take a group of stars to Germany during the Christmas season to lift the morale of the U.S. Airmen involved in the round-the-clock airlift. Hope quickly agreed, giving up his and Dolores's plans to take the family to Lake Tahoe for the holidays. Hope would celebrate Christmas in December with the troops for many, many more years, celebrating the holidays with his family on New Year's Day at the family estate.

Bob Hope was no fool; he saw the commercial value of doing his radio show live from Berlin. It would certainly detract from the Berle television show. Through Symington, he arranged to do just that, again demonstrating the perks available to those on the "in" side of the political lay of the land.

Loaded up with celebrities from Hollywood and Washington, Hope departed for Europe. The Truman administration provided Vice President Alben Barkley and General Jimmy Doolittle, who had engineered the famous B-25 raid over Tokyo in World War II. Hope recruited Jinx Falkenburg and husband Tex McCrary, songwriter Irving Berlin, a bevy of Radio City Music Hall Rockettes, network news commentator Elmer Davis, and all the cast and crew of the Swan Soap Show with the exception of Doris Day, who respectfully declined—not wanting to travel across the ocean by plane. Singer Jane Harvey replaced Doris along with guitarist Tony Romano, who would become a regular with Hope. Dolores went along, but the children remained at home.

Secretary Symington and all of Hope's yes-men accompanied the comedian aboard the Constellation set aside for Symington's personal use.

During Hope's Christmas tour of Air Force facilities in England and Germany, I happened to be on duty as an air traffic controller at Celle, a small town near Hannover where the Americans operated an airlift from the British Occupied Zone of Germany. The USAF flew C-47 and C-54 cargo planes, stripped of all but bare essentials, back and forth between Celle AFB and one of the three airports in Berlin controlled by the American, French, and British occupation forces—usually Templehof Airport inside the American Zone of the divided city.

Celle seemed always to be overcast and more often than not during the winter of 1948-49 the planes took off and landed in near-zero visibility. The planes, coming and going, were supposed to be stacked at 500-foot intervals. During severe weather conditions, those intervals were sometimes lowered to 200-300 feet, stacked as high as oxygen would allow. The potatoes and coal went out on schedule, regardless of the weather. The planes went out loaded, returning empty from Berlin. Landing and take-off intervals were very risky. As one plane rose into the air outbound for Berlin, another touched down at the other end of the runway on the return trip.

It was tricky business. Bob Hope had priority clearances on his Christmas trip. Hope and some of his biographers have claimed that the Russians tried to shoot down American planes. One can only imagine what an international crisis that would have precipitated. During my stay in Germany, until the blockade was lifted in 1949, I never heard of such an incident. Planes crashed all the time—usually overshooting or undershooting the runway on landings or failing to lift off at the end of the runway due to overloading. The pilots and crews of those planes were heroes.

Bob Hope did not mix with the enlisted men at Celle. The closest we got to him was seeing his show on stage—and we all loved it. During World War II and the Berlin Airlift, I saw Bob Hope at Air Force bases five or six times. His shows were topical. His scouts prepared dossiers on the local nightclubs, bars, and hooker hangouts. This information was cleverly woven into his gags and monologues by his writers. Every airman felt that Hope had actually been to these places. His jokes at March Field, Victorville AFB, Wiesbaden, Celle, and Berlin were the same—merely adapted to the local scene.

Guys would sit around in the PX after a Hope show and compare notes from Hope visits at other bases in previous years. The material never changed, but he represented home and we ate it up.

He socialized with the brass in their homes and officers' clubs. If, by chance, someone persuaded him to visit an enlisted men's club, he brought along photographers to make sure it was well documented.

In Berlin he did his show for the men at the Tatania Palast Theater. Then he and Dolores joined General Lucius Clay, the Allied Commander in Europe, for a big Christmas party in Bob's honor. The Secretary of War, Secretary of the Air Force, U.S. Ambassador to the Soviet Union, Irving Berlin, and all their wives joined in the festivities.

He assured his sponsor of several million more listeners by doing his regular Tuesday night show from Berlin with this opening:

> "This is Bob—here in Berlin to entertain the men in the airlift—Hope saying I'm here with Swan Soap in lots ..."

When the Clay party broke up, someone reminded Hope that he had promised an enlisted man, an Armed Forces Radio Sgt. Kelso, that he'd try to stop in for a few minutes. By the time he showed up, only the men on the overnight shift were listening to AFRS.

Actress Constance Bennett's husband, General Coulter, commanded the American Forces at Celle. Once again Hope was wined and dined by the VIP reception committee—not the enlisted men.

Yet, to his credit, he never failed to spend Christmas with the troops wherever they were stationed around the world until his health, his doctor, and his wife finally grounded him twenty-four years later.

Rating high with the troops, the Bob Hope Show did not

fare so well with radio audiences. He began 1949 trailing Jack Benny, Fred Allen, Edgar Bergen, and Fibber McGee and Molly in the ratings. Milton Berle dominated television on Tuesday nights, also drawing from Hope's audience.

Still disgruntled with Milton Berle for daring to slot himself opposite him on Tuesday nights, Hope made numerous derogatory comments about Berle. He threw darts at Milton, disguised as jokes. "Berle," he complained, "memorized an entire one-hour television show every week and loused it up for all the rest of us . . . Uncle Miltie became 'Mr. Television.' "

He went on to add that, " . . . while Milton Berle was Mr. Television, there were only about twelve television sets in the U.S. that worked, and they cost so much that the guys who owned them couldn't afford to go to the movies."

Motion picture producers and studio heads worried about "Uncle Miltie" and that "damned tube!" Network radio executives fingered worry beads and wrung their hands in tandem with the big Hollywood studios. When Bob Hope mentioned television to his bosses at Paramount Pictures, they nearly had apoplexy. Radio had a lot more to worry about. It wouldn't be long before someone in the motion picture industry would see the value of selling off their backlog of motion pictures to television for hefty profits.

That idea would eventually bring about one of the biggest lawsuits in motion picture history when the unions representing actors, writers, and directors took the studios to court for a "residual" every time their pictures were shown on television. Radio had no such option. Radio could not be seen on television.

Bob tested the television waters in 1949 by appearing on "The Ed Sullivan Show" on CBS. He thought he'd made the biggest mistake of his life. "I can tell you," he said, "that I got hate letters from motion picture exhibitors from every state in the union." Television, like anything new, threatened movie theaters. They detested Ed Sullivan and Milton Berle because they represented the strongest competition ever to hit the film industry.

Of course, we think it is silly today. Despite almost every home having one or more television sets, there are more motion picture screens and more movies making more money than ever. Television thrives—and radio makes more money than it did when it ruled the airwaves, only they make it by other methods: political talk, news, advice—and music.

When tape recorders were introduced, the record industry went berserk, then converted to tape and made more money than ever. When CD's were introduced, the cassette manufacturers went ballistic. Cassette sales went sky high when enterprising manufacturers brought out a line of combination CD/Tape Decks which allowed the taping of CD's—and so it has always gone.

NBC's Niles Trammel warned Bob Hope, "Television is just a baby. We'll call you when it needs changing." Hope realized that, "If the network is so worried about television, maybe there is something to it."

During the summer of 1949, Bob went into a joint oil venture with Bing Crosby, each putting up $50,000. The first hole drilled spouted enough water to turn West Texas into an oasis. Hope, feeling the pinch of losing fifty grand, resisted when Crosby started working on him to match another $50,000. "I let him talk me into it—against my better judgment," Hope later confessed. This time Crosby's intuition did better. The second hole brought in a gusher worth seven million dollars to be split between the two golfers.

At the same time, *The Paleface* was being praised by some critics as his funniest film to date. It also filled up the theater seats and box-office tills to the tune of seven million.

One of Hope's most severe critics, Bosley Crowther of the *New York Times,* failed to find anything he liked in *The Paleface:*

"If the new Bob Hope picture, *The Paleface* goes down in history books as a memorable item, it will not be because it stands forth as a triumph of comic art. Even with Mr. Hope in it, having great fun pretending to be an itinerant chicken-livered dentist in perilous Indian country in the old Wild West, this new picture is just a second string 'road' show at best, conspicuously lacking the presence of Bing Crosby and Dorothy Lamour . . .

"Neither is it worthy of historical note because of the fact that it generously offers Jane Russell, star of *The Outlaw,* a chance to reform. Miss Russell, while blessed by nature with certain well-advertised charms, appears to be lacking completely even a modest ability to act."

A 36-city tour starting in the South, then moving up into New England and back to the West Coast, made Bob $700,000 richer. Bill Faith figured his take at $11,000 a day.

His next picture for Paramount, *Fancy Pants,* which costarred Lucille Ball, did not go before the cameras until after the spring thaw. Hope decided to use that time to do another whirlwind tour, covering fifteen states in sixteen days.

Hope did not know how to ride a horse and the script of *Fancy Pants* required that he do just that. Lucille Ball was supposed to be teaching him how to ride a bucking bronc, using a wooden barrel put together to simulate a wild mustang. Bob did not fare well and ended up in Hollywood Presbyterian Hospital in traction, yet still found a way to milk a lot of publicity from his hospitalization, at the expense of Paramount's new boss, Henry Ginsberg. He took out an open letter addressed to Ginsberg, certain to hype *Fancy Pants:*

"If your economy-minded production heads had used a real horse instead of putting me over a broken-down barrel, I would not have landed on my back on Stage 17 with an injury which you will see from the bill, was not cheap . . . When I woke up in the hospital, four nurses were standing over me, a doctor was feeling my pulse, and another doctor was busy on the phone checking with the Bank of America on how much we could go for . . . The more X-rays they took the more the doctor looked worried. It seems they couldn't find much wrong with me and the doctor had promised his wife a new mink coat. He finally got desperate one day when he thought

I was asleep. I heard him scream at the X-ray people: 'Find something even if it's on another patient.'

"But I could see that I had them over a barrel at this point—if the word is not too sensitive for you."

He goes on to say that during occupational therapy (for which the bill was $1,400), the occupation he picked up was horse playing, "and we both know it's not a poor man's pastime. Please understand that this puts me in deep debt to you, almost as deep as you are to the doctors."

Hope ends the letter: "Yours in our great work, Bob Hope."

Chapter 29

In September 1949, the last Bob Hope radio season sponsored by Lever Brothers began with an indication of things to come. He told his audience, "... I like television ..."

American audiences found television exciting, but they still adored Bob Hope. A poll taken by Dr. George Gallup in September 1949 indicated as much. In Gallup's press release, dated September 18, he said:

> "All America loves a laugh, and almost every American has his own idea as to who is the funniest laughmaker ever in the business. But the reigning comedian, in the public's mind, is Bob Hope. He outdistances his closest rivals in the American Institute of Public Opinion's first "comedy star derby"—with stage, screen, radio, or television stars all included—by a commanding ratio of almost 2-1/2 to 1. Next come Milton Berle, Jack Benny, Red Skelton, and Fibber McGee and Molly—all close on the heels of each other."

Television had certainly caught the imagination of American audiences, with an estimated two and one half million sets already in the nation's living rooms in late 1949. Milton Berle dominated television as the number one comedian on the small screen.

While Berle's face came into America's living rooms on Tuesday nights, *Motion Picture Daily* reported that Bob Hope led all others in box office appeal. His latest release, *The Great Lover,* packed theaters—but not on Tuesday nights. People stayed home to watch "Uncle Miltie," which continued to irritate Hope.

Bob, Dolores, Tony, and Linda were joined by country and western star Jimmy Wakely, Patty Thomas, and pianist Geoff Clarkson on a Christmas trip to Alaska, where Hope and his entertainers—including Dolores as the female singer—did twelve shows in three days, beginning at the Anchorage base hospital.

Hope, still ignoring his own health, caught a virus which cost him the use of his voice. The year had been both good and bad for the reigning comedian. His difficulties with NBC, Lever Brothers, and Paramount Pictures were chronicled from time to time in the trade publications and mainline press—but no one dared expose his womanizing. He should have thanked his lucky stars that Seymour Hersh or Kitty Kelly did not choose him as a biographical subject.

Sometime in early February, while on tour, he made one of his writers angry. The writer, in turn, had a few drinks and decided to get even. Getting even meant calling up Dolores and exposing an affair between Bob and actress Gloria DeHaven. After a tryst at the Carter Hotel in Cleveland, Ohio—where Gloria was a guest on a live Broadcast of Bob's radio show—the writer made the phone call which sent Bob to the doghouse.

Barbara Payton, an aspiring teenaged actress from Texas, hit Hollywood during the late forties, seeking a career in motion pictures. Unfortunately for her, the Hollywood wolves were haunting the airports, train station, and bus depots, looking for young, naive, and ambitious beauties willing to do anything for so much as a walk-on in pictures. They might be nobodies in Hollywood, but back in Texas or Louisiana when a hometown girl wiggled across a hotel lobby on film, she became a big fish in a little pond.

I interviewed writer Nancy Bacon, who ghosted Barbara Payton's autobiography, *I Am Not Ashamed*. Although the book was written years after the affair with Hope ended, she had no respect for him.

"Nancy," she said, "Bob and I would be having sex and he'd stop to tell me about a weird game he and Bing Crosby played." The "game," according to Payton, had to do with Bing and Bob seeking out young virgins (before they were corrupted by others) and deflowering them.

"Bob," she declared, "would call me on the spur of the moment and demand that I come immediately to Fort Worth or Dallas or God only knows where. He would give me the airline, the flight number, and departure time from Los Angeles. I would be met by a limousine and whisked off to his hotel. My room was either next to his with adjoining doors or on the same floor. I never spent any time in my room except when Bob wanted to hang out with the boys."

Hope, she declared, "always treated me in a grandiose manner. I never wanted for anything material. Not really. He just didn't like to part with cash."

Barbara, more famous for her torrid affair with Bob Neal, met Hope in Dallas at the end of his spring 1949 tour of the country. Fred Otash, the famous (some say infamous) Hollywood private eye and *Confidential Magazine*'s chief investigator, researched Barbara's claims of her romance with Hope and on the basis of his investigation, *Confidential* paid her big bucks for the story.

I ghosted Fred's first book, *Investigation Hollywood,* and had access to all his *Confidential* files as well as those involving Jimmy Hoffa and the Kennedy brothers. Hope tossed a big party for himself in his suite at the Baker Hotel in Dallas. Neal brought Barbara up for a drink. Thanks to her abilities on the couch and in the boudoir, Barbara had been given some pretty good parts in pictures, in which her costars were Robert Montgomery, Gary Cooper, James Cagney, and Gregory Peck—all of whom she claimed to have slept with. None bedded her quicker than Bob Hope. She spent that first night with him, and thus began their romance.

Bob and Barbara shared another interest—drinking. Barbara's health and life were eventually destroyed by booze and drugs, but Hope merely went through a phase during his affair with her—and probably drank to keep her from drinking alone.

Wherever Bob appeared outside Los Angeles, Barbara would always be found nearby. Their affair was no secret to the writers who traveled with him, but Bob wrote the checks that kept them in the niceties of life, so no one ever squealed except for the Gloria DeHaven tryst—and he didn't discover the culprit until a number of years after the writer left his employ.

When *Sorrowful Jones* premiered at the New York Paramount in June 1949, Barbara accompanied Bob with Doc Shurr (to serve as Bob's cover). Bob and Barbara did all the New York nightclubs together and yet no reporter or columnist tipped off Dolores. They probably had too much respect for her. As Barbara told Nancy Bacon, "I'm sure his wife knew about us. I don't see how she couldn't. We were so public. I think she knew her husband was an alley cat who always came home when he got hungry. She had all the security any woman could want. Why rock the boat?"

When Hope returned to Hollywood he rented an apartment for Barbara, only a few minutes from Paramount where he and Lucille Ball were shooting *Fancy Pants*.

"You see this bed?" she said, directing Nancy's attention to a sagging king-sized bed that had seen better days. "Bob bought me this bed because the one in my apartment couldn't accommodate him. People don't realize how big a man Bob Hope is. He's no runt, that's for sure." She had kept the memento of happier days all those years.

After a big fight, Bob dumped Barbara Payton, replacing her with Marilyn Maxwell—another gorgeous Hollywood blonde with a wonderful heart and high ambitions. Barbara went on to marry Franchot Tone, an excellent actor, and tried to resurrect her film career. She could not, however, escape her alcoholism and lust for men. She found her match in a former prizefighter-turned-actor, Tom Neal. Their affair destroyed her marriage.

When she committed suicide in 1966, she'd not even made it to her fortieth birthday.

Marilyn Maxwell, accustomed to liaisons with famous men, had been married to actor John Conte. Following their divorce less than a year after the end of World War II, she took up with Frank Sinatra—very much a married man. This fact has been verified enough times to be part of the Hollywood archives of philandering.

Nancy Sinatra, Sr., had occasion to look into the glove compartment of Frank's car just before Christmas, finding a slender jewelry box. A gorgeous diamond bracelet lay cold and glittering on the soft velvet lining. Believing the expensive jewelry to be a surprise Christmas gift for her, she put it back where she found it.

Christmas came and went and still Frank did not present her with the diamond bracelet. Perhaps he meant it for a New Year's Eve surprise when the Sinatras were having a big bash at their house.

The bracelet appeared on New Year's Eve, but not as a gift to Nancy, who received the surprise of her life when she went to greet Marilyn Maxwell in the foyer. As Marilyn started to remove her full-length mink coat, the diamond bracelet from Frank's glove compartment clung lovingly to her slender wrist.

Mrs. Frank Sinatra pointed to the front door. "How dare you!" she said in cold fury. "Get out of my house now! Now!" Frank's dalliance with Hollywood's beauties had been exposed to his wife for the first time. Others would follow, beginning with Ava Gardner, while he still wore his wedding ring.

Sinatra tired of Marilyn Maxwell and all other women in his life when Ava Gardner came on to the scene. Enter Bob Hope. Marilyn would become, and remain, a part of Bob Hope's life longer than any other woman outside his marriage.

January 1950 did not begin well for Hope. He'd gone down to Palm Springs to get in a little golf. The Bing Crosby-sponsored Pro-Am Pebble Beach Tournament was coming up and he wanted to make a big show when he confronted Crosby. The press always gave both men plenty of coverage.

Bob had other worries. Business problems. Lever Brothers

were disgusted with his total abandonment of all rules and structure. The sponsor wanted him to stay in one place—broadcast out of the studio especially set up for him in Hollywood—and stop gallivanting around the world. His demands, to them, were enormous and they weren't interested in spending additional sums just so Bob Hope could say, "Look where I am now!" With the military broadcasts becoming less important, Bob had taken up going to college campuses, perhaps remembering how popular the big bands had been doing their live broadcasts from Notre Dame, Duke, and other well known campuses.

Jimmy Saphier, having a sense of timing not unlike Hope's, decided to confront Bob about television. During one of Hope's practice sessions in Palm Springs, with the Crosby bash in Pebble Beach coming up, Saphier approached the comedian, setting forth his opinion that "It's time for television."

"Not on your life," Hope declared. "They couldn't pay me enough money."

Saphier went to Hugh Davis, a vice president of Foote, Cone, and Belding, a major advertising agency, and told him that he believed Bob could be had if the price suited him.

"What's he want?" Davis asked.

"I'll let you know."

Saphier went back to Hope and brought the subject up again. "How much is enough?"

Hope, wanting to end the conversation once and for all, responded quickly, "Fifty thousand dollars."

Saphier, having gone into further discussion with Hugh Davis, also knew that one of the agency's major clients, General Electric, would like to have Bob Hope host a show for it's Frigidaire division.

"Bob wants fifty thousand dollars."

"For one show?" Davis asked.

"Yup," Saphier said with inner assurance.

No performer had ever been paid so much for one appearance on television. Davis quickly thought it over—there would be great publicity value in having Bob Hope debut for Frigidaire.

Refrigerators were part of the American home—the same as Bob Hope. What a tie-in.

"Let me think it over," he told Saphier.

Bob had quite a bit to drink that afternoon and by the time he and some of his writers, along with Saphier, were headed out toward Riverside, en route to Los Angeles on Route 60, he was feeling as high as the 75 to 80 miles per hour his new Cadillac was travelling.

He lost control of the car and ended up flipping upside down and rolling over several times before coming to rest in a citrus grove. Hope's alcoholic condition was never an issue. At Riverside Community Hospital the doctors and nurses were too busy asking for autographs to worry whether Bob Hope had too much to drink and damned near killed a carload of people.

With a broken shoulder, Bob Hope would not be playing the Crosby Pro-Am in Pebble Beach.

During his recuperation he finally discovered a reason to do television: Frigidaire's $190,000 package, which consisted of $40,000 for the first show and $150,000 for four additional shows.

Meanwhile Bob took Les Brown and Jane Russell along to fulfill a $50,000 per week gig at the Paramount Theater in New York City. He simply could not resist Broadway. While on the East Coast he emceed the White House Correspondent's annual get-together. Stuart Symington presented him with the Air Force's highest civilian award, which pleased Bob. However, nothing pleased him quite as much as catching sight of Charles Luckman, who'd recently left Lever Brothers without explanation, at a table amongst the celebrated audience. After taking jabs at the politicos, including President Harry Truman, who seemed to have more fun than anyone else, Hope zeroed in on Luckman.

"I hear," Hope said, as though it had just occurred to him, "that Lever Brothers is behind a Broadway show called *Where's Charley?*"

Red-faced and furious, Luckman avoided Hope the rest of the evening. Hope always got even—and usually in public.

When someone asked him why he'd been so mean, the comedian said, "I was just kidding."

Bob couldn't have cared less what Luckman or Lever Brothers thought of him. His next stop would be Broadway—again. His first week at the Paramount brought in $141,000, a Paramount record.

The *Daily Mirror* critic, Alton Cook, who had seen Hope perform many times, caught his new Paramount appearance and it caused him to speak fondly of Bob's maturity:

> "Bob has mellowed considerably in the decade since he has been away from Broadway stages ... his charm has increased ... The test is that he stays on the stage without much assistance for 40 whole minutes, a very long time for anyone to remain the life of the party and get away with it."

While in New York he adopted a new charity—Cerebral Palsy. After performing at P.S 135, with all the attendant publicity, he advised Mack Millar to be sure that he appeared for Cerebral Palsy throughout the tour that followed his appearance at the Paramount. Bob also allowed Leonard Goldenson, head of United Paramount Theaters, to talk him into becoming national chairman of Cerebral Palsy—primarily as a spokesman to raise money. It didn't matter to Hope that he wouldn't be paid a salary because the publicity only served to keep his name and face in public view. He held that post until 1954 before relinquishing it to Bill Ford—of the Detroit Ford automobiles.

When Marilyn Maxwell arrived in New York, Bob dropped Jane Russell. Marilyn appeared with him on stage throughout the rest of the tour, across country from Rochester, New York, to three stops in Kansas before returning to the West Coast. He also took along a young unknown singer from Floral Park, Long Island, by the name of Tony Bennett.

Marilyn Maxwell soon began to appear wherever Hope did a show, and later in his films. He seemed almost to flaunt her to the point that Marilyn once confessed to an intimate that "I'm sure he'd marry me—but everybody in Hollywood would hate my guts for breaking up his *happy* marriage.'' That she was madly in love with Bob, there can be no doubt—even though married to another man at the time and proudly displaying her wedding ring at every occasion (as though that might stop the gossips).

He barely made a pit stop in Toluca Lake before he was aboard a plane to New York to begin rehearsals for his big television debut for Frigidaire. The ad agency, along with NBC-TV, spent thousands of dollars on full-page ads to promote the show, dubbed ''Star Spangled Rhythm.'' It guaranteed Hope maximum coverage on his big night—live from New York.

Bob should never have feared television. Surrounded by the likes of Bea Lillie, Douglas Fairbanks, Jr., the Mexico City Boys Choir, dancer Hal LeRoy, Dinah Shore, pianist Maurice Rocco, and singer Bill Hayes, he glistened like a diamond set in platinum.

The show went out live from the new NBC television studio atop the New Amsterdam Hotel to the network's twenty-seven regular stations, and rebroadcast to another eighteen NBC affiliates the following week. Hope, in fine fettle despite a case of stomach butterflies, stopped the show:

> ''What a fine-looking audience . . . Now, ladies and gentlemen, doing this big special Easter show on television is a high point for me . . . for years I've been on radio . . . you remember radio . . . blind television . . . but I want to tell you that Frigidaire has been a brick about the whole thing . . . especially where the money is concerned . . . ah, the money . . . are you listening, Washington? . . . Yes, Frigidaire has been very generous with me . . . they told me I could have my salary any way I wanted it . . . big or little cubes.''

No one ever covered a commercial, or got as many laughs in the doing, as Bob Hope. He walked away from that show with a much healthier respect for his future. He could do ninety minutes of live television and now even he knew it. Once he got over the early jitters, he'd managed to sail into his material like an old sea captain in uncharted waters. It didn't matter that critics quibbled over his salary. Someone once said that when critics can't find anything else to write about they complain that the entertainer was paid too much.

The most important review of his first major appearance on television came from the *New York Times* critic, Jack Gould:

"What the viewer saw was the true Hope of the old *Roberta* and Palace days, the master of ceremonies who was relaxed and leisurely and never in a hurry. Here was the polished clown in the tradition. His impishness had the light touch, and his gags were sent across the footlights with the deftness of deliveries. To the audience at home he communicated that priceless feeling that they, too, were conspirators in the make-believe while to his supporting company he conveyed that esprit and cohesion which is the trademark of the born showman."

Having been baptized in the video waters, Hope would never be the same again. A new frontier loomed in the horizon and, as Hope said, "What makes Berle think there isn't room for another 'uncle'?"

Uncle Bob???

Chapter 30

Bob's initial enthusiasm for television waned a bit after he read all of the reviews. He couldn't wait to get back to California and Paramount, where he truly did reign as king of comedy.

"The next time I do a television show," he told one of his writers, "I'm going to be surrounded by 'real' talent."

He called Saphier on the phone. "See what you can do for the Mother's Day show."

"What do you mean," Jimmy asked.

"I mean, like I'd like to have Sinatra and Ella Fitzgerald and Peggy Lee. You know, big names."

"Sure, Bob," he said. "I'll see who's available on short notice."

It really rubbed him the wrong way that some of his competitors thought he'd asked for and received too much money for his first show. He suspected Milton Berle was stirring up trouble. At the same time, he did not want an open fight with any other comedians because he knew how brutal they could be to their fellow performers if pushed.

He had an idea, but first he needed to take care of preproduction matters involving his next picture, *The Lemon Drop Kid*. He'd already set his costar—Marilyn Maxwell.

Returning to New York, he threw himself into the upcoming Mother's Day show. Less nervous, when the show aired he poked fun at both himself and television:

> "It's amazing how many people see you on TV. I did my first television show a month ago, and the next day five million television sets were sold . . . The people who couldn't sell theirs threw them away."

Marilyn Maxwell had been around Hollywood for several years and wasn't exactly a household name. When Hope told the studio that he wanted her as a costar, the executives were against it. "Who the hell is she?" a guy from the front office asked.

"I worked with her in New York. She's good. I want her and that's enough for me." And he got her.

It didn't matter that Marilyn Maxwell did not have star quality. She certainly had her other attributes. Also, the supporting cast had enough talent to lend credibility to the picture: Lloyd Nolan, Fred Clark, Bill Frawley, and Jane Darwell.

Bob wasn't the least bit pleased with the first cut of *The Lemon Drop Kid*. Paramount took an "I told you so," position, referring to Marilyn Maxwell rather than finding fault with Hope.

Bob insisted that the picture not be released until there had been some reshooting and major script changes. Frank Tashlin came aboard to do the rewrites while Evans and Livingston, the famous songwriting duo, wrote another surefire Hit Parade tune—"Silver Bells," which has become as perennial as "White Christmas."

About the same time *The Lemon Drop Kid* was being filmed, Lever Brothers dropped Bob's radio show. The happy marriage had finally developed into what the divorce lawyers call "a state of irreconcilable differences."

The marriage of Hope and Lever Brothers did not go through an ordinary default. The matter ended up with civil litigation in the California State Superior Court, where Bob Hope's kingdom ended. The Superior Court sided with Lever Brothers. Bob's contract with the sponsor dictated that he could only perform in "live broadcasts." Bob decided that he would, in defiance of Lever Brothers, pre-record his show when he had a conflicting commitment.

Lever Brothers, by dropping the king of comedy, saved a lot of money. His salary at that time was $22,500 per broadcast—with option clauses, more than a million dollars during a season run.

It was openly whispered around town that despite public statements that blond Jan Sterling would be his leading lady in *The Lemon Drop Kid*, she never was given serious consideration by Hope.

I interviewed Marilyn Maxwell for a magazine article in the early 1970s, when we met at a big charity function at the Century Park Hotel in West Los Angeles, which involved Bob Hope, Barry Goldwater, and a lot of military and Washington bigshots. She gave me a surprisingly honest insight into her long relationship with Bob Hope that night. To this day I do not know why she opened up the way she did about her personal life.

Marilyn had arrived with actor Guy Madison, who, at one time, had been the most beautiful young hunk in Hollywood. On that particular night Guy was anything but beautiful. He'd lost a lot of weight and by the time he left Marilyn and me, he'd more than slaked his thirst for that ninety-proof stuff. Drunk and disoriented, he wandered off to find other amusements, leaving Marilyn and me alone.

Shortly after Guy left us, Bill Shatner stopped for a moment and said hello to Marilyn. I remember it well because I made the error of mistaking him for Johnny Bench, the popular catcher with the Cincinnati Reds. He wasn't too amused.

Marilyn and I sat side by side in two overstuffed chairs, typical hotel lobby fare, and drank our drinks. For some reason our conversation got around to children. She wanted to know if I was married and did I have any children. My answer to both was yes.

She had a very handsome young son and showed me a picture

of him. After we ran out of family banter, I asked her what brought her to this charity affair.

"Oh, Ray, Bob and I go way back. I'm sure you know that."

I did—or at least I'd heard about it.

"A romance?" I asked.

"You might call it that." She took a sip of her drink.

"Serious?"

"I thought so for a while, but you've got to understand Bob Hope."

"Meaning what, exactly?"

"Meaning that he is very much a married man."

Marilyn laughed and changed the subject. She had the warmest, sexiest, and most totally unpretentious laugh I'd ever heard—almost as if she actually enjoyed laughing. I interviewed her a couple of other times. I always thought she'd be an interesting subject for biography, but she felt if she did a book it would have to be honest, and the last time I asked, she said, "I wouldn't want to hurt my son. He'll hear enough if he hangs around Hollywood long enough."

I wanted to know more about Marilyn and Bob Hope. Her story was not unlike that of Barbara Payton with one exception: she thought of all the women Hope had dated, she might be the one he'd been most serious about. "I think he loved me in the European manner. He saw nothing wrong with having a mistress and a wife at the same time."

Of Dolores, she said, ". . . she has a great hold over him through her religion. Bob couldn't give a hoot if he ever went to church, but she sees that he donates a lot of his time and money to the Catholic Church, especially that one out in the Valley."

"St. Charles?"

"That's the one."

Marilyn told me the story of *The Lemon Drop Kid*. "Bob's partners talked about Jan Sterling, but I had an inside track. We were sleeping together. We only did a couple of pictures together, but I traveled with him on USO tours and personal appearances—and did television specials."

She said that she owed a lot to Bob Hope. "I'm not the only

one," she confided, "who got a step up the ladder by sleeping with Bob Hope, and there were plenty of women willing to share his bed. Who knows," she added, "I might have done a television series with him. We talked about it, but I don't think he ever liked the idea of doing a weekly show."

He frowned on those who did so, Marilyn said. "He thought Milton Berle was a prostitute to television. I don't think I ever heard him say a nice world about Miltie throughout the years I've known him. Actually, I believe the only comedians he had any respect for were George and Gracie. Bob had his own idea about family values."

Marilyn said she always believed that Dolores Hope knew when it was time for Bob to cease a relationship. "I know that's what happened in my case," she said. "I was getting too close to just who the man was and Dolores never wanted anyone to be that close except herself."

I was stunned that Marilyn Maxwell would offer me such personal information. At the time I'd never had any work of consequence published, mostly writing columns and feature stories for magazines and the *Citizen News,* Hollywood's daily paper. I think she just saw me as someone to talk to, having been abandoned by her escort and finding herself alone that evening in the lobby of the hotel. She told me something very strange that night, however. "You know, Ray, the most misunderstood man in this town is Rock Hudson. I might have married him . . . he's been so good to me and to my son—like an older brother. I can't think of him as a father image. There's too much of the little boy in him. But you can certainly put this in your story, if you really are going to write one. Rock Hudson is the best friend I've ever had."

"Not Bob Hope?"

"Rock Hudson. First, last, and always."

I never did write the story because I didn't know where to start, but after Marilyn Maxwell died, I heard that she'd asked that Rock Hudson be made guardian of her son. I knew then that she truly did consider him the best friend she had because she would never have left that boy in the custody of anybody she didn't trust.

* * *

In September, Bob did his third special for Frigidaire. His guests were Bob Crosby, Dinah Shore, and Lucille Ball. The *San Francisco Chronicle*'s Terence O'Flaherty gave it a rave review:

> "I love you, Bob Hope. Last night the cinema kid with the ski-shoot nose gave a little peek of what television is going to be when the big entertainers move in and take over. For the first time, 'The Star Spangled Revue' turned out to be something approximating the grandiose title of the show. Hope himself had good material to work with and he looked happy about it . . . all in all it was 'one fine, fat show,' as my neighbor, Mrs. Pellachotti, expressed it, and she is a very particular woman."

Bob's television, radio, and motion picture life was once again interrupted by the big guns of war. During the summer of 1950, North Korea invaded their neighbors to the south and the United States found itself embroiled in another Pacific War, via the United Nations, in a "police action" to defend South Korea. Before any peace declaration could be declared, China joined sides with North Korea and most of the rest of the world signed up with the United Nations.

Bob Hope found himself in North Korea entertaining the troops once again at war at Christmastime of 1950. His good friend, Secretary of the Air Force Stuart Symington, placed two C-54 cargo planes at Hope's disposal for his tour of Korea and Japan. With so much space available, he took along more than four dozen entertainers—including his concubine of the moment, Marilyn Maxwell. Since Marilyn had a commitment in Pittsburgh, she promised to join Bob in Hawaii.

Gloria DeHaven filled in adequately for Marilyn in every department until the blond Maxwell, freed up from her other obligations, joined him for the shows at Pearl Harbor and the rest of the South Pacific tour. With Maxwell on the scene, DeHaven found herself on a plane back to the States.

General Douglas MacArthur and his wife hosted a luncheon for Hope and nineteen other members of his troupe at the American Embassy in Tokyo.

Hope and his gang put on a hell of a show at the Ernie Pyle Theater before more than 3,000 GI's stationed in the Tokyo area. Later that day, he and Marilyn Maxwell wowed another 10,000 troops with their sexually-laden routines. The GI's loved it. Hope brought a taste of home with him. Sushi was okay, but these were steak-and-potato guys—plus Marilyn Maxwell for dessert.

Dolores Hope could not have been happy to read an October 27, 1950, headline in the *Los Angeles Times:*

BOB HOPE AND MARILYN MAXWELL IN WONSAN BEFORE LEATHERNECKS

Bob continued to enjoy special privileges. He did not bunk down with the troops. Aboard the U.S.S. *Missouri,* he was assigned the suite belonging to General MacArthur.

Larry Gelbart was among the writers accompanying Bob Hope to Korea. He had been a mainstay and rescued Hope's show on more than one occasion due to his uncanny ability to prepare a monologue at a moment's notice. If Hope didn't give much credit to the writers who made him look great, what those writers saw—especially Gelbart—gave them their well-deserved rewards later on. For Larry Gelbart, the recognition came because he paid attention to what he saw in Korea—and out of that situation emerged "M*A*S*H", a smash movie which later segued into the most successful television series since the invention of the format.

When Hope returned to the United States he was sought out by powerful gossip columnist Louella Parsons and grilled about his "affair with Marilyn Maxwell." Miss Parsons, a devout Catholic and close friend of Dolores Hope, looked at cheating on one's wife as the most cardinal of all sins.

Dorothy Manners, Miss Parsons' faithful assistant, remembered that Hope more or less told Louella to mind her own business—which took some telling, because Louella was known to kill careers at any stage of their existence. She single-handedly destroyed popular and talented actress Ingrid Berg-man, a married woman who gave up her husband and family to have a baby with Italian film director Roberto Rossellini.

Dolores begged Louella to go easy on Bob, so when the item appeared in the Hearst newspaper syndicate under Parsons' byline, it was softened up to protect Dolores:

A LOUELLA PARSONS EXCLUSIVE

"In an exclusive interview with Dolores Hope, I have learned that there's absolutely no truth to the current rumors that Bob Hope and his leading lady, Marilyn Maxwell, are serious about each other just because they have been seen together so much. 'Our marriage is stronger than ever,' Mrs. Hope assured me."

Robert Slatzer, Bing Crosby's biographer and a close friend of Hope's youngest brother, George, revealed confidences to both Arthur Marx and to me which more than confirmed the rumors of Bob Hope's sexual aggressiveness:

"Whenever Bob left Hollywood to do personal appear-ance tours or camp shows, he didn't take girls with him nor did he want local talent to service his sexual needs. He used a lot of young starlets and wannabes in his shows and films—most of them were not actresses and so therefore were used mostly to spruce up the scenery. If they were willing, George would collect their names and file them for future reference—sometimes I did the same thing. He made sure a certain amount of these girls were sent ahead and set up in his hotel where he had easy access."

These girls were for sex and sex alone. They were not the Marilyn Maxwells or Barbara Paytons. Those two were special and when they were along, the showgirls were either kept to a minimum or not sent out at all.

Slatzer recalled a particular set of twins who worked every Crosby and Hope picture. Rumor had it that one of them, who lived a block or so away from Hope in Toluca Lake, was much admired by Hope.

The girls always had to be beautiful if they were sent ahead to put some zing in Bob's life on the road. He liked beauty contest winners and gorgeous young starlets. Not only were they able to perform in the bedroom, but he'd put them in the show. He once said, "They don't have to have talent. The guys in the service couldn't give a damn whether they could act. They had tits and nice asses—that's what I gave them and that's what they wanted."

On one of the tours to Ohio in the early fifties, when Slatzer was working in the publicity department at Paramount Studios, he recalls " . . . a Miss Universe contest down in Long Beach, won by a gorgeous brunette from the State of Ohio. I was standing in front of Hope's dressing room when his brother Jack came out and said, 'I wonder if you'd be interested in doing Bob a favor."

"What is it?" Slatzer asked.

"There's this girl, you know, and she just won the Miss Universe contest."

Jack Hope presented Slatzer with a note and photograph of the new Miss Universe. "Take the afternoon off. Run down to Long Beach and give her this note. You can take Bob's Cadillac convertible."

The note read: "This is Jack Hope. I'm Bob Hope's manager. We'd like to talk to you about appearing on one of Bob's television shows."

It wasn't the first time Slatzer had been sent on such a mission. "The girl," he said, "couldn't believe it at first, but I convinced her that it was the real thing and that Mr. Hope really wanted to meet her."

The girl, all aflutter, would have left immediately, but she had a stage mother who interceded. She snatched the note from her daughter's hand and told Slatzer, "Well, you can tell Mr.

Hope to look elsewhere. My daughter is not going anywhere with you."

A somewhat bewildered Slatzer asked why not. Most mothers he'd encountered were anxious to rush their daughters into Hope's arms—if it meant a part. Either that or there were no mothers around to chaperone their budding starlet daughters.

"But why wouldn't you want your daughter to have such a great opportunity?" Slatzer asked.

"I'll tell you why not," the mother said, as though fire were slipping off the tip of her tongue. "I've heard of his philandering around with young girls from beauty contests, and I am *not* allowing my daughter to be on his show."

The irate woman thrust the note into Slatzer's hand and turned to walk away.

"But, Mother," the girl pleaded, tears running down her cheeks. "I want to be in Mr. Hope's show."

Slatzer said, "That time the virgin got away."

But there were more girls available than not, so Bob Hope had no shortage of beauteous variety to accompany him on his sojourns both in America and abroad.

To placate his wife, Bob continued his charitable appearances for Dolores's religious associations. It was a small price to pay for being forgiven so many transgressions. At the moment his thoughts turned to Marilyn Maxwell. One down—one in the bag.

Chapter 31

Throughout the filming of *My Favorite Spy* with Hedy Lamarr, Bob made no secret about his affair with Marilyn Maxwell. I spent quite a bit of time with Hedy when she was dating a young actor named Burt Lange who'd come to Hollywood from Chicago. Hedy loved to talk about the men in her life, especially if she'd had a couple of cocktails.

This was a number of years after she'd made the picture with Hope. At the time, Hedy was occupying the old Hedda Hopper house in the 1700 block of Tropical Drive in Beverly Hills. Bob Hope had definitely never been one of the men in her life.

"I never knew him that well," she said. "We didn't travel in the same social circles. We did our scenes. He went wherever he went and I came home.

"I never understood what women saw in him unless it was his money, and from what I learned from women he'd dated, he didn't like to spend it. And besides," she added, "that Maxwell woman—you know, the blonde. She was always on the set with Bob."

I asked Hedy if it embarrassed her and she laughed loudly.

"Heavens no, darling. Why should I be embarrassed? I wasn't married to him."

My Favorite Spy turned out to be just another "Bob Hope romps around with a beautiful girl" picture.

Bob continued to romp with Marilyn Maxwell, both in Hollywood and abroad. He couldn't wait to get out of town after the completion of *My Favorite Spy,* and had his agent arrange a tour of Great Britain. He arrived in London with Marilyn Maxwell wrapped in full-length mink, with one arm clinging to Hope's.

Dolores never expressed any reaction to Bob's cavorting in public, but she must have suffered untold private agonies. During his crossing of the Atlantic in April 1951 he made quite a public spectacle of himself, displaying Marilyn Maxwell as though she might become the next Mrs. Bob Hope. Word quickly got back to Dolores in Hollywood that Bob was making a fool of himself. Theresa DeFina, Dolores's mother, told one of Bob's secretaries that Dolores couldn't take it any longer. She contacted him aboard the *Queen Mary* before it docked at Southampton and, according to Theresa, told him that, ". . . he was publicly humiliating her and his adultery had to stop."

Bob never mentioned the call to Marilyn. In London the forerunners of the paparazzi flashed pictures of Bob and Marilyn around the clock, which included their trip to Ireland, where Bob was supposed to have asked Marilyn to marry him. She is reputed to have turned him down. She understood that you can sleep with an icon, but you can't break up his marriage. It isn't socially accepted—or wasn't in the Hollywood of the fifties.

As a diversion from critics of his companionship with Marilyn Maxwell, Bob was happy that he'd been allowed to enter the 1951 British Amateur Golf Championship; he received a star's reception when he arrived at the Royal Portcawl Golf Course in Glamorgan. Thousands of fans overran the links to glimpse one of their own who had made it big in American motion pictures. They didn't seem to care that they might damage the golf course. Some of them wouldn't have known a golf club if it hit them in the face. They screamed and they yelled out his name.

He made an easy target as he exited his limousine wearing a blue and red shirt, yellow jersey, traditional grey slacks, tartan socks, and a tartan tam-o'-shanter set at a cocky angle. The only thing that could ruin his entrance did. Someone said, ''Mr. Hope, only one time before has a celebrity caused so much of an uproar at the British Amateur.''

Sobered somewhat, Bob feigned a smile, and waved to the crowds to the left and to the right. ''Who?'' he asked, as though tossing an aside.

''Oh, Mr. Crosby. Yessir. Mr. Bing Crosby himself. He made a big splash here last year.''

Hope, as sharp as a tack, quickly responded, ''Yes, but he dropped out after 16 holes. Don't tell him, but he'll turn green when he hears that I completed the first round.''

Bob's boast was premature. He did not complete the round. The game turned against him on the 17th green. After a three-hour marathon, Chris Fox, a nondescript 41-year-old man from Yorkshire, beat him two and one.

Fortunately, he had Marilyn Maxwell at his elbow to ease his loss. Acting the clown in failure, Bob did all he could do to be funny, but it backfired. The British newspapers torpedoed him, stating that he demeaned the honor of the championships. British actor David Niven, coming to Bob's defense, asked an obvious question: ''What does the British press have against Bob Hope? Just how unsporting can sportswriters get?''

Bob discovered more happiness upon returning to Hollywood and jumping right into *Son of Paleface* with Jane Russell, Roy Rogers, and Trigger, Roy's horse. He never took criticism easily. Everyone had to love Bob Hope as much as Bob Hope loved Bob Hope. It hurt him deeply anytime he found that not to be true.

Back home in Toluca Lake again, he felt safe from British critics who ''don't understand how we operate here in the good old United States of America.'' He said it with the patriotism of a U.S. Marine raising the flag on some isolated Pacific Island in World War II.

In Hollywood, rumors flow faster than the Los Angeles River during a rainstorm, subsiding just as quickly. The tabloid stories from England became the subject of telephone gossip and whispers. Someone certainly must have had the guts to tell Dolores. If so, she never let on publicly. I seriously doubt that Bob Hope would ever have divorced Dolores for any reason. He well knew he had a jewel in Dolores. No other woman would have tolerated his philandering. She would simply have filed for divorce, taken her share of the loot (which would have been a queen's ransom), and split.

Dolores hung in there during the hard times, so why give up an empire and suffer the same indignities that all the other ex-Mrs. Moviestars went through?

Dolores turned more and more to the Catholic Church for consolation and reassurance, her faith in God stronger than in her marriage.

Evie Wynn, one of Van Johnson's wives, once told me that "When Van left me and we got divorced, *our* friends were immediately *Van's* friends. That's the way it is in Hollywood."

As a personal observation, I believe that Bob Hope loved Dolores from the beginning and loved her throughout their long marriage. He came from an old world tradition that allowed the man to play as long as he didn't do anything to embarrass his family. Dolores, being a devout Catholic, understood that. All Catholic women did.

Bob never doubted his marriage—not as long as Dolores remained the loyal wife who supported her husband no matter what. It never occurred to Bob that she would ever draw a line in the sand. And she never did, though she came close on numerous occasions.

Bob Slatzer worked with Bob's brother George at Paramount Pictures and, on occasion, in the services of Bob Hope. Slatzer recalls one instance when Dolores's temperature might have exploded into an inferno.

"George and I put together an independent film production company. Both of us were working at General Services Studios at the time, so we spent a lot of time together. George also continued working for his older brother's company and on a more personal level at the same time.''

Bob Hope did some pretty brazen things in those days, one of the most outrageous, according to Slatzer, was putting various girls up in apartments within walking distance of his estate in Toluca Lake. Part of George's job, sort of as a gofer for Bob, was to deliver envelopes with cash in them to these girls so they could pay their rent. This became a monthly chore.

On one occasion, George had some difficulty explaining to his wife why he had these envelopes full of money. She'd caught him with a girl just before the money passed hands. George, not wanting any further domestic problems over Bob's girls, devised a plan that brought Slatzer into the equation.

''For a period of time,'' Slatzer recalls, ''George would pick up the envelopes from Bob, or someone designated by Bob, and drop them off to me for delivery. When George explained his situation, I agreed to help him out as a friend. I didn't want him to have trouble with his wife because of his brother's illicit interludes. I saw no problem for myself. Just doing a favor for a friend.

''The envelopes, as I recall, were filled with fifty- and one-hundred-dollar-bills.'' Slatzer always counted the money out with George to make sure that both knew how much was being delivered in case someone should cry foul.

''After a while both George and I knew the exact addresses of the girls so it became routine. Pick up, count, and deliver.

''Hope's name was never mentioned. George merely said, 'Take care of this for The Boss, okay, Bob?' Okay. No problem.

''This went on for quite a while. Weeks turned into months until it got to be part of my life's duties, so to speak.''

All went well until a couple of nights after Slatzer had made his last drop for the month.

''It must have been two-thirty or three in the morning when my phone rang, sounding like a fire alarm, and brought me wide awake—very fast. I grappled for the phone in the dark and finally got the receiver to my ear. 'Hullo . . .' ''

''Bob, this is George. You get your fucking ass out of bed

right now. You've fucked up this whole deal. What'd you do, spend the money on some broad?''

Bob Slatzer says, ''I had no idea what the hell he was talking about. I wasn't even awake, really, and he was going off like the Fourth of July. Then he says, ''You know that girl in 301?''

''Bob's girl?''

''The same. Well, her landlord called Bob at the Moorpark house and is raising hell because the broad didn't pay her rent. Now get this. The girl says she didn't receive no rent money from The Boss, which means she's saying you didn't deliver.''

''That's bullshit,'' Slatzer said. ''I delivered just like I always do. One, two, three—all of them right on the button. She's lying. As a matter of fact, I broke all the rules. I not only handed it to her, she invited me in for a cup of coffee. I can even tell you the brand if you want to know.''

''Well,'' George said, ''we better get over to Bob's house right now, because we're going to have a meeting in The Boss's office.''

The two men met and drove together to the Hope residence where they found Bob Hope in a very agitated state. In the car, George explained that Dolores, not Bob, had received the phone call from the landlord ''and now she wants to know what's going on.''

In Hope's office his brother George and Slatzer sat like two little boys waiting to be disciplined, not knowing what might be coming next. Bob paced the floor, fully dressed, as if he were addressing a board of directors meeting.

Hope spoke first to Slatzer, his voice cold, nasty, and irritating. ''Did you give her the money or didn't you?''

''Yes sir,'' Slatzer responded, ''just as I do every month. Same routine. Nothing any different than any other time.''

Slatzer says, ''I think he believed me. He'd just been caught in a situation where his wife caught him with his hand in the wrong cookie jar and he was looking for a way out.''

''Yeah, yeah,'' Hope said, changing direction. ''I know how these broads are. Sometimes they spend the money and don't pay the rent. It's not the first time it's happened, but it's the first time anybody ever called my home—or my wife—to complain. Stupid broad!"

"So," blurted Slatzer—and to this day he doesn't know why he said it—"what do you want with those kind of girls in the first place?"

Hope turned and gave Slatzer a look that seemed to ask, Who let you out of the nuthouse? But instead he said, "Listen, you take care of your business and I'll take care of mine."

Afterward, Hope apologized for getting Slatzer out of bed in the middle of the night, then brought Dolores into the room and directed his statement toward Slatzer. "I wish you would ask your women not to call my house in the future. Go take care of the matter and if you need money, I'll advance you some. You have no idea the misunderstandings this caused."

Fake apologies were made all around. George and Slatzer went home, the worse for wear, and Slatzer told me, "For a while I wasn't on the Hopes' invitation list, but eventually that blew over. Nobody can tell me Dolores didn't know the whole thing was a sham."

The girl later admitted to George that she had spent the money on clothing and groceries. "Bob," she said, "is too damned cheap to give me money for clothes. I just thought maybe I could put the landlord off for a month. How was I to know that the son of a bitch would call Mrs. Hope?"

Women and fun aside, Bob Hope had put in a very tough two years. When he returned from Europe there were lines under his eyes from lack of sleep. His jaws reflected a tired, worn-out body that had been overworked and under-rested. His doctor, friends, and family begged him to slow down, to stay home for a while. He promised to let up with his work schedule, but really didn't. He finished up the year for Chesterfield, did a fourth Frigidaire television spectacular, and completed another film.

Hope's year ended with a visit to Washington, D.C., where President Harry S. Truman presented him with the USO's highest honor on the anniversary of his first radio broadcast from

March Field, California, in 1941. The plaque referred to Hope as the ''GI's Guy.'' That he was and always would be. With future wars to come in the 20th century, no entertainer, male or female, would be more familiar to the American fighting men and women scattered around the globe.

Bob went directly from *Son of Paleface* into the production of *Road to Bali,* the sixth of the Paramount series. It was fun to be back on familiar ground with Lamour and Crosby and all the barbs between the two guys and the outrageous pranks they pulled on their lovely female costar. *Road to Bali,* the first ''Road'' picture to be shot in Technicolor, became another Hope-Crosby-Paramount venture, with Dorothy Lamour again left out of any ownership. Not only did the twosome make a partnership deal with the studio, but they managed to keep the copyright for themselves—almost unheard of in motion picture history.

Bob, as usual, inserted barbs into the script—all directed at Bing. In one scene Bing says to Bob, ''I've got a dame lined up for you.''

Hope's rapid response, ''A dame! What's wrong with her?''

In the end Bing ends up with two girls. Yeah—he got Lamour *and* Jane Russell, who magically appeared when Bob did a bit of hocus-pocus over a woven basket. Much to Bob's surprise, Jane slipped onto Bing's free arm.

''Hey,'' Bob asked of Bing, ''what are you going to do with two girls?'' He looked like he wanted to cry.

''That's my problem,'' said Bing jauntily as he sashayed out of the scene with a beauty on each arm.

The picture had been a romp because every actor in Hollywood would give his eye teeth to do a cameo in a Hope/Crosby/Lamour road picture. This one sported, in addition to Russell, Humphrey Bogart, Dean Martin, Jerry Lewis, and band-leader Bob Crosby (Bing's younger brother).

Bogart, one of the most mischievous actors ever to tread the boards, rigged up a scene in which Bob was offered the opportunity to react to Bing's winning Best Actor for his portrayal of Father O'Malley in *Going My Way.* During a scene that can only be referred to as hallucinatory, Humphrey Bogart forgets his Oscar and Bing picks it up.

"Gimme that!" Hope said, grabbing for the statuette. "You've already got one!"

That scene added word of mouth dollars at the box office— and it was well worth the seeing.

Something else of note happened during the filming—or rather, at the end of filming—of *Road to Bali*. Bing Crosby had never appeared on television. Hated it. Wanted no part of it. Like many other movie stars, he thought it could only harm him at the box office, so he shied away from the camera with the little red light.

Bob Hope had been selected to emcee what turned out to be a fourteen-hour TV marathon, the purpose of which was to help toward the $750,000 fund needed to send American athletes to the 1952 Helsinki Olympics.

In the closest gesture toward real friendship between the two men, Bing agreed to appear with Hope on the long, grueling marathon. The show ran so long that *Road to Bali* missed a full day's shooting. Paramount insisted that Hope and Crosby absorb the costs, but the two men couldn't have cared less. Dorothy Lamour had agreed to be a cohost and the performers who helped raise more than a million dollars for the 333-member Olympic team were the Tiffany and Harry Winston of show business: Frank Sinatra, Milton Berle, Peggy Lee, Burns and Allen, Frankie Laine, Martin and Lewis, Georgie Jessel, Donald O'Connor, Abbott and Costello, Eddie Cantor, the Ritz Brothers, Fred MacMurray, a dozen famous sports stars, a couple of dozen jazz groups, and big bands.

Bob never had to leave home to do it, and most of all he had Crosby on his own home turf. The show was broadcast from the El Captitan Theatre (home of Bob's shows) and carried by both NBC and CBS.

Bob and Bing continued their high jinks on and off the golf course. And there were plenty of charity golf tournaments, which both men readily accepted. What the hell, they got paid for having fun, and the charity involved received a share of the profits.

Bob managed to get in two weeks at the London Palladium, where the hard-nosed critics were most kind. One tough critic said it for everyone:

"A brilliant Palladium bill is headed by Bob Hope, surely the most endearing of the American comedians. His very entrance is a joy as he ambles on, jaw-shutting, eyes-roving, abounding in that old indefinable heartwarming quality of your true star comedian. Mr. Hope is funny to look at, funny to hear, funny without effort, and without flagging. What matter how many joke writers assist?"

All very nice, but Hollywood again beckoned. He had rehearsals for a new show called "The Colgate Comedy Hour" for NBC. Bob loved the format because he didn't like doing weekly television, which is somewhat strange, because he never minded weekly radio at all.

"The Colgate Comedy Hour" went on the air for the first time on Sunday, September 10, 1950, from 8:00-9:00 P.M. opposite Ed Sullivan. The show furnished a lot of firsts for the Guinness Book of Records: First starring vehicle for Eddie Cantor, Fred Allen, Abbott and Costello, Spike Jones, Tony Martin, and Ray Bolger—and was the first commercial series to originate in Hollywood on September 30, 1951, as well as first network telecast on November 22, 1953.

The idea was to rotate autonomous shows, beginning with Eddie Cantor, Martin and Lewis, and Fred Allen. By the time Bob Hope came aboard in 1952, any number of big names had hosted the show. It had a successful five-year run.

Bob not only landed a new toothpaste, but really threw his hat into another ring. As he liked to say, "The best is yet to come—and it's me!"

Chapter 32

Bob Hope steered clear of political jokes that made reference to Senator Joseph McCarthy, the Communist-baiting demagogue from the State of Wisconsin. Since 1952 was a presidential election year, no comedian in his right mind wanted to be branded as a "leftist." The McClellan House Un-American Activities Committee had already done a great deal to harm Hollywood by labeling anyone who might ever have spoken to someone who knew someone who once stumbled into a Communist meeting. The entire entertainment community was scared as hell.

In 1948 a second-year congressman, Richard M. Nixon of California, teamed up with Senator Karl Mundt of South Dakota. From that pairing, and out of the House Committee on Un-American Activities, came a proposed bill which, in its original form, provided for:

> ". . . the registration of all Communist Party members and required a statement of source of all printed and broadcast material issued by organizations that were found to be Communist fronts."

Under the proposed bill, the identification of a group as a Communist front might be made by a Subversive Activities Control Board, which, in turn, would investigate a group at the request of the Attorney General. This language amounted to a noose around the First Amendment to the Constitution.

Although the bill made it through the House, the Senate had the good gumption to kill it. Yet, a bill of even stronger language passed both House and Senate as the McCarran Act a couple of years later—about the same time that Senator McCarthy was stirring up a hornet's nest about Communists. There were more hornets than Communists in his bag of wind. The Hollywood community was awestruck. Only two or three years earlier, we had counted the Soviet Union as an ally, but times had quickly changed. Hitler and Mussolini were dead. Communism became the new boogie man.

Hollywood's biggest stars, directors, and writers were brought before Washington investigative committees and each asked the same question: ''Are you now or have you ever been a member of the Communist Party?''

Ronald Reagan, President of the Screen Actors Guild, kept in close contact with Senator Joseph McCarthy's committee as well as other congressional committees looking under rocks and beds for Communists and Communist ''sympathizers.'' He was always on the lookout for ''actors who might have Communist affiliations.'' Salem had moved to Hollywood.

Actress/Director Lee Grant, whose husband was blacklisted took the Fifth Amendment, refusing to give the names of suspected Communists before the House Un-American Activities Committee in the fifties, and found herself out of work for twelve years. Larry Parks, who'd only recently appeared in two highly acclaimed film biographies af the late Al Jolson, found himself and his wife, Betty Garrett, personae non grata in Hollywood. A few brave producers used writers like Dalton Trumbo to write screenplays, giving screen credit to writers of lesser stature.

Bob Hope did not want to walk into that spiderweb, so he avoided the Communist controversy for a long time. He especially feared the powerful senator from Wisconsin. If

McCarthy uttered the word "Communist" in the same breath with your name, you were toast. Although many of his fellow Republican actors like Reagan, George Murphy, Cecil B. DeMille, and John Wayne were behind McCarthy all the way, Hope preferred, for the sake of his career, not to poke fun at a rattlesnake.

Finally, however, Bob simply could not let the blowhard demagogue continue to go unchallenged; sometime in 1952 he began to needle McCarthy. In one of his monologues, for instance, he began, "Senator McCarthy got off the train in Washington, D.C., and spent two days at Union Station investigating redcaps . . ."

He received some criticism for his McCarthy cracks, but nothing serious. Bob Hope could get away with material no other comedian would dare use.

A big fan of General Eisenhower, Bob jumped on the bandwagon to support his candidacy when President Truman declined to run again. He apparently knew the mood of the American people because the most popular American General since George Washington beat Democratic candidate Governor Adlai Stevenson of Illinois, not just once—but twice—to become the first Republican president in 20 years.

Eisenhower, a golfer, became the first president with whom Bob Hope had a genuine personal relationship. They shared political philosophy and a good joke and were enthusiastic golfers—both quite good.

In November, General Eisenhower became the new president, based a great deal on his promise to "go to Korea." He made no promise beyond that—and the American public embraced their wartime hero to lead the country in peace. Bob Hope joined the ranks. He became "Bob, so this is peace, Hope" and found a whole new application for old jokes brought out, rearranged, and presented in contemporary fashion.

Bob did something unheard-of during the presidential political conventions of 1952. He decided to accept his network's idea of adding color to the Democratic and Republican conventions, both held in Chicago. He brought along his wife and children, making it a family event and allowing his children to see history in the making. This was Bob Hope the family man at his best. His commentary during those two meetings would make an excellent study for stand-up comics on how to ad-lib your way through the landmines of comedy clubs.

At the Republican convention he brought the house down with "The way Taft and Eisenhower campaign managers are ballyhooing their respective candidates, you'd think they had transfusions from Cecil B. DeMille . . ."

He saved something for the Democrats when they arrived a couple of weeks later. "This town was known as the Windy City even before the politicians arrived . . ."

Bob had his own political campaign going on at the same time. Prior to his election as President of the American Guild of Variety Artists that summer, one Chicago columnist said that if Hope got elected, "At long last everyone would address him as 'Mr. President.' "

After an absence of several years, Bob Hope returned to the Academy Awards Ceremony at the Pantages Theatre in Hollywood on March 19, 1953, with actor Conrad Nagel co-hosting from New York. Hope had been snubbed by the Academy Committee because he had signed up with NBC to do television shows. By 1953 the big "backlog" deal had been made between the film studios and the television industry; much, but not all, was forgiven. That year the show was televised for the first time and Joan Crawford, a Best Actress nominee for *Sudden Fear,* actually showed up. She would probably have enjoyed the show more from her bedroom, since Shirley Booth walked off with the statuette for her brilliant performance in *Come Back Little Sheba.*

Hope had zingers for one and all after Charles Bracket, President of the Academy, opened the evening by presenting Hope with an honorary award.

"All over America," he began, "housewives are saying, 'Honey, put on your shirt, Joan Crawford's coming over.' Television—that's where movies go when they die . . . Jack Warner . . . he still refers to television as that furniture that stares back."

Looking out over the sophisticated, fancily dressed assemblage, he quipped, "It looks like a PTA meeting in Texas."

He regurgitated his old Bette Davis garage joke about the Oscar table but the joke, having been used too often, flopped.

Bob managed to have his girlfriend, Marilyn Maxwell, do a duet with him of "Am I in Love," one of the nominated songs, which brought sniggers from some tables.

Cecil B. DeMille's epic, *The Greatest Show on Earth,* won Best Picture but not Best Director (that went to John Ford for *The Quiet Man);* Gary Cooper took the Best Actor Oscar for *High Noon.* The big surprise came when Anthony Quinn was announced as Best Supporting Actor in *Viva Zapata,* when everyone expected Richard Burton to win for his performance in *My Cousin Rachel.*

Hope continued doing two pictures a year for Paramount in conjunction with his own company. In 1953 his first release was *Off Limits,* his second and last film with Marilyn Maxwell. Their affair also took a nosedive when Marilyn decided she wanted to get married and knew that she'd never be anything more than a mistress to Hope, no matter how much love he professed for her. The following year she did, indeed, marry. Bob didn't lose any time finding a new playmate, Jeannie Carmen, who would become famous as a close friend and confidante to Marilyn Monroe.

But other things happened to Bob in 1953 that were equally important. For one thing, he gained easy access to the White House and President Eisenhower. He merely picked up the phone and dialed the White House operator and was connected to whoever he asked for.

Hope always laughed when he told of having such easy accessibility to the president. "Hell," he said, "I knew him when he was a general and really had power . . . I played golf with him yesterday, and it's hard to beat a guy who rattles his medals while you're putting . . . he had Senator McCarthy's picture painted on the ball."

Eisenhower, a more moderate fellow (who seemed to have difficulty making up his mind whether to accept the Republican or Democratic nomination for president, since both parties made overtures), did not like Senator Joseph McCarthy and no doubt gave Hope the go-ahead to "let the damned rabble-rouser have it."

Beginning with Eisenhower, Bob Hope was close to every Republican president thereafter, but not even Ronald Reagan could claim him as a close friend. Eisenhower could.

President Eisenhower received only warm, cuddly comments in Hope's monologues. As a for instance, at the end of his second term, during one of Bob's television monologues, the following is typical of his commentary about Eisenhower over the years:

> "Ike left today on a good will tour . . . that means, 'How much and for how long?' Nixon briefed him on South America . . . but he's going anyway . . . Ike's not afraid. He's been through two wars and Ladies Day at the Gettysburg Country Club . . ."

Hope reveled in power and being on a first-name basis with the president of the United States gave him more power than he'd ever enjoyed in the past—political power which, after all, is the only power that counts. Arthur Marx states in his book that, "I personally know writers who've had portions of their manuscripts censored by book publishers in order to please Mr. Hope."

To back up his claim, Mr. Marx stated, "In the early seventies I had a contract to write a biography of Bob Hope for Norton. I signed it and deposited the advance, which was considerable. Then Evan Thomas, editor-in-chief at Norton at the time, called me to say, 'A word of advice about the Hope book! Take it easy on the guy. If you knock him, the people who like him won't buy it, and the people who don't like him won't buy it anyway.' "

Marx told Mr. Thomas that, ". . . if I can't tell the truth about him, there's no point in writing it." Marx fulfilled his contract with a biography of Sam Goldwyn instead.

Hope really revved up his engines in 1953. He'd taken on a five-day-a-week, fifteen-minute morning radio show sponsored by General Foods for which he received an unheard-of two million dollars. The same corporation began sponsorship in January 1953 of Hope's radio show, now broadcast on Wednesdays, as well.

His second film from Paramount in 1953, *Here Come the Girls* was a real laugher. His co-stars were Rosemary Clooney and Tony Martin. In *Portrait of a Superstar,* Charles Thompson quotes Rosemary:

> "Oh yes! One of the world's worst pictures! Here come the girls—there went the girls ... it was a very fast, nothing at all film. But it was funny, because Bob was doing about twelve other things at the same time. It seemed to me that he would show up for about an hour a day and we would shoot around him the rest of the time."

When the Friars Club gave Hope a second "roast" in February, Crosby's chair once again stood empty. Bing just didn't consider Bob Hope his equal, which had been and would continue to be made obvious by his snubs and snide remarks over the years.

Crosby wrote a highly successful autobiography in 1953, *Call Me Lucky.* Once he saw how well Crosby's book had been received, Bob Hope contacted Jack Goodman, editor-in-chief at Simon and Schuster, about writing his autobiography, which ended up being called *Have Tux, Will Travel.* Publication was preceded by an arrangement with the *Saturday Evening Post* to serialize the forthcoming book in a series of articles published between February and April 1954 as "This is on Me."

During my research for this book, I read both *Have Tux, Will Travel,* and "This is on Me." This effort, with all due respect to Pete Martin, who was always a highly respected celebrity profiler, read more like the "Local yokel makes it big—but is still a local yokel!"

There was no real reference to Hope's womanizing throughout his career. For Hope to admit that "I'm no angel" totally understates the facts. Leo Rosten, writing for *Look* magazine in September 1953, said of Hope:

"A tie-fumbler and a neck-stretcher, he ogles the dames and hints at midnight seductions, but you know he'll end up with candied cashew nuts and a uke. He is Penrod playing Don Juan. The minute a babe sails into view, he breaks into a leer, but he breaks into a sweat if the girl so much as flutters her lashes. His leer, indeed, shows the triumph of innocence over intention; his type gets seasick in a boudoir."

Based on all the revelations by the women who have come forward and revealed their trysts with Hope prior to publication of the book and articles, Leo Rosten was either naive or looking at Bob Hope through the eyes of a fan.

Represented as autobiographical, the book and articles omitted, in part, the following incidents:

1. A sensational court battle between Bob and his sister-in-law (Jim's wife).

2. Hope's lawsuit against *Life* magazine critic John Crosby, in which he alleged that Crosby had "maligned" him in a piece entitled, "Seven Deadly Sins of the Air," in a November 1950 issue of the magazine. Hope requested two million dollars, but later dropped the lawsuit after private meetings with the publisher. Hope stated that he withdrew the suit because "the offending paragraph had been left in the story inadvertently and there was no intention to harm him." Andrew Heiskell promptly made a public statement on behalf of *Life* magazine in which he praised Hope.

3. A $100,000 lawsuit brought in 1950 by the Forest Hotel in New York for a crack made in one of his monologues during a Paramount Theater appearance: "I got into town today and the Mayor gave me the keys to the city, and I checked into the Forest Hotel," he quipped, "where they gave me a cell. The maid changes rats every day." The hotel accused him of slander. Rather than face the unfavorable publicity,

Hope's attorneys advised him to settle out of court. As usual in such cases, the amount of settlement was not revealed, but it did include court costs.

Bob completed another Colgate Comedy Hour in early 1953 and went back out on tour. He did a charity golf tournament at the famous Greenbriar Hotel in White Sulphur Springs, West Virginia. He had as a partner the late abdicated King Edward VIII of England, who became the Duke of Windsor over "the woman I love."

Bob had been seeing a gorgeous blond model, Jeannie Carmen, who happened also to be a pretty impressive golfer with a figure rarely seen on any course.

I asked Jeanne how she'd happened to meet Bob Hope.

"I met him," she said, "on audition for his first color television show for Frigidaire. Actually I'd been very sick that week and didn't look well, but Bob wanted me for the show. I don't know why. It wasn't really a part, just a couple of lines. The producer and director and everyone else kept saying they wanted another girl, but Bob insisted, 'I want Jeanne Carmen.' He'd heard about my golfing, and I think that did the trick. After he found out I played a 77 handicap he wouldn't settle for any other girl. He had a thing about golf."

Jeanne says she was given lines for the part, "which I immediately blew because I was a model, not an actress. I think the lines were, 'Here comes Beau Geste,' or something like that which I fucked up royally. The entire set cracked up which embarrassed me to death, but in Bob's eyes I'd done nothing wrong. He definitely had tuned his antenna into me. I learned about his real intentions later on."

She remembers that they were having a break between scenes and she'd gone down into the audience and sat down with the crowd. "All of a sudden Bob comes walking down the aisle, got right next to me, and said, 'Hi.'

"I said, 'Hi,' back."

Bob said, "I hear you're a great golfer."

"That's true. I am."

"How would you like to play sometime?"

She said, "Sure. Why not? Little did I know," she says, "that his 'playing' did not necessarily mean golf. At 17 I'd only been away from home in Arkansas a short time. I'd taken off at 13, moved to St. Louis and from there to New York, still not a very hep girl. Bob Hope was the first star I ever met—I mean, actually knew to talk to.

"I hitchhiked from St. Louis to Manhattan and the very next day I had a dance part in a Broadway show called *Burlesque* starring Bert Lahr. Starting at the top, right?

"I always liked Bob. I've never been part of the intelligentsia, but I've always been different than other girls from Arkansas. I had something that caused me to appreciate good stuff, and I thought Bob really had something—so funny. I'd never heard anyone so clever and I thought, God, his jokes are fabulous. Little did I know that they were not his jokes. I soon discovered that he had eight of the best writers in the world and he used to test his jokes out on me.

"I'm sure that thirty years earlier, when he started out, he wasn't nearly as funny because he couldn't afford those expensive writers."

Jeanne had quite a reputation as a golf "trick artist," but Bob didn't know that until she told him.

"Really?" he asked. "I never met a girl trick artist before. What kind of tricks can you do?"

"I laughed. I wasn't too young to understand a double entendre but I thought he'd merely made a play on words, being known as a quick-witted guy. "I had no idea there was anything more than making a joke in his question."

It didn't take long for her to learn that Hope didn't joke when it came to young girls.

"He asked me out to dinner and I accepted, still not aware that my idea of dinner and his were two different entrees."

"How about coming over to my hotel? I'm at the Waldorf."

"Sure," she said, expecting the hotel's restaurant. "Here I was in New York trying to be the sophisticated Manhattanite. I was, in the only word I know to explain myself, *dumb!*"

Jeanne arrived, went to the Waldorf restaurant, and inquired as to Mr. Hope's table. The maitre d' checked the reservation list and, glancing up at the blond beauty, took a second good look and nodded. "I don't see Mr. Hope's reservation, but I'm sure it's an oversight," and proceeded to lead Jeanne to a "reserved" front table.

"I'd never been so catered to in my life. After a while I began to understand that just the mention of Bob's name brought out the best silver, the best table . . . just cater, cater, cater."

As the maitre d' moved toward his station, he spotted Bob Hope just outside the vestibule. "It was so funny," Jeanne recalls. "The maitre d' ran out in the hall to tell him I was there, calling out 'Mr. Hope, Mr. Hope . . . your lady . . . your lady friend is waiting for you.' The look on Bob's face is one I'll never forget as he peered into the door, searching. I still don't know why he got that look on his face, but I'll never forget it as long as I live. Nevertheless, the Hope name got me the best seat in the house. I only said that Bob Hope would be arriving soon and to let him know where I'd been seated."

Jeanne says, "Bob's face turned a not-so-delicate shade of purple and he made some small talk with the maitre d' before disappearing toward the elevators."

The maitre d' returned to Jeanne and said, "Mr. Hope will be right down."

"I thought Bob looked more than a little bit nervous, but chalked it up to overwork. The maitre d' muttered something about Mr. Hope's beard, and I thought to myself, who the hell is he kidding? Everybody knows Bob Hope. I tell you I was that green. I thought a beard meant, you know—like on Santa Claus or something." She soon discovered that it had another meaning and in this case the 'beard' turned out to be one of Bob's agents, Jimmy Saphier."

Bob hadn't planned dinner in the restaurant, nor had he planned for Jeanne to say a polite good night and return to her own apartment after dinner.

"We didn't get together intimately right away. We dated a couple of times when he happened to be in New York. Funny thing is, I was so dumb that I didn't even know the sonofabitch was married. I had a career that took up all my time, so I didn't read a lot of movie star stuff. Remember, I wasn't an intellectual from Harvard or Yale, merely a little old girl from Little Rock, Arkansas.

"Nobody," she says, "was nicer than Bob Hope, and good looking until he developed a stomach pouch, which he tried to hide by wearing the famous girdle that everybody talks about.

"One night in New York, after we'd been seeing each other for a while—and we still hadn't slept together—he took me out to a nightclub. I can't even remember where, but it had the biggest dance floor I'd ever seen. The minute we walked in, the band struck up 'Thanks for the Memory.' Bob grabbed me around the waist and took me out on the floor, sweeping me right into a waltz. I couldn't believe he did that. What a hell of a good dancer he was. Now I'm an Arkansas hick and I don't know ballroom dancing, although I'd already danced in a Broadway show. Give me the numbers to do and I know routines. That's a little bit different. Even in the Broadway show, they made me the comedienne because when the girls were all going this-a-way, I went that-a-way. I never could, and still can't, walk out on a dance floor with somebody who says, 'Let's dance,' and do it.

"Bob and I were all over the floor. Finally he said, 'What's the matter, honey, don't you know how to dance?'

"No," I said. "I don't know how to dance."

"Well, don't worry about it, honey. Just follow the old boy."

Jeanne says, "There was just no hope for me and I'm sure everybody had their eyes on us. Finally he saw the futility of it and escorted me back to the table. But you know something? It never even bothered him. He didn't appear to be the least bit embarrassed. He took it all in stride. It just never occurred to him to be irritable with me.

"When Bob returned to California he asked me to keep in touch with him at the studio by telephone. I did that, and I reversed the charges. I'd always tell the long distance operator, 'Reverse the charges to Robert Hope.' The dumb operator would invariably ask, 'You mean Robert Hope the movie star?' I stunned them even more when I calmly responded, 'No, Bob Hope the plumber!' Bob said to call collect, so I did as he asked."

Jeanne claims that she never even considered that Bob might be married. He certainly never mentioned a wife. "Maybe I was innocent, but if he had a wife, why would he tell me to call him collect at the studio? It also never occurred to me that calling him collect might get into the gossip columns.

"Back in those days we didn't have the paparazzi. Photographers protected people like Bob Hope. I remember once with Frank Sinatra when a photographer came up and asked, 'May I take your photo, Mr. Sinatra?' Everything seemed so innocent. But I did use that plumber thing all the time. How could anybody not know Bob Hope?"

In New York Bob pulled out all his seductive magic trying to get Jeanne up to his hotel room. By the time he succeeded she'd known him long enough to know what he meant. "I can tell you one thing, sex with Bob wasn't anything to write home about. I don't even remember the first time we did it, but I think it was during one of his stays at the Waldorf-Astoria. That's where he usually stayed in New York. He'd be in and out of town. Marilyn Maxwell had broken off their relationship. He really loved that woman. I met him on the rebound while he still carried a torch for her. She's probably the one woman who might have lured him away from his marriage. He really had a thing for her. Marilyn traveled a lot with him."

I asked Jeanne why she never did the USO tours with Bob.

"He tried to get me to go on trips with him and I don't know why I didn't. I was ambitious and dedicated to my work. I was young and hadn't traveled much, if any. And I was afraid. I kept asking myself, 'How can I do this?' I modeled every day and I liked that. I had not a clue that Bob's stuff out there with those soldiers could have done more, in one trip, than modeling could have done for me in a thousand years, that it would have brought me all kinds of good publicity. It would have been incredible. No one had ever done those trick shots into the audience with rubber golf balls. I turned him down one time and Anita Ekberg went on that trip. She soon became a big star.

"Anyway, I had my own career—a little television, some modeling, and, of course, my golf exhibitions, which were bringing me somewhere between 30 and 50 thousand dollars a pop. Not bad for a country girl. I had no ambitions to travel the world.''

She did go on a trip with Bob that is memorable.

''Bob asked me to accompany him to White Sulphur Springs, West Virginia, to a golf tournament at the Greenbriar Hotel. He was playing in a couples match with the Duke of Windsor, who'd brought along his wife—I think she more or less chaperoned him. Some kind of big charity event. Bob did a lot of those when I knew him.''

Bob flew into New York to meet Jeanne and they flew down to White Sulphur in a private plane.

''I do recall that he was too cheap to get me my own room at the Greenbriar. He said he didn't see any need to pay for two rooms. Frankly, I don't think he paid for any of it himself. After all, he was a celebrity and it was a celebrity event.''

Bob gave her an ultimatum: ''Sleep with me or sleep on the couch!''

''I did sleep with him that night but refused to have sex. He didn't get pushy or anything. When I said no, that was it. I sort of respected him for that, which made it easier for him when we were back in New York at the Waldorf.

''Celebrities never impressed me as being superior beings. When I met the Duke of Windsor, I said, 'Hi, Dukie.' No big deal. He seemed to enjoy the informality.

''I am by nature not a temperamental person unless I'm drinking pink champagne, which seems to cause me to do strange things, but Bob sort of brought out something in me that nobody else did. I'd do crazy things. I remember at the Greenbriar. Bob sat on my left and the Duke of Windsor on my right. The Duchess had a young guy with her. The Duke didn't seem to mind. Actually, he appeared to be having a good time. We were seated at a very long table with perhaps a dozen people in the party. We were dining and drinking champagne. I'd downed several pink champagnes when Bob said something cutesy to me which I can't even remember, but it pissed me off so much that I jumped up and as I shoved the table away from me the whole damned thing turned over and spilled drinks all over everybody on the other side of the table, including the Duchess and her young stud.

"I got up and stalked out of the room, my head high like a star of stage, screen, and television, without so much as a glance back, and returned to our room. I hadn't been there more than a minute before Bob came rushing in and said, 'You've got to come back down. Go change clothes and come back with me now.'

"He kept saying, 'Don't be shy. Don't be afraid. Don't be ashamed. Nobody's mad at you. They all love you.'

" 'Nope! I'm not coming down.' I don't know if I was embarrassed or what the hell. It didn't bother me that they were the Duke and Duchess of Windsor. I always felt I was as good as anybody. I was one of them. I think I was still angry with Bob. It took me a while to forgive him over some silly something or other.

"You know," she said, "all these women in his life and I don't know what the attraction could have been. There was nothing sexual about him. When I hear about all these other women I just wonder what he had that attracted us. He always admitted to being the cheapest guy in the world. He told me once that he'd do anything to get something for free."

Jeanne played golf—once—with Bob's great nemesis, Bing Crosby. "I can tell you," she says, "Bing Crosby was a bit of a prick. I played a round of golf with him and some other big shots one time and he became furious with me because I played so much better. He couldn't stand that I beat him, but nobody in the group played better. I was a great golfer in those days. Nothing made me nervous. That's what I did. I could put a ball anyplace I chose, anytime. Bing Crosby couldn't handle that.

"I later played a number of charity golf tournaments with Bob, but always paid my own plane fare. The only time he ever popped for a ticket was when he picked me up in the private plane in New York for the trip to White Sulphur Springs. I think he promoted that, too.

"He called me up once and wanted me to come over to Toluca Lake to see his house and the putting green in his backyard. Out of curiosity I went, and the next thing you know we were making love in the bedroom. I suddenly wondered how I would feel if my husband had another woman in my bed. I think Bob liked the excitement of taking chances.''

Bob had bragged to everyone at Lakeside about his great golfer friend, Jeanne Carmen. Someone suggested if she was so great, why didn't Bob have her over and put some money on her ability? Bob bet a bundle. After making love that afternoon, he told her to get in shape because he had set up an exhibition for her to show her stuff.

"I laughed at him. For Christ's sake, I *was* in shape. I golfed every day. However, on the appointed day for this great exhibition, cupid shot me in the rear end and spoiled the whole thing.

"I'd been golfing regularly at Hillcrest Country Club and they had a sixteen-year-old champion there. I mean, this kid was a hunk and looked a lot older. I'd been hot for him and so that particular morning he and I ended up at a hotel—the only cherry I ever got. And it almost got me into a pack of trouble. His mother found out and wanted me to marry him. Afterward she used to follow me around the golf course and ask, 'Are you Jeanne Carmen?' 'Yes.' 'Do you know my son, so and so?' 'Yes.' 'Are you having an affair with him?' 'Oh, no. Not me. You got the wrong girl.'

"The kid and I returned to Hillcrest and he took off. I went to my appointment at Lakeside with Bob.

"I mean to tell you, I have never played such bad golf in my life. I probably went farther than the golf ball when I swung the club. The balls went left, they went right. I think I even missed a couple of times. I'd made such mad love to the kid from Hillcrest that I had no strength left.

"Bob was furious. Not that I played bad golf, but that he lost so much money on me. Nothing ever seemed to make him angry except losing his money. He just kept asking me, very softly, 'What's the matter, honey?' I whispered back, 'It's a long story, Bob. I'll tell you later.' ''

The incident ended their affair, as it were. Bob drove her to the garage where her car waited.

"He let me out of the car, tossed my clubs out on the ground, and said, 'I'll see you sometime.' He pulled his car forward, revved the engine, put it in reverse, and took his foot off the brake. Whack! He drove right over my golf clubs—bag and all. They bent into what looked like horseshoes. Bob laughed like all hell as he drove away. I can still see him waving and laughing."

He called Jeanne a couple of times afterward and invited her over to the house, but she declined.

"I ran into him once in Palm Springs afterward. I'm driving down this dark street at night. I could see the image of the back of the head of the driver ahead of me and thought, that looks like Bob Hope. So I honked my horn. Now we're talking about a very dark street, late at night. The car ahead of me stopped and the driver got out and indeed it was Bob Hope. He came back and stuck his head in my window and, recognizing me, asked if I'd like to come up to his place for 'a drink or something.'

"Can you imagine a big star like Bob Hope hearing someone honk a horn behind him in the black of midnight, then getting out of the car to see who it is? He seemed never to be afraid of anything. It totally amazed me. But he never acted like a star with me. He seemed so unspoiled."

Jeanne lived next door to Marilyn Monroe and she moved to Phoenix, Arizona, to avoid the press after Marilyn's death. One day she read in the paper that Bob Hope was in town, staying at the Camelback Hotel. "I thought I'd give Bob a call, not even sure they'd put my call through, but they did right away.

"Bob said, 'Hi, honey. What are you doing here?' We talked for a while and then he said, 'Damn! It's too bad you didn't call earlier. I woke up with the biggest hard-on you've ever seen. I wound up having to drop a window on it.'

"I said, 'Bob, I don't recall it being that big!' He got a big laugh out of that and then I started laughing so hard I couldn't stop and I couldn't tell him why. I had to hang up.

"I got to thinking, the bottom line with Bob, to me, is that he cheated like it was going out of style and nobody seemed to care. I don't remember any of his women ever bragging about him being great sex. He wore that girdle with the staves and that's not very sexy when he takes his clothes off in front of a girl. Women aren't turned on by men wearing girdles. Maybe that's why he always liked young, innocent girls. He could impress and control them.''

Chapter 33

Bob brought a great deal of personal experience into his next Paramount release, *Casanova's Big Night*. If ever someone understood the role, he did. Artistically, the picture flopped, but still made three million at the box office. It had a hokey double ending. In one version Hope addressed the audience from the screen, declaring, "Now an alternative ending written, directed, and produced by Bob 'Orson Welles' Hope."

Casanova's Big Night more or less capped off Bob's personal opinion of himself. Arthur Marx gave a classic example of Bob's ego, recalling that when *Have Tux, Will Travel* was published, Bob not only plugged the hell out of his book but insisted that NBC urge their other stars on the network to do likewise.

"Jack Goodman," Marx says, "Simon and Schuster's editor-in-chief, told me that Hope's constant plugging was responsible for the book's initially selling five thousand copies a day."

Groucho Marx went out of his way to boost Bob's book on his show, "You Bet Your Life," which happened to be one of the most popular and longest-running shows on both radio and television. When Arthur wrote the biography of his father, *Life With Groucho,* Bob, despite the urging of Simon and

Schuster, which published both books, would not plug Arthur's biography.

On one show Bob had Hedda Hopper as a guest star. "What's that you've got under your arm?" he asked the great gossip columnist.

"Oh," said Hedda, producing Arthur's book, "that's a new book—*Life With Groucho.*"

Bob's responded coldly, "Well, you ought to read my book, *Have Tux, Will Travel.* You'll learn all about your favorite comedian."

The end of radio, as a forum for comedians, signaled the end of an era. The morrow would toss radio back into the days of the crystal set for guys like Bob Hope. He knew it. But as long as he could squeeze a buck out of radio, he would keep it somewhere on his agenda.

Motion pictures, he knew, could only grow bigger and better with all the new technologies being developed every day. Eddie Foy had been one of America's great vaudevillians, beloved by audiences yet plagued by personal demons. Mel Shavelson and Jack Rose had written a screenplay based on Foy's troubled life and times. They had no financing, a small matter once Bob read the script. He loved the idea of getting his teeth into a "really serious" character. He agreed to do the picture, making a deal which gave Hope Enterprises the bulk of ownership (44%) with the balance divided between the writers and Paramount Studios.

Jimmy Cagney reprised his role as George M. Cohan gratis because, "When I was breaking in as an actor, I could always get a square meal and a place to flop at the Foys'." It was payback time.

Some of Hope's writers felt that Bob Hope playing the black side of Foy's character would be like looking in the mirror and imitating himself. A number of Hope's writers secretly harbored intense hatred for their employer because of the very reasons Hope wanted to do the part, the things they believed Hope had in common with Eddie Foy: overly self-important, angry, condescending, and often just plain nasty and mean-spirited.

When the film was released in 1955, Bosley Crowther, in his *New York Times* review of *The Seven Little Foys,* showed little amusement or tolerance for the picture:

> "The impression the viewer is likely to get of the popular card from this report, which Mel Shavelson and Jack Rose have written, directed, and produced, is that he was just a bit of a nitwit, operating in a fog of conceit, shy of the normal compassions and wholly committed to the gag. He bore, in short, a strong resemblance to the stock screen character of Mr. Hope . . ."

The critic at the New York *Daily News* thought otherwise, concluding that: ". . . for the first time in his career, Hope isn't playing Hope on the screen. He's acting and doing a commendable job."

One memorable scene in the film took place when Bob, as Eddie Foy, is begging a judge to let him have his children back after they'd been removed due to violation of child labor laws. Bob's good friend and inspiration back to the early days of his "Road" films, Barney Dean, died the night before the scene was to be shot. Hope says it was the toughest scene he ever had to do—very emotional, very personal, very real.

During the spring of 1954 Bob became bored without a new front to conquer. He decided it was time to hit the road and break in some new material. Having more or less received the green light from the Eisenhower White House to take off on Senator Joseph McCarthy, Bob honed his wit and went after the demagogue in his own backyard although he did not at first consider it such a good idea.

One of Bob's senior writers, Mort Lachman, handed Bob some last minute material before he took to the road. Hope took one look and asked, "What the hell is this?"

Lachman said, "Just take it Bob. Trust me."

"Who the hell wants to hear anything else about that sonofabitch McCarthy? Besides, you want your boss sent to the federal penitentiary?'' Hope knew that decent, honest people were being accused or indicted and, worse, destroyed by the renegade senator's finger-pointing.

"Trust me, Bob. Besides," he said, baiting Hope, "what is more important to you, staying out of jail or getting a laugh?"

"Forget it," Hope said.

Mort slipped the material into Bob's bag anyway. Two days later Mort was awakened at two in the morning by a call from Bob. "Send more McCarthy zingers," he said. "They're great. I did a few at the state fair tonight and they were terrific! The audience went crazy!"

"What state fair?" Mort asked.

"Wisconsin State Fair," Bob said.

"Wisconsin? That's McCarthy's home state! You've got more guts than I have—they could ride you out on a rail!"

"Just send more!" Bob said and hung up.

He began one of his routines at the fair by announcing, "I almost didn't get to the fairgrounds tonight because of the jam-up of cars. Ever since McCarthy started that investigation, the traffic lights have been afraid to turn red," . . . "I have it on good authority that Senator McCarthy is going to disclose the names of two million more Communists. He just got his hands on a Moscow telephone book."

The crowds might have loved it but one ultra-conservative newspaper banner-lined: BOB HOPE IS A COMMUNIST!

Bob wrote the publisher a rather long, tongue-in-cheek rebuttal. Hope says, "In the very next edition that same paper headlined: BOB HOPE IS NOT A COMMUNIST! No one escaped the Hope humor once he'd figured out the sort of animal he needed to unravel. Joe McCarthy became easy prey compared to some of Hope's other targets. Fortunately, he always said, the presidents he knew all had a good sense of humor. "Otherwise," he snapped, "I'd be doing time."

During the opening negotiations to renew his contract with NBC, the critics were giving him their annual going-over about the "sameness" of his show. NBC told him to let the network worry about the critics. His sponsors were happy and the ratings were good. NBC's attitude? Don't rock the boat.

Bob felt the boat needed rocking. He, more than anyone else, knew that he had to do something different. While many of the radio comedians coming into television were settling into situation comedy shows, that was the last thing he wanted.

"I need something new. Something fresh." An invitation to emcee a Royal Command Performance in London gave him the excuse he needed for a break. His network executives did not find his next suggestion amusing in the least. He told NBC to cancel his November special because he intended to do a whole new show from Europe with an international flavor. He expected, he told the network bosses, to recruit people like Orson Welles and Edith Piaf—and maybe his old friend, Maurice Chevalier.

He told Jimmy Saphier that if NBC didn't like it, then let them sue. His rationale, which Saphier had a hell of a time selling to NBC, was that American television was "old." He figured that the European stars had never appeared on American television. By this time Orson Welles had taken up residence in Paris.

NBC had no choice since Hope's ultimatum meant he simply wasn't doing a November show. Hope was the number one star on the network, so the executives sweated out his "unbelievable stupidity."

He created an international situation in France and almost didn't get access to Paris. His writers despaired in his presence. He pushed everyone like a madman, but by the time he completed his mission he had a show which indeed included Maurice Chevalier, Bea Lillie, the 182-voice Cologne Maile Choir, Laine Dayde, the famous Parisian ballerina, two gorgeous blondes (Moira Lister and Shirley Eaton), and Reginald Gardiner, a rather stiff-upper-lip English actor with a fantastically dry wit.

NBC aired what can only be described as a mishmash of Europeans making their first American television appearance.

Hope claimed to be making history. The *Washington Star* critic aptly placed the hodgepodge of a show in its proper perspective:

> "If this is history, Arnold Toynbee has been ploughing a long furrow in the wrong field."

After watching the show from the comfort of his own home in Toluca Lake, Bob became depressed. He even considered retiring until his doctor told him there was absolutely nothing wrong with him and to get the hell out of the office and go to work.

Finding no sympathy from Dr. Hearn, Bob did what he always did—he jumped in four directions at the same time. He called a press conference to announce the signing of a brand new five-year contract with NBC to do eight colorcasts a year.

He said he would be making *That Certain Feeling* with Eva Marie Saint, adding that he also had plans to do a picture in Europe with Katharine Hepburn based on a story by Ben Hecht. The male lead had originally been offered to Cary Grant. Substituting Bob Hope for Cary Grant gave Ben Hecht indigestion to say the least.

Things got so bad that at a final conciliatory meeting in Bob's Dorchester Hotel suite in London, Ben Hecht in effect told Bob to let his "hokey" writers finish the script. He'd had it. Hepburn had the same feelings as Hecht but was too much of a traditionalist to walk out on her contract or bad-mouth a costar.

Ben Hecht did not mess around. He immediately wired a letter back to Hollywood to be published immediately on the back page of the *Hollywood Reporter:*

> "My dear partner Bob Hope:
> "This is to notify you that I have removed my name as author from our mutilated venture, *The Iron Petticoat.*
> "Unfortunately your other partner, Katharine Hepburn, can't shy out of the fractured picture with me.
> "Although her magnificent performance has been

blow-torched out of the film, there is enough left of the Hepburn footage to identify her for her sharpshooters.

"I am assured by my hopeful predators that *The Iron Petticoat* will go over big with people 'who can't get enough of Bob Hope.'

"Let us hope this swooning contingent is not confined to yourself and your euphoric agent, Louis Shurr."

[Signed] BEN HECHT

Ben Hecht was a writer and playwright of considerable stature both on Broadway and in Hollywood. Someone who could handle himself well and did not need Bob Hope in order to sustain life and limb had finally taken him on in public. Not just a critic who could be easily dismissed as having a bad day, Hecht, a giant among giants, had been the highest paid screenwriter in Hollywood when Bob Hope was fiddling around with *The Big Broadcast of 1938*.

Undaunted, however, Hope took his own full-page ad in *The Hollywood Reporter*:

"My dear Ex-Partner Ben:

"You once wrote *The Front Page,* and now you've followed it up with the back page.

"The first thing I did on hearing of your withdrawal from *The Iron Petticoat* was to seek out my other fan, Doc Shurr . . . I handed him your ad. He read it under water and came up with this comment: 'The billing is now strengthened.'

"I am most understanding. The way things are going you simply can't afford to be associated with a hit.

"As for Kate Hepburn, I don't think she was depressed with the preview audience rave about her performance.

"Let's do all our correspondence this way in print. It lifts *The Iron Petticoat*."

BOB (Blow-Torch) HOPE"

Ben Hecht won the argument, hands down. Bob, way out of his league, should have ignored Hecht's letter. Instead, he made a fool of himself in print. The picture went down faster than the *Titanic*.

Bob picked up his paycheck and said, "Next!"

"Next" became the Eva Marie Saint co-starrer, although there is some conjecture about which film began or was completed first between *That Certain Feeling* and *The Iron Petticoat*. In either event, Bob, playing opposite a true dramatic actress, did not come off in synchronized fashion with his co-star, just as he hadn't with Katharine Hepburn.

George Hope asked Bob Slatzer to accompany him back to Cleveland to set up for the film's premiere. Since Bob came from Cleveland and Eva Marie from Bowling Green, Ohio, it figured that a premiere in Cleveland would get loads of favorable publicity.

Bob Slatzer says, "It didn't take me long to figure out why Bob always left Dolores in Hollywood when he hit the highway.

"George, myself, and our wives checked into the same hotel where Bob and Eva would be staying while in Cleveland, the Carter. George called me aside, away from my wife, and whispered, 'Don't say anything about the girls in front of our wives.'

"I had no idea what the hell he was talking about. What girls did he mean? I didn't see any girls.

"On the first day of rehearsal I noticed three Vegas-type girls hanging around. They might have been fans, for all I knew. As a nice gesture I said hello to one of them, but George quickly pulled me aside.

" 'I told you. Keep away. They belong to The *Boss.*' "

Slatzer finally got the picture. The three girls were also guests at the Carter Hotel, courtesy of Bob Hope. "One," says Slatzer, "was on the floor above Bob, another on the floor below, and the third in a room near Bob's suite. Bob never played with the local talent. He always imported his playmates."

Hope, who could call the president of the United States on his private line, could not persuade the Soviet Union to let him do a television broadcast live from Moscow. His every effort met with the usual "Nyet! Nyet! Nyet!" Still, he kept it in mind that one day they would see it his way.

Being an Englishman by birth, Bob Hope should have known that during the somewhat conservative 1950s he needed to be careful not to offend the British royal family. But he dared to be foolish. During one of his specials in the fall of 1955 he made some comments about Princes Margaret and Group Captain Peter Townsend.

In his monologue, Hope quipped:

"Next time I'm in London I expect to see the Princess's handkerchiefs hanging out of the Palace to dry . . . Townsend should have known better than to try to play the Palace—I never could."

The Canadian stations that carried the show were deluged with complaints about his inappropriate remarks. The *Toronto Telegram* trashed Hope, declaring that his monologue was ". . . in extremely poor taste, off-color, and not very funny . . ."

Bob's feeble attempts to justify himself fell on deaf ears.

Meanwhile he kept jumping from picture to picture. He decided to make *Beau James,* based on the playboy (and very shady) former Mayor of New York, Jimmy Walker, who had been the darling of Manhattan's gangsters during the Roaring Twenties. Hope seemed always to forget, when he played real people on the screen, that they were not fictional characters. His costar, Alexis Smith, appeared on screen as either a cold, conniving woman, or snobbish society type. Hope's comedic talents playing against a blank wall did not work. The critics did not treat him as kindly as he thought they should, either.

Paris Holiday, in which he chose as his costars busty Anita Ekberg and the French comedian Fernandel, also went down the drain. Neither man understood the other's language or sense of timing. For the first time, Hope publicly admitted that he'd made a mistake. He took full responsibility, because the film had been his idea in the first place.

"*Paris Holiday,*" he said somewhat in jest, "set a new record: three men were killed on the picture, all of them auditors. The cost went a million dollars over budget, but it was all

United Artists' fault. Handing me the money to make a movie is like asking Dean Martin to tend bar.''

Not even the presence of luscious Anita Ekberg could save the picture. A dog is a dog. Adding insult to Bob's already frayed psyche, Fernandel demanded an extra ten grand in addition to the $100,000 he had already received for the film—and he wanted it immediately and in cash.

In the midst of all this madness, Bob was asked to emcee the Academy Awards for the 1954 crop of films. The event took place on the evening of March 30, 1955, at the RKO Pantages Theatre near Hollywood and Vine. Thelma Ritter co-hosted from New York. Seldom has there been an Oscar night in which so many truly great stars handed out awards: Grace Kelly, Eva Marie Saint, Edmond O'Brien, Rod Steiger, Lee J. Cobb, Dorothy Dandridge, Nina Foch, Jane Wyman, Jan Sterling, Humphrey Bogart, Katy Jurado, Marlon Brando, Claire Trevor, Karl Malden, Audrey Hepburn, Bing Crosby (in the company of starlet Kathryn Grant, 30 years his junior and soon to become the second Mrs. Crosby), Frank Sinatra, Donna Reed, William Holden, Bette Davis, Lauren Bacall, and Merle Oberon.

Academy President Charles Bracket introduced Hope, who immediately wisecracked, ''Welcome to *You Bet Your Career.*'' In fine form, he continued, ''Cecil B. DeMille is about to make *The Eight Commandments.* He couldn't get two of them past the Breen Office,'' he added, naming the censors.

He then exchanged some classic patter with Thelma Ritter. When Bogart came up on stage to make a presentation, he joshed Hope, ''Who does your make-up,'' he asked, ''Abbey Rents?''

Hope had a grand time with Bing Crosby, who presented the music awards as the two men swapped wisecracks as though they were in a new film called *The Road to Hollywood.*

Crosby and Brando were equally favored to win Best Actor, Bing for *The Country Girl* (Grace Kelly had already won Best Actress for the same film) in which he played a broken-down drunk, Brando for his portrayal of a dock worker in the dynamic *On the Waterfront*. When Brando's name was announced he was so nervous he almost swallowed a mouthful of gum.

The only near-calamity came when Bob Hope bade Oldsmobile farewell as a sponsor. Network affiliates misunderstood and cut away from the balance of the show. Some of them never did get back in time for the Best Picture award, which went to *On the Waterfront*.

Bob finally got his visa to the Soviet Union approved, after what can only be described as an international lack of understanding as to Bob Hope's importance—especially to Bob Hope. In the interim, President Eisenhower won his second term in a landslide victory over Adlai E. Stevenson, making Ike the first Republican to win a second term since William McKinley in 1900. Hope also tripped over to London to do a special film for one of Prince Philip's charities. Some said he was atoning for his Princess Margaret offense. However, according to English biographer Charles Thompson, Hope turned down performing at a Windsor Castle staff Christmas party at which both Queen Elizabeth and Princess Margaret were in attendance.

Bob didn't make another picture for quite some time, but he did intensify his focus on the Soviet Union and a Moscow premiere of *Paris Holiday*. While in London filming a television special, and sneaking a premiere of *Paris Holiday,* he personally went to the Soviet Consulate in London to apply for sixteen visas for himself and his entourage. He quickly learned that when a Soviet said ''Nyet,'' it meant no, not without approval from ''higher authority.''

He'd hired Ursula Halloran, a good-looking young recent graduate of Penn State University, to handle his New York publicity. He got Ursula on the phone and ordered her down to Washington, D.C., to see if she couldn't speed things up at the State Department. He then prevailed upon Irving R. Levine, the distinguished NBC correspondent in Moscow, to use his contacts behind the Iron Curtain to help arrange things.

Jock Whitney was the United States Ambassador to the Court of St. James. Thanks to Eisenhower, Bob Hope had great connections at the ambassadorial level. He merely picked up the hotel phone, called the embassy, and enlisted Whitney's assistance. He put a lot of oars in the water, but so far the boat simply wasn't moving off the political sandbars.

Whitney promised to speak with Jacob Malik, the Soviet Ambassador to Great Britain, when he saw him that evening at a cocktail party. Bob Hope smiled. In the bag.

Malik asked Whitney, "What does Mr. Hope want to do? Does he want to entertain our troops in Red Square?"

Bob returned to California empty-handed and hadn't been home a week when he received a phone call from NBC's Washington headquarters. The Soviets had approved six visas, not sixteen, and he would be limited to seven days in Moscow to do whatever it was he had to do. Seven days. One week.

Bob leaped with joy. Seven days? Great. Didn't God create the universe in six days? Bob Hope could certainly do a television special and orchestrate a film premiere in seven.

Chapter 34

Bob's major decision concerned the six visas: to whom would the extra five be awarded? He decided that he would need writers, opting for Mort Lachman and Bill Larkin. Then he settled on British cameraman extraordinaire Ken Talbot and two press agents, Arthur Jacobs from United Artists Pictures and Ursula Halloran. Some eyebrows were raised at the inclusion of Ursula, but nobody openly questioned her presence.

He went through a debriefing by the U. S. State Department as to what he could and could not do, where he could and could not go, and what he would not be able to say. The Soviets were sticklers for rules and regulations.

When the Soviet Aeroflot jet arrived at the Moscow airport, Hope and his party were met and greeted by Irving R. Levine from NBC along with several magazine writers, correspondents, and Russian government agents including an interpreter/guide who would shadow Hope night and day during his stay in the Soviet Union.

The Soviet Minister of Culture insisted that all filming be done in Moscow, developed by Soviet experts, and not allowed out of the country until it received the Soviet seal of approval.

Bob kept saying, yeah, yeah, yeah. He knew the value of

having the first American television show filmed entirely inside the Soviet Union. He did not fare as well with his hoped-for premiere of *Paris Holiday*. The Ministry held its nose and said, "Nyet!"

The Soviets made his trip miserable. The game of spying became daily fare for Hope and his small troupe. He returned to his room one night to discover it had been rummaged through and the contents of his briefcase scattered about without any attempt to cover up the deed.

His hosts rejected his doing a special show for English-speaking residents of the city in a public hall. Ambassador Llewellyn Thompson opened up his own house to bring a bit of home to those who found themselves isolated in Moscow due to their work. Hope received a welcome comparable to those he received from American troops around the globe.

The Soviets were happy to provide a cameraman to shoot the Moscow circus, a Russian fashion show, violinist David Oistrakh, ballerina Galina Ulanova, Popov (clown par excellence), and comedian Arkadi Raikin. But they made him pay for footage of the Ukrainian State Dancers. They didn't let Communism interfere with a capital venture.

On the night before Hope's departure, three bureaucrats from the Ministry of Culture cornered him and gave him some Soviet "advice." They liked his show, but had a couple of suggestions on how to improve it.

"What's the problem?" Hope wanted to know.

He was told that the show would be a better one if he omitted a couple of jokes. One of them cited the following:

> "The Russians are overjoyed with their Sputnik. It's kind of weird being in a country where every other ninety-two minutes there's a national holiday. Anybody without a stiff neck is a traitor. It's a big topic of conversation everyplace but the dog show."

" 'Traitor,' " the man advised, "is a very serious charge in Russia."

Hope tried to explain that in America exaggeration was one

of the basic forms of comedy, but received a cold shoulder. The man continued, "Perhaps you could eliminate all references to the Sputnik. It is not really a subject for comedy."

Bob told a few jokes and the bureaucrats laughed, but told him he'd receive a list of offensive jokes before he left Moscow the next day. He required Hope's personal word that the $1,200 for developing film would be paid before releasing the edited show.

Back in Hollywood, Hope edited the special and inserted some "different" material, probably just as offensive to the Ministry of Culture. He'd accomplished his coup, for which he received both the Peabody and Sylvania merit awards.

Hope always found time for the troops, no matter what engagements were slotted into his schedule. During Christmas 1957 he took a group along with him to Alaska, Korea, and Japan. They included columnist Mike Connolly from the *Hollywood Reporter,* gossip columnist Hedda Hopper, and one of filmland's reigning sex symbols, Jayne Mansfield.

In his book *Don't Shoot, It's Only Me,* Hope says:

> "Jayne Mansfield . . . had her bed and her swimming pool built in the shape of a heart. When she put on a silky, flimsy gown and stepped out on a stage in front of a few thousand lonesome GI's a million miles from home, they could see everything they were fighting for. Of course, in 1957, America wasn't fighting for anything. But the men were."

Hedda Hopper harbored a personal dislike for Jayne Mansfield because Jayne enjoyed a close relationship with Hedda's archenemy, Louella Parsons. Hedda never missed an opportunity to claw Jayne. During a show in Japan, Jayne walked out onto the stage in a gown that seemed to expose Mts. Everest and McKinley in one fell swoop. The GI's went berserk. Hope said, "The GI's took so many pictures, Kodak stock went up ten points."

Hedda Hopper seethed. After the show she coldly said to Jayne, "Darling, let me give you some professional advice. You're too talented to show that much. Stop over-exposing yourself." Jayne smiled, not anxious to fight with the influential gossip. Hedda went to the NBC representative, Norman Morrell, there to make sure they had the right kind of material to put together a stateside show, and complained about "the scandalous attire that woman is wearing."

Hedda's powerful column, originating with the Los Angeles Times-Mirror Syndicate, could help or harm a show. Neither Hope nor NBC cared to have Hedda say anything bad about a show that would eventually be televised as a special back in the States.

Norman advised Jayne that the dress might wear well with the troops, but he'd have to cut her out of the television special if she insisted on wearing it. Jayne, never to be outdone by anyone in the sex department, appeared on the next show in a dress that went all the way to the top of her neck, zipped up the back so tight that when she turned a profile to the troops she out-pointed her critics, a strategy that captured her audience while the cameras continued to flash.

One of the more confusing aspects of Hedda and NBC's complaints about Mansfield had to do with Hope's first "Overseas Christmas Shows" in 1954 when Hope, unable to get Marilyn Monroe or Jeanne Carmen, settled for a beauty contest winner from U.C.L.A. She went on to fame as Anita Ekberg. The interesting aspect, however, had nothing to do with the girl, but with her attire.

Ekberg came out on the stage in Thule, Greenland, before several thousand GI's in sub-zero weather. She wore a fur coat, looking more like a large, woolly worm than an exquisite beauty. However, according to Hope, "She took off the coat and stood there in a low-cut gown that showed cleavage that made the Grand Canyon look trivial. It was bedlam. Hedda Hopper, who had insisted on going along for a "scoop," found no fault with Anita's revealing attire.

When the edited show aired as a Hope "Colgate Comedy

Hour'' in January, 60 percent of all American television sets were tuned in that night.

These Christmas shows often presented problems other than dodging bullets, sludging along in the mire, or performing in sub-zero weather. On one trip to Europe, Bob was set to do a show for American troops at Moron, Spain. He collapsed in the mess hall and was immediately hospitalized. His brief appearance on stage, as the show went on without him, brought thousands to their feet, stamping and cheering for the man who had brought so much of home to so many away from home.

By the following day he had recovered and was rehearsing for the show that night at Torrejon Air Base. Jimmy Saphier came to Bob and told him that Gina Lollobrigida, in Spain filming *David and Bathsheba,* would guest star on the show for $10,000—in cash on the barrelhead. The money had to be wired from a Los Angeles bank. Jack Hope, Bob's brother, picked up the cash at a local bank, brought it to Gina's hotel room, and counted it out in hundred dollar bills—American. Of course, it was only one percent of Bob's take when the show aired on NBC later as a Christmas special.

A year later Bob, after suffering numerous other collapses and near-collapses, fuzzy vision, and spurts of high blood pressure, entered Columbia Presbyterian Hospital in New York to be examined by a number of the world's most renowned eye specialists. The results were not encouraging.

"You've got to slow down," Dr. Stuart Cosgriff advised.

Bob asked him to cut the sermon and shoot it to him straight. "What's the matter with me, Doc?"

The doctor explained that Hope suffered from a vascular circulatory problem. If he would just relax and work less, he might get some of his lost sight back. For a man as active as Bob Hope, whose eyesight as much as his timing sustained his career, the doctor's prognosis came as a shock.

Dolores put her foot down. Bob Hope, like the war-worn battleship that he was, was effectively placed in mothballs. It was a major blow and only the beginning of the eye problems that would plague Bob for the rest of his life.

* * *

Bob found himself co-hosting the Academy Awards at the RKO Pantages Theatre once more on March 26, 1958. His co-hosts were James Stewart, Rosalind Russell, David Niven, and Jack Lemmon. One of the presenters that night, Lana Turner, left her gangster boyfriend, Johnny Stompanato, steaming with rage at her Beverly Hills home. The publicity attendant to their romance had rocked Hollywood and by Good Friday, only a few days away, the world's media would forget the Academy Awards when it learned of the slaying of Stompanato in Turner's bedroom.

Bob Hope, the last of the emcees for the evening, commented about his recent trip to Russia, and in a sense reminding the Academy that he had never "won" an Oscar. "They didn't recognize me there, either. At least here they let the losers stay in town. They had a TV in every room, only it watches you."

The Academy adopted some new rules that year, one of which stated that, "No one may be nominated for an Oscar if he has admitted Communist Party membership and has not renounced that membership, if he has refused to testify before a Congressional Committee, or he has refused to respond to a subpoena from such committee." Within a year the rule was quietly rescinded.

Toward the end of the fifties, President Eisenhower opened the door to American disaster in Vietnam by sending the usual "technical advisors" to Saigon (under the SEATO Treaty), a move that seemed to precede American involvement. Little did Bob Hope or anyone else know that the bloody battles in Vietnam would become the Hope Diamond in his entertainment crown.

Busy making three films in a row plus television specials, Bob rather expected that Richard Nixon, Eisenhower's vice president, would follow Ike into the White House. Otherwise he gave little or no particular attention to politicians. Eisenhower had not been the best president in terms of comedy material.

Alias Jesse James (co-starring Rhonda Fleming), *The Facts of Life* (Lucille Ball) and *Bachelor in Paradise* (with Lana Turner) rolled out in succession.

Bob Hope and Lana Turner were the most mismatched co-stars imaginable. Ever the sophisticated, glamorous, and opinionated actress, Lana did not take to Bob's off-color jokes nor his bawdy sense of humor. They barely spoke off the set and Lana could not wait to get home in the evening, as she told her hairdresser, to "get in a hot tub and soak away any lingering stench of that awful picture and that pompous ass, Bob Hope."

Of the three films, only one is much remembered. *The Facts of Life* is considered the best picture in which Bob Hope ever appeared. The combination of Ball and Hope created a feeling in the audience that those two people could be you and me. The only problem, for the times, happened to be that they were married—but not to each other.

Bob didn't like the script, but Lucille Ball did. Lucy had one objection. "I am not going to play Dorothy Lamour in Bob's 'Road to Infidelity.' "

The script, based on Noel Coward's *Brief Encounter,* was written, by Frank Panama and Norman Frank, who understood Hope because of their previous writing assignments on the "Road" pictures at Paramount. Bob and Lucy had co-starred in three previous films, so each felt comfortable with the other.

The Facts of Life proved to all skeptics that Bob Hope was capable of serious comedy and did not need one-liners and punch shots to relate to an audience. That he worked better with Lucille Ball than any other of the many beautiful women who shared the big screen with him stands as a testament to the professionalism of both. Lucille Ball from Metro, like Betty Hutton at Paramount, could slapstick you right out of your boots, then turn around and give you a scene registering a ten on the Kleenex meter. Bob played the domesticated puppy opposite her in a manner that made women want to take him home to cuddle.

* * *

For the second year in a row, the Motion Picture Academy selected Bob to emcee the Oscars, but again surrounded him with co-hosts. He returned to the RKO Pantages on April 6, 1959, in the company of David Niven, Tony Randall, Mort Sahl, Laurence Olivier, and Jerry Lewis. One might think the Academy trusted Bob, but worried whether or not his vision might fail him during the show. The problems with his eyes had been in the headlines of every major publication in the country, though his doctors made it publicly plain that relaxation and some tranquilizers would eliminate any serious problems.

Hope opened the show with, "We have a great show tonight . . . Ed Sullivan is in our audience . . ." The celebrated audience roared. "I'll be followed by David Niven . . . if the balloon arrives on time." Jayne Mansfield modeled the winning Cecil Beaton gown, created for *Gigi,* although it was reported by a somewhat jealous Sheilah Graham that Beaton didn't want Jayne because her figure was "too much" for his gowns. Jerry Lewis, the final emcee, made such a fool of himself when Susan Hayward was awarded the gold statuette for her chilling performance in *I'll Cry Tomorrow* that the critics en masse condemned him—none more than Dorothy Kilgallen, who criticized "his cheap give-the-little-girl-another-hand treatment of Susan Hayward, who scarcely needed an assist from an egg-laying comedian in her hour of triumph."

The following year the Academy returned to its senses by selecting Bob Hope to be the sole host and emcee when the show would air for the first time on ABC television instead of Bob's home network, NBC.

After commenting about the striking Screen Actors Guild, Bob reached his stride. "How about the pictures this year? Sex, persecution, adultery, cannibalism—we'll get those kids away from those TV sets yet . . ."

Caught flat-footed when Academy president B. B. Kahane came out to announce him as the winner of the annual Jean

Hersholt Humanitarian Award (his fourth honor from the organization), Bob turned to him and said, "I'll get you for this . . . I don't have writers for this type of work . . ."

Bob proved that his eyes were just fine and the Academy needn't have worried so much. With Hope at the helm, it was one of the better ceremonies of the decade.

Hedda Hopper, who seemed always to have something to complain about, didn't disappoint. She severely criticized the Academy voters for giving the Best Actress nod to Simone Signoret because of her leftist political views.

"I never minded when the Democrats won, but I drew the line when Simone Signoret hit the jackpot. I'm as broadminded as anyone, but that was ridiculous . . ." Hopper was so angry she resigned from the Academy (not for the first time, either).

On his 1959 Christmas tour to Alaska, Bob again brought along Jayne Mansfield. He said, "I always liked to take Jayne to the cold country. If she stood next to an iceberg we got instant hot water." As always, the photographers followed Jayne around, but Hope never seemed to mind the extra attention they gave her. He liked Jayne.

At King Salmon on Christmas Day, they performed in a hangar on the flatbeds of two trucks which served as a stage. Jayne and Bob had a skit in which they came on stage from opposite sides. Mickey Hargitay, Jayne's muscleman husband, assisted her up onto the truck bed. Wearing an ultra-low-cut pink gown, Jayne leaned up and forward as Mickey guided her. What Hope and several thousand anxious servicemen saw was two enormous nipples followed by Jayne Mansfield—a vision in pink. The GI's went crazy. Sex-starved and homesick, Jayne Mansfield warmed their hearts better than any Christmas eggnog.

Few people knew that Jayne had a wonderful singing voice. But that night as she sang *White Christmas* at a private party, even a hardened base commander wiped tears from his cheeks.

After her death, Hope released a statement:

"She had joy, that girl. She had bounce. She was an upper all the way. She had fantastic style. I could never figure her out. One minute she was the most naive little girl in the world and the next minute you had the feeling she was putting the whole world on. She had a pool that was pink and heart-shaped—and that was Jayne—pink and heart-shaped. I really miss her."

Chapter 35

The sixties opened with a bang for Bob Hope. Although his friend, Richard Nixon, was defeated in the presidential sweepstakes by Senator John F. Kennedy from Massachusetts, he found plenty of jokes at the new president's expense. Bob soon learned that the young president had his own style of wit and humor and loved nothing more than repartee.

Kennedy hadn't been in office long when the Academy of Motion Picture Arts and Sciences called on Bob, as they would again the following year, to be the solo emcee and host for the 1960 Oscar presentations. Hedda Hopper had a long list of complaints, beginning with the moving of the awards to April 17, a date she considered far too late in the season. Worse, from her point of view, was that the ceremony was not in Hollywood but of all places, in the Santa Monica Civic Auditorium.

"If Dalton Trumbo gets an Oscar for either *Exodus* or *Spartacus,* the roof may blow off the Santa Monica Auditorium!" Trumbo was one of the writers blacklisted as a result of the House Un-American Activities Committee witchhunts of the fifties.

The new president of the Academy, Valentine Davies, introduced Bob Hope, who quickly got down to business as only he could. "The members of the Academy will decide which actor and actress has the best press agent. I didn't know there was any campaigning until I saw my maid wearing a Chill Wills button." Wills had been nominated in the Best Supporting Actor category for his performance in John Wayne's *The Alamo*.

Hope brought the crowd to a roar when he defined the five nominated films:

> "How about those movies this year? *Exodus*, the story of the Republican Party; *Sons and Lovers*, the Bing Crosby family; *The Apartment*, the story of Frank Sinatra (recalling the famous wrong-door raid on Marilyn Monroe by Frank and Joe DiMaggio, Marilyn's estranged husband); *Never on Sunday*, about a Greek coffee break . . ."

To the surprise of no one, Elizabeth Taylor won best actress for *Butterfield 8* (an award most thought should have gone to her the previous year for "Maggie the Cat" in the film adaptation of Tennessee Williams' play, *Cat on a Hot Tin Roof.*)

The title song from Bob's movie, *The Facts of Life*, was nominated, but lost out to "Never On Sunday."

It is not known if Hedda Hopper had any influence on the Academy, but the following year the 1961 awards were handed out on April 9, 1962—a week earlier—but still at Santa Monica Civic Auditorium. Hope, the sole emcee, had yet another of his movie title songs nominated, *Bachelor in Paradise*. The award went to "Moon River" from *Breakfast at Tiffany's*.

The new Academy president, actor Wendell Corey, declared, "While we hope you'll be entertained, this is essentially a news event . . ." and he introduced Bob Hope.

> "Welcome to Judgment at Santa Monica. I'm something new—a method loser . . . Jackie Gleason can't be here . . . he's afraid of planes . . . and vice versa. *The Hustler*— that's about Bing's obstetrician."

As Bob approached 60 he was itching to get back into the swing of things. He already kept a pace that outdistanced younger men, but then Bob Hope wasn't an ordinary man. While some people required a full night's sleep, Bob just began to wake up after midnight. George Burns, who knew Bob Hope all the way back to vaudeville, once said, "Bob can go to four different cities in one day and entertain in each. But he sleeps, you know! He gets on a plane, closes his eyes, and goes to sleep. Then he gets up in front of an audience, makes them scream, and goes back on the plane and goes to sleep again."

The long-awaited new "Road" film finally became a reality, but only as a shabby imitation of the other six. Panama and Frank wrote and produced *The Road to Hong Kong,* made in England at Shepperton Studios. Dolores insisted that Bob combine a family vacation with his movie-making, so he gathered up his wife and the four children and took them with him to London.

Bing brought Kathryn, who was very near the birth of her second child, and their son Harry.

It became quite a hassle taking the long drive from the Dorchester Hotel every day out to the studio near Staines in Surrey. Mel Frank wanted his stars closer to the studio, not only because it would be easier on the wives and children, but more importantly so that he could get together with the two men to discuss the picture on a daily basis after the set shut down. Mel found the ideal place—Cranbourne Court. The estate boasted 25 acres and 22 bedrooms. There were golf courses nearby for Bing and Bob, plus an in-house butler.

Originally Mel had thought only of Bob's family but when Hope complained about the size of the place, Crosby suggested they all move in together. "My God," he said, "we could wander around here for days and never even run into one another." Bob popped for a Rolls Royce to cart the men back and forth to the studio. It would be the closest that Bing and Bob would ever come to real friendship and only lasted for the duration of shooting the picture.

To his credit, Bob Hope fought valiantly to have Dorothy Lamour return to reprise her usual role, but Crosby wouldn't hear of it. "She's turned into an old hag," Bing said, refusing to budge one inch. "People aren't going to come out to see an over-the-hill broad."

Never had there been a more classic example of the double standard. Both Bing and Bob were ten years Dottie's senior. Not only did Bing not want her but according to Hope biographer Bill Faith, neither Norman Panama nor Melvin Frank was interested in Lamour as the female lead. The United Artists contract stipulated that no Lamour, no *Road to Hong Kong*.

Crosby wanted a young sex goddess, Hope wanted Lamour, the producers wanted anybody but Lamour. In the end it turned out to be a miserable set and a lousy picture.

Hollywood had treated Dorothy Lamour so shabbily that she escaped to Baltimore with her husband and two young sons. Her son Tommy once told me that Crosby never treated his mother as an equal. "But," he added, "my mother always looked at the positive side. She was shocked when they offered her almost a walk-on in the picture."

When Lamour found out that she had been replaced by Joan Collins, she was so upset she refused even to consider being in the picture. Only because of Bob's persuasion did Dorothy agree to come to England and do a song and dance routine with him in a cameo. But she never got over Bing's mean-spiritedness.

After the film was completed and everyone had gone home, Hope persuaded Dorothy to come to the West Coast to be part of his television show promoting the picture, but when she approached Bing about being on *his* show, he said there wasn't any room. So sorry.

All throughout his show, Bing talked about Lamour and even used life-sized blow-ups of her in skits.

The film had a gaggle of cameos, including David Niven, Frank Sinatra, Zsa Zsa Gabor, and Peter Sellers. The funniest scenes involved guest stars. In one scene Sellers, playing a doctor from India, does an eye exam on Hope which involves a cobra. After the snake slithers back down into the basket, Bob asks Peter, "What would you do if it bit you?"

"Very simple. I'd cut the wound and suck out the poison."

Bob persisted. "But what if it's in a place where you can't reach with your mouth?"

"That," responded Sellers, "is when you find out who your friends are."

Crosby and Hope spent hours thinking up gags to play on one another. Joan Collins never understood Crosby and he couldn't have cared less. To him she was merely a necessary piece of the scenery.

Mel Frank surprised both Crosby and Hope in one instance. The scene called for Bob and Bing to argue which one would have Joan on which day as they ticked off the days of the weeks. In the middle of the scene, two astronauts walked onto the set—much to the confusion of Crosby and Hope, because there were no astronauts in the script.

When the two men looked up from their argument they found Joan Collins hugging and kissing the astronauts, who turned out to be Frank Sinatra and Dean Martin under those space helmets. All four men cracked up.

Upon hearing that Zsa Zsa Gabor was in London Bing called her up and invited her out to pull a gag on Hope. "You'll be dressed up as a nurse and in this scene Hope is in a coma. I want you to kiss him on the lips."

She did and Hope quickly opened his eyes and found himself face-to-face with Gabor. The episode ended shooting for the day. Crosby doubled up on the floor he laughed so much. Then both men took off for the golf course. Nobody could keep a straight face after seeing the complete shock and surprise registered on Bob's mug when he recognized Zsa Zsa.

Gabor later said, "It was the first and, I will tell you, the last time I ever kissed Bob Hope!"

Most of the great humor took place between scenes. Some of the outtakes would make a good two-hour television special.

Despite the so-so reviews, the picture made a lot of money, but it truly signaled the end of an era. The first "Road" picture had been made 22 years earlier and somewhere along the way the road narrowed, the hips widened, and the jowls sagged a bit. Nevertheless, the picture became a fitting epitaph for the seven-film series.

                                    *   *   *

Denounced by many of his past writers for being cheap and
stingy, Hope was now carrying forty or so writers on a payroll
that topped half a million dollars a year. Instead of slowing
down his pace as his family and doctors insisted, he had merely
started to gear up for new ventures with sharper, brighter writers
kicking out "Hope humor" by the carload.

Bob was sharply reminded of the passing years when his
son Tony graduated from Georgetown University during the
summer of 1962. The whole family joined Bob and Tony in
Washington where Tony received his liberal arts bachelor's
degree while Bob was handed an honorary doctorate in humane
letters.

Bob receiving a degree of any kind drew surefire media
coverage, plus the enormous amount of press releases being
whizzed out of his Hollywood and New York offices. Although
it was Tony's show, his father stole some of the thunder by
being asked to address the several thousand graduates and their
families. He had come prepared, and would have gone away
disappointed had he not been asked to speak:

> "My advice to young people going out into the world:
> don't go. I was out there last week and the stock market
> was down so far I came right back in . . ."

Several years earlier Bob had begun to press, through his
public relations people, to have a gold congressional medal
struck in his honor. As always, Bob was his own best press
agent. He knew how to work a room and the U. S. Congress
was a room with a very small audience compared to those Hope
usually entertained.

Feeling physically better than he had in some time, he decided
to take Dolores and the three younger children on a yacht tour
of the Alaskan waters. While aboard the yacht he received a
radio message that his brother Jack had been rushed to a hospital
in Boston suffering from acute hepatitis.

Bob was at his brother's bedside when he succumbed to the disease late in the day on August 6.

According to Bill Faith's account, the black sheep brother, Jim, had written a family tell-all book. A set of the galleys rested on a nearby table in the death room. Jack had been reading the manuscript at Jim's request. Faith further alleges that the publisher refused to publish the book without a foreword by Bob Hope.

When Jim nixed the idea the publisher is reputed to have said, "No Bob Hope foreword, no deal." The book had a clever title, *Mother Had Hopes.* When Jim died his wife, Wyn, is supposed to have delivered one of two existing copies to Bob, who locked it up in the Hope vault. What Wyn did with the other copy remains a mystery.

Jack's death brought Bob ever closer to his own mortality, something that bothered him a lot even though he did not like to discuss anything to do with the hereafter. But someone had to take over the awesome responsibilities that Jack had shouldered. The most likely candidate was Mort Lachman, who took on the chores.

One of Mort's first duties involved a film script submitted by producer Harry Saltzman. "Would Bob," he asked, "consider a location film in Africa?"

Anita Ekberg had been proposed as a likely costar. Bob liked Anita, so he read the script carefully and decided that perhaps a change of scenery might do him some good.

By the time the pre-production work had been completed, a civil conflict erupted in Kenya which caused great concern for the safety of the actors and film crew.

Bob went to United Artists and offered a way out. "Why don't we do it on location—in England?"

Eventually a totally human-built jungle sprang up at the Pinewood Studios near London. Hope liked working in the jungle next door to one of the swingingest metropolises in Europe.

As if Jack's death hadn't cast a pall over his life, while filming *Call Me Bwana,* Monty Brice (Fanny's brother) died of a heart attack on the set. Monty had been Barney Dean's replacement. On that same evening Hope received a call to his Dorchester Hotel suite advising him that Mack Millar, who worked so tirelessly to fulfill Bob's dream of a congressional gold medal, had died at his Coldwater Canyon home in Beverly Hills of a heart attack at the age of fifty-seven. Monty was seventy-one, but fifty-seven? Two deaths in one day came as a major jolt to Bob's inner security.

Just prior to all these events, Bob had agreed to do a new book for Doubleday regarding his trip to Russia called *I Owe Russia $1,200*. The book, dedicated to his brother Jack, became an immediate bestseller. To further his quest for the congressional gold medal, Bob, through Mack Millar, had negotiated a deal with one of the most prestigious weekly newspaper inserts, *The American Weekly*. They promised to run a full fifteen-page center-spread of Bob's life and career as an entertainer in order to influence Washington legislators.

Bob also committed himself to something he always swore he would never do—a weekly television show. Jimmy Saphier negotiated an unbelievable long-term deal with Chrysler Motor Company involving an hour-to-ninety-minute weekly show. Bob would receive $25,000 for shows that he merely introduced and $500,000 for any show in which he personally starred. The shows were to have the highest calibre scripts by the best writers available. Not since Martin Manulis's "Playhouse 90" had there been such an effort to bring quality drama to television. Not only did the truly good writers show an interest, but also the quality actors expressed a desire to get in on the ground floor.

Hope starred in his first production under the new Chrysler contract, along with Barbra Streisand, James Garner, Dean Martin, and Tuesday Weld. It was well written by Mort Lachman, Lester White, and Norman Sullivan. Taking on another of the late Jack Hope's chores, Lachman produced the show.

Variety gave the show a thumbs-up:

"Bob Hope, who is giving his all for Chrysler this season as host of an anthology series and star of a monthly variety, teed off with one of his own crackerjack comedy stanzas. It remains to be seen whether the dramatic entries can sustain this momentum, but in any case Hope's own specials can be counted on to be surefire winners . . .''

Call Me Bwana could have used some mature writing. the *New York Times* gave the picture a swift kick in its credits:

"Bob Hope, one of the world's most celebrated traveling men, undoubtedly took the wrong turn when he hit the trail toward Africa in *Call Me Bwana* . . . Mr. Hope has been called many things in films, but *tired* must be the word for him, his writers, and his cast in this pseudo safari."

The Vietnam build-up, which began under President Eisenhower in 1954, now claimed a large contingent of American servicemen. On his annual Christmas tour, scheduled for the Far East to include Guam, Japan, the Philippines, Korea, Taiwan, and Okinawa, Bob took along Janis Paige, Anita Bryant, and Amachee Chabot (a U.S. Miss World contestant), plus Jerry Colonna and the Les Brown band.

Lana Turner, who'd expressed displeasure at working with Bob Hope, went along as a surprise gift for the troops and turned out to be the consummate professional by appearing on stage and doing her routine even when her voice became so hoarse she sounded more like Louis Armstrong. Of course, she'd been brought up at Metro-Goldwyn-Mayer under the tutelage of Louis B. Mayer, who believed that unless you were on your deathbed, you performed.

The tour turned out to be a great one for Bob and garnered an Emmy for his NBC documentary coverage of our troops in the Far East.

Good things happen. Bad things happen. During the summer of 1962, several months before the Far East Christmas tour, the Congress of the United States finally voted a gold medal for Hope which President John F. Kennedy presented to him in the presence of his family and more than a hundred congressmen in the Rose Garden of the White House.

On the back of the medal it said:

> "Presented to Bob Hope by President Kennedy in recognition of his having rendered outstanding service to the cause of democracy throughout the world. By Act of Congress . . ."

President Kennedy said the medal reflected ". . . the great affection all of us hold for you, and most especially, the great appreciation we have for you for so many years going so many places to entertain the sons, daughters, brothers, and sisters of Americans, who were very far from home."

Hope responded in kind: "Thank you for this great honor, Mr. President. I feel very humble, but I think I have the strength of character to fight it . . . This is a great thing. There is only one sobering thought: I received this for going out of the country. I think they are trying to tell me something."

Bob never wasted an opportunity to break up a solemn situation, which is one of the reasons he deserved the high honor. Wherever he went on his trips to war zones and far-flung posts, he always encountered a certain depression—whether it be the wounded in hospitals or just plain homesick guys and gals far from home on Christmas—and he had in his bag of tricks the penicillin of optimism: humor, the best remedy for whatever ailed these gallant young people.

Bob would not let up. He insisted on loading up his schedule. He did a benefit in Dallas, Texas and began what would become a series of Bob Hope remembrances when he gave $300,000 to Southern Methodist University's new Owen Art Center for the Bob Hope Theater.

While playing golf in Palm Springs one day in late October his eye hemorrhaged again and he immediately grew dizzy. His doctor quarantined Bob to a dark room and almost total immobility and quiet. No telephones, no conversations, no nothing. It shook him up pretty good. What if it had been a stroke?

Bob was no fool. He knew he'd been playing with fate and eventually it might catch up with him. For a change he obeyed.

Bob told his press agent he'd get the next plane out of Los Angeles because he wanted to see Dr. Reese at Columbia Presbyterian Hospital in New York for further examination of his eye condition. He returned after being told that surgery would not correct his eye problems but that a Swiss surgeon in San Francisco, Dr. Dohrmann Pischel, had some new invention or other that might stop the hemorrhaging—but there were no guarantees.

While resting at home in Toluca Lake, trying to decide whether or not to risk another disappointment, Bob, along with the rest of the world, suffered an irreversible shock. On November 22, 1963, President John F. Kennedy met up with Lee Harvey Oswald at Daley Plaza in Dallas, Texas.

VIETNAM &
REDEMPTION

Chapter 36

President Lyndon Baines Johnson was a totally different species of president than John Fitzgerald Kennedy. Kennedy represented, as he clearly enunciated in his inaugural address, a new generation of Americans, born in the twentieth century. Whereas Kennedy offered the country "Camelot," President Johnson gave us Texas barbecues and an explosive expansion of what became known as the Vietnam War.

Bob Hope and Johnson were as opposite as east and west. Johnson did not play golf and exhibited none of the niceties of a modern president.

Bob had some personal problems of his own to deal with. A first session with the photocoagulation gun treatment on his eye did not produce the desired results and he returned to San Francisco for a second attempt, uncertain whether he would come home with better vision or possibly even blind.

The dark glasses provided by Dr. Pischel were specially designed to have pin-hole clarity in the center of the lenses, much like the cardboard pin-holes advertised on television to replace glasses. The cardboard focus was fun for kids, but not suitable for anyone in need of real glasses. In Bob's situation, he had no choice. Either he wore the glasses prescribed or gave up all hope of being able to read again.

The operation took place on December 10, 1963. Plans for a Christmas tour of American bases around the world had already been made and he feared that he might have to cancel for the first time since he began the holiday treks. Mort Lachman and others involved in pre-show preparations had serious doubts as to whether Bob would be up to the tough pace and schedule involved in a heavily scheduled Christmas tour. At the very last minute, when it looked as though there would be no Bob Hope Christmas Caravan, Bob gave Lachman the go-ahead. He would follow doctor's orders and rest up for a week to ten days and would catch up with everybody else in Ankara, Turkey, in time to do the first show. A military ophthalmologist accompanied Bob throughout the tour.

Bob opened his monologue with, "I'm glad I could make it ... I just thought you'd like to see a new kind of turkey..." He responded to the thunderous applause by forgetting his eye problems and gave the guys one hell of a show. He told the ophthalmologist who cautioned him to be careful not to aggravate his eye condition, that "Compared to what these kids are missing I'm one hundred percent healthy!" And he meant it.

The new year did not bring Bob any personal blessings. *TV Guide,* in its second edition of that year, really went after him in a way no other magazine had dared to do in the past. A feature article by Dwight Whitney blasted Hope's personal behavior:

> "... It has been estimated that in the 25 years since old Ski-Nose first rose to fame on the coattails of Bing Crosby during the 'me and Bing era,' he has raised close to a quarter of a million dollars for worthy causes ... traveled to almost every country in the world, often to entertain troops at Christmas, a time when any sensible father of four contrives to stay home. His stature as the world's foremost funny humanitarian has put in his pocket more brass hats, politicos, industrial wheelhorses, and Russian

generals than any comedian since Will Rogers . . . he is
sometimes called upon to facilitate matters which have
baffled the State Department. The wonder is that Mrs.
Hope has managed to preserve her own individuality, and
by doing so has freed him to live the sort of life he wants,
a nuance by no means lost on him. She is the rock, the
mother of their four adopted children, the presider over
the home he needs to come back to. They are separate
but equal. He fills the house with his golfing pals; she
invites men of the cloth. Bob has long since become
inured to arriving at his Palm Springs house late at night
to find a strange priest walking the grounds . . ."

The article shook the Hope household, especially Bob. He
resented the intrusion into his private world, but like it or not,
Dwight Whitney had opened a door to what many privately
thought was a strange marriage indeed. Had Dolores opted out,
public opinion would have been squarely on her side and the
mainline press would have gone on an anti-Bob Hope feeding
frenzy to equal or surpass any tabloid coverage. That is the
nature of the press/celebrity relationship—always extremely
fragile.

Bob had completed another below-par film with an insignificant co-star, Lilo Pulver, which went nowhere in quick time.
Actually, he had begun to tire of movie-making. He'd seen the
problems that other stars were having in sharing in the profits.
The new "Hollywood" bookkeeping seemed always to indicate
that packed movie houses made no profit. In other words, the
lawyers and CPA's had devised a peculiar "double-entry"
method of recording profits. One entry said "big grosses," the
other showed "runaway post-production costs."

Bob considered it plain cheating. Even as an independent
producer he knew that if you didn't police the costs and profits,
someone would take your socks when you looked the wrong
way for a second. He didn't need that. He'd found a lot of
other ways to control both his business ventures and the income
derived from such activities.

I'll Take Sweden, starring Bob, Dina Merrill, and Tuesday

Weld, was not a Bob Hope film. Dina Merrill was not his kind of costar. He preferred them younger and more voluptuous. Dina, although an excellent actress, came off as the society woman that she was in real life, so the usual Hope humor did not go over with the public as it had in the past. It didn't make much of an impression on Bob, either. He seemed to be just walking through his pictures, grabbing the money and moving on to the next project. The love he'd once had for moviemaking now focused on television and what had come to be his first love, the boys in uniform.

The Vietnam War was custom-tailored for Bob Hope. He could handle television, personal appearances, and any number of myriad, far-flung enterprises as long as he had "my boys." Bob offered something that no commanding officer could ever give—hope and Hope humor. It had worked for him since 1941 and energized him in a way that no medication ever could.

Bob's first trip to entertain the troops in Vietnam came about at Christmas 1964. In addition to his "repertoire" group of Les Brown and his band and Jerry Colonna, Bob took along his son Tony, Anita Bryant, Jill St. John, Anna Maria Alberghetti, Janis Paige, and Ann Sydney, the current Miss World.

Bob Hope, television and Vietnam became a psychological *ménage à trois*. Vietnam, our first "televised war," permitted Bob to bring into America's living rooms the real horror of jungle warfare.

Aware of the possibility of an attack from North Vietnam, the perimeter of the Bien Hoa Air Base, near Saigon where Bob and his group did their first show inside Vietnam, was totally surrounded by men armed with every kind of weapon from side arms to rocket launchers. Hope had never been so protected. He would soon find out that wherever he went in Vietnam he was in a war zone. His life, and the lives of his troupe, was in constant danger. Bob began his monologue with what was now proving to be a tried and true opening:

"... Hello, advisors ... I understand the enemy is very close ... but with my act they always are ..."

A short show ran two hours. Bob just refused to cut his monologue as long as 23,000 young heroes were willing to give and take banter with him. Finally, he simply had to move on to Saigon.

Hope soon learned how Vietnam differed from the other wars he'd covered. Rapid communications were not limited to the United States; the North Vietnamese military could track his every movement with ease. South Vietnam was infiltrated with Viet Cong informers. When Hope and his gang arrived at the Caravelle Hotel he discovered that the officers' quarters in the Brinks Hotel, just across the street, had been almost destroyed when a station wagon filled with high explosives went off during a Christmas party, killing and injuring many officers.

Garrick Utley of NBC news came up to Bob later at a party at General Maxwell Taylor's and asked if he was going to the hospital to visit the seventy-five people injured in the Brinks billets.

Bob, Les, and Jerry left for the hospital immediately where only Hope, of the three, gained entry into the burn ward. Bob says that the burn wards are always the hardest to deal with. He recalls with clarity that night and one particular young man who'd suffered cuts and burns over much of his face and body:

"... One kid was bent over while a doctor was working on his head and when he heard someone say 'Bob Hope,' he jerked his head away from the doctor and looked up at me, his face covered with blood. He said, 'Merry Christmas' as if he really meant it and I don't suppose I will ever forget the way he said it. It still chills me."

Bob had plenty to be thankful for as he attended a Midnight Mass conducted by Cardinal Spellman, Archbishop of New

York. He'd promised Dolores that he'd attend Mass—a promise he kept.

The military, in order to protect Hope's entourage, set up double stages for each show. In other words, there were two possible places where he might perform and one was chosen at the last possible moment. Hanoi Hannah, a second cousin to Tokyo Rose from World War II, never failed to announce the exact location of Bob's show on her daily radio broadcast. No one ever knew how she managed to have that information, but it re-affirmed the fact that South Vietnam had an unbelievable infiltration of civilian Viet Cong.

Several years after his first show, Bob received a note from Lt. General Jonathan O. Seaman in which he notified Hope that he'd recently read a translation of a document captured several days earlier. He ended his note to Bob with, "This quote should interest you: 'Attack on Brinks BOQ missed Bob Hope by ten minutes due to faulty timing devices.' "

If anybody doubts that Bob Hope went into active war zones, they simply didn't understand the man's single-minded objective in the Vietnam War—to go anywhere, under any circumstances, at any hour of the day or night to entertain American troops.

When Bob returned to Los Angeles, the brass breathed a sigh of relief. Nobody wanted North Vietnam to take out Bob Hope.

Back in the USA, Hope came face-to-face—probably for the first time—with the real split in America over the Vietnam War. Demonstrators from both sides filled college campuses and federal property and marched in the streets. It was the time of burning draft cards and "Hell no, I won't go!"

The highlights of Bob's Christmas tour became the focus of his 90-minute Chrysler extravaganza in January 1965. He had never devoted so much attention to the troops themselves in a special and Chrysler officials were nervous, as were some of Bob's advisors, given the mixed feelings in the country. Bob knew, despite the split, that most people supported the troops whether they agreed with the president or not.

Bob prevailed and the show, according to the Nielsen ratings, was watched by more people than any other Bob Hope television special.

After such a head-on collision with the horrors of a very bloody war, the Academy Awards ceremonies on April 5, 1965, at the Santa Monica Civic Auditorium gave Bob some much-needed comic relief.

At the outset a war of words erupted when Audrey Hepburn did not win a nomination for Best Actress for her role as Eliza Doolittle in *My Fair Lady*. The film received twelve nominations.

As a rebuke to the members of the academy, the *Los Angeles Times* carried the following front page banner-line:

Academy Nominations Upset
JULIE ANDREWS CHOSEN
AUDREY HEPBURN OMITTED

When *Daily Variety* alibied that Marni Nixon warbled the songs and perhaps that was why the members had ignored Hepburn, Warner Brothers Pictures fired off an immediate response: "If that's true, next time we have some star-dubbing to do out here we'll hire Maria Callas!"

Great lady that she was, Audrey immediately stepped in to present the Best Actor Oscar when Patricia Neal suffered several strokes just prior to the night of the awards. Ironically, it went to her costar in *My Fair Lady,* Rex Harrison.

Bob marched out into the fray and opened the ceremonies: "Welcome to Santa Monica on the Thames. Tonight Hollywood is handing out foreign aid. Before you can pick up your Oscar, you have to show your passport."

When Hope introduced Audrey Hepburn the audience lost all of its decorum, probably out of guilt. Jumping to their feet, they hooted, howled, applauded, and gave the English actress a rousing ovation—no one more enthusiastically than Julie Andrews. Upon receiving his gold statue from Hepburn, Harrison said, "I feel in a way I should split it in half between us."

At the end of the ceremonies, Bob Hope came out on stage to say something and the orchestra began to play so loudly that he couldn't be heard. When the mistake was realized and corrected, Hope quipped, "That's the loudest background music I ever heard . . . the losers will now join hands and march on the British Embassy."

But, as almost always, Hedda Hopper had the last word:

"No American actor won. Either the rules will have to be changed or our actors will have to try harder. And did you notice that Oscar went home with those who acted, produced, and directed good, clean family-type pictures? Proving that not only the rest of the country but Hollywood itself doesn't go for all that overabundance of sex and stripping."

One wonders what invective Miss Hopper might have injected into the Academy Awards in the nineties.

Bob's love for golf led Chrysler to bring about The Bob Hope Desert Classic, with Bob as its president. That Palm Springs tournament has long since surpassed the Bing Crosby Pebble Beach Tournament, and has become one of the major golf tournaments of the Pro Golfers Association. Every year celebrities join the top golfers of the country for the most glamorous pro-am tournament ever presented. The parties and events surrounding the tournament have become the greatest social events of the Palm Springs winter season. All of the money, of course, goes to charity.

Chrysler did not like Bob's idea of following up his Vietnam Christmas television show with another in March. The executives still worried about the country's attitudes toward the war. The last thing they wanted was a boycott of their products because of Hope's fervor for Vietnam.

Bob adamantly defended his decision in an interview with Associated Press writer Bob Thomas:

> ". . . if the Commies ever thought we weren't going to protect the Vietnamese, there would be Vietnams all over . . . Like it or not, we've fallen heir to the job of Big Daddy in the free world."

Bob more or less walked through *Boy, Did I get a Wrong Number,* a picture with Elke Sommer and Phyllis Diller, growing ever more tired of motion pictures.

A very savvy man when it came to what did and what didn't work in entertainment, Bob had come to realize that he had peaked as a movie star. He'd had his day and he had a platter full of moneymaking ventures, owned more real estate than any human being needed, and was certainly financially secure. Vietnam would be his great accomplishment in the third phase of his life. Although it wasn't a known fact at the time, Bob Hope accomplished something that four presidents would be unable to do—he came away from Vietnam a winner, no small feat for an English import.

Chapter 37

As the Vietnam War grew, so did Hope's family. Tony graduated from Georgetown and married a nurse. Linda completed her studies at St. Louis University with a degree in English and returned to Los Angeles to teach at Our Lady of Queen of Angels High School in downtown Los Angeles where her students were predominantly Hispanic.

Bob had become adept at speaking to the students and parents upon the graduation of his progeny. When Kelly graduated from St. John's Vianey Catholic High School in Los Angeles, his father gave the commencement address in which he told the assemblage:

> "I think it's great that our young men and women are concerned about people's rights, because that's the American way, and that's why the world looks to us for help. Americans need the new ideas of its young people . . ."

Bob's Chrysler shows were rolling right along and his life seemed to be settling into a steady pace for the first time in his long career. He spent more time at home, but continued to do benefit performances, for which he usually received a fee.

Bob Slatzer relates a Milton Berle story about Bob Hope:

"One night Milton and I were having dinner at the Magic Castle in Hollywood. We got to talking about Hope, and Milton said Bob called him up one night and said, 'Milton, I'm supposed to appear out in West Los Angeles at some function tonight and I've got a bad sore throat and don't feel good. Feel like hell. I'm wondering if you'd cover for me. All you have to do is tell a few jokes—you'll be on the agenda for an hour. That's about it.'

"Milton told me he did it, smoked a cigar, and went to bed. The next morning he gets a phone call from Hope. 'How'd it go, Miltie?'

'Went fine, nice audience.'

'Did you get the check?'

'What check?'

Hope said, 'Well, my fee is $25,000. They were supposed to give you a check for me.' Milton said, 'Bob, I don't know anything about it. You never mentioned money to me.'

Hope ended the conversation pretty fast. He said, 'Well, thanks, Miltie, I'll take care of it.'

Milton said, 'Can you imagine? I thought he was doing it for nothing. I certainly didn't expect anything.' "

That's a great story, but Bob never turned down anyone for a charity appearance—whether he got paid or not. He has always loved to perform for causes, which may be the reason he became so attached to the kids in Vietnam, a cause that overwhelmed him with compassion.

Christmas 1965 found him back in the Southeastern Pacific and the jungle warfare of Vietnam. He took along a group of 63, covered more than 23,000 miles in 12 days, made 19 stops doing 24 shows. He visited Thailand, South Vietnam, the Philippines, the South China Sea, and some remote islands. In addition to Les Brown and his Band of Renown, he took along Jerry Colonna, singer Jack Jones, film star Carroll Baker, Miss USA, and a bevy of chorus girls. Nightclub chanteuse Joey Heatherton filled out the entourage. During a recent telephone conversation, Joey told me that "Bob Hope did more than anyone to enhance my career. I think he's wonderful."

In Di An the Viet Cong were everywhere. As Hope exited a latrine just before showtime on Christmas Day, he made a joke about a soldier being loaded down with artillery. "Afraid it will blow away, son?"

The young GI reminded Bob that he had entered an "active zone," and that ". . . We're not only surrounded by Charleys, there may even be some in your audience."

One wonders why thousands of men would subject themselves to almost instant death in order to see Bob Hope. Perhaps one of his writers, Mort Lachman, came even closer than he intended when asked to sum up Bob's charisma as he appeared before the troops:

> ". . . There is something hysterical, religious, fanatical, and overwhelming about their fervor . . . it inspired Bob . . . to perform almost beyond endurance . . . Bob . . . is not a religious man, but there is a spiritual, missionary quality to these Christmas trips which is strangely contagious . . ."

While his romance with the troops blossomed, a different situation existed back home. Americans were not committed to fighting 9,000 miles away in a country most had never even heard of. Bob did not escape public and critical wrath. As much as he had done over the years to bring a bit of home to America's servicemen and women, their parents seemed averse to hearing about the war on Bob's television specials.

Despite the criticisms, his Christmas special drew 55 percent of the viewing audience. He couldn't understand the ambivalence of "the people back home." Hope had not as yet begun to see the futility of the war. Almost right up to the end he believed the Johnson and Nixon administrations were shooting straight. The fact that the Pentagon was party to the delusion must have come as a great shock to him. General Westmoreland, Commanding General of all forces in Vietnam, came home less than a hero. A CBS special on Westmoreland stained his name forever. Hope had deeply admired Westmoreland. He has never publicly said much about the general since his retirement from active service.

In late March 1966 President Johnson honored Bob Hope by presenting him with a medal at an event celebrating the silver anniversary of the USO. Bob seemed somewhat at a loss for words. He merely said, "Thank you very much, Mr. President." However, he quickly recovered and said, of Johnson, "Pretty crazy drop-in, isn't he?" A little applause, some whistles, and Texas-style hooting brought Bob back to his senses and he rattled on for some time, using a good-humored President Johnson as his foil. Johnson laughed until he shook. Both Hope and the president were in vintage form.

By April 1966 Hope had several reasons to hang around Los Angeles. For one thing, and it was beginning to be a habit, Bob's name appeared as the emcee for the annual Oscar presentations at the Santa Monica Civic Auditorium on April 18.

Hedda Hopper wasn't there to complain, having died a couple of months prior to the event. Her only competition, Louella Parsons, arrived in a wheelchair. An era was slowly passing into history.

On the podium Bob took a potshot at George Hamilton, who was dating Lynda Bird Johnson, daughter of the president. Said Hope of George, "If he plays his cards right, he may be the second Hamilton in the White House." (Actually he might have become the first. As Secretary of the Treasury, Alexander Hamilton never occupied the White House, despite his ambitions to do so.)

Arthur Freed, the reigning head of the Academy, presented Bob with his fifth honor, the prestigious Thalberg Award.

As Bob became more associated with the Vietnam War and defending the American position in Southeast Asia, talk behind the scenes focused on politics. George Murphy was already a U. S. Senator from California and Ronald Reagan showed an affinity for public office. His 1964 speech endorsing Barry Goldwater for president had caught the attention of political king makers. Would Bob Hope be interested in running for public office? For president on the Democratic ticket?

Bob joked, "Why would I want to be president? The American people love me. I'd like to keep it that way."

In 1966 Bob wrote another best-selling book, *Five Women I love; Bob Hope's Vietnam Story,* a chronology of his 1964-65 Christmas tours to the Vietnam war zones. He eloquently presented the raw-bone differences between Americans on the home front and those at the "hot front":

> ". . . These kids seem to be a lot more optimistic about this country than a lot of our citizens here at home. In their everyday job of fighting this treacherous war they know there's no alternative . . . they know if they walked out of this bamboo obstacle course, it would be like saying to the Commies—'Come and get it.' "

Ironically, less than ten years later that's exactly what happened. The United States abdicated a losing cause as the North Vietnamese took Saigon, leaving behind many friends and the memory of 58,000 gallant youngsters.

Whether on stage with Viet Cong in the bushes and B-52's flying out to bomb the Ho Chi Minh Trail or visiting quickly erected combat zone medical facilities, Bob knew how to be honest without being somber. The situation with demonstrators against the war intensified daily back in the states. During one of his monologues at Bien Hoa, Bob brought the home front to Vietnam:

> "Our Government's got a new policy about burning draft cards . . . Now they say, 'If he's old enough to play with matches, draft him . . . You've seen some of these guys with the shoulder-length hair. I guess they'd rather switch than fight."

When Bob's show took place aboard the aircraft carrier U.S.S. *Ticonderoga,* the destroyer *Turner Joy* and supply ship *Sacramento* pulled abreast of the carrier to hear the show over loudspeakers. Those with binoculars had the privilege of both listening and watching. Bob quipped, "I've played water holes before, but this is ridiculous!"

Hope hopscotched about South Vietnam, sometimes just behind enemy assault, sometimes a few minutes ahead—and all too often had to take cover when all hell broke loose. His arrival at Da Nang was almost burlesque. His entourage deplaned from a C-130 in a rainstorm. Long, black limousines escorted the group across the tarmac to helicopters, which flew them eight miles to an enclave of mud and mire where thousands of Marines had been sitting in the mud since morning, drenched to the skin.

Just as he prepared to go on stage someone handed him a telegram. Upon opening it he read the following message:

> "Along with thousands of brave young Americans, their families and friends, I'm glad that Christmas brought Hope to Vietnam. Please accept my thanks—and pass along my appreciation to your wonderful company. Lyndon B. Johnson."

President Johnson was indeed grateful for Bob Hope because Bob's shows were about the only good news he received from the war front.

Before continuing his tour, Hope received a request to fly immediately to the military hospital at Clark Field, north of Manila in the Philippines, where hundreds of severely wounded men from Vietnam were being treated. Jerry Colonna recalled the situation:

> "They were in terribly bad shape, under heavy sedation, and they hardly knew we were in there. That was the tough one to see. Bob very seldom speaks his mind about this sort of thing, but I knew by his expression and the tone of his voice that he was really shook."

Some photographs of Bob during the 1965 tour reflect the physical ailments he suffered. His gaunt facial expression in one photograph in which he wears a dark coat over his shoulders is reminiscent of a tired and worn-out President Franklin Roosevelt at a meeting with Churchill and Stalin toward the end of World War II. Suffering from exhaustion, Bob should have been home in bed, but he plowed on as though there would be no end to his quest until he became a battle casualty himself.

He contended that the kids in Vietnam had more spirit than those he entertained in World War II. In the latter there had been a common goal with the people at home. Beat the Axis and come back to a hero's welcome for a job well done. In Vietnam they faced a different kind of enemy, one that was alien to the American way. There would be no joyous welcome back to the States. Some of the guys in their second and third tours had spread the word—don't expect a hero's welcome. Yet they fought on. Hope respected that.

"It is," he told one friend, "like a salmon swimming upstream to die. It has to be done."

On April 10, 1967, Bob found himself before another glittering audience at the Santa Monica Civic Auditorium, once again host of the Academy Awards. As he surveyed the mass of glamour and ego he thought about the differences between Hollywood and the trenches of Vietnam. Here, he had to be funny or bomb. In Vietnam he just had to show up and dodge bombs along with the other guys. In his heart he preferred Vietnam.

"What tension, what drama," Bob said in reference to an impending strike, "and that was just waiting to see if the show would go on. Pretty soon we're going to have another category, Best Performance by a Governor," referring to fellow actor Ronald Reagan, then Governor of California. "But let's get on with this farcical charade of vulgar egotism and pomposity."

Many of the winners did not even attend the ceremonies to pick up their Oscars, including Elizabeth Taylor and Sandy Dennis. Taylor's excuse? Richard Burton didn't like to fly.

Hope's alibi for Elizabeth? ". . . leaving Richard alone in Paris is like leaving Jackie Gleason locked in a delicatessen."

When Dick LaPalm suggested to Bob that he ought to permit the release of an LP of his USO shows in Vietnam, Hope agreed. He associated that with his radio days when audiences sat by their consoles on Tuesday evenings and rocked with laughter at his humor. So why not put out an audio disc with the money earned going to support the USO?

The record, entitled *The Road to Vietnam,* fell on deaf ears. Some found it distasteful. The recording was released in time for the Christmas trade, which turned out to be a public relations fiasco. Too many American homes displayed gold stars.

Hope took a lot of flak for being "commercial," which wasn't anything new. He could handle criticism that involved making money, but the accusation that he was profiting from the death of the servicemen he entertained caused him to bristle. His critics ignored the reasons for which the record had been made, or the fact that Hope hadn't made a penny from the venture. The men and women who had already served in Vietnam and returned to the States appreciated the recording and that meant everything to Bob Hope.

Bob made only one picture in 1966, *Eight on the Lam,* also starring Jonathan Winters and Phyllis Diller. Jill St. John played the "beautiful doll" in the film which came from an original story by Arthur Marx and Bob Fisher.

In his Hope biography, Arthur says that when NBC renewed his contract they had a specific stipulation which did not appear in print. If NBC was to be involved in the financing of any of Hope's future films, Bob could not play the romantic lead. They felt his age precluded romance with a beautiful young woman.

Since Bob no longer did anything more in films except keep contractual commitments, it didn't bother him that someone else might get the laughs. His dedication, certainly during the sixties and into the early seventies, was to Vietnam and the boys at the front.

His 1966 Christmas tour to Southeast Asia differed from the previous ones in several ways. Sadly—his *gumba,* Jerry Colonna, suffered a stroke following a performance in one of the Hope Chrysler television specials, which left him partially paralyzed with a speech impairment and confined to the Motion Picture Country Home and Hospital in Woodland Hills, California.

Bob very much liked working with Phyllis Diller, so he recruited her to go along on the trek along with Joey Heatherton, Anita Bryant, Raquel Welch, Miss World of 1967, and singer Vic Damone. Les Brown and his band had become permanent fixtures on the Hope trips. He did something else different this time when he brought Dolores and their two youngest children, Nora and Kelly. It was the first time he'd taken the younger kids into a war zone, but he explained that it was time he spent Christmas with his own children.

One of the highlights of the trip came when Bob asked Dolores to sing *White Christmas.* She'd never lost her sense of professionalism and, as a mother who had time and again explained to her children that their father was off entertaining the children of other mothers and fathers, she had a mother's compassion for the men gathered by the thousands in front of the stage. She delivered that compassion and understanding through the lyrics of the song. Silence prevailed until she sang the last phrase; then she received an ovation unlike anyone in the troupe had ever heard at any troop entertainment stop throughout Hope's career.

During a news conference at Pleiku a *New York Times* reporter dared ask a question that few would have ventured. Did Hope consider himself a hawk or a dove?

Bob bristled with anger, gritting his teeth. He'd never been publicly called to identify his feelings, but he didn't flinch. "If it means that I want to see this thing brought to an early end— then I'm a hawk!"

By Christmas of 1967 the situation had so deteriorated in Vietnam that the Government feared Bob might come to harm, so he and his people were quartered in Bangkok and flown into Vietnam daily on U.S. Air Force planes to do their shows and then returned to Thailand at night. To the troupe, it seemed odd not being awakened in the middle of the night by a rocket attack.

Starting in Da Nang, Bob took his gang on a merry-go-round of 26 performances.

In his book, *The Show Business Nobody Knows,* columnist Earl Wilson, who went along on this jaunt, best described what went on from an outsider's point of view:

> "On the morning of December 28, 1967, our C-130 transport plane, with several millions of dollars worth of entertainers aboard, was just lifting off the runway at Cuchi, Vietnam, when the Viet Cong snipers shot at us ... Bob Hope, riding shotgun up in the cockpit, did not do anything heroic. Nor did Les Brown or Phil Crosby. Nor did any of us bravely seize Raquel Welch in our arms to protect her. Her husband, Pat Curtis, was sitting beside her, as he had been during the whole tour ... Besides, we didn't know we'd been fired on until the pilot, Lieutenant Colonel Bob Parker, told us ... and counting about fifty bullet holes in our plane, said we had perhaps been hit not only at Cuchi but also at Chu Lai and Da Nang ... 'It was small-arms fire. It could have come from rifles five hundred yards or more away.' ... 'Is it dangerous?' we asked him ... 'Not until it hits you,' he answered ominously ... 'Sniping never bothers me,' Bob said. 'After all, I used to play vaudeville at the Palace ...'"
>
> ... It was all carefully planned to enable the boys to escape the world of war for a few hours, and there was no political conversation or harangue ... even on those hot days and nights, the troupe would end the show with *White Christmas* and *Silent Night* ... as thousands of GIs bared their heads ... The wounded soldiers lay in hospital cots or sat in wheelchairs in the front rows. It was difficult for us to control our tears ... we tried to keep our lips from quivering ... a voice over the speaker

interrupted the show to say: 'All medics report immediately.' Standing on the back steps of the stage, I could see stretcher-bearers rushing battle casualties from the helicopter to the hospital a few hundred yards away. Many of those wounded men died as our show was in progress.''

As a New York newspaper man, Earl Wilson wasn't accustomed to what he encountered in Vietnam with Bob Hope and came away convinced that he'd been witness to something special—a special kind of man—Bob Hope.

''He never got temperamental, never got out of line. He bent all his efforts toward trying to make people laugh. The good he has done, the laughs he has brought those boys, cannot be appreciated by those who have not seen his military audiences close up. I did.''

Aware that the GI's already knew about the October march of more than 50,000 anti-war protesters on Washington, D.C., he explained to a group of battle-worn Marines that, ''I bring you great news from the land of liberty. It's still there, even if you have to cross a picket line to enjoy it . . . But don't worry about the riots in the States. All of you will be sent through survival school before you go back there.''

Silent Night had become the showstopper at every performance, sung that Christmas by Barbara McNair.

Bob managed to get in some political zingers declaring that Ronald Reagan ''is the only man who doesn't know he's running for president.''

Arthur Marx says that stateside, GI's were not as appreciative of Bob Hope's trips as they had been in the past. He stated in his biography of Hope that ''Resentment against Hope was beginning to grow—possibly because the GI's were beginning to feel he was having fun and making a profit from the war, while they were suffering and risking their lives.''

The Soviet-controlled newspaper *Izvestia* must have been worried about Bob's influence on the morale of the Viet Cong because throughout 1967 they ran articles condemning his trips and shows, declaring him an ''agent for the Pentagon and its dirty war." *Izvestia* told its readers that "Bob Hope plays the unattractive role of a comedian without principles."

Bob made a joke of the Communist propaganda. "I think they're sore over the $1,200 I never paid them for material they never delivered."

The 1967 Christmas show had a profound effect on Raquel Welch, who was more accustomed to the bright lights of a sound stage than the burning sunshine and drenching rains of Southeast Asia. Upon her return to the States she expressed her feelings about the war and the kids fighting there:

"It was very frightening to me and some of the other ladies, because it was really like throwing raw meat to a lot of hungry lions. The press fantasized that this was a very licentious experience for all these boys. But it wasn't at all. I don't mean to make them out to be Pollyannas, but really, the expression was much more urgent than a boy-girl kind of thing; it was like home . . . Bob Hope, America . . . and home. They were all kids . . . They were all babies; they could have been my younger brothers, barely shaving . . . fresh-faced kids that were out there fighting that war. It was the first time that it dawned on me and I was overwhelmed . . ."

Raquel said it all, critics of Hope and the war notwithstanding. These kids were only the instruments of war, not the war itself. The war was political.

Chapter 38

As the Vietnam War descended into a deeper morass, the mood of the country became more depressed, brewing anger and deep resentment toward the government. America wanted out of the war. By 1968 it had become obvious that we would not win the war, no matter how much our leaders lied to us and how hard we tried—wanted—to believe the lies.

Students continued to protest the war, now often joined by their parents. It was a year in which the war in Vietnam drove President Lyndon Johnson out of office. In the spring he announced that he would not seek reelection. He'd not only seen the losing of a war, but he'd lost the guts to continue fooling the American people.

The Democratic Convention in Chicago turned into a rout with fighting inside the convention hall and in the streets, disrupting the normal business of the city. It was a year that saw civil rights leader Martin Luther King assassinated on the balcony of a Memphis motel by an angry racist, setting off rioting in the streets and the burning of buildings across the country. Senator Robert F. Kennedy of New York, brother of the martyred President John F. Kennedy, was assassinated in the kitchen of the Ambassador Hotel in Los Angeles just after winning the California Democratic Presidential Primary.

America was a nation needing to focus more on the war within than the war in Vietnam. Republican Richard M. Nixon and Democrat Hubert H. Humphrey won their respective party's presidential nominations. Nixon won a stunning victory and would become the new president, saddled with the debacle that had become Vietnam and the burden of preventing the country from exploding into flames from coast to coast.

Bob Hope, like most people, thought he would never live to see the day that the country would be so divided. People were talking about race wars openly. Not since the Civil War had insurrection been so much on people's minds.

Bob Hope went on record during an interview published in *Variety* in early January of 1968, expressing his views about the Vietnam conflict:

> Hope said that he shared the belief of General Westmoreland that the war should be escalated . . . While admitting he was talking for himself and not the generals, Hope said he was expecting something big to happen soon. Maybe not THE BOMB, but crippling air strikes in hot pursuit of the enemy into bordering neutral countries. He doesn't share the beliefs that this being a presidential election year has anything to do with military strategy. "We are out to win it, and as soon as we can. To save American lives. The thinking in Washington is getting more hawkish."

His president apparently did not share Bob's view of eventual victory.

Bob's life had become golf, television specials, Vietnam, Oscar, and family. During the 1968 Awards Ceremony in Santa Monica on April 10, he made a misstatement that drew heavy criticism. Originally set for April 8, the awards were set back two days out of respect for Martin Luther King. A pall hung over the civic auditorium.

Bob opened the ceremonies:

"Welcome to the Academy Awards, or, as it's known at my house, Passover. About the delay of two days—it didn't affect me, but it's been tough on the nominees. How would you like to spend two days in a crouch? We also voted a special Oscar to the ABC programming department. They just committed harakiri. The delay also hurt Kodak, the sponsor's image. This show took three days to develop."

Hollywood, some for show and some for real, was in a state of mourning for the fallen leader. Many workers in the film industry—not just stars, but carpenters, electricians, writers, hairstylists, and, many others had marched or claimed to have marched with Martin Luther King in Alabama. They'd been to Selma, been in the crowd of 100,000 who'd gathered in the Great Basin in Washington, D.C. to hear him speak. Hope offended them. It was not the first time he'd been insensitive; in Vietnam the previous Christmas he'd made his "long hair" statement. He blamed his writers in both instances.

The star-studded audience gasped. Gregory Peck had just delivered a somber message:

"This has been a fateful week in the history of our nation and the two-day delay of this ceremony is the Academy's way of paying our profound respect to the memory of Dr. Martin Luther King, Jr. Of the five films nominated for Best Picture, two dealt with the subjects between the races. We must unite in compassion if we are to survive."

Bob Hope seemed not to say the right things throughout the evening. At the end of the show he closed with:

"Clichés have been replaced. Films reflect the human condition. The moguls shared something with the man in Atlanta—they had a dream. Rioting and indifference are equal sins."

His last sentence reminded the audience that there were thousands of American boys being slaughtered every day in Vietnam—and he never apologized for the reference. Bob meant no disrespect to Dr. King. He knew that many of those in the auditorium were anti-Vietnam and that they ought to be reminded not to blame the GI's.

Interestingly enough, *In the Heat of the Night,* a film about racism in the south, won for Best Picture; Rod Steiger won Best Actor for his portrayal of a rednecked southern sheriff in the same film, and Katharine Hepburn won the Best Actress award for *Guess Who's Coming to Dinner,* a film concerned with interracial marriage.

Bob already had an edge with the incoming Republican Administration of Richard Nixon. He had made friends with Spiro Agnew, the new vice president, when Agnew served as Governor of Maryland. He'd known the new president when he served as Eisenhower's vice president for two terms. If there was ever any doubt about Hope's politics, it disappeared during the Nixon administration.

Bob had one film released in 1968, *The Private Navy of Sgt. O'Farrell,* co-starring Phyllis Diller with Jeffrey Hunter and Gina Lollobrigida as the love interests. He made one picture during the year, *How to Commit Marriage,* which, many of his fans believe, was the best picture he made after the ones with Lucille Ball. He played Jane Wyman's husband. Jackie Gleason and Hope are bitter enemies, but their children fall in love and, with love conquering all, everything turns out okay.

At a time when Hollywood leaned more toward bawdy films, it was great family fare and did well for Bob's image as well as his bank account, but his health broke down during filming. Problems arose with his eyes again, which sent him to bed for a time. His film career was near an end. He would star in only one more picture, *Cancel My Reservation,* which Warner Brothers released in 1972.

He'd had a great ride in the movie business, but without Louis Shurr, who died just prior to his 1968 Christmas trip, he lost all interest in making pictures.

Bob found one event in 1968 to make him happy. In October, his eldest daughter Linda became engaged to Nathaniel Greenblatt Lande, the son of a prominent Augusta, Georgia, doctor. He and Linda had met at Universal Studios where he worked as a producer.

By the time Bob took off for points Pacific for his 1968 tour, a dialogue had been initiated between North Vietnam and the United States in Paris which became known as the ''Vietnam Peace Talks.'' Napalm had become a new method of heating up the jungles while torture by North Vietnamese interrogators of American prisoners of war equaled and surpassed that of the Japanese at Bataan during World War II.

Film star Ann-Margret and former Los Angeles Rams football player Rosey Grier headed up a brilliant troupe which included a bevy of leggy dancers billed as ''The Golddiggers,'' Linda Bennett, the Four Honeys, and Dick Albers—all accompanied by Les Brown and his big swing band.

Hope's show covered the entire Eastern Pacific from Korea to the tip of Vietnam, but always the focus was on South Vietnam where the hot war had exploded. No part of the peninsula was safe from the fighting, not Vietnam, Cambodia or Laos. Chaos, rather than containment had become the order of the day.

The Bob Hope ''Follies'' began in Japan and went on to play Korea, Taiwan, Thailand, Vietnam, Okinawa, the Philippines, and Guam. The troops understood Hope's sense of humor and played straight man for him en masse. At Kishine a big banner greeted him with: WE LOVE YOU BING!

Hope promptly ad-libbed, ''Aha! I've fallen in with a bunch of Commies!''

Known to walk into an orthopedic ward and announce, ''It's only me, Bob Hope, don't get up,'' the patients in one facility topped Bob with a welcoming sign reading, WELCOME BOB

HOPE. WE WOULD STAND UP AND SALUTE, BUT AT THE MOMENT WE'RE ALL HUNG UP.

On their first day in Vietnam, Hope expected to put on three shows: Bienhoa, Camranh Bay, and Long Binh. After losing one engine en route, they only made it to Bienhoa, where he opened his monologue with, "One of our motors went out on the way in, and I had quite a laundry problem." The men forgot their own problems and had a rousing good time. Their laughter peaked to a crescendo when Hope quipped, "Actually, I'd planned to spend Christmas in the States, but I can't stand violence. Besides, it was the perfect time to come to Vietnam— the war has moved to Paris."

No one worked harder on the tour than Bob. He was the first up and the last to bed, "working the room," so to speak, and every hospital ward possible. He never complained about his own problems and he had them—especially with his eyes. The man was approaching 65 and throughout his life he had worked like a demon—first to achieve fame, then fortune, and now causes, none more sacred to him than bringing a smile to the faces of war-tempered youth.

Bringing Rosey Grier along presented a possible problem for Hope. Rosey's anti-war stance had been well publicized, especially after the assassination of Robert F. Kennedy. He managed to avoid controversy by fitting right into the routines and sketches like everyone else. At the end of the trip, en route back to the United States from Guam, he did reveal his feelings, which Bob related in his best-selling book about the dozens of Christmas shows he'd put on for American servicemen and women over the years. Quoting Hope, Rosey summed it up:

> "Even though I was against the war, I thought we ought to let the soldiers know that we were not deserting them, that they were our brothers and our sisters. The anti-war battle we were fighting at home was not against the soldiers and the nurses; it was against the power that sent them there and the attitudes that sent them there. I went with Bob because I felt he was doing something I could relate to. I wanted to show the servicemen we cared about

them. That we didn't care why they were there, we cared about *them*. I wanted the soldiers to know where I stood. Even though I didn't approve of the war, I approved of them as human beings, doing what the government asked of them because they were citizens of our country. And I approve of that.''

Hope added, "So do I, Rosey. So do I.''

Bob and Dolores relaxed on New Year's Day as they rode down Colorado Boulevard in Pasadena on a beautiful day filled with sunshine and the grandeur of the annual Rose Parade which preceded the Rose Bowl football game. Bob and Dolores, in fact, were Grand and Mrs. Marshal of the event watched by an estimated 100 million viewers around the world—certainly Bob's greatest audience on television.

Chrysler furnished its prize vehicle, an Imperial convertible, and to the gross embarrassment of the automobile company, the car's motor stopped in the middle of the parade. Disaster was avoided when five long-haired teenagers volunteered to push the Grand Marshal's stalled vehicle to the end of the parade. A grateful Bob Hope gave the boys five prime seats to the game, including his and Dolores's as a reward.

Linda Hope's wedding was the social event of the young year when she and Nathaniel walked down the aisle of St. Charles Borromeo Church in North Hollywood where all of the Hope children, along with their mother, attended Mass every week. Bob gave away the bride. The religious ceremony quickly gave way to a lavish reception under a gigantic tent erected on the Hope estate in Toluca Lake.

The mingling guests made up a who's who of Hollywood and the Republican Party, including Bob's close friend and golfing buddy, Vice President-elect Spiro Agnew (representing the President-elect) and his wife. Also attending were California Governor Ronald Reagan and his wife Nancy, California Senator George Murphy, Generals Jimmy Doolittle and Omar Bradley, Cardinal McIntyre, head of the Los Angeles Catholic

Diocese, Jules Stein, head of the famed MCA talent agency, Danny Kaye, Gregory Peck, Jack and Mary Benny, Danny Thomas, Loretta Young, Irene Dunne, Earl Wilson, Ed Sullivan, Bob Considine, Bing and Kathryn Crosby, Dottie Lamour and her husband, Bill Howard.

Bob had never thrown such a large party at his own home and he wasn't about to pass up the opportunity to get "on" and stay "on" for as long as possible. He delivered some choice barbs at his "A" list guests.

His youngest daughter, Nora, already engaged to Sam McCullagh, did not escape her father's good humor. "Why don't you two get married right away," her father snapped, "before we have to strike the set?"

Of the new Vice President-elect, he said, ". . . there's the kind of golfer I go for—not a very good one."

His annual January Christmas television special on NBC, with the war edited down to fit the television format aired on January 16. The fifth show turned out to be even more popular with the television audience than the previous one, which gave Bob a lift. He held the strong belief that more Americans supported the war effort than opposed it. In his mind he tried to justify that position through the ratings of his Chrysler special.

Shortly thereafter, Hope became a patient at the Jules Stein Eye Clinic at UCLA where he spent three days after which he went home and canceled all appearances that were not absolute priority. That didn't stop him from visiting his old friend, former President Eisenhower, in his hospital room at Walter Reed Hospital in Washington, D. C. Ike's condition wasn't good. He had a history of heart problems dating back to his years in the White House. On March 30, 1969, a saddened Bob and Dolores Hope returned to Washington for the State Funeral given the former president.

No sooner were the services for Ike completed than Bob received word that his youngest brother, George, was in the hospital in California undergoing abdominal surgery. He and Dolores returned to California immediately and rushed to George's bedside. The surgery had been successful and Bob breathed a sigh of relief.

Forgetting his eye surgeon's advice, Bob stepped up his pace. Two days later he attended daughter Nora's formal engagement party, and in rapid succession taped a television special for Chrysler, showed up at Mort Lachman's engagement party, saw Dolores installed as Honorary Mayor of Palm Springs, and on April 14 presented the Jean Hersholt Humanitarian Award to fellow globe-traveler Martha Raye at the Academy Awards ceremonies. It was the first time in several years that Hope did not host the event, held that year in the Dorothy Chandler Pavilion of the Music Center in downtown Los Angeles.

On April 27, while accepting an honorary degree at the University of Miami in Oxford, Ohio, Bob suffered another eye attack and rushed immediately to New York, where he underwent eye surgery performed by his good friend, Dr. Algernon Reese. Dr. Reese bluntly advised his patient that he would not be able to perform photocoagulation on him again. All Bob had left was scar tissue. A week later, back in Toluca Lake, he and Dolores decided it might be the right time to take a vacation. Dr. Reese had suggested a full month, which they spent in Aruba, San Juan, and the Bahamas.

Within a few days of their return, Bob was flying all over the country, participating in charity golf tournaments, making speeches, performing at benefits, and receiving awards—one of which was a thirteenth honorary degree bestowed upon him by Bowling Green University.

During Bob's acceptance speech his brother, Ivor, suffered a heart attack and died. Bob wasn't told until after the festivities were completed. Bob took Ivor's death badly. He had been like a father to Bob. It seemed that all of his friends and family were dying.

He didn't feel like being funny, but he felt compelled to keep a commitment to the U.S. Air Force to perform at the Pike's Peak Festival in Colorado Springs. No longer the big draw he had once been, it discouraged him to learn that advance ticket sales were lousy. But, to Bob, a commitment was just that.

Just as had occurred in Ohio when Ivor died, during Bob's first show at Colorado Springs, his brother George died from throat cancer in Los Angeles. Unable to continue, Bob got in touch with Danny Thomas, who immediately rushed in to complete Bob's remaining shows. George's death left Bob absolutely devastated. He'd lost his oldest and youngest brothers within a week of each other.

For the better part of a month after George's funeral, Bob went into semi-seclusion, canceling all appointments except the most important. He did make a quick trip to Washington to meet with the Pentagon brass regarding the 1969 Christmas tour to the Far East.

Nixon, trying to emulate Eisenhower, ran a campaign that promised to end the war in Vietnam. Actually, he escalated the hostilities by ordering the bombing of Cambodia and Laos, along the border of Vietnam, in areas he would later describe as "sanctuaries" overrun with Vietcong. Nixon had the same problem as Johnson—he lied to the American people by denying that there was any bombing of Cambodia, while veterans of Vietnam were returning to the United States with the truth on their lips.

Yet, Bob Hope defied this reality when he appeared before students on Southern college campuses. When asked if he didn't find more and more students opposing withdrawal from Vietnam, Bob bristled. "It's just small minorities on campus who make headlines. And the news media is guilty of blowing every anti-war event way out of proportion."

Even his good friend Stuart Symington favored getting out of Vietnam right away without further loss of life. Bob couldn't understand how Symington could possibly not fight to the end.

On October 15, 1969, a coalition of high-ranking Democrats, ministers and priests, and university presidents united together in demanding a moratorium against the war.

Bob shrugged off any suggestion of a moratorium. In a speech the day before the proposed moratorium, he said:

". . . tomorrow is the moratorium period. A lot of kids will be out of school, and a lot of professors won't be teaching . . . The president would like nothing better than a cease fire, but the Democrats won't stop sniping . . . what

I resent is their moratorium against soap and water . . .
I don't know what's happening to the kids in this country . . ."

Contrary to his past history of refusing to involve himself
deeply in politics, Bob let President Nixon appoint him national
chairman of a pro-administration event called "National Unity
Week," which was supported by the American Legion, Veterans of Foreign Wars, and Americans for Responsible Action.
They would stage rallies across the country during the week
prior to a major anti-Vietnam War demonstration in Washington
on November 15. Bob made a series of speeches across the
country in which he backed Nixon and the war and debunked
the anti-war demonstrators as "misguided youth."

At one point he verbally attacked NBC News for televising
"rigged film clips from Vietnam," and accused the network
of emphasizing stories that suggested black soldiers in Vietnam
were not being treated with the same respect as whites.

Despite the efforts of Bob Hope and Vice President Agnew,
who were alternating on a daily basis pushing the administration
line while severely criticizing the "peaceniks," as the protesters
were now being referred to, the anti-war movement was on the
move. On November 15 the most gigantic demonstration in the
history of the Republic took place in Washington, D.C., when
more than 250,000 joined together, clearly demonstrating that
the Vietnam War had punctured the conscience of the country.
Many prominent scholars were comparing the schism to the
Civil War.

In Seattle, Washington, on that same day, Bob Hope's show
was picketed by hundreds of people of all ages and walks of
life. During an interview after the show, Bob said, "Hell, I'm
for peace, but not at all costs. Why don't they march against
the North Vietnamese? Why don't the dissidents march against
them? Lots of our kids are being killed. And who's doing the
killing? The Communists are the ones who need the demonstrations."

Bob was picking on the wrong group. He should have been
addressing both the past and present administrations who car-

ried on a war without fighting the enemy on his own turf. Had either Johnson or Nixon systematically bombed the cities of North Vietnam, the United States might have had a chance to win and the demonstrators might well have gone away.

Privately, Bob probably entertained such thoughts himself.

Bob may also have been considering his own mortality, having recently lost so many of his friends and family, when he decided that the 1969 Christmas tour would not be just to the Far East, but world-wide. His doctors thought him foolhardy to take on such an arduous journey in light of his delicate eyesight. He now needed very large cue cards in order to perform. But no one could deter him. If this might be his final tour, and he wasn't conceding that at all, then he wanted it to be world-wide.

The 1969 Christmas tour kicked off with a dinner at the White House at the invitation of President and Mrs. Nixon. The first family was treated to a wonderful preview performance in the Blue Room by Bob and his entire package of entertainers, all of whom had been invited to the dinner.

The next morning the troupe met at Andrews Air Force Base, ready to depart for Berlin. According to Bill Faith, the only person missing was Bob Hope, who remained in his hotel, refusing to get out of bed, and did not begin to rouse until Mort Lachman advised him that Secretary of Defense Melvin Laird, General Westmoreland, Secretary of State Rogers, and others were waiting to bid him a safe journey.

"No kidding," Bob said and quickly pulled himself together, arriving at the airport only one hour late. Bob doesn't mention such an incident in *The Last Christmas Show,* which gives his account of the Christmas tours he made to entertain servicemen and women throughout the world.

They landed at Templehof Airport in Berlin at 7:00 A.M. the following morning, did their Berlin shows, and took off for Rome after an evening reception hosted by Major General R. J. Ferguson, commander of the U. S. forces in Berlin. The two-hour flight to Rome got them to Italy by 10:00 P.M. but a misguided bus driver lost his way, causing the group to arrive at their hotel sometime between 2:00 and 3:00 A.M. the following morning. Despite the difficulties, they were on stage for a scheduled 9:00 A.M. show, bringing Christmas cheer from America to several thousand sailors and Marines aboard the aircraft carrier U.S.S. *Saratoga*.

In addition to his regulars, Bob brought along German film beauty Romy Schneider, Connie Stevens, The Golddiggers, dancer Suzanne Charney, Miss World of 1969, the Piero brothers, and Irv Kupcinet, a popular gossip columnist from Chicago.

The cast and crew proceeded on to Turkey, the Persian Gulf, Bangkok, where they presented Teresa Graves (of *Laugh In* fame), and the coup of all coups—the first man to set foot on the moon, American astronaut Neil Armstrong. At the end of each show the girls were all but ignored while the GI's pushed and shoved in order to speak with Neil Armstrong. These guys were kids and kids still loved heroes.

Bob faced a double shock at Lai Khe, where he put on his first show inside Vietnam during the 1969 trip before an audience of the 1st Infantry Division. The show almost didn't go on. Earlier in the day a sweeping search party discovered Viet Cong with a complement of Cong rockets hiding out in the jungle near the stage. Obviously, Bob Hope was their target.

With more than 10,000 men and women waiting to see the show, Bob walked out on stage and said, "The president said to me, 'I have a plan to end the war.'"

Expecting laughs from this perceived tongue in cheek remark (actually, he was serious), it shocked him when the troop booed him. He was glad to bid Vietnam goodbye when they did the last show at Long Binh and flew out to Guam. Bob still couldn't understand what had happened, but the kids in Vietnam did. Many of them were replacements—fresh kids who only a few months earlier weren't even in the service. Some had been part of the anti-Vietnam demonstrations stateside.

Bob was still thinking in terms of World War II. Compared to Vietnam, that war could be dubbed "The age of innocence."

A tired and weary Bob Hope and company returned to Los Angeles with plenty to think about. Bob needed to edit the film

for the television Christmas special to air on January 15, 1970—
with the boos edited out. Who could blame him for that? He
saw no reason to fan the flames at home by showing how
disillusioned the kids in Vietnam had become.

Chapter 39

After being booed by the troops in Vietnam, suffering with the problems with his eyes, and losing so many of those near and dear to him, Bob began to reflect on his own mortality. He toned down some of his more commercial activities and turned to doing more "good things."

He had been especially close to and fond of President Eisenhower and was one of the few outside the family who called him "Ike" without recrimination. So no surprise was expressed when he set out to promote enough money to complete a hospital at Palm Springs in Ike's name, which eventually became the Eisenhower Medical Center.

The Hopes pledged, through fund-raising benefits, to bring in a cool $2.1 million dollars, one-third of the overall cost to complete the first phase of building by the end of 1971. In spite of failing eyesight, slipping popularity, and numerous other plagues, Bob set to work renting the Grand Ballroom of the Waldorf-Astoria and picked up the $70,000 tab for a dine-and-dance soiree on January 20, 1970, at $1,000 per seat, raising $1.5 million dollars. Entertainment by Bob Hope, Raquel Welch, Bing Crosby, Johnny Cash, and Ray Bolger gave the 1500 guests a bang for their bucks.

Additionally, he convinced other well-known penny pinchers, like Irving Berlin, to get on the bandwagon. Berlin gave $125,000, as did Frank Sinatra and Fritz Loewe. Upon his death, Loewe left all his royalties from *My Fair Lady* to the Eisenhower Hospital.

Bob had been criticized for not using more blacks in his television show and on Christmas trips. Being from Ohio, a state that integrated its schools long before it became the law to do so, Bob knew that there had always existed elements on both sides of the issue ready to leap into potentially explosive situations.

Sure enough, a writer by the name of Lucius E. Lee, in a Columbus, Ohio, *Call & Post* article, complained about the dearth of black faces at the televised edition of the dinner, which aired on February 16. Bob had his brother Fred get in touch with the writer and tried to alibi out of the situation. Bob even wrote a personal letter explaining that he had made an effort to get Dr. Ralph Bunche and that George Foreman was somewhere amongst the 1500 guests. He said he'd had to cut the original footage and Foreman, unfortunately, ended up on the cutting room floor.

Bob is, and always has been, pure Anglo-Saxon WASP. That is no secret, but no one ever brought it quite to the fore as that particular columnist did. Behind the scenes it shook him up because the last thing in the world he wanted to be branded was "racist," considering all of his trips to entertain the troops where thousands upon thousands of blacks were serving their country.

He joined 15 cohosts for the Academy Awards on April 7 at the Dorothy Chandler Pavilion. "Welcome to the Academy Awards," he said, "or as it is known at my house, *Mission Impossible.*" All of the cohosts did their thing, but Bob Hope had the last words: "The show ran two hours and twenty minutes—which is the longest any show has run on ABC without being canceled."

Hope was getting warmed up for Houston where, in May,

he put on one of the grandest shows ever to grace the Astrodome to raise money for a youth center memorializing astronaut Ed White, one of three men who died atop the launch pad awaiting lift-off.

Les Brown, with Hope as always, provided all of the music for the show with Hope emceeing and introducing the star-studded celebrity volunteers for the cause, including Cary Grant, who never did personal appearances ("Only Bob Hope could get me to do this"), Gregory Peck, David Janssen, Dottie Lamour, Joey Heatherton, Glen Campbell, and Robert Goulet.

Among others who appeared were O. J. Simpson (known then for his exploits on the football field), Trini Lopez, and the Step Brothers.

Bob still hadn't given up on the war in Vietnam and along with Televangelist Billy Graham he agreed to host a July Fourth variety show on the Mall in front of the Washington Monument in the nation's capital where Martin Luther King, Jr. had gathered a giant force for civil rights prior to his assassination. Two former presidents, Truman and Johnson, and Ike's widow, Mamie Eisenhower, were named honorary chairpersons of the event.

The organizers of the event were all pro-Vietnam War, a fact that the *Washington Post* took issue with in an editorial two weeks before the event.

"The suspicion . . . is that any effort to make something different out of this year's Fourth of July observances is going to take on the trappings of a pro-war rally in support of President Nixon's Vietnam policy . . . It needs a broader mix . . . not just Democrats and Republicans but of dissenters as well as supporters . . . Hubert Humphrey, to take one example, or George McGovern . . ."

Humphrey and McGovern were quickly added to the list. Bob Hope did not wish to take on one of the most powerful newspapers in the country. Even that wasn't enough to satisfy the *Post* and the publisher made that plain in another editorial.

The *Dallas Times Herald* defended Bob Hope, comparing him to Will Rogers and stating in part, "He has the national image and respect. He has the same intense love for his country, and he has the guts to stand up to any heckling hippie."

Bob called a press conference for the purpose of suppressing talk about the rally being "anti-dissident," but it did little good.

Finally he told the assembled media, "Don't worry. We'll have over 400,000 people out there—the biggest crowd that has gathered for any show . . . bigger than Woodstock!"

Throughout the day, on the Fourth of July, anti-war protesters drank wine, smoked pot, danced naked, and disrupted the assemblage in any way they could—even to shouting obscenities and making lewd gestures to the Reverend Billy Graham as he delivered his sermon for the day. They did everything possible to destroy the rally, which had been officially proclaimed "Honor America Day."

Even as Bob came out on stage to introduce the acts that night, demonstrators had to be quelled by the District Police for tossing bottles, cherry bombs, and whatever else they could do to disrupt the evening.

The 350,000 folks who came didn't pay them any mind. They'd come to see and hear Dinah Shore, Sugar Ray Robinson, Dorothy Lamour, Glen Campbell, Connie Stevens, Jack Benny, Kate Smith, Red Skelton, Pat Boone, Barbara Eden, and at least a dozen other celebrities.

No sooner did Bob get out of one situation, however, than he was involved in another. He allowed *Life* reporter Joan Barthel to travel with him over a weekend of speaking appearances for which he received his usual fee of $25,000. It is normal for celebrities to be paid for speaking—they rightfully capitalize on their name value. It has been done as long as there have been celebrities.

Bob, however, got in hot water for some of his words. At South Bend, Indiana, during halftime of a game between Notre Dame and Georgia Tech, the Irish University presented a "Salute to Bob Hope." Prior to Hope's arrival, the Reverend

Theodore M. Hesburgh, the university's president, made the following statement:

". . . the great majority of Notre Dame students and faculty . . ." wanted the United States to withdraw from Vietnam.

Even the Fighting Irish football captain had something to say, declaring the war to be ". . . a waste—Americans are dying for nothing."

On one of the rare occasions when Dolores publicly commented about her husband's dalliances, she told the *Life* reporter: "I think he's a great man. No person living has the kind of unspotted life that is the perfect example of clean living."

In an unguarded moment, Bob let the reporter inside his political psyche:

". . . Americans are marvelous; they're very grateful . . . there's only about one percent of the college kids that protest . . . the FBI knows it. I've looked into the Kent State thing . . . I know it for sure—that that wasn't just students there. And if they were students, they were led . . . hooked up with subversive forces. I know something about that, but I can't talk too much about it . . ."

He went on to say that he believed in a Communist conspiracy in the United States. Bob loved to brag about his "inside information." He further told the reporter:

"You see these kids up on the Sunset Strip . . . smoking this stuff . . . Seventy-five or eighty percent of them have a social disease . . . I know an awful lot about this because I'm close to a lot of people in law enforcement agencies."

When Bob got up to speak at Notre Dame a large section of students stood up, with thumbs down, and loudly booed him. Later, as the limousine carried Hope and the reporter away from the football stadium, Bob explained to her that, "They weren't booing me, you know. They were cheering for Moose

Krause (Notre Dame's athletic director).'' Ms. Barthel wasn't buying that.

At another location, Bob referred to the war in Vietnam as ''a beautiful thing'' for which ''we paid in a lot of gorgeous American lives, but we're not sorry for it.''

Bob was angry with the adverse publicity and complained that the reporter had misquoted him. Barthel won the argument because she had taped his entire speech. *Life* received dozens of angry letters in response to the article which appeared in the January 19, 1971, issue.

Interestingly enough, Arthur Marx, who later wrote a very raw exposé of Bob Hope's private life, was asked to script, along with his writing partner Robert Fisher, what would turn out to be Hope's last feature film, *Cancel My Reservation*.

The director, Paul Bogart, had never directed anything comparable to a Bob Hope comedy and he had reservations about accepting the assignment. He said that Hope's costar, Eva Marie Saint, convinced him that it would be a great film and they'd have a lot of fun doing it. On her say-so, he signed the contract.

Problems arose immediately. Bogart couldn't believe the number of writers on Bob's payroll, all of whom seemed to have an opinion about the script. Bogart said, ''The script kept getting thicker and thicker until it was about the size of a Manhattan phone directory . . . Hope and I disagreed on everything.

''His least attractive aspect is that he has no respect for his coworkers . . . especially his writers and directors . . . Unless they are the 'good old boys' who belong to his club . . .''

During the last days of shooting in Rockefeller Plaza, Bogart, having had it up to his ears with Bob's temperament, let loose his own tirade. Arthur Marx quotes Mr. Bogart extensively in his book, summing up the director's frustrations:

''. . . Bob kept us waiting for several hours . . . and I'm starting to feel feverish . . . very close to pneumonia. I started to explain to him, 'This is what we're going to do, Bob,' and he said, 'I don't see it that way.' Well, I completely lost my cool and started to scream, 'Well, how do you see it, Bob? Tell-me-how-you-fucking-well-see-it, Bob.' And before he could even answer I said, 'You know what, Bob? You're boring. This whole thing is boring' I could hear myself saying that over and over again, 'You're boring, you're BORING, FUCKING BORING!' "

Bogart's speech was delivered in the presence of a large crowd. The whole thing so upset him that his doctor ordered him into the hospital for three weeks to recover. Needless to say, he was never again on Bob's invitation list.

To the surprise of almost everyone, Warner Brothers booked the film into Radio City Music Hall. Film critic Pauline Kael's review called the film "a new low."

Two days after the film opened, the Rockettes went out on strike and the theater closed down for the first time ever. According to Paul Bogart, the decision to close the theater was the best thing that ever happened to *Cancel My Reservation* .

Trying to make up for past mistakes and to seem more "hip to the scene," Bob was very careful about his selection of personnel to accompany him to the Far East in 1970, taking along Johnny Bench, the Cincinnati Reds' popular catcher, film actress Ursula Andress, black entertainer Lola Falana, singers Gloria Loring and Bobbi Martin, Miss World, and the Gold-diggers.

The dress rehearsal was held in the U. S. Military Academy at West Point, where Hope entertained the cadets and socialized with the brass, which was his usual routine whether stateside or abroad.

In Vietnam, Bob broke in some marijuana jokes. During one skit with Johnny Bench, he said, "It's a great sport, baseball. You can spend eight months on grass and not get busted."

On another occasion he said, "The British have given us a

sight that makes us think we must be stoned even when we're not: Engelbert Humperdinck.''

In a sense, Hope was acknowledging an open secret. This was the first war in which thousands of GI's left the country clean and returned addicted to some form of drugs. No one had dared talk about it in the past, but when Bob popped the cork on drugs it made more news than any of his usual jokes.

Before the 101st Airborne Division, he quipped, ''I guess you guys are too busy to be bothered by things like mosquito bites. I hear you go in for gardening. The commanding officer says you grow your own grass . . . In one barracks I passed, a group of GI's was watching *Twelve O'Clock High* and they didn't even have a TV set . . .''

Bob was talking about real life and the men seemed to understand that he was trying to reach them where they lived. They appreciated that. Word spreads quickly in the military and, having already heard that Bob's jokes had a ''high'' flavor this time around, the crowds were larger than ever.

But NBC had a peacock fit, and they weren't alone. Back home as the film was edited for the usual NBC Chrysler Christmas Special, Bob ran into flak of another kind—political. The footage had already been previewed for the press. Associated Press writer Bob Thomas asked, ''Bob Hope doing marijuana jokes for the troops?''

Bob tried to explain his position by discussing the realities in Vietnam. One of Hope's publicity experts was able to spin the story so the blame was shifted to the military. Nevertheless, the executives at NBC were interested in entertainment, not truth, so they cut out all references to pot. Bob later went on the Johnny Carson show and discussed the pot jokes that had been cut from his show.

Jack Gould, of the *New York Times,* defended Hope in an article entitled, ''Some Like it Pot and Some Don't'':

''. . . Hope told it as he found it during his conversation with Carson: the troops in Vietnam did respond to quips on pot, which even the Pentagon admits is heavily used there, and everyone did want peace and wanted to come

home . . . But more by manner than word, he left no
doubt of the war's unpopularity among the troops he
encountered . . . As a patriot and performer, Hope's cre-
dentials are impeccable . . . if in his own way he can also
incorporate the accompanying elements of significance,
sans strictures by either NBC or the Pentagon, he could
be even more of a national asset than he is.''

It wasn't going to be a good year for Bob Hope if early
events were any barometer. The New York City Council of
Churches had voted him its Family of Man Award in February
which had been awarded to Presidents Kennedy, Eisenhower,
Nixon, and Johnson in the past. Lutheran minister Richard
Nenhaus objected because ''Mr. Hope has uncritically supported the military establishment.''

Neuhaus collected enough votes on the Board to override its
previous decision, which was finally given posthumously to
Whitney Young, Jr.

The response to the change of recipients sent the editorial
scribes into a frenzy. In an effort to play it low key, Bob
publicly supported the Board's decision to reverse.

Former Republican presidential nominee Barry Goldwater
stood tall for Bob Hope and rightly so. Bob had vociferously
supported Goldwater in his presidential bid.

Nothing, however, would have a worse effect on Bob Hope
than the death of Marilyn Maxwell on March 21, 1971, at age
49. Marilyn's fifteen-year-old son Mathew Davis found his
mother dead from a heart attack in her Beverly Hills home.

Bob delivered the eulogy at Beverly Hills Community Presbyterian Church, which was jam-packed with her famous
friends, fans, and curiosity seekers. He said of his former lover,
''If all her friends were here today we'd have to use the Colos-
seum.'' He added that she ''had an inner warmth and love for
people . . . Who would have thought that this little girl from
Clarinda, Iowa, would do this much and go as far as she did?''

He did not stay long afterward, departing in a black limousine
for his home in Toluca Lake.

The Oscar Awards on April 15 were telecast by NBC from the Dorothy Chandler Pavilion and boasted thirty-three co-hosts. Bob was reduced to presenting, along with Petula Clark, the Oscar for Art Direction—a far cry from his previous one-man show. Hope had swung so far to the right politically that his time on stage was limited. The booing he'd heard in Vietnam and Notre Dame was now coming from the celebrity audience. Hope hadn't the faintest idea why his peers would give him the raspberry—but they did, for the first time throughout all of his years before the Oscar microphones.

George C. Scott refused to show up or to accept the award if he won for Best Actor. He did not show up; he did win. The shocker came when Charles Champlin, always a friend to show people, wrote in the *Los Angeles Times:* "Bob Hope's mono-logue—weary, bitter, and excruciatingly unfunny—was an embarrassment to everyone."

Before another year passed Bob Hope would find himself the center of an international escapade that left some high-ranking Washington Administration and Diplomatic officials at a loss for words.

Bob said he was only trying to help end the war, and obtain the release of American POW's in North Vietnam.

Even President Nixon was unaware of a financial deal Hope tried to negotiate with a North Vietnamese representative in a secret meeting in Vientiane.

Chapter 40

It all began innocently enough. Bob Hope wanted to obtain a visa from North Vietnam in order to go to Hanoi to entertain American prisoners of war and hopefully arrange for their release. As outrageous as it might sound, Bob Hope thought he could accomplish that.

There are a number of versions of what happened. In his book, *Don't Shoot, It's Only Me,* Bob placed blame on his publicity director, Bill Faith:

> "In my innocence, through my publicity man, Bill Faith, I arranged to go to Thailand for a secret meeting with our ambassador to Laos, Leonard Unger, who had contacts with the North Vietnamese. That gives you an idea of the kind of war this was. You arranged a secret meeting through a publicity man."

In his biography of Hope, Arthur Marx suggests a somewhat different scenario:

> ". . . Bob got the notion that he could do something to help free the American POWs held in North Vietnam . . .

he felt he could get friendly with Hanoi's top officials and talk them into releasing the American men they were holding . . .''

Bill Faith, in his *Bob Hope, A Life in Comedy,* tends to support Arthur Marx. Since Faith was with Hope at the time, it seems he would have had a bird's eye view.

In *The Last Christmas Show,* a book written by Bob Hope and Pete Martin, Hope sets forth a slight variance from the other books:

"I called in Bill Faith, my PR man, and we secretly arranged a meeting with the U.S. Ambassador to Thailand, Leonard Unger. He was all for the idea, and arranged for me and Bill to fly to Vientiane, Laos, to meet with the North Vietnamese consul there, Nguyen Van Thanh . . . The whole thing was very hush-hush. No one in the troupe—never mind any of the bigwigs back in the States—knew I was going. I wanted to do the whole thing strictly as a private citizen.''

Upon his arrival in Vientiane aboard an unmarked CIA plane, Bob was met by Admiral John McCain, Jr., who was attired in civilian clothes. According to Hope, American Embassy officials were also involved in the clandestine meeting.

Nothing came of Hope's offer, although he kept trying to get the visa which was repeatedly turned down by Hanoi. The most intriguing aspect to the story is that Hope admits "President Nixon knew nothing of our efforts.''

In other words, while the president of the United States and his Secretary of State, Dr. Kissinger, were negotiating a delicate peace treaty with the North Vietnamese in Paris, Bob Hope took it upon himself to play diplomat in Laos.

The war was winding down with or without Bob's intervention, but when he returned to the United States and continued to hound Washington to arrange a visa for him to go to North Vietnam, Secretary of State Rogers called him in for a visit and told him that the president, through Henry Kissinger, had made an offer of $2.8 billion dollars to the North Vietnamese in "relief aid" to bring the war to an end.

The United States had capitulated and Bob Hope was told, in so many words, to forget it. He left Washington, disappointed that he hadn't been able to contribute more to bringing home the POWs, quickly changing his focus to Nixon's successes on other international fronts.

The 1972 Christmas tour would be the end of Bob Hope's relationship with Vietnam. It was his third war—and the worst, in his opinion. The publicity preceding "The Last Christmas Show," was astronomical. There had never been so much advance publicity for one of his shows. The media, aware of his attempted diplomatic coup the previous year, looked upon this trip as that of an old warrior reviewing the troops for the last time before retirement. However, there were no American ground troops remaining in Vietnam.

Dolores accompanied her husband on this tour, along with comedian Redd Foxx, Lola Falana, Los Angeles Rams quarterback Roman Gabriel, nightclub chanteuse Frank Jeffries, some beauty contest winners, and Les Brown.

In Vietnam, Hope repeated his farewell message wherever he appeared "Now that the war is winding down, I want to say I do appreciate you fellows hanging around here—just for me."

Bob always played to an American audience and when, during a performance in Thailand, he joked, "When I came out of a temple recently, I found two Thai families in my shoes who refused to evacuate." The Thais' sensitivities had been invaded by Hope and it created an international to-do that ended with the American Ambassador to Thailand issuing a formal apology to the Thai people on behalf of the United States Government.

Hope's tour, filled with nostalgia and tears, ended aboard an aircraft carrier with Dolores Reade Hope singing *White Christmas*. For Bob Hope, the war was over.

Shirley Eder covered Hollywood for many years, living and

working out of Detroit, Michigan. She filed her account of Hope's last Vietnam tour on December 28, 1972:

> "With difficulty I'm trying to choose the one standout moment of the entire trip—there were so many. When we started out on the plane, Hope's producer, Mort Lachman, told me there is usually one thing or one spot during a performance that grabs you more than any other. He was right . . . when Dolores came out just before the finale . . . Six thousand boys and men stood up when she made her entrance, then sat down again and were very still while she sang *White Christmas* . . . I looked around at all those young men, many of them with their heads lowered, trying to hide their emotions. Hundreds sat with tears streaming down their faces, especially when Dolores ended the song . . . At this point I looked away from them, as they tried to look away from their shipmates, because the tears were streaming down my face, too."

Over the next three or four years, Bob spent Christmas with the veterans in military hospitals around the country—swapping stories about past wars, recalling incidents, being a veteran among veterans and feeling comfortable doing so.

However, Bob Hope wasn't finished by a long shot. "I'll never quit," he said. "I'll probably he telling a joke on my way to the grave."

Christmas Day 1973 found Hope enjoying a family Christmas at home in Toluca Lake for the first time in a quarter century. His children had grown up believing that Christmas was January first.

The day after Christmas, however, Bob was off on another "tour." He visited veterans' hospitals in San Francisco and Bethesda, ending up at the Long Beach Veteran's Hospital, where he entertained a large contingency of vets, most of whom suffered both physically and mentally from the ravages of the Vietnam jungles.

He developed a new joke formula for the stateside hospital patients. For instance, in Long Beach:

"Over two thousand veterans call this place home—at least that's what they call it when the nurses are in earshot . . . A nurse! That's a girl in a white uniform who can take your temperature and give you one—both at the same time . . . To give you an idea how cute the nurses are in this hospital . . . someone hung a bunch of mistletoe in surgery and they had to operate on one poor guy twice. Once to cure what was wrong with him—once to get his lips unpuckered."

Bob hadn't wanted to become involved with the military back in 1941 when he did that first show at March Field, California. During those days he could have cared less about war and soldiers. He has reflected on his "military career" on several occasions:

"When I started this thing, I never believed I'd get hooked on it. And the gratification was tremendous, from both the parents and the boys. Today I can't take a trip anywhere without the pilot saying, 'I saw you in North Africa' or Germany or England . . . It's a warm feeling . . . when we were at war I got the same feeling . . . they let you know that you were doing something for somebody and that you were doing some good. It was a package of love, so far as I was concerned."

With the war over Bob would have more time for golf, family, golf, television and . . . golf.

Chapter 41

When Bob closed the door behind him on Vietnam, ending an NBC "Last Christmas Show" special, his seventieth birthday loomed ahead.

He had reasons to be happy. He'd just received an honorary doctor of law degree (his twenty-second such honor) from Pepperdine College in Malibu and had begun a project of magnificent proportions—a new home in the hills above Rancho Mirage, California, rumored to be the size of a department store. Why build such an enormous living accommodation in the desert when he already had a large estate in the San Fernando Valley with its own putting green and a golf course within walking distance? "I need room to grow," he said, winking.

Asked if his brand of humor was being eclipsed by the new, more caustic comedians, he pondered for a moment and answered "Sure ... Mort Sahl ... I thought when he came on the scene, he brought a new approach to comedy ... it's great .... There are a couple of young guys ... that's always welcome."

He put forth the argument that "the kids today" had been "exposed to so much dirt" that they knew all the old jokes by heart and weren't interested. He blamed that on television. Even the most backwoods hick had a television set. "I talk about sex," he added, "because that's what they're interested in."

He swore he didn't tell "really blue" jokes, but anyone who attended any of his warm-ups prior to going on the air, knew better. One-liners, such as *"Super Fly* was a movie about Tom Jones's tailor" or "The girl in *Deep Throat* should get Best Supporting Gargle," abounded.

In the September 1973 issue of *Esquire,* Michael Rogers says:

"Hope unswervingly grooms every moment he spends in the public eye. In some places, the patina is wearing thin; his humility, for example, is by now so smooth and practiced that it somehow never rings completely true. But the real character residing beneath the ten thousand interchangeable one-liners, the humble platitudes, the good works, the McCarthy era politics, the one-man humor industry is difficult to assess fairly, unless that assessment is that there comes a time in every man's life when he retires—whether he realizes it exactly or not."

Bob staunchly defends his great wealth, declaring that "I have worked hard all my life. I don't have a penny I didn't earn. There's none of that bullshit about limousines ... We take a limousine when we go to a dinner, where it'll expedite things better, but nobody's got a limousine to go to the golf course ... Everybody stays kind of like they were ..."

Bob would have plenty of time in what everyone thought would be the waning years of his life to reflect on friends and enemies. He had three wars to look back on and write about. His personal memoirs, if told truthfully, would detail the American twentieth century, both morally and politically, and would take years to write.

He had enemies, some disguised as friends, but his real friends stayed with him always. It didn't matter to Bob that General Westmoreland took the greatest hit for Vietnam, or that he didn't like Nixon's lying to the American people. They were his friends.

His closest friend, which might surprise many, was Spiro T. Agnew, Richard Nixon's disgraced vice president. Hope and Agnew were not just political cronies—they played golf together regularly. Bob built a new home in Rancho Mirage, and Agnew settled down in the Palm Springs area after leaving Washington. The two men had many things in common. More importantly, Hope trusted Agnew. Ninety out of a hundred people would have answered "Crosby," if asked who Bob considered his best friend. They would have been wrong. Bob never trusted Crosby, nor Crosby Hope. They were too competitive for that. Agnew seems to have loved playing straight man to Hope.

When talk show host Lou Gordon asked Hope, referring to Agnew, "How can you remain friends with a thief and a scoundrel?", Bob responded, "If you were my friend in the same position, I would still be your friend."

Bill Murray, preparing a piece for *Playboy Magazine,* spent a good deal of time with Bob and didn't hesitate to ask the tough questions—questions Bob would have refused to answer in the past. Bob confessed that the comedian with the bluest material, Lenny Bruce, was his favorite—which might lend some substance to some of Hope's critics who accused him of infusing too much off-color material into his own monologues.

If Bob had neglected his family during all of those years making movies, making money, doing television, making money, entertaining the troops and making money, in his semi-retirement he really plunged into family life. During the summer of 1973, after taping a Fourth of July *Stars and Stripes Show* in Oklahoma City," Bob came back to Toluca Lake and surprised Dolores with what Bill Faith describes as "the largest gathering of family in Hope history." He atoned big-time and Dolores, no doubt, was finding renewed faith in her rosary.

According to Faith:

"Bob had invited every living member of the clan for a monster reunion. The children alone, when all were

assembled ... numbered 50 ... grandchildren, grand-
nieces ... grandnephews ... from Ohio ... Illinois ...
California ... running everywhere ... exploring the
grounds .... swimming with Uncle Bob ...''

Apparently having discovered the joys of family, Bob took
to it like a guppy to water.

Bob did not slip into total retirement—he cut back his appearance schedule to "only 250 days a year," which gave him 115
free days and more time at home. Dolores once told a friend,
"I'm so used to him being gone it sometimes surprises me to
meet him at the breakfast table in the morning."

He never tired of making money and quickly signed a new
television contract—with Texaco, Incorporated, which demanded very little of his time compared to his previous long-
term television commitments. He would be required to package
seven hours of shows, mostly comedy specials, annually for
three years. He received $3,150,000 a year for three years plus
a hefty additional sum to do spot commercials. Not bad for a
semi-retired "veteran." Additionally, he soon negotiated
another contract with NBC valued at $18,000,000 according
to the media.

It seemed, however, that no matter what good news Bob
received, he had reached an age where friends and relatives
were departing life for a different kind of retirement.

Nothing ever hit him any harder, outside of losing a family
member, than the death of Jack Benny from pancreatic cancer.
He knew Jack had been ill, but nothing had indicated that death
was imminent. When Bob addressed the galaxy of stars at
Benny's funeral, he appeared solemn and still stunned at the
loss of a man he had known since their days in vaudeville:

"How do you say goodbye to a man who is not just a
good friend, but a national treasure? It's hard to say no
man is indispensable. But it is true just the same that
some are irreplaceable ... Jack had something called

'genius' ... was blessed with it. He didn't just stand on
the stage—he owned it''

Bob never had much stomach for firing his employees personally. He paid people to do that sort of thing. In the past his
brother Jack played the heavy. When Jack died it fell on Mort
Lachman's shoulders. Then when Bob signed his new contract
with Texaco, he wanted to shed a lot of his longtime work
crew, including Mort Lachman, Lester White, and Norman
Sullivan. These were men who went way back, some of them
to Hope's inception into show business. He claimed that Texaco
wanted them out and made a lot of excuses about their not
being "fresh" or "with it."

Lachman and the others got wind of what Bob had in mind
and it fell to Bill Faith's partner in the publicity department,
Ward Grant, to take the hit when time came to slash the payroll.
Bob could have made room for his friends who stuck by him
all those years. He could well have supplemented their income
or paid it out of his own pocket and never missed a nickel, but
he chose not to do that.

It says something about the man that he would cling to a
Spiro Agnew—actually a Johnny-come-lately in his life—in
favor of the men who helped make him into a national icon.

On April 8, 1975, Bob found himself once again at the
Dorothy Chandler Pavilion along with Sammy Davis, Jr., Shirley MacLaine, and Frank Sinatra as they co-hosted the Oscar
Awards via the NBC Television Network. The only thing missing to make it a true classic was Dean Martin.

Rain marred the parade of celebrities, umbrellas covering up
many famous faces. The rain gave Bob Hope his opening line:
"I didn't know Dustin Hoffman *(Rainman)* had that much
power," he began. "If Dustin wins, he's going to have a friend
pick it up ... George C. Scott. I think *Godfather II* has an
excellent chance of winning. Neither Mr. Price nor Mr. Waterhouse has been heard from in days. I'm wearing a tuxedo with
a bulletproof cummerbund. Who knows what will happen if
Al Pacino doesn't win?''

Vietnam garnered more serious attention than Oscar, starting with a commentary by Peter Davis, producer of *Hearts and Minds,* which won for best documentary. He set the tone when he said, "It's ironic to get a prize for a war movie while the suffering in Vietnam continues."

Adding fuel to the growing fire, Bert Schneider, Davis's co-producer, said, "It is ironic that we're here at a time just before Vietnam is about to be liberated. I will now read a short wire that I have been asked to read by the Vietnamese people from the delegation for the Viet Cong at the Paris peace talks:

"Please transmit to all our friends in America our recognition of all that they have done on behalf of peace and for the application of the Paris accords on Vietnam. These actions serve the legitimate interests of the American people and the Vietnamese people. Greetings of friendship to all American people."

There were a lot of ultra-liberals in Hollywood whose sympathies lay more with North Vietnam than South. Even so, the audacity of reading a telegram from the Viet Cong to the world on the Oscar Show was way beyond the pale of anything that preceded it, including Jane Fonda, who was expected to make political statements, whether popular or not.

The wire so incensed Bob Hope that he actually became physical with Oscar producer Howard W. Koch, demanding that he immediately go out on the stage and do a disclaimer. Shirley MacLaine, one of Hollywood's most outspoken anti-war actors, shouted at Koch, "Don't you dare!"

Bob wouldn't let up. Furious, he wrote his own disclaimer and presented it to Frank Sinatra, who was next on the agenda to present the writing awards.

"If you don't go out there right now and read this," Bob demanded, "then I'm going to do it myself."

Sinatra took the paper from Hope and walked to the podium. "Ladies and gentlemen," he said, "to deviate a second, I've been asked by the Academy to make the following statement regarding a statement made by a winner:"

"We are not responsible for any political references made on the program and we are sorry they had to take place this evening . . ."

An enraged Shirley MacLaine met him as he came off stage and yelled, "Why did you do that? You said you were speaking on behalf of the Academy . . . Well," she shouted, "I'm a member of the Academy and you didn't ask me. It was arrogant of you and Bob Hope not to submit it to the Board of Governors first."

Sinatra escaped Shirley's wrath by scooting back out on stage to make another presentation.

Bob continued to rave about Schneider's "cheap, cheap shot."

John Wayne joined Hope in his denunciation, declaring, "That producer was a pain in the ass and out of line and against the rules of the Academy."

Later, at the Governor's Ball, Bob made a nuisance of himself trying to get the revelers to read the handful of telegrams he said he'd received from viewers in protest. Nobody paid much attention. Shirley MacLaine, having cooled down since her earlier tirade, laughed. "Bob Hope's so mad at me he's going to bomb Encino."

Bob believed in his brand of patriotism and took a dim view of anyone who refused to see it his way. In his mind everyone had to be a captain—never abandoning ship.

Bob's first presentation for Texaco, a two-hour special, was nostalgic, featuring clips of his quarter of a century in television and highlighting almost a hundred skits in which celebrity guests appeared.

The reviews praised his stamina and energy over the years, dishing up kudos where kodos were due, but overall it was just considered Bob Hope, doing what Bob Hope does. Some thought it pure hokum and criticized him for being "too establishment."

Today's comedians, by contrast, are totally anti-establishment

—as was Mort Sahl and Lenny Bruce, the two political come-dians that Hope most respected. Bob just never could bring himself to be too cruel to politicians. He enjoyed their company. That was part of his brand of patriotism. Also, having access to the country's leaders contributed more than a little to his monologues.

Bob finally received a high school diploma at age seventy-two. It went up on the wall along with 32 degrees he'd already received—degrees which, he said, came "from places I couldn't get into legitimately."

He continued having influence with the Republican Administrations in Washington and still knew how to commandeer an Air Force plane for his personal use. Bob introduced President Ford at the Kennedy Center gala which officially kicked off the Bicentennial. President Ford arranged for an Air Force Jet to stand by to fly Hope off to Los Angeles and return to Washington to attend a couple of state dinners honoring Queen Elizabeth and Prince Philip, who were on an official visit. The Queen dubbed Hope an Honorary Commander of the British Empire.

An eighth "Road" picture was called off when Bing Crosby suffered a severe injury while performing with Bob Hope in a charity event to celebrate Crosby's 50 years in show business.

Bing had just finished a song, Bob and Pearl Bailey having already gone down below the stage to their dressing rooms, adjacent to the orchestra pit. Bing, acknowledging the audience applause, misstepped and fell 25 feet down onto the concrete floor of the orchestra pit. The studio audience gasped; Bob Hope turned ashen and rushed out to Crosby's side. Blood gushed from Bing's forehead.

Bob later discussed the accident with a reporter: "We heard this tremendous crack, followed by a horrible thump. I don't know how he survived the fall. The stage was exceptionally high because a special platform had been built for the television people. The scenery must've slowed him up enough because it was a hell of a long way down."

Bing's injury was indeed serious. He'd severely crushed a disc in his spine which kept him in traction for months.

* * *

On October 10, 1977, Bing Crosby completed a great run at the London Palladium with Rosemary Clooney as his featured guest. Afterward, Rosemary returned to the United States along with Bing's wife, Kathryn. Bing's son, Harry, Jr. (named after his father), was set to enter the London Academy of Music and Dramatic Arts. Bing went on to Spain to get in a few rounds of golf, intending to return home to Hillsborough in the San Francisco Bay area after a brief vacation. Before leaving London, Crosby pre-taped his Christmas television show (which would air after his death).

In their biography, *Bing Crosby, the Hollow Man,* Robert Slatzer and Don Shepherd detail Crosby's final moments and the aftermath:

> "... On Friday, October 14, 1977, Bing had just finished the seventeenth hole at the La Moralejo Golf Club when he was felled by a massive heart attack. His golf partners thought he had slipped and fallen, but he didn't move, and he never regained consciousness. He died en route to the Red Cross Hospital in Madrid."

Dolores Hope's mother, Theresa DeFina, had died, a couple of days earlier and the Hopes were already in mourning. Bob, in New York for a charity benefit, was contacted at his Waldorf Towers Hotel suite by telephone. The voice on the other end said, "Bing Crosby has just collapsed and died on a Spanish golf course. It was a heart attack."

Bob slumped down in his chair, stunned beyond belief. He later told Charles Thompson, "It was the strangest feeling I've ever had. My head felt like someone had wrapped a steel band around it. It was an incredible sensation. Even when I lost my mother and my brothers it didn't affect me that way. My head was completely tight; it was a great shock."

Bob had been preparing a television special based on his and Bing's escapades in the "Road" films. Bob begged off from his evening engagement, simply too shook up to attend.

No one represented Bob Hope's generation more than Bing Crosby. The two men thought of each other as indestructible and, like John Adams and Thomas Jefferson, each expected to hear of the other's demise before he, too, decided to go. Bob, however, had no intention of going anywhere and would outlive Crosby by decades.

Bing left very specific directions in his will. He didn't want anybody at his funeral except his wife and children. Kathryn made exceptions to include Bob and Dolores Hope, Phil Harris, Rosemary Clooney, and other members of Bing's family. Bing's dislike for Dorothy Lamour seemed to have affected his wife's thinking. Under no conditions would she consider inviting Dorothy Lamour. Lamour begged Hope to intervene, but he refused. "It wouldn't be right for me to interfere," he told Dorothy.

With the media around the world deluging Hope for a statement, he finally gave in to the pressure and dictated the following remarks to Ward Grant, for release to all media:

"The whole world loved Bing with a devotion that not only crossed international boundaries, but erased them. He made the world a single place and through his music, spoke to it in a language that everybody understands . . . the language of the heart . . .

"No matter where you were in the world, because of Bing, every Christmas was white And because we had him with us . . . it will always seem a little whiter.

"The world put Bing on a pedestal. But somehow I don't think he ever really knew it. Bing asked the world, 'Going my way?' and we all were . . .

"Yesterday, a heart may have stopped, and a voice stilled, but the real melody Bing sang will linger on as long as there is a phonograph to be played . . . and a heart to be lifted."

Howard Koch, again producing the Oscar extravaganza, selected Bob Hope to be the sole emcee and host of the presentation on March 29, 1978, at the Dorothy Chandler Pavilion, televised once again over the ABC network.

It seemed that the Academy Awards was becoming the great American forum for dissension and protest. A large contingent from the Jewish Defense League were out in force to picket Vanessa Redgrave, known for her anti-war and leftist opinions. Vanessa arrived in the company of several black bodyguards. Blacks in Media Broadcasting Organization ("BIMBO") protested that the Academy adds "racism, segregation, and a totally negative image of blacks" to the show "but honors white glory, success, and superiority."

Vanessa Redgrave's Oscar for Best Supporting Actress for her role in *Julia,* and her politically-charged acceptance speech, left even Hope speechless. In some ways, it was the dullest Academy Awards in history. It couldn't hold a candle to some previous ones, and to others yet to come, at which Bob Hope would not be an emcee. Hope's dominance of the Oscar Awards was over. Indeed, new blood was already being lined up for the following year, and every year thereafter. Johnny Carson was about to become the next reigning "Master of Oscar Ceremonies."

Chapter 42

Bob felt slighted when President Jimmy Carter did not invite him to his inauguration or ask him to emcee his inaugural ball. Bob got even. Carter gave him plenty of material from which to do entire monologues. He loved going after Carter, Miss Lillian—the president's mother—and "first brother" Billy Carter. To Hope, Carter was a Democrat from Georgia and that alone gave him some satisfaction.

Some of his shots included the following:

"Jimmy Carter's a very religious man. I know, because every time I eat a peanut—I feel immortal . . . I love Billy Carter. I had an uncle just like him. He drank so much that when he died and they cremated him, his liver burned for three months . . . Billy's got a new book coming out—with or without crayons . . . I hear we're not going to give the Panama Canal back until the year 2000—so I guess they're going to mail it to them . . . I think they ought to fill it with sand—and let Amy play in it . . . or fill it with beer—and let Billy play in it . . . Or fill it with money—and let Bert Lance play with it . . ."

Bob's seventy-fifth birthday became an almost year-long bash. Everybody wanted to be a part of the celebration. The USO wanted to combine it with their new World Headquarters in Washington, D. C., to be called "The Bob Hope U.S.O. Center."

The affair began as a three-hour gala at the Kennedy Center, bringing stars from every walk of life—vaudeville, radio, movies, television, politics, diplomacy, military—all who touched and were touched by Bob Hope. The excitement went on for two days.

Invited guests included Pearl Bailey, John Wayne, Lucille Ball, Danny Thomas, Sammy Davis, Jr., Elizabeth Taylor, Redd Foxx, George C Scott, Eliott Gould, Telly Savalas, Alan King, Marie and Donny Osmond, Dorothy Lamour, the Muppets, Carol Lawrence, Kathryn Crosby, and Fred MacMurray.

On the first day, May 24, the Hopes were given a lunch by the wives of congressmen and then driven by limousine to the White House, where 500 famous and important personages had gathered as a surprise for Bob.

The new Democratic Administration had gotten Bob's message. President and Mrs. Carter, along with their daughter Amy, headed the welcoming committee for Bob and Dolores in the East Room of the White House.

President Carter presented himself as somewhat of a standup comedian in his own right:

> "I've been in office 489 days ... In three weeks more I'll have stayed in the White House as many times as Bob Hope has ... Bob has a second career, making commercials. But it's not true that he sold Pepsodent to George Washington ... We all know *he* was a Lemon Pledge man ..."

Hope, elated that a Democratic president would get into the comedy ring with him, rose to the occasion and launched into his own monologue:

"I've never seen so many freeloaders in my life . . . What a kick it is to shake hands with the president and the First Lady . . . Thank you, President and Mrs. Carter, for loaning us your house . . . God knows, we paid for it."

By the time the two-day bash ended, Bob had been praised and feted by dozens of other famous names, including Vice President and Mrs. Mondale, *Washington Post* publisher Katharine Graham, Barry Goldwater, General Omar Bradley, Cyrus Vance, W. Clement Stone, Averell Harriman, Nelson Rockefeller, George Murphy, Henry Kissinger, and George Meany.

On the second day, Bob, Dolores, their daughters, grandchildren, and Fred (Bob's only surviving brother) were seated in the House of Representatives gallery at the invitation of the Speaker, Tip O'Neill. Congressman Paul Findley opened the ceremonies:

"He is a great physician. He has eased the pain of inflation and taxes, something no member of this House has ever done. He never hurt anyone, except when we laughed too hard. Christmas away from home, whether in the cold reaches of Germany during World War II, or the sweltering heat of Vietnam years later, was still enjoyable and memorable to millions of American men and women because Bob Hope was there . . ."

Everyone wanted to be part of the tribute, all of which was duly recorded for posterity in the Congressional Record. A future Speaker, Jim Wright, waxed eloquent as did many congressmen.

Congressman (and former Senator) Claude Pepper of Florida brought the House into unanimous agreement when he said, "Bob, if you want to endear yourself further to everybody, just assure us before you leave that you won't run against any of us."

A long parody of "Thanks for the Memory" was read and

a couple of verses sung (against all House rules) by Rohert Michel of Illinois, who had the best singing voice in Congress:

> "Thanks for the memory,
> Of places you have gone,
> To cheer our soldiers on,
> The President sent Kissinger,
> But you sent Jill St. John,
> We thank you so much . . ."

And as always happens in the House of Representatives— the Speaker, Mr. Tip O'Neill of Massachusetts, had the last word:

"I must explain to our guests, particularly, that singing in the House, and speaking in a foreign language, are not customary in the House.

"Also, you may be interested to know that in my 25 years in Congress, and I know there are members senior to me here, never before have I ever witnessed anything of this nature.

"The rules say that nobody can be introduced from the gallery, and that rule cannot be waived. Presidents' wives and former presidents merely sit there. I have seen distinguished visitors who have come to the House sit in the galleries, but never before have I seen anything compared to what is transpiring on the floor today.

"It is a show of appreciation, of love and affection to a great American, and I think it is a beautiful tribute."

The only sour note was the absence of both Hope sons-in-law. Linda and Nat were divorced and Nora and Sam were getting a legal separation. Hope could certainly state that his was the typical American family.

Bob continued doing television shows and golfing with presidents and pros. Probably his greatest access to the White House came during the administration of Dwight Eisenhower, but Hope and Ronald Reagan shared something more relative— they were both veterans of movies and television.

Bob's birthdays became cause for reminiscing with various magazine and newspaper writers. On the occasion of his eighty-third birthday he sat down with Margy Rochlin of the *Los Angeles Times Magazine*. Ms. Rochlin led off her piece with a question to Hope's daughter Linda, who manages Hope Enterprises.

Linda, a savvy lady who no doubt knows her father as well as anyone in the world, was asked what she would envision should she involve herself in a project about her father. She thought it would be about an aging man who makes desperate attempts to attract a younger woman to boost his failing ego.

"I would like to see him expose the softer, gentler side of himself. I would like to see him take risks. His image is very much that of the ladykiller—your basic Loni Andersons and Brooke Shieldses and all these young girls kissing him. That's not something that really happens to people who are 83, 84. It could certainly have humor, but you'd have to be able to see the underbelly, see the pain, for it to really work."

Ms. Hope, was in essence saying, hey—this is my father. He's human. He's sinned—and he's triumphed. He's a good man. I love him. One believes that she would like to share that humanity and love with everyone else.

The Rochlin interview with Bob took place while he was on a work/vacation trip to do a television special from Tahiti. The two were seated in a cabana on the small South Pacific Island of Moorea.

Hope recounted that he sometimes made big boo-boos and the censors were always ready to snip out blue material, but he admitted to making a big mistake the previous Fourth of July at a $1,000-a-plate function aboard the yacht *Princess* when he said the Statue of Liberty had AIDS:

"Nobody knows if she got it from the mouth of the Hudson or the Staten Island Ferry."

Bob laughs. "Yeah, that got me in trouble. It was like an intimate thing, and somebody there reported it. It was kinda sneaky on my part, but I thought the joke was funny."

Bob loved homophobic and ethnic jokes and told them often in private. Occasionally he slipped and told one in public— and they always got him in hot water.

During another February 1987 interview, with Jim Myers of *USA Today*, Hope diverted the writer's attention by telling jokes. Commenting on the long TV mini-series "America," Hope quipped, "The Russians could never occupy America— unless they managed to sneak up while we're watching a fourteen-and-a-half hour mini-series."

On former President Ford's golf game: "He's still so dangerous Oliver North tried to sell him to Iran for the Gulf War."

Referring to the Americas Cup, he said, "Vanna White got so excited she learned how to spell 'boat'."

Hope approached his eighty-fourth birthday boasting a career unequaled by anyone, even his good friend George Burns: 400-plus television shows, 1,145 radio shows, thousands of personal appearances, USO tours, and 58 films. *USA Today* claimed that more people had seen Bob Hope than any other entertainer in history.

During the Iran/Contra scandal Hope gave Ronald Reagan an easy pass. "How could I knock him?" he said. "I've known him for 46 years. He's like a brother."

With the Vietnam conflict relegated to history, Bob Hope still believed in the American goal: "If the politicians had given it to the military, it would have been over in two weeks and we'd have saved three million lives."

To show Bob's political clout, even into his late eighties, his son Anthony J. Hope was nominated by President George Bush (also a golfing buddy of Bob's) to become chairman of a new National Indian Gaming Commission.

The appointment caught the U.S. Senate off guard, because

that body would be required to hold confirmation hearings on the nomination.

Although Tony Hope had been a Washington attorney for several years, he admittedly was no expert on Indian affairs. He had limited political experience and had made an unsuccessful run for Congress from the San Fernando Valley in 1986, a race he lost by a 50-34 percent final tally.

Manny Fierro, executive director of the National Indian Gaming Association, objected to the appointment, stating that it amounted to a political appointment. "We certainly think he should have some experience in the field," he added.

Tony Hope countered, "I'm absolutely qualified," detailing his experience in dealing with less-developed countries as vice president for finances of the Overseas Investment Corporation from 1975 to 1977.

"The Indians have sovereign rights they are trying to protect against erosion from the more powerful entities that surround them. I want to help the Indians by promoting gambling on reservations."

Tony had received previous political appointments from President Ronald Reagan—to the Amtrak Commuter Board and the Grace Commission to curb government waste.

Bob Hope couldn't escape criticisms, directed at himself, his shows, his trips, or his family. In 1990 he ran into another flak attack in connection with several thousand acres of mountain land, part of which was situated in an area known as Corral Canyon, on the western end of the San Fernando Valley. Some of the letters to the editor of the *Los Angeles Times* viciously attacked Bob for profiteering at the expense of nature. One writer complained, "Bob Hope views his land . . . as a potential golf course. But when I look at his land in Corral Canyon, I see a place of beauty and my real home. I grew up in Corral Canyon, and as a boy I used to explore its cliffs and caves, untouched by mankind since the Chumash Indians first walked there . . ."

Another wrote, ". . . long ago I tired of Hope and his worn-out *shtick* . . . The man has become a national bore . . . but

he has the right to profit as much as he can from his investments . . ."

A woman from Agoura, California, said: "I would like to
clarify a few things about Hope's Jordan Ranch controversy.
There is no donation of land to the park service—not even one
single acre."

One irate citizen spoke the thoughts of many when she wrote:
"Bob Hope, through the courtesy of friends in high places, has
been elevated to what passes for the aristocracy of this country.
It's too bad he never heard of *noblesse oblige.*"

Hope has received it all: Plaudits, brickbats, honors, and
rotten tomatoes.

His most recent honors include being made an "honorary
veteran" of the U.S. Armed Forces—an honor never before
given to any civilian in the history of the Republic. Pope John
Paul II has just named him a "Papal Knight," an honor
bestowed upon those with "unblemished reputations."

In 1991, Graydon Carter, a writer and publisher, came from
the East Coast to Palm Springs to do an interview with Bob
for a piece he was writing, "Palm Springs Past: Grooming and
Tomcatting Tips from Bob Hope."

Carter ends his article with himself and Hope driving late
at night in downtown Palm Springs:

"The only thing that disturbs him from his evening con-
stitutional is the sight of a men's clothing store . . . He
oohs and aahs over the merchandise and makes a mental
note to stop by the next day. His thoughts are interrupted
once again, this time by the approaching sight of a trio
of blond girls in too-tight, too-short cutoffs. He glances
appreciatively, then nudges his visitor. 'What do you
say?' he whispers. 'You feel lucky tonight?' "

Epilogue

TOLUCA LAKE, CALIFORNIA — SUNDAY, JULY 27, 2003: 9:30 PM.
Comedian Bob Hope died peacefully tonight at his Toluca Lake, California, home, surrounded by those he loved most—his family. He celebrated his centennial on May 29, 2003.

Eras come and go with the passing of celebrities and political figures on the world stage; masterpieces are created but once. They are often copied, but never duplicated. Bob Hope will always be a masterpiece. His creativity, his volume of work, and the love of his fellow human beings belong uniquely to him.

This book, started in 1995 and finished in 1998, was thought at the time to be the last word on the life of this fabulous man. But although he did retire from entertaining, he never gave up making public appearances. For the next eight years he traveled extensively with his lovely wife, Delores, enjoying the many accolades showered upon him from the ordinary people whose life he enhanced for eighty-five-plus years. He made us all laugh at times when world conditions lent themselves more to mourning than happiness.

Millions upon millions of servicemen and -women, from every country on earth, have had their spirits lifted during their most trying times when Bob Hope beamed a radio broadcast, hosted a television show, starred in a new movie, or—most important of all—made an impromptu appearance, parachute prop trailing behind him, at some far-flung spot in the darkest parts of a savage jungle, scorching desert, or godforsaken outpost near the North Pole. Despite his celebrity and notoriety, Bob Hope was, in the hearts of his fans around the world, a man for all people.

Hope had only one ambition from the beginning of his career back in Cleveland, Ohio: to play the Palace Theater on Broadway. Throughout his life he never wavered in believing that "being successful in vaudeville is the only true measure of a comedian's ability."

He made it to the Palace and then some. In truth, he didn't always please his peers—especially when he co-starred with them, for Bob never failed to commit larceny during a scene.

Ethel Merman, in her autobiography, has a few choice words—hers, not his—to describe when they appeared together in the Cole Porter Broadway musical, *Red, Hot and Blue*. Merman and Hope sang a duet of Porter's "It's De-Lovely":

> "De-Lovely" caused a bit of friction between Bob and me on occasion. He, whether out of insecurity or because he liked to fool around, began playing to the boxes and otherwise distracting the audiences. At one point a titter arose at the wrong moment and I looked down to discover him lounging at my feet. I didn't mince words when we exited.

After giving Hope a good tongue-lashing, she went directly to the show's producer and exhibited her famous Merman temper. "If that so-called comedian ever behaves like that again, I'll use my shoe to remodel that ski nose of his." The message got through to Bob. He gave up the lounge act during the run of the show.

Eddie Fisher remembers Hope for his generosity. "While I was in London, Bob Hope had called to ask me to join him in

North Africa, where he was entertaining American troops." Fisher explained that he had a conflict, due to a gala commitment in Monaco.

"That's not a problem," Hope said, "I'll send a plane and get you back in time for your appearance." Hope arranged for a U.S. Air Force transport to fly from North Africa to London to pick up Fisher. Fisher did his songs for the troops and within minutes was back on the plane, en route to his Monaco gig. When Bob Hope wanted something done, it got done. He really loved his ability to order up government transportation. Few entertainers have that kind of clout.

Comedian and talk-show host Joan Rivers, known to have a barbed tongue when referring to other celebrities (although, when I appeared on her show with one of my books in 1992, she neither trashed the subject of my book—Jayne Mansfield— nor did anything other than make me feel like the most important person on camera), claims that Bob Hope was high on her role model list. "No entertainer in American history has ever achieved more. Bob was the *only* one who was ever supremely successful in every medium: vaudeville, radio, movies, and TV. You probably think it was all a walk in the park for Bob. Wrong. In his early days, Bob considered *sleeping* in the park."

Every comedian took potshots at Hope simply because he was Bob Hope. They told jokes, narrated events involving Hope, and probably made up a great deal of the repartee. Hope returned the banter in kind. Like all comedians, Hope sometimes "borrowed" jokes. Broadway gossip columnist Walter Winchell once accused Bob of stealing a line from one of his columns to include in a routine. Bob was indignant. Winchell, when proven wrong, refused to apologize—Winchell did not apologize to anyone. However, a few weeks later, in a backhanded manner, he scribed "bouquets" to Hope in one of his columns.

Bob Hope was the last of the great comedians from vaudeville who went on to other venues of entertainment when vaudeville became extinct. Along with Jack Benny, Red Skelton, Burns and Allen, Milton Berle, and Lou Costello, who knew how to please a crowd without vulgarity or smut, Bob Hope understood the relationship between the comedian and the audience. He disdained the lack of moral responsibility in most of today's cable "comedians." A few years ago, he said, "If a fella has to be smutty to get a laugh, he doesn't deserve a forum."

No one, however, will ever remember Bob Hope as a prude. Far from it. His shows were sexy and sometimes suggestive— but always in a subtle manner. He followed the old show business axiom that says "When lovers close the bedroom door you don't have to jump in bed with them to get the idea."

The great comedians always made themselves the butt of the joke, and Hope was a master at making himself look the fool. If he picked on politicians—especially presidents and world leaders—his barbs were nonpartisan and rarely if ever did the politicos feel insulted. As former First Lady Nancy Reagan said upon hearing of his passing, "Ronnie and I never took offense at Bob's remarks. We knew it was all in fun."

Bob Hope knew every president personally, beginning with Franklin D. Roosevelt, who first invited him to entertain the troops overseas. He performed for eleven presidents and often joked that he "entertained five or six." Starting with President Eisenhower, he also played golf with most of them. He joked about his golf games with Gerald Ford. "Yes," he said, "I played golf with President Ford—and survived." (Ford had a reputation for shanking the ball into the crowd, often nailing a spectator. Hope's affectionate barb delighted him.)

Hope had close relationships with Presidents Eisenhower, Nixon, and Reagan. Ronald Reagan, onetime president of the Screen Actors Guild, knew Hope long before Reagan became two-term Governor of California and, later, two-term President of the United States.

Bob Hope's record sixteen hostings of the Academy Awards ceremonies has led to serious consideration of erecting a statue of him in the lobby of Hollywood's new Kodak Theater, the permanent home of the awards.

Hope has received more awards of his own than anyone else

in the world. *The Guinness Book of World Records* credits him as the most-honored entertainer in history, with more than two thousand awards and citations for humanitarian and professional efforts, including five Oscars (honorary), 44 honorary doctorates, and seven civilian medals. The one he valued most was presented to him on October 29, 1997, at age ninety-four, by the United States Congress: "Honorary Veteran of the United States Armed Forces."

Bob, Dolores, and their family were escorted into the U.S. Capitol's Rotunda as the United States Army Band played, "Thanks for the Memory." For an hour House Speaker Newt Gingrich, Congressman Robert Michel, and a bevy of U.S. senators, including Arlen Specter, Trent Lott, Max Cleland, and the late Strom Thurmond, lauded Hope's service to his adopted country and his contributions to the morale of American armed forces both at home and abroad over a period of six decades—a record of service that is not likely ever to be equaled by any other entertainer.

On March 15, 1997, Bob and Dolores flew to New Orleans where Bob was honored with the naming of the U.S. Navy's new Military Sealift Command (MSC). Dolores christened the USNS *Bob Hope* (T-AKR 300) at the Avondale Shipyards. The *Hope* became the first of (to date) seven fighting vessels now known as the *Bob Hope* class.

The Honorable John H. Dalton, secretary of the navy, principal speaker for the occasion, spoke of Bob as a *military hero*. "We can never repay him for his contributions to the men and women in uniform, but we can show our appreciation with a class of ships named in his honor. This is our way of saying 'thanks for the memories.' "

Not only did Hope now have his own fleet, but he had the brass on hand to prove it. Dozens of admirals and generals witnessed the launching of "old ski nose's" armada, including General William Westmoreland (ret.), whom Hope had come to know well during the Vietnam War (and with whom he became somewhat disenchanted, as he became displeased with many Washington and military bigwigs when he discovered that the government hadn't been totally straightforward with him about the progress of the war).

Hope's Navy! Milton Berle, always quick to needle the competition, said, "Give Hope a navy and we might need bomb shelters in Hollywood. Especially along comedian row."

Berle, probably more than any other of Bob's contemporaries, enjoyed booby-trapping his old friend. He loved to create situations designed to make Hope squirm. He swore the following to be true (though it probably isn't). Hope, according to Berle, while on a road tour was caught red-handed with a chorus girl when Dolores unexpectedly showed up. Berle, with an almost straight face, declared, "Bob sat straight up in the bed, raised his right hand, and without cracking so much as a wrinkle, said, 'Dolores, I swear to God it's not me!' " True or not, Berle got a lot of mileage out of it.

Hope gave as good as he got, and sometimes he gave much more. The kids—and some not so kiddish any longer—could always count on him for a boost. Bob developed a theory that he couldn't be everywhere at the same time, so he didn't mind slipping some of his humor between the ears of new comedians. His good friend Rosemary Clooney once told me that if Hope could have packaged his humor we'd be eating "Bob Hope Funny Bunnies" for breakfast.

Phyllis Diller, who co-starred in three films with Hope, gives him credit for helping her continue a career that didn't seem destined to go much farther than her native Ohio. Sometime during the late 1950s Phyllis had been struggling along as a minority-of-one standup female comedian and not getting much traction along a road dominated by male comics. She'd been appearing at an East Coast nightclub for more than a week and was, as she put it, "bombing like a B-52." Disgusted, she was about ready to give up her life as the Erma Bombeck of the club circuit when someone told her Bob Hope was in the audience.

"Hope was my idol. I tried to sneak out the stage door when someone said Bob Hope wanted to speak to me."

Hope caught her before she could escape. "You were wonderful!" he said.

Phyllis swears to this day that "Bob turned my life around. He gave me the confidence to go on." He could have brushed her off as just another night at the comedy store, but somehow he sensed she needed a boost and gave it to her. His reward? A lifetime of gratitude and appreciation for "giving the kid a boost."

In a post-mortem piece on Hope, Alicia Potter makes a point that is true about Hope and all comedic entertainers: they model themselves on their predecessors—Woody Allen imitated Hope, and Hope imitated Chaplin. Hope, however, did more than imitate. He studied the work of his comedic peers. He once said, "I don't envy other entertainers. I watch what they're doing right and try to do it better. After all, there are only so many basic jokes. It's not the joke. It's the delivery." With Bob, delivery was only an element. He thoroughly understood the human condition. He seemed to subconsciously question his jokes. "Would I laugh at that?" seemed to be his standard of acceptance or rejection of material.

Bob would show up, often alone, sit in the back of a club or theater, and observe audience reaction to the comedian on the stage. He told the late Marc Anthony, one of his writers, "I almost want to cry when I hear a good joke delivered incorrectly."

Although a total competitor, he loved other comedians and wanted to know what they were doing. "Who knows," he said, "I might be missing something." That remark reminds me of an experience I had with the great operetta composer Rudolf Friml. Friml's home, high up on Appian Way in the Hollywood Hills, hovered above Hollywood like a classical European retreat. Several contemporary rock groups of the early sixties moved into houses across the road from him, including The Mamas and the Papas. One afternoon I was sitting with Friml and some friends when suddenly one of the groups began a very loud rehearsal. Someone said, "Close the windows. This kind of music will disturb Rudy."

Friml, shaking his head, said, "No! No! Let's listen. I might learn something."

Friml, the great classical musician, and Bob Hope, everyman's comedian, each wanted to know what the modern audience wants to hear.

I first met Bob Hope during World War II while serving in the U.S. Army Air Corp just prior to being shipped out to Tinian, a small island, part of the Mariannas, now part of Micronesia. He came with his radio show to the Army Air Corps base outside Victorville, California. I will never forget his entrance. He did not arrive on stage from the wings. While we waited for the show to start there occurred a loud clamor in the back of the theater. When we turned to look, there came Bob Hope, dragging behind him an open parachute (which became one of his entrance props).

I heard him comment to a second lieutenant accompanying him down the center aisle towards the stage, "Are we still in the United States?" I knew immediately that these guys were gonna love him—and we did. He poked fun at the local watering hole, the brass, and the desert heat. He touched on our everyday lives and the human condition in general.

After the show, I had an opportunity to speak to him. I never had a chance to ask about Hollywood or his work because he peppered me with questions. How long had I been in the service? Had I been overseas yet? How long had I been at Victorville and where did I come from? When was the last time I'd been home? Did I ever get homesick for West Virginia? He also gave me a wicked wink and said, "I once knew a girl from West Virginia." He cocked his head in Hope fashion and sighed, "Boy, were those the days. Hey kid, enjoy yourself while you're young." He was only in his forties himself.

The next time I saw Hope, he'd come out to March Field to do a show after the war. His routine hadn't changed. He still poked fun at the brass and dispersed knowing information about the local bars and clubs.

In 1948 I volunteered for duty as an air traffic controller for the Berlin Airlift. By then President Harry Truman had signed an order making the U.S. Air Force an autonomous branch of the armed forces. While at Westover Field, Massachusetts, awaiting shipment to Germany, Hope showed up to do his radio show and give us a big send off. After the show he stopped backstage to talk to some of us and spotted me.

"Don't I know you, kid? Where are you from?"

"Yes sir, Mr. Hope. We met at Victorville."

"Oh, yeah—the kid from West Virginia. When was the last time you were home on leave?"

I assured him I'd had a two-day stopover en route to Westover and that I'd had a good visit with my mother.

"I'll bet she writes you often."

I said, "Yes sir, she sure does."

"Well," he said, clapping his hand on my shoulder, "you see that you write her back. Folks at home worry about their kids, and when they don't hear from you, they worry."

I couldn't believe that anyone as famous as Bob Hope would give a damn whether my mother wrote me or not.

During the Berlin Airlift, I was stationed at Celle, Germany, in the British Occupation Zone. The commanding general of our base just happened to be married to the glamorous motion picture star Constance Bennett. Through her efforts, it was arranged for Bob's overseas troupe to do a show at Celle during his tour of American bases in Germany.

I'd been a singer in civilian life and appeared with some of the military service club bands while in Europe. Being part of the local base entertainment, I had a chance to be backstage when U.S.O. troupes came through. Hope came to do a show at Celle, or "smelly Celle" as we called it, and did his usual shtik, coming down the aisle of the theater, dragging an open parachute behind him. I'd seen him do it three or four times already, so it was no big surprise. However, he made jokes about how he bailed out to avoid being shot down by the Russians and just happened to land in Celle. The guys all went bananas over him—they related to that. After all, we were just a few kilometers from the very tense border between the British zone and the Russian-occupied eastern zone.

After the show, Hope sought me out. "Hey, Sarge," he said, "you're the kid from Charleston, West Virginia."

"That's me," I said.

"You writing to your mother?"

"Twice a week."

"Hey, does the Air Force know you're following me around?"

He was that kind of guy around the troops. He made it personal—like being part of your family—and that went a long way to bring a feeling of home to all of us in the military, whether it was in a war zone, a stateside base, or facing the Russian border during the Cold War.

There's always been a lot of talk about how much money Bob made on his NBC specials from military bases and his trips overseas. I hope he made millions because just having him there was as American as mom and apple pie. He was the mailman, the Western Union delivery guy, and the nice guy down the block who just happened to be passing through with some good cheer from the folks at home.

As I write this, I've been channel-surfing, listening to celebrities sing his praises on all the talk shows, knowing that many of them barely touched his life, if at all, but they all want to be remembered as being a part of the Bob Hope Era. Nothing wrong with that. They're just like the ordinary Joes who say, "Did I ever tell you about the time I met Bob Hope?"

It reminds me of all the folks I've known in Hollywood over the past forty-five years who enjoy letting you know of their arm's-length relationship with someone in "the outfit." It creates a sort of intimacy with the Mob without participating in the sausage factory that produces that dark side of Americana.

Associating ourselves with Bob Hope is the flip side of that. (As Paul Harvey always says, "And now here's the rest of the story.") Bob Hope made us feel good. No one ever took his business to the public the way Hope did. He never had to coerce us. We waited in long lines to see him, set our clocks, tape recorders, and VCRs to make sure we didn't miss him in person, on radio, in the movies, and on television.

The outpouring from the world when he turned one hundred years old on May 29, 2003, was comparable to a presidential inauguration. Bob Hope's is one of the most recognizable faces around the globe, comparable in stature to Muhammad Ali and President John F. Kennedy. His face represents Americana as much as Norman Rockwell's *Saturday Evening Post* covers and the faces on Mount Rushmore.

The bells toll his passing as they would that of a monarch, for he was and always will be the King of Comedy.

Although he was ailing and frail during the late nineties, when his very good friend Rosemary Clooney invited him to be a guest at her wedding—she and longtime boyfriend, Dante Di Paolo, were getting married at Maysville, Kentucky, Rosie's hometown—Bob and Dolores surprised the town by flying in from Hollywood to honor their friend. Hope's appearance nearly upstaged the nuptials. Rosemary Clooney was rarely upstaged by anyone, but she was thrilled that her hometown loved Bob Hope as much as she did.

Bob Hope would go to the wire for a friend. Not too long before her untimely death in an automobile accident along a fog-shrouded highway between Biloxi, Mississippi, and New Orleans, Jayne Mansfield was involved in a bitter custody dispute with her husband, Matt Cimber. She had been charged in the custody papers as being an unfit mother. Jayne called all of her personal friends, seeking letters of recommendation as to her motherly abilities and concern for her children.

I was Jayne's press secretary at the time. On the telephone Bob said that if Jayne would prepare a letter for him to sign and send it over to his house, he'd be happy to take care of it for her. Paul Blane, Jayne's road manager was in town and was dispatched from Jayne's pink palace to Bob Hope, who was at the time rehearsing that night's show.

When Paul arrived Bob asked the guys to excuse him. Paul relates it best:

> Bob took me off to a side room and we talked for something like twenty minutes about Jayne's situation. He said that he loved Jayne and would do anything to help her out, "but frankly, Paul, I don't know that I've ever been in her house. I've seen all her children, of course, but never

in a home setting. I don't have the faintest idea how she mothers her children. But I want to help her."

Hope signed the letter and returned it to Paul. His parting words to Blane were, "If I go to jail over this, you're going with me." They both laughed nervously.

The point is, if Bob Hope was your friend, he wouldn't care what you'd done. If he could help, he would, and in this instance his word helped Jayne keep custody of her youngest son.

Since this book (minus this epilogue) was completed five years ago, it has become a joke among my friends that Bob Hope simply wasn't going anywhere—that I would die and Bob would read the book. By the generous grace of God, I am still here, but I'll bet that between U.S.O. shows in heaven, Bob will take time out to see what's been said about his life. I can almost hear him say, "Yeah, that's right"—"No, that's not exactly the way it happened" and "Now why in the hell did he have to say that?" All with good humor and understanding that we're all just ordinary human beings trying to do what it is we do, and hoping that somewhere, somebody will say "good job."

To Bob Hope, I say, "Good job, kid!"

P.S.: Borrowing from Hope's opening line at every base he ever appeared with his show, I can imagine him saying something like, "This is Bob I-just-landed-in-Heaven Hope. You know what Heaven is . . . that's another way of saying, 'I think I boarded the wrong plane.' "

God bless and keep you, Bob Hope. I know the angels are fluttering their wings in applause.

FILMOGRAPHY

Two Reelers

1. *Going Spanish*

   Starring : Bob Hope, Leah Ray.

   Director : Al Christe
   Script   : Art Jarrett and William Watson
   Studio   : Educational Films
   Released: 1934

2. *Paree, Paree*

   Starring : Bob Hope and Dorothy Stone, with Charles Collins, Lorraine Collier, Billie Leonard

   Director : Roy Mack
   Script   : Cyrus Wood
   Original material: *Fifty Million Frenchmen* by E. Ray Goetz, Herbert Field, and Cole Porter.
   Studio   : Warner Brothers
   Released: 1934

3. *The Old Grey Mayor*

> Starring : Bob Hope and Ruth Blasco, with Lionel Stander, Sam Wren, and George Watts

> Director : Lloyd French
> Script   : Herman Ruby
> Studio   : Warner Brothers
> Released: 1935

4. *Watch the Birdie*

> Starring : Bob Hope, Neil O'Day, Arline Dintz, with Marie Nordstrom and George Watts

> Director : Lloyd French
> Script   : Jack Henley and Dolph Singer
> Studio   : Warner Brothers
> Released: 1935

5. *Double Exposure*

> Starring : Bob Hope and Johnny Berkes, Loretta Sayers, Jules Epailley

> Director : Lloyd French
> Script   : Jack Henley and Burnet Hershey
> Studio   : Warner Brothers
> Released: 1935

6. *Calling All Tars*

> Starring : Bob Hope and Johnny Berkes, Oscar Ragland

> Director : Lloyd French
> Script   : Jack Henley and Burnet Hershey
> Studio   : Warner Brothers
> Released: 1936

7. *Shop Talk*

Starring : Bob Hope

Director : Lloyd French
Script   : Jack Henley and Burnet Hershey
Studio   : Warner Brothers
Released: 1936

Feature Motion Pictures

1. *The Big Broadcast of 1938*

   Actors : Bob Hope, W. C. Fields, Shirley Ross, Martha Raye, Dorothy Lamour, Lynn Overland, Ben Blue, Grace Bradley, Leif Erikson, Kirsten Flagstad, Rufe Davis, Lionel Pape, Tito Guizar, Russell Hicks, Dorothy Howe, Patricia "Honey Chile" Wilder, Leonid Kinskey and Shep Field and his "Rippling Rhythm" orchestra

   Director : Mitchell Leisen
   Producer: Harlan Thompson
   Script : Ken Englund, Walter De Leon and Francis Martin (original story by Frederick Hazlitt Brennan—adapted by Russell Crouse and Howard Lindsay)
   Studio : Paramount
   Released: 1938

2. *College Swing*

   Actors : Bob Hope, George Burns, Gracie Allen, Edward Everett Horton, Martha Raye, Ben Blue, Florence George, Jackie Coogan, Betty Grable, Cecil Cunningham, John Payne, Jerry Colonna, Robert Cummings, Tully Marshall

Director : Raoul Walsh
Producer: Lewis Gensler
Script : Francis Martin and Walter De Leon (adapted by Frederick Hazlitt Brennan from a Ted Lesser idea)
Studio : Paramount
Released: 1938

3. *Give Me A Sailor*

Actors : Bob Hope, Betty Grable, Martha Raye, Clarence Kolb, Jack Whiting, Emerson Treacy, Nana Bryant, Bonnie Jean Churchill, Kathleen Lockhart, Edward Earle, Ralph Sanford

Director : Elliott Nugent
Producer: Jeff Lazarus
Script : Frank Butler and Doris Anderson (adapted from a play by Anne Nichols)
Studio : Paramount
Released: 1938

4. *Thanks for the Memory*

Actors : Bob Hope, Shirley Ross, Otto Kruger, Charles Butterworth, Laura Hope Crews, Hedda Hopper, Roscoe Karns, Emma Dunn, Edward Gargan, Eddie "Rochester" Anderson, Patricia "Honey Chile" Wilder, Jack Norton, William Collier, Sr.

Director : Goerge Archinbaud
Producer: Mel Shauer
Script : Lynn Starling (adapted from Albert Hackett and Frances Goodrich's play, *Up Pops the Devil*)
Studio : Paramount
Released: 1938

5. *Never Say Die*

> Actors   : Bob Hope, Martha Raye, Paul Harvey, Ernest Cossart, Andy Devine, Siegfried Rumann, Alan Mowbray
>
> Director : Elliot Nugent
> Producer: Paul Jones
> Script   : Don Hartman, Preston Sturges and Frank Butler (adapted from a William H. Post play)
> Studio   : Paramount
> Released: 1939

6. *Rhythm Romance*

> Actors : Bob Hope, Shirley Ross, Drummer Gene Krupa and his Orchestra, Rufe Davis, Una Merkel, Wayne "Tiny" Whit, Bernard Nedell, Frank Sully, Harry Barris, Dudley Dickerson, Clarence H. Wilson, Pat West, Richard Denning, Sam Ash, Lillian Fitzgerald
>
> Director : George Archinbaud
> Producer: William C. Thomas
> Script   : Wilkie C. Mahoney and Lewis R. Foster (adapted from a play by Gene Fowler and Ben Hecht)
> Studio   : Paramount
> Released: 1939
> *Original title: *Some Like It Hot*

7. *The Cat and the Canary*

> Actors   : Bob Hope, Paulette Goddard, Douglass Montgomery, John Beal, Nydia Westman, Gale Sondergaard, Willard Robertson, George Zucco, Elizabeth Patterson
>
> Director : Elliot Nugent
> Producer: Arthur Hornblow, Jr.
> Script   : Lynn Starling and Walter De Leon (adapted from the John Willard play of the same name)

Studio : Paramount
Released: 1939

8. *Road to Singapore*

Actors : Bob Hope, Dorothy Lamour, Bing Crosby, Charles Coburn, Anthony Quinn, Jerry Colonna

Director : Victor Schertzinger
Producer: Harlan Thompson
Script : Don Hartman and Frank Butler (adapted from a story by Harry Hervey)
Studio : Paramount
Released: 1940

9. *The Ghost Breakers*

Actors : Bob Hope, Paulette Goddard, Anthony Quinn, Richard Carlson, Willie Best, Paul Lukas, Pedro De Cordoba

Director : George Marshall
Producer: Arthur Hornblow, Jr.
Script : Walter De Leon (adapted from the play by Charles W. Goddard and Paul Dickey)
Studio : Paramount
Released: 1940

10. *Road to Zanzibar*

Actors : Bob Hope, Dorothy Lamour, Bing Crosby, Eric Blore, Una Merkel, Joan Marsh, Luis Alberni, Iris Adrian, Douglas Dumbrille, Noble Johnson

Director : Victor Schertzinger
Producer: Paul Jones
Script : Don Hartman and Frank Butler (adapted from *Find Colonel Fawcett,* a story by Sy Bartlett and Don Hartman)

Studio   : Paramount
Released: 1941

11. *Caught in the Draft*

Actors   : Bob Hope, Dorothy Lamour, Eddie Bracken,
Lynne Overman, Paul Hurst, Clarence Kolb, Phyllis
Ruth, Arthur Loft, Irving Bacon, Edward Dearing

Director : David Butler
Producer: B. G. DeSylva
Script   : Harry Tugend (special dialogue by Wilkie C.
Mahoney)
Studio   : Paramount
Released: 1941

12. *Nothing but the Truth*

Actors   : Bob Hope, Paulette Goddard, Leif Erikson,
Edward Arnold, Willie Best, Helen Vinson, Grant Mitchell, Glenn Anders, Charles Kolb, Catherine Doucet

Director : Elliott Nugent
Producer: Arthur Hornblow, Jr.
Script   : Ken Englund and Don Hartman (adapted
from James Montgomery's play from an original novel
by Frederic S. Isham)
Studio   : Paramount
Released: 1941

13. *Louisiana Purchase*

Actors   : Bob Hope, Vera Zorina, Victor Moore, Dona
Drake, Irene Bordoni, Maxi Rosenbloom, Raymond
Walburn, Frank Albertson, Phyllis Ruth, Jack Norton,
Donald MacBride, Margaret Hayes, Barbara Britton,
Dave Willock, Jean Wallace

Director : Irving Cummings
Producer: Harold Wilson

Script : Joseph Fields and Jerome Chodorov (adapted from the musical comedy by Morrie Ryskind from an original story by B. G. DeSylva)
Studio : Paramount
Released: 1941

14. *My Favorite Blonde*

Actors : Bob Hope, Madeleine Carroll, George Zucco, Gale Sondergaard, Edward Gargan, Victor Varconi, Isabel Randolph, Dooley Wilson, Minerva Urecal, Monte Blue

Director : Sidney Lanfield
Producer: Paul Jones
Script : Frank Butler and Don Hartman (adapted from a story by Melvin Frank and Norman Panama)
Studio : Paramount
Released: 1942

15. *Road to Morocco*

Actors : Bob Hope, Dorothy Lamour, Bing Crosby, Dona Drake, Anthony Quinn, Laura La Plante, Mikhail Rasumny, Yvonne De Carlo, Monte Blue

Director : David Butler
Producer: Paul Jones
Script : Frank Butler and Don Hartman
Studio : Paramount
Released: 1942

16. *They Got Me Covered*

Actors : Bob Hope, Dorothy Lamour, Otto Preminger, Lenore Aubert, Florence Bates, Eduardo Ciannelli, Donald Meek, Marion Martin, Philip Ahn, Walter Catlett, Mary Treen, John Abbott

Director : David Butler

Producer: Samuel Goldwyn
Script   : Harry Kurnitz (adapted from a story by Leonard Q. Ross and Leonard Spiegelgass)
Studio   : Goldwyn-RKO
Released: 1943

17. *Let's Face It*

Actors   : Bob Hope: Betty Hutton, Phyllis Povah, Zasu Pitts, Dave Willock, Eve Arden, Marjorie Weaver, Raymond Walburn, Arthur Loft, Dona Drake, Joseph Sawyer

Director : Sidney Lanfield
Producer: Fred Kohlmar
Script   : Harry Tugend (adapted from a musical play by Herbert and Dorothy Fields and Cole Porter, original material from a play by Norma Mitchell and Russell G. Medcraft)
Studio   : Paramount
Released: 1943

18. *The Princess and the Pirate*

Actors   : Bob Hope, Virginia Mayo, Walter Slezak, Walter Brennan, Marc Lawrence, Victor McLaglen, Hugo Haas, Mike Mazurki, Maude Eburne, special cameo by Bing Crosby

Director : David Butler
Producer: Samuel Goldwyn
Script   : Everett Freeman, Don Hartman and Melville Shavelson (adapted by Allen Boretz and Curtis Kenyon from an original story by Sy Bartlett)
Studio   : Goldwyn-RKO
Released: 1944

19. *Road to Utopia*

Actors   : Bob Hope, Dorothy Lamour, Bing Crosby, Douglas Dumbrille, Hillary Brooke, Robert Barrat, Jack

LaRue, Robert Benchley (voice-over narration), Nestor Paive

Director : Hal Walker
Producer: Paul Jones
Script   : Melvin Frank and Norman Panama
Studio   : Paramount
Released: 1946

20. *Monsieur Beaucaire*

Actors   : Bob Hope, Joan Caulfield, Marjorie Reyn-
olds, Patric Knowles, Joseph Schildkraut, Cecil Kellaway, Constance Collier, Reginald Owen, Mary Nash,
Hillary Brooke, Douglas Dumbrille

Director : George Marshall
Producer: Paul Jones
Script   : Norman Panama and Melvin Frank (adapted
from the Booth Tarkington novel)
Studio   : Paramount
Released: 1946

21. *My Favorite Brunette*

Actors   : Bob Hope, Dorothy Lamour, Lon Chaney,
Jr., Peter Lorre, Charles Dingle, John Hoyt, Frank Puglia,
Willard Robertson, Ann Doran, special cameo by Bing
Crosby

Director : Elliott Nugent
Producer: Daniel Dare
Script   : Jack Rose and Edmund Beloin
Studio   : Paramount
Released: 1947

22. *Where There's Life*

Actors   : Bob Hope, Signe Hasso, George Coulouris,

William Bendix, John Alexander, George Zucco, Joseph
Vitale, Denis Hoey, Harry Von Zell

Director : Sidney Lanfield
Producer: Paul Jones
Script : Melville Shavelson & Allen Boretz (adapted
from an original story by Melville Shavelson)
Studio : Paramount
Released: 1947

23. *Road to Rio*

Actors : Bob Hope, Dorothy Lamour, Bing Crosby,
Frank Faylen, Gale Sondergaard, Frank Puglia, Joseph
Vitale, Jerry Colonna, Nestor Paiva, The Andrews Sis-
ters, The Wiere Brothers, Tan Van Brunt

Director : Norman Z. McLeod
Producer: Daniel Dare
Script : Jack Rose and Edmund Beloin
Studio : Paramount
Released: 1948

24. *The Paleface*

Actors : Bob Hope, Jane Russell, Iris Adrian, Robert
Armstrong, Jack Searl, Robert Watson, Charles Trow-
bridge, Joseph Vitale, Jeff York, Clem Bevans, Iron Eyes
Cody, Stanley Adams

Director : Norman Z. McLeod
Producer: Robert L. Welch
Script : Frank Tashlin and Edmund Hartmann (Spe-
cial dialogue by Jack Rose)
Studio : Paramount
Released: 1948

25. *Sorrowful Jones*

Actors : Bob Hope, Lucille Ball, William Demarest,

Mary Jane Saunders, Thomas Gomez, Bruce Cabot, Paul Lees, Tom Pedi

Director : Sidney Lanfield
Producer: Robert L. Welch
Script : Edmund Hartmann, Melville Shavelson, and Jack Rose (adapted from a play by Damon Runyon)
Studio : Paramount
Released: 1949

26. *The Great Lover*

Actors : Bob Hope, Rhonda Fleming, Roland Culver, Roland Young, Jerry Hunter, Richard Lyon, Karl Wright, Jackie Jackson, Jim Backus, George Reeves, Sig Arno

Director : Alexander Hall
Producer: Edmund Beloin
Script : Melville Shavelson, Edmund Beloin, and Jack Rose.
Studio : Paramount
Released: 1949

27. *Fancy Pants*

Actors : Bob Hope, Lucille Ball, Jack Kirkwood, Bruce Cabot, Hugh French, Lea Pennman, Joseph Vitale, Eric Blore, Norma Varden, John Alexander, Ida Moore, Colin Keith-Johnston

Director : George Marshall
Producer: Robert Welch
Script : Robert O'Brien and Edmund Hartman (adapted from the Harry Leon Wilson novel, *Ruggles of Red Gap*)
Studio : Paramount
Released: 1950

28. *The Lemon Drop Kid*

   Actors : Bob Hope, Marilyn Maxwell, Jane Darwell, Lloyd Nolan, Fred Clark, Andrea King, William Frawley, Jay C. Flippin, Sid Melton, Harry Bellaver, Ida Moore

   Director : Sidney Lanfield
   Producer: Robert L. Welch
   Script : Edmund Hartmann, Frank Tashlin, and Robert O'Brian. (Special dialogue by Irving Elinson, adapted from the Damon Runyon short story by Edmund Beloin).
   Studio   : Paramount
   Released: 1951

29. *My Favorite Spy*

   Actors : Bob Hope, Hedy Lamarr, Arnold Moss, Francis L. Sullivan, John Archer, Stephen Chase, Morris Ankrum, Luis Van Rooten

   Director : Norman Z. McLeod
   Producer: Paul Jones
   Script : Jack Sher and Edmund Hartmann
   Studio   : Paramount
   Released: 1951

30. *Son of Paleface*

   Actors : Bob Hope, Jane Russell, Bill Williams, Roy Rogers, Paul E. Burns, Lloyd Corrigan, Harry Von Zell, Douglas Dumbrille, Iron Eyes Cody

   Director : Frank Tashlin
   Producer: Robert L. Welch
   Script   : Robert L. Welch, Frank Tashlin, and Joseph Quillan
   Studio   : Paramount
   Released: 1952

31. *Road to Bali*

Actors   : Bob Hope, Dorothy Lamour, Bing Crosby, Ralph Moody, Murvyn Vye, Leon Askin, and Peter Coe. Cameo appearances: Humphrey Bogart, Bob Crosby, Dean Martin, Jane Russell, Jerry Lewis

Director : Hal Walker
Producer: Harry Tugend
Script   : Hal Kanter, Frank Butler, and William Morrow (adapted from an original story by Harry Tugend and Frank Butler)
Studio   : Paramount
Released: 1952

32. *Off Limits*

Actors   : Bob Hope, Marilyn Maxwell, Mickey Rooney, Stanley Clements, Eddie Mayehoff, John Ridgely, Marvin Miller, Carolyn Jones

Director : George Marshall
Producer: Harry Tugend
Script   : Jack Sher and Hal Kanter
Studio   : Paramount
Released: 1953

33. *Here Comes the Girls*

Actors   : Bob Hope, Arlene Dahl, Tony Martin, Millard Mitchell, Rosemary Clooney, Fred Clark, William Demarest, Robert Strauss

Director : Claude Binyon
Producer: Paul Jones
Script   : Hal Kanter and Edmund Hartman (adapted from an original story by Edmund Hartman)
Studio   : Paramount
Released: 1953

34. *Casanova's Big Night*

> Actors : Bob Hope, Audrey Dalton, Joan Fontaine, Arnold Moss, Basil Rathbone, Hope Emerson, John Carradine
>
> Director : Norman Z. McLeod
> Producer: Paul Jones
> Script   : Edmund Hartmann and Hal Kanter (adapted from an original story by Aubrey Wisberg)
> Studio   : Paramount
> Released: 1954

35. *The Seven Little Foys*

> Actors : Bob Hope, George Tobias, Milly Vitale, Richard Shannon, George Tobias, Lydia Reed, Billy Gray, Jimmy Baird, Linda Bennett, James Cagney (as George M. Cohan)
>
> Director : Melville Shavelson
> Producer: Jack Rose
> Script   : Jack Rose and Melville Shavelson
> Studio   : Paramount
> Released: 1955

36. *That Certain Feeling*

> Actors : Bob Hope, George Sanders, Eva Marie Saint, David Lewis, Pearl Bailey, Al Capp, David Lewis, Florenz Ames, Jerry Mathers
>
> Director : Norman Panama
> Producer: Melvin Frank and Norman Panama
> Script   : William Altman, Norman Panama, I. A. L. Diamond, Melvin Frank (adapted from the Jean Kerr and Eleanor Brooke play, *King of Hearts)*
> Studio   : Paramount
> Released: 1956

37. *The Iron Petticoat*

Actors   : Bob Hope, Katharine Hepburn, James Robertson Justice, Noelle Middleton, David Kossoff, Robert Helpmann, Alexander Gauge, Alan Giggord

Director : Ralph Thomas
Producer: Betty Box
Script   : Ben Hecht
Studio   : Metro-Goldwyn-Mayer
Released: 1956

38. *Beau James*

Actors   : Bob Hope, Alexis Smith, Vera Miles, Darren McGavin, Paul Douglas, Jimmy Durante, Joseph Mantell, Walter Catlett

Director : Melville Shavelson
Producer: Jack Rose
Script   : Melville Shavelson and Jack Rose (adapted from the biography of New York Mayor Jimmy Walker, written by Gene Fowler)
Studio   : Paramount
Released: 1957

39. *Paris Holiday*

Actors   : Bob Hope, Anita Ekberg, Fernandel, Martha Hyer, Anita Ekberg, Andre Morell, Preston Sturges, Alan Gifford

Director : Gerd Oswald
Producer: Robert Hope
Script   : Dean Riesner and Edmund Beloin (adapted from an original story by Robert Hope)
Studio   : United Artists
Released: 1958

40. *Alias Jesse James*

Actors : Bob Hope, Rhonda Fleming, Jim Davis, Wendell Corey, Will Wright, Gloria Talbot, and Mary Young. Cameos: Bing Crosby, Jay Silverheels, Gail Davis, Fess Parker, Hugh O'Brian, Roy Rogers

Director : Norman Z. McLeod
Executive Producer: Bob Hope
Producer: Jack Hope
Script : Daniel D. Beauchamp and William Bowers (adapted from an original story by Robert St. Aubrey and Bert Lawrence)
Studio : United Artists
Released: 1959

41. *The Facts of Life*

Actors : Bob Hope, Lucille Ball, Don Defore, Ruth Hussey, Philip Ober, Louis Nye, Peter Leeds, Marianne Stewart, Robert F. Simon, Louise Beavers, Mike Mazurki

Director : Melvin Frank
Producer: Norman Panama
Script : Melvin Frank and Norman Panama
Studio : United Artists
Released: 1960

42. *Bachelor in Paradise*

Actors : Bob Hope, Lana Turner, Jim Hutton, Janis Paige, Don Porter, Paula Prentiss, John McGiver, Virginia Grey, Clinton Sundberg, Florence Sundstrom

Director : Jack Arnold
Producer: Ted Richmond
Script : Hal Kanter and Valentine Davies (adapted from an original story by Vera Caspary)

Studio   : Metro-Goldwyn-Mayer
Released: 1961

43. *Road to Hong Kong*

Actors   : Bob Hope, Dorothy Lamour, Bing Crosby, Robert Morley, Joan Collins, with cameo by: Frank Sinatra, Peter Sellers, David Niven, Dean Martin, Dave King, Zsa Zsa Gabor, Jerry Colonna

Director : Norman Panama
Producer: Melvin Frank
Script   : Melvin Frank and Norman Panama
Studio   : United Artists
Released: 1962

44. *Critic's Choice*

Actors   : Bob Hope, Lucille Ball, Rip Torn, Marilyn Maxwell, Jim Backus, Jessie Royce Landis, Dorothy Green, Rick Kellman, Jerome Cowan, Marie Windsor, Stanley Adams, Lurene Tuttle

Director : Don Weis
Producer: Frank P. Rosenberg
Script   : Jack Sher (adapted from a play by Ira Levin).
Studio   : Warner Brothers
Released: 1963

45. *Call Me Bwana*

Actors   : Bob Hope, Anita Ekberg, Lionel Jeffries, Edie Adams, Percy Herbert

Director : Gordon Douglas
Producer: Albert R. Broccoli
Script   : Johanna Harwood and Nate Monaster
Studio   : United Artists
Released: 1963

46. *A Global Affair*

Actors : Bob Hope, Lilo Pulver, Elga Anderson, Michele Mercier

Director : Jack Arnold
Producer: Hall Bartlett
Script : Charles Lederer, Arthur Marx and Bob Fisher (adapted from an original story by Eugene Vale)
Studio : Metro-Goldwyn-Mayer
Released: 1964

47. *I'll Take Sweden*

Actors : Bob Hope, Dina Merrill, Tuesday Weld, Jeremy Slate, Frankie Avalon, Rosemarie Frankland

Director : Freddie De Cordova
Producer: Edward Small
Script : Bob Fisher, Arthur Marx and Nat Perrin
Studio : United Artists
Released: 1965

48. *Boy, Did I Get a Wrong Number!*

Actors : Bob Hope, Elke Sommer, Cesare Danova, Phyllis Diller, Kelly Thordsen, Marjorie Lord, Terry Burnham, Benny Baker, Harry Von Zell, Joyce Jameson

Director : George Marshall
Producer: Edward Small
Script : Albert E. Lewin, Burt Styler and George Kennett (adapted from an original story by George Beck)
Studio : United Artists
Released: 1966

49. *Eight on the Lam*

Actors : Bob Hope, Jonathan Winters, Phyllis Diller, Jill St. John, Shirley Eaton, Kevin Brody, Stacey Maxwell, Debi Storm, Glenn Gilger, Austin Willis, Peter

Leeds and special appearances by Avis and Robert Hope (Bob Hope's grandchildren)

Director : George Marshall
Producer: Bill Lawrence
Script : Burt Styler, Albert E. Lewin (story) Bob Fisher and Arthur Marx
Studio : United Artists
Released: 1967

50. *The Private Navy of Sgt. O'Farrell*

Actors : Bob Hope, Jeffrey Hunter, Phyllis Diller, Gina Lollobrigida, Henry Wilcoxon, Mylene Demongeot, William Wellman, Jr.

Director : Frank Tashlin
Producer: John Beck
Script : Frank Tashlin (adapted from an original story by Robert M. Fresco and John L. Greene)
Studio : United Artists
Released: 1968

51. *How to Commit Marriage*

Actors : Bob Hope, Jane Wyman, Maureen Arthur, Jackie Gleason, Leslie Nielsen, Paul Stewart, Irwin Corey

Director : Norman Panama
Producer: Bill Lawrence
Script : Michael Kanin and Ben Starr
Studio : Cinerama
Released: 1969

52. *Cancel My Reservation*

Actors : Bob Hope, Eva Marie Saint, Forrest Tucker, Ralph Bellamy, Doodles Weaver, Keenan Wynn, Henry

Darrow, Betty Ann Carr, Anne Archer, Chief Dan George

Director : Paul Bogart
Executive Producer: Bob Hope
Producer: Gordon Oliver
Script : Robert Fisher and Arthur Marx
Studio : Warner Brothers
Released: 1972

Kensington Profiles:
The Rich and Famous

__The Richest Girl in the World
  by Stephanie Mansfield
    0-7860-1027-4   **$6.99**US/**$8.50**CAN
At thirteen, Doris Duke inherited a $100 million tobacco fortune. By
the time she was thirty, she'd lavished millions on her lovers and
husbands. Now, read one of the most fascinating stories of our time—
the story of a woman who lived a life of incredible excess, a woman
in search of the love all the money in the world couldn't buy.
A Book-Of-The-Month Club Selection

__Fergie: The Very Private Life
  by Madame Vasso and David Leigh
    0-7860-0376-6   **$5.99**US/**$6.99**CAN
Madame Vasso, Fergie's former personal spiritual advisor and close
friend, witnessed the devastating crash and burn of the Dutchess'
golden life firsthand. Learn all about Fergie and Di's violent rivalry
over John F. Kennedy, Jr., the outrageous Fergie photos that shocked
the queen, the private bedroom scandals that ended in a very public
divorce, plus much, much more!

Kensington Profiles:
The Trial of the Century

Get Healthy
With Kensington Books

BOOK YOUR PLACE ON OUR WEBSITE AND MAKE THE READING CONNECTION!

We've created a customized website just for our very special readers, where you can get the inside scoop on everything that's going on with Zebra, Pinnacle and Kensington books.

When you come online, you'll have the exciting opportunity to:

- View covers of upcoming books
- Read sample chapters
- Learn about our future publishing schedule (listed by publication month *and author*)
- Find out when your favorite authors will be visiting a city near you
- Search for and order backlist books from our online catalog
- Check out author bios and background information
- Send e-mail to your favorite authors
- Meet the Kensington staff online
- Join us in weekly chats with authors, readers and other guests
- Get writing guidelines
- AND MUCH MORE!

Visit our website at
http://www.kensingtonbooks.com